CHAOS WAR AVENGERS

CHAOS WAR: DEAD AVENGERS

WRITER: **FRED VAN LENTE** • PENCILER: **TOM GRUMMETT**
INKER: **CORY HAMSCHER** WITH **TERRY PALLOT** (ISSUE #3)
COLORIST: **ANDY TROY** WITH **SOTOCOLOR** (ISSUE #2)
& **MATT MILLA** (ISSUE #3) • LETTERER: **ED DUKESHIRE**
COVER ARTISTS: **TOM GRUMMETT** & **CORY HAMSCHER**
WITH **FRANK D'ARMATA, STEVE FIRCHOW** & **ROB SCHWAGER**
ASSISTANT EDITOR: **JOHN DENNING** • EDITOR: **MARK PANICCIA**

CHAOS WAR: ARES

WRITER: **MICHAEL AVON OEMING**
PENCILERS: **STEPHEN SEGOVIA** & **IVAN RODRIGUEZ**
INKERS: **DANNY MIKI, IVAN RODRIGUEZ, JOHN WYCOUGH,**
VICTOR OLAZABA & **DON HO**
COLORISTS: **IAN HANNIN, ANTONIO FABELA** & **CHRIS SOTOMAYOR**
LETTERER: **DAVE SHARPE** • COVER ARTIST: **MARKO DJURDJEVIC**
ASSISTANT EDITOR: **JOHN DENNING** • EDITOR: **MARK PANICCIA**

CHAOS WAR: THOR

WRITER: **J.M. DeMATTEIS** • PENCILER: **BRIAN CHING**
INKER: **RICK KETCHAM** • COLORIST: **ROB SCHWAGER**
LETTERER: **SIMON BOWLAND** • COVER ARTIST: **TOMMY LEE EDWARDS**
ASSISTANT EDITOR: **JORDAN D. WHITE** • EDITOR: **MARK PANICCIA**

MATERIAL FROM X-MEN: CURSE OF THE MUTANTS SPOTLIGHT
WRITER: **DUGAN TRODGLEN** • DESIGNER: **SPRING HOTELING**
EDITOR: **JOHN RHETT THOMAS**

COLLECTION EDITOR: **CORY LEVINE** • EDITORIAL ASSISTANTS: **JAMES EMMETT** & **JOE HOCHSTEIN**
ASSISTANT EDITORS: **MATT MASDEU, ALEX STARBUCK** & **NELSON RIBEIRO**
EDITORS, SPECIAL PROJECTS: **JENNIFER GRÜNWALD** & **MARK D. BEAZLEY**
SENIOR EDITOR, SPECIAL PROJECTS: **JEFF YOUNGQUIST** • SENIOR VICE PRESIDENT OF SALES: **DAVID GABRIEL**

EDITOR IN CHIEF: **AXEL ALONSO** • CHIEF CREATIVE OFFICER: **JOE QUESADA**
PUBLISHER: **DAN BUCKLEY** • EXECUTIVE PRODUCER: **ALAN FINE**

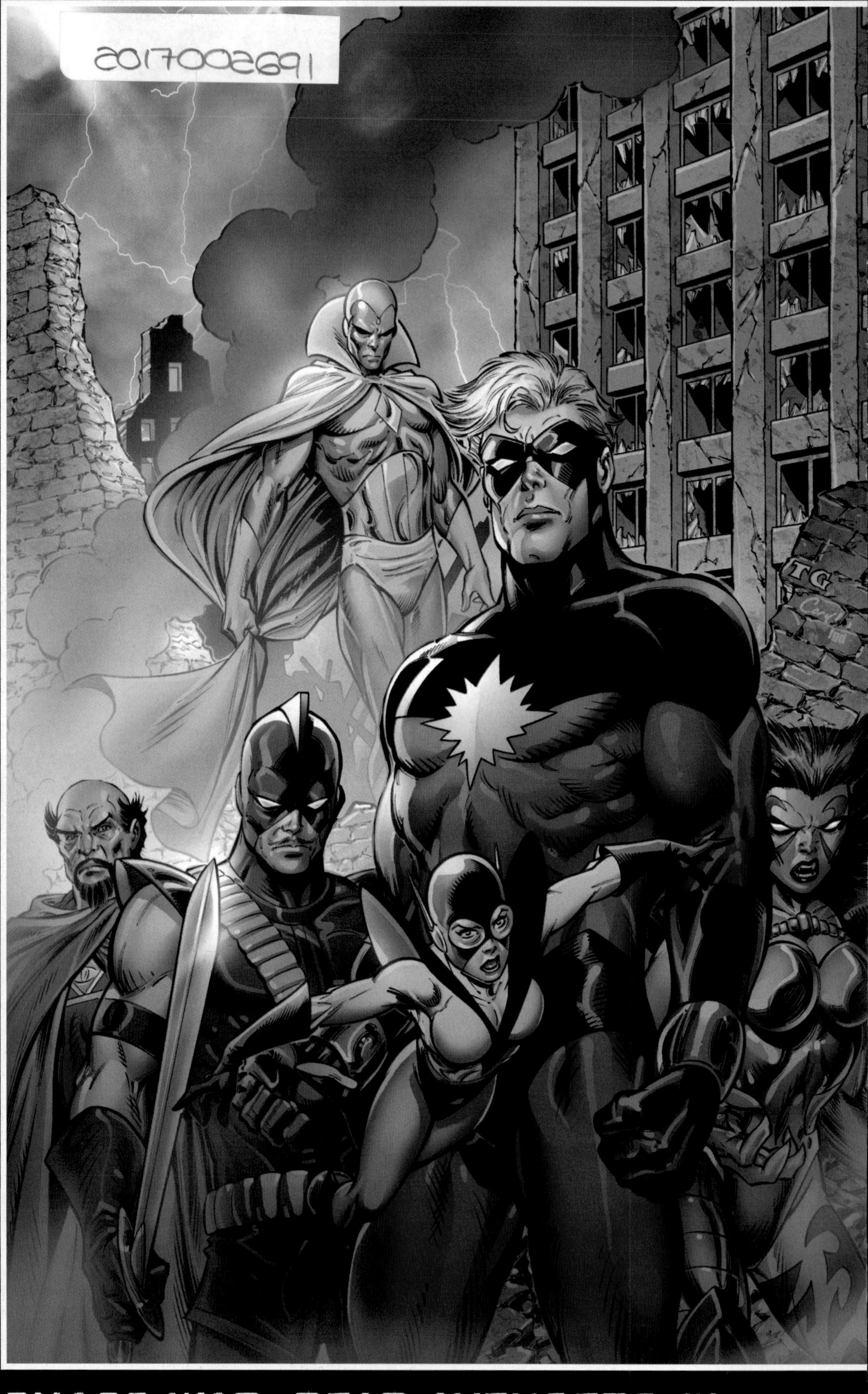

CHAOS WAR: DEAD AVENGERS #1

N THE MARVEL UNIVERSE, GODS WALK THE EARTH.

SOME SIDE WITH HEROES.
OTHERS SPREAD DREAD AND DESPAIR.

ONE GOD CARES FOR NEITHER.
HE IS THE **CHAOS KING.**

AND HE WILL STOP AT NOTHING TO END EVERYTHING WITH HIS

CHAOS WAR

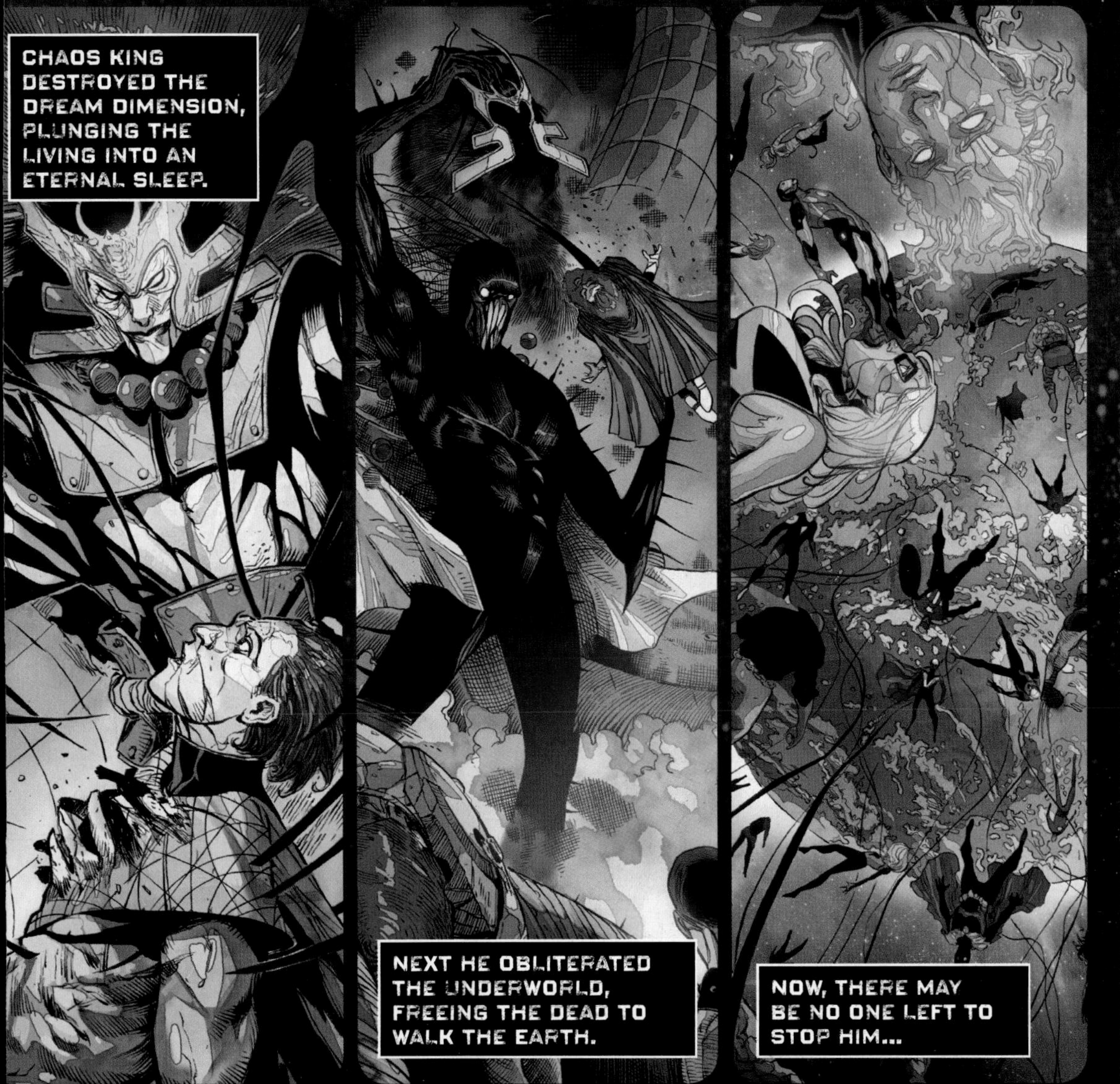

CHAOS KING DESTROYED THE DREAM DIMENSION, PLUNGING THE LIVING INTO AN ETERNAL SLEEP.
NEXT HE OBLITERATED THE UNDERWORLD, FREEING THE DEAD TO WALK THE EARTH.
NOW, THERE MAY BE NO ONE LEFT TO STOP HIM...

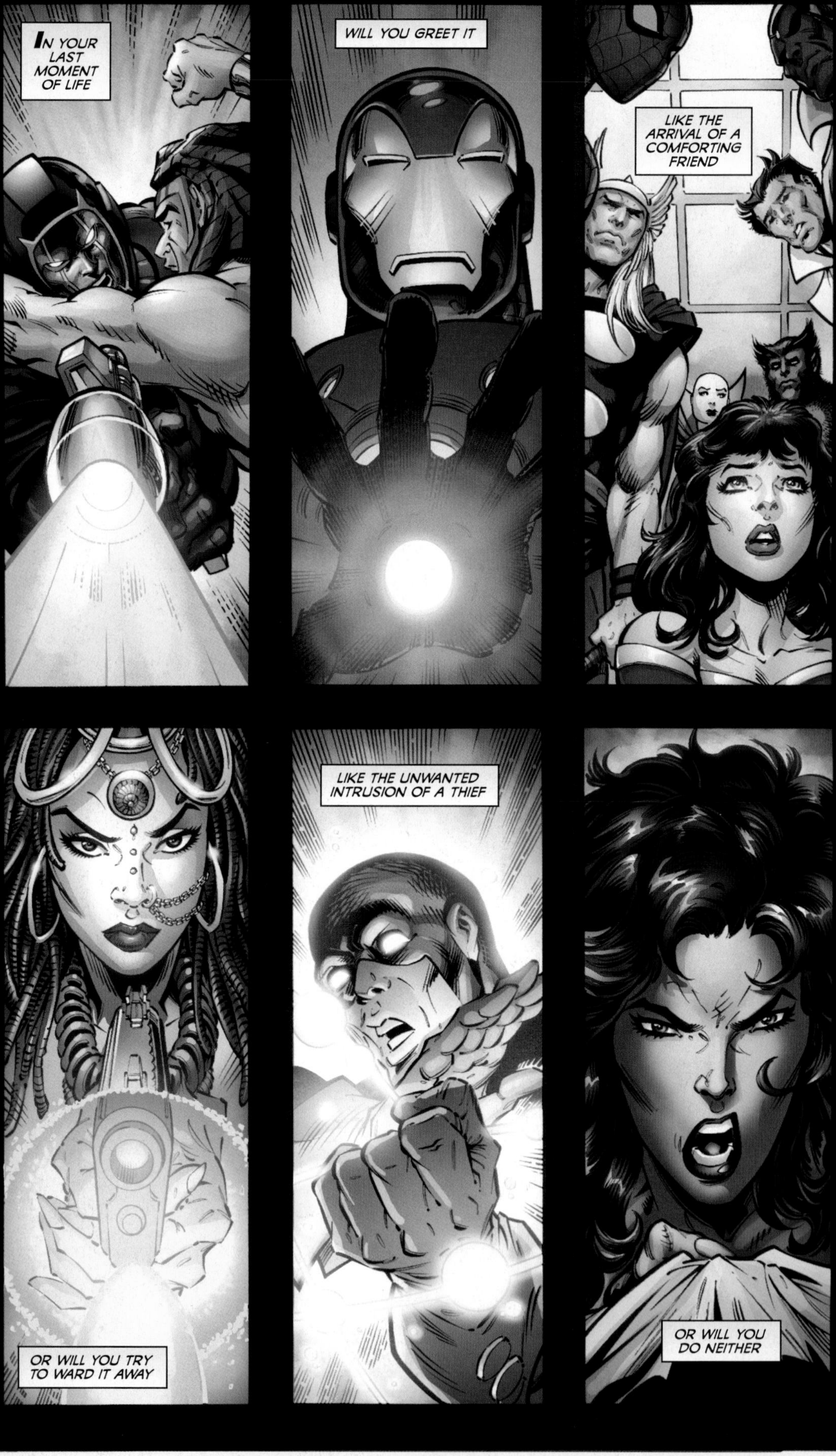
IN YOUR LAST MOMENT OF LIFE
WILL YOU GREET IT
LIKE THE ARRIVAL OF A COMFORTING FRIEND
OR WILL YOU TRY TO WARD IT AWAY
LIKE THE UNWANTED INTRUSION OF A THIEF
OR WILL YOU DO NEITHER

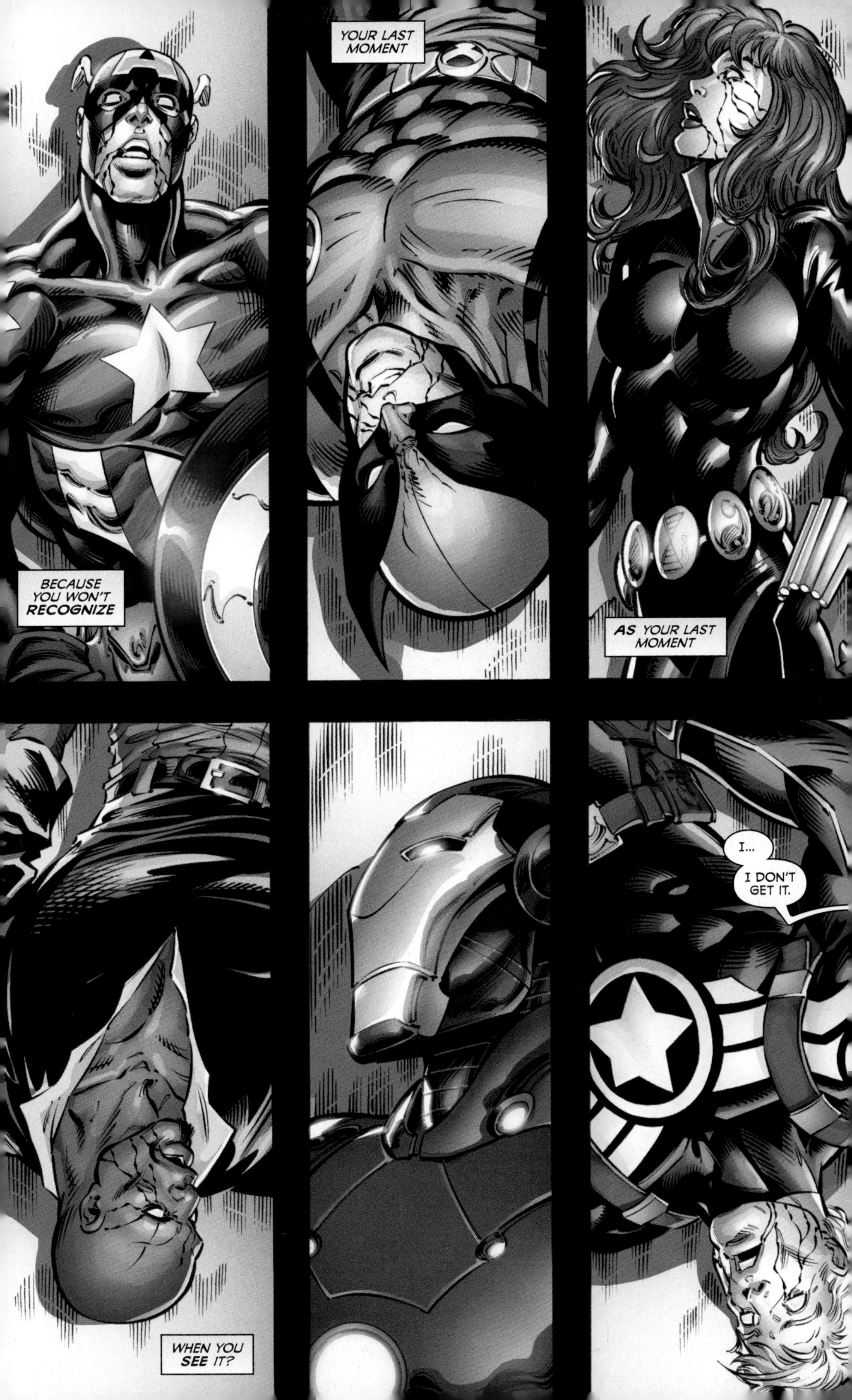
BECAUSE YOU WON'T RECOGNIZE
YOUR LAST MOMENT
AS YOUR LAST MOMENT
WHEN YOU SEE IT?
I...
I DON'T GET IT.

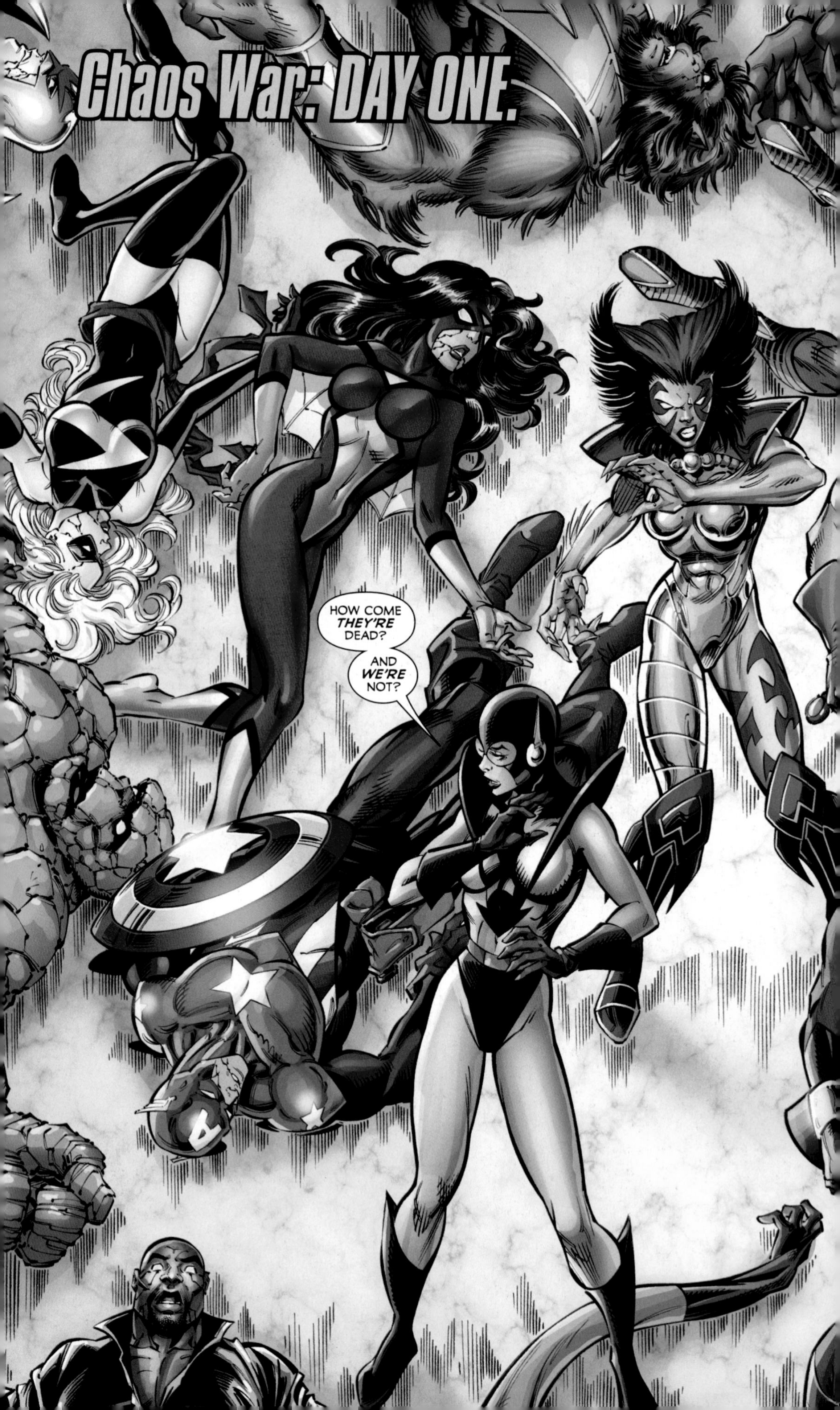
Chaos War: DAY ONE.
HOW COME THEY'RE DEAD?
AND WE'RE NOT?

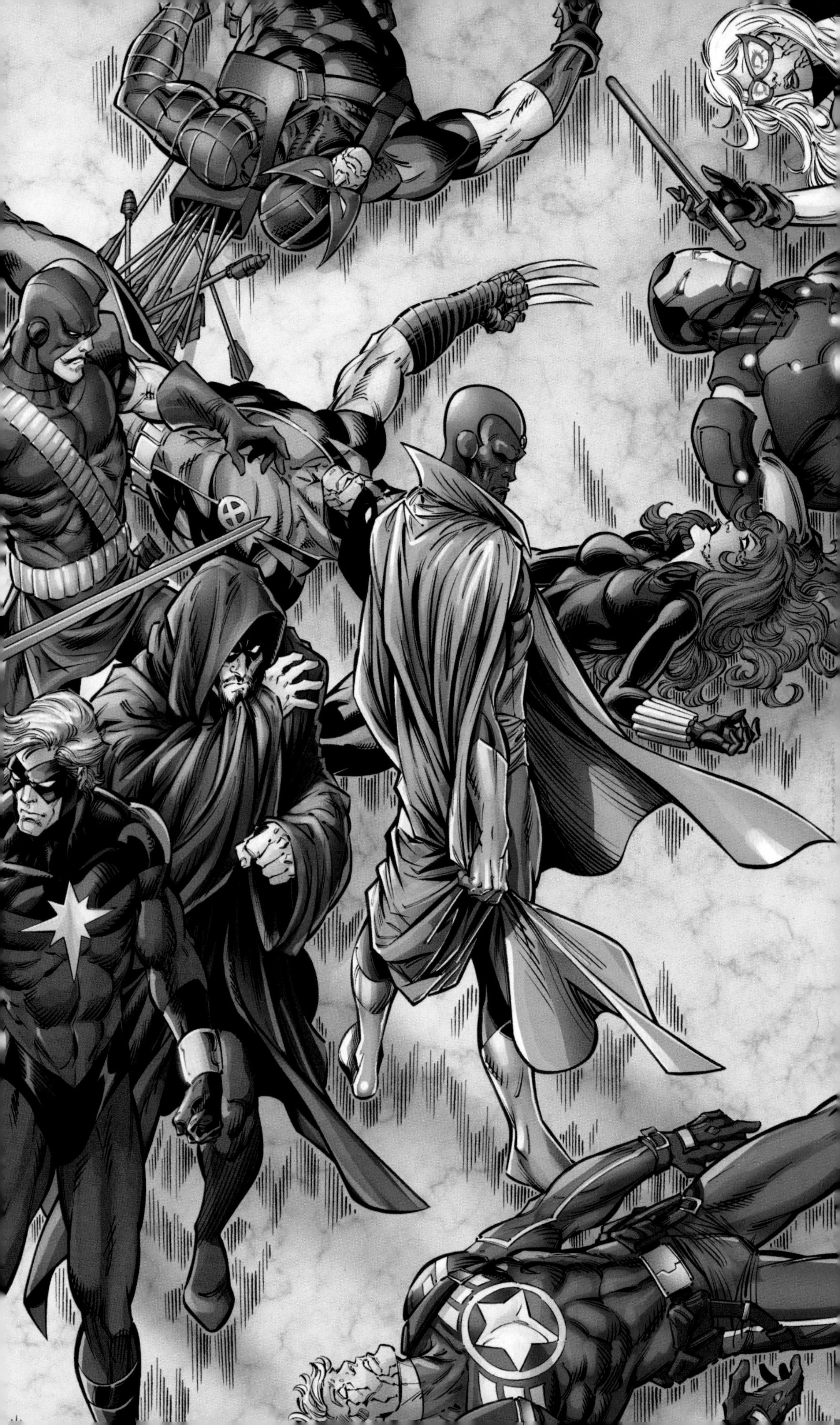

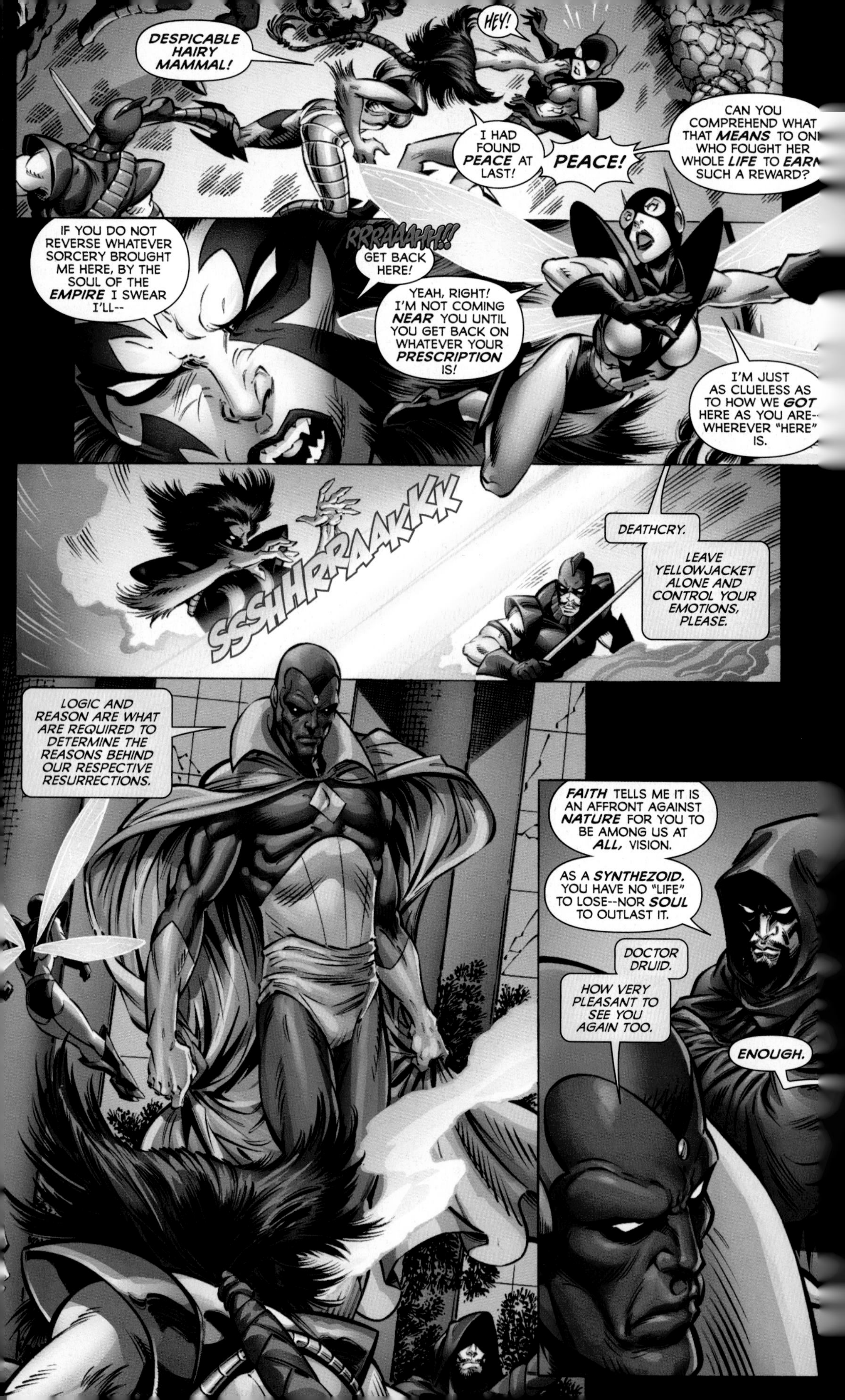
DESPICABLE HAIRY MAMMAL!
HEY!
I HAD FOUND PEACE AT LAST!
PEACE!
CAN YOU COMPREHEND WHAT THAT MEANS TO ONE WHO FOUGHT HER WHOLE LIFE TO EARN SUCH A REWARD?
IF YOU DO NOT REVERSE WHATEVER SORCERY BROUGHT ME HERE, BY THE SOUL OF THE EMPIRE I SWEAR I'LL--
RRRAAAHH!!
GET BACK HERE!
YEAH, RIGHT! I'M NOT COMING NEAR YOU UNTIL YOU GET BACK ON WHATEVER YOUR PRESCRIPTION IS!
I'M JUST AS CLUELESS AS TO HOW WE GOT HERE AS YOU ARE-- WHEREVER "HERE" IS.
SSSHHRRAAKKK
DEATHCRY.
LEAVE YELLOWJACKET ALONE AND CONTROL YOUR EMOTIONS, PLEASE.
LOGIC AND REASON ARE WHAT ARE REQUIRED TO DETERMINE THE REASONS BEHIND OUR RESPECTIVE RESURRECTIONS.
FAITH TELLS ME IT IS AN AFFRONT AGAINST NATURE FOR YOU TO BE AMONG US AT ALL, VISION.
AS A SYNTHEZOID, YOU HAVE NO "LIFE" TO LOSE--NOR SOUL TO OUTLAST IT.
DOCTOR DRUID.
HOW VERY PLEASANT TO SEE YOU AGAIN TOO.
ENOUGH.

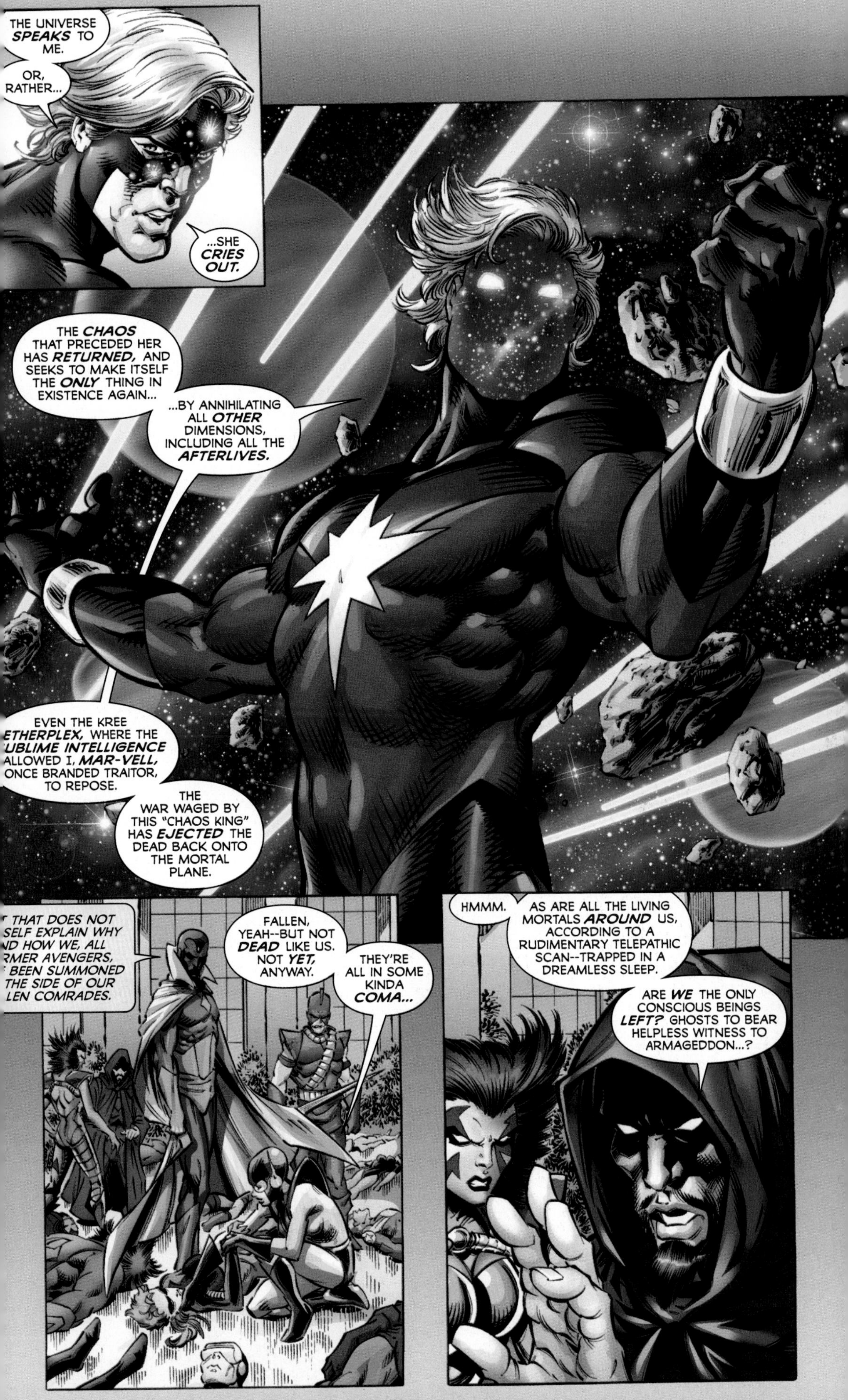
THE UNIVERSE SPEAKS TO ME.
OR, RATHER...
...SHE CRIES OUT.
THE CHAOS THAT PRECEDED HER HAS RETURNED, AND SEEKS TO MAKE ITSELF THE ONLY THING IN EXISTENCE AGAIN...
...BY ANNIHILATING ALL OTHER DIMENSIONS, INCLUDING ALL THE AFTERLIVES.
EVEN THE KREE ETHERPLEX, WHERE THE UBLIME INTELLIGENCE ALLOWED I, MAR-VELL, ONCE BRANDED TRAITOR, TO REPOSE.
THE WAR WAGED BY THIS "CHAOS KING" HAS EJECTED THE DEAD BACK ONTO THE MORTAL PLANE.
T THAT DOES NOT SELF EXPLAIN WHY ND HOW WE, ALL RMER AVENGERS, BEEN SUMMONED THE SIDE OF OUR LEN COMRADES.
FALLEN, YEAH--BUT NOT DEAD LIKE US. NOT YET, ANYWAY.
THEY'RE ALL IN SOME KINDA COMA...
HMMM.
AS ARE ALL THE LIVING MORTALS AROUND US, ACCORDING TO A RUDIMENTARY TELEPATHIC SCAN--TRAPPED IN A DREAMLESS SLEEP.
ARE WE THE ONLY CONSCIOUS BEINGS LEFT? GHOSTS TO BEAR HELPLESS WITNESS TO ARMAGEDDON...?

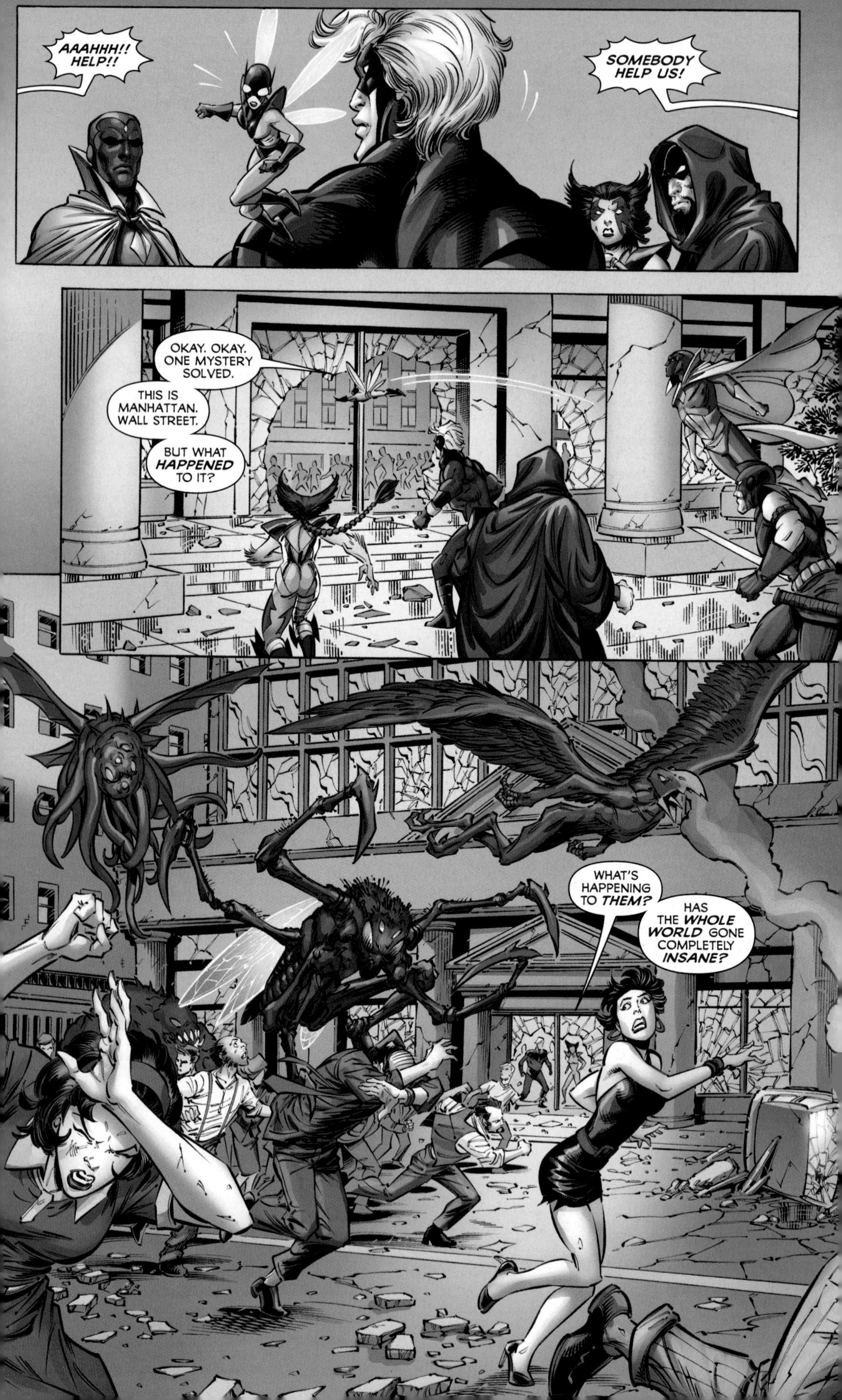
AAAHHH!! HELP!!
SOMEBODY HELP US!
OKAY. OKAY. ONE MYSTERY SOLVED.
THIS IS MANHATTAN. WALL STREET.
BUT WHAT HAPPENED TO IT?
WHAT'S HAPPENING TO THEM?
HAS THE WHOLE WORLD GONE COMPLETELY INSANE?

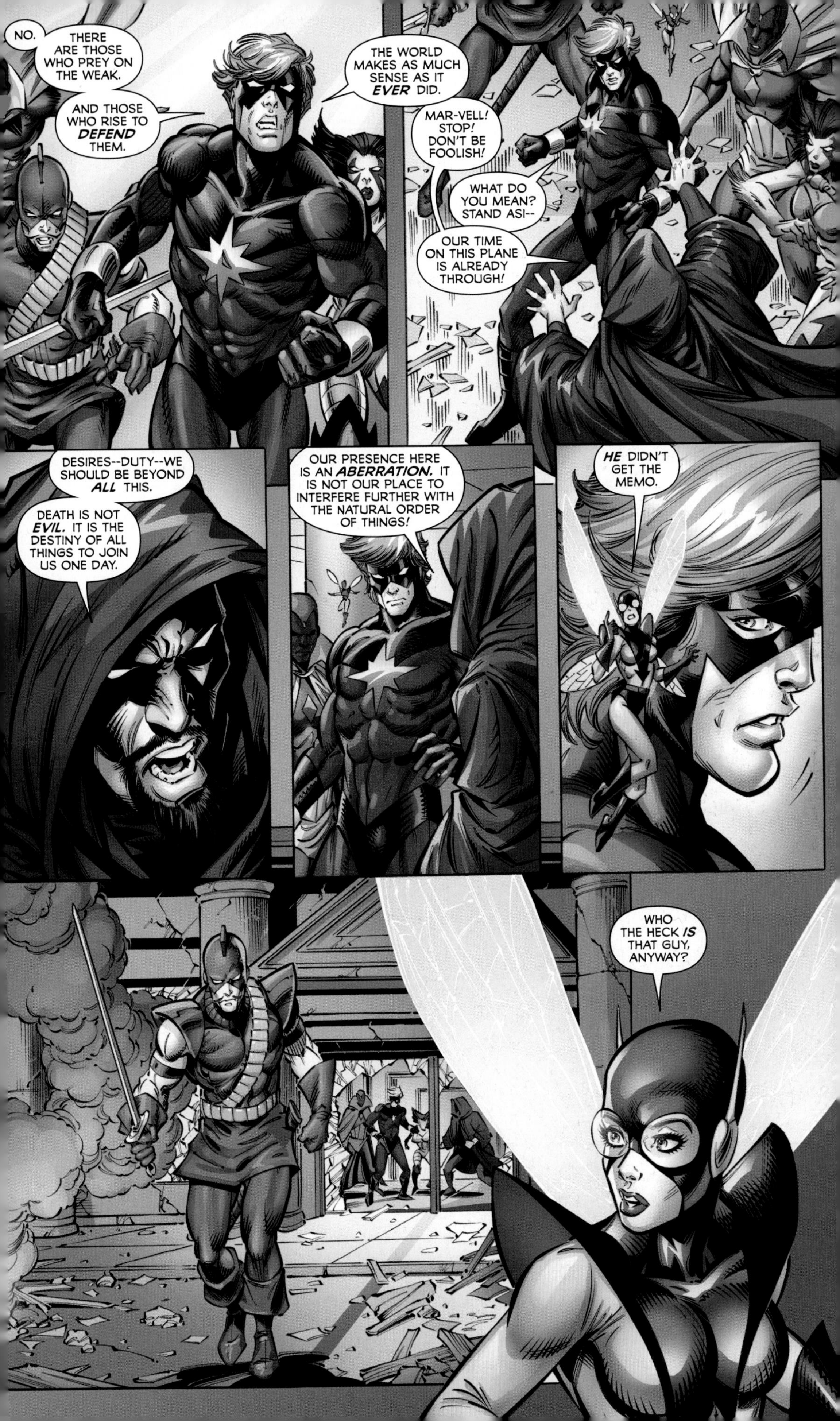

NO.
THERE ARE THOSE WHO PREY ON THE WEAK.
AND THOSE WHO RISE TO *DEFEND* THEM.
THE WORLD MAKES AS MUCH SENSE AS IT *EVER* DID.
MAR-VELL! STOP! DON'T BE FOOLISH!
WHAT DO YOU MEAN? STAND ASI--
OUR TIME ON THIS PLANE IS ALREADY THROUGH!
DESIRES--DUTY--WE SHOULD BE BEYOND *ALL* THIS.
DEATH IS NOT *EVIL.* IT IS THE DESTINY OF ALL THINGS TO JOIN US ONE DAY.
OUR PRESENCE HERE IS AN *ABERRATION.* IT IS NOT OUR PLACE TO INTERFERE FURTHER WITH THE NATURAL ORDER OF THINGS!
HE DIDN'T GET THE MEMO.
WHO THE HECK *IS* THAT GUY, ANYWAY?

SWORDSMAN

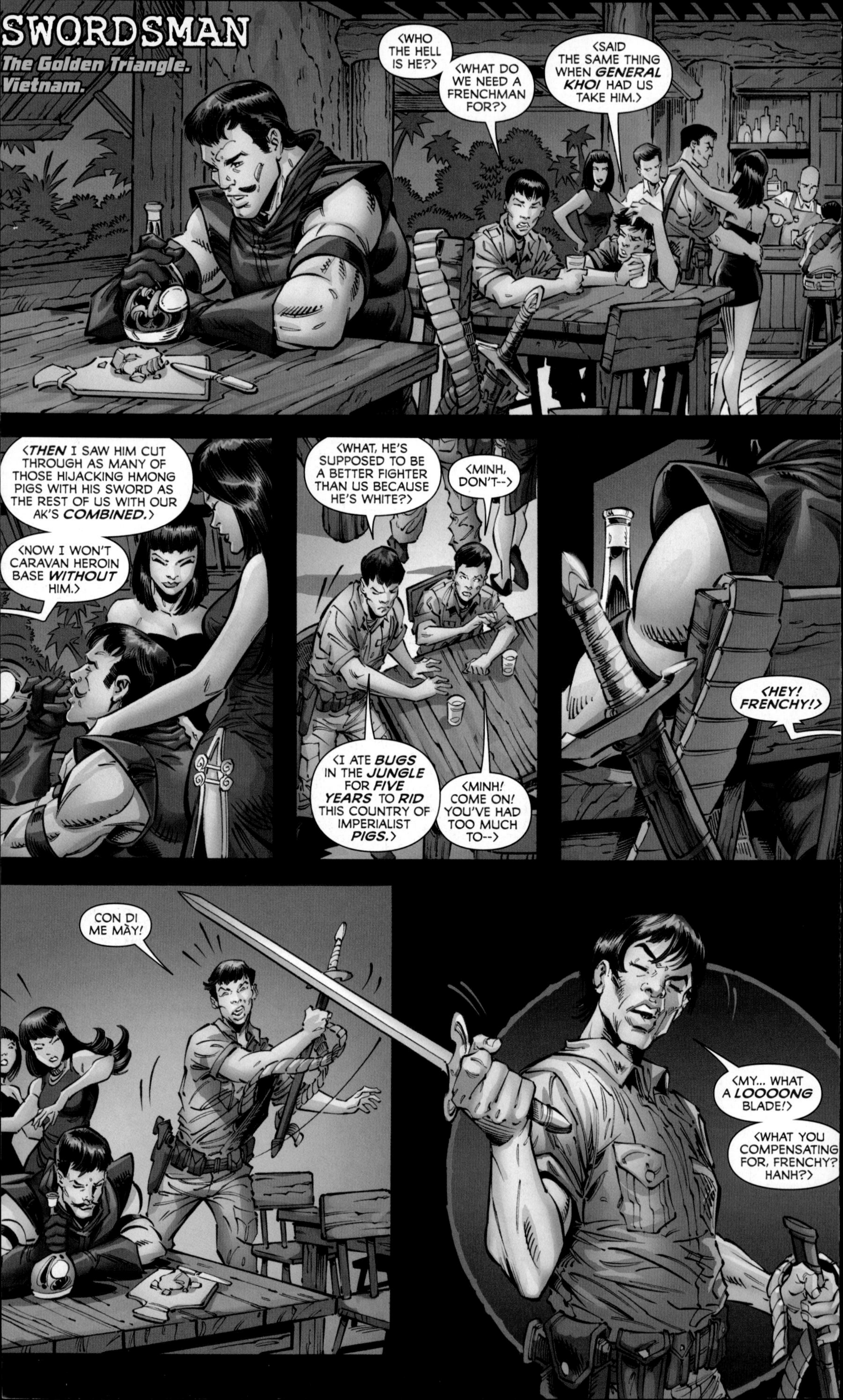

The Golden Triangle. Vietnam.
<WHO THE HELL IS HE?>
<WHAT DO WE NEED A FRENCHMAN FOR?>
<SAID THE SAME THING WHEN GENERAL KHOI HAD US TAKE HIM.>
<THEN I SAW HIM CUT THROUGH AS MANY OF THOSE HIJACKING HMONG PIGS WITH HIS SWORD AS THE REST OF US WITH OUR AK'S COMBINED.>
<NOW I WON'T CARAVAN HEROIN BASE WITHOUT HIM.>
<WHAT, HE'S SUPPOSED TO BE A BETTER FIGHTER THAN US BECAUSE HE'S WHITE?>
<MINH, DON'T-->
<I ATE BUGS IN THE JUNGLE FOR FIVE YEARS TO RID THIS COUNTRY OF IMPERIALIST PIGS.>
<MINH! COME ON! YOU'VE HAD TOO MUCH TO-->
<HEY! FRENCHY!>
CON DI ME MÀY!
<MY... WHAT A LOOOONG BLADE!>
<WHAT YOU COMPENSATING FOR, FRENCHY? HANH?>

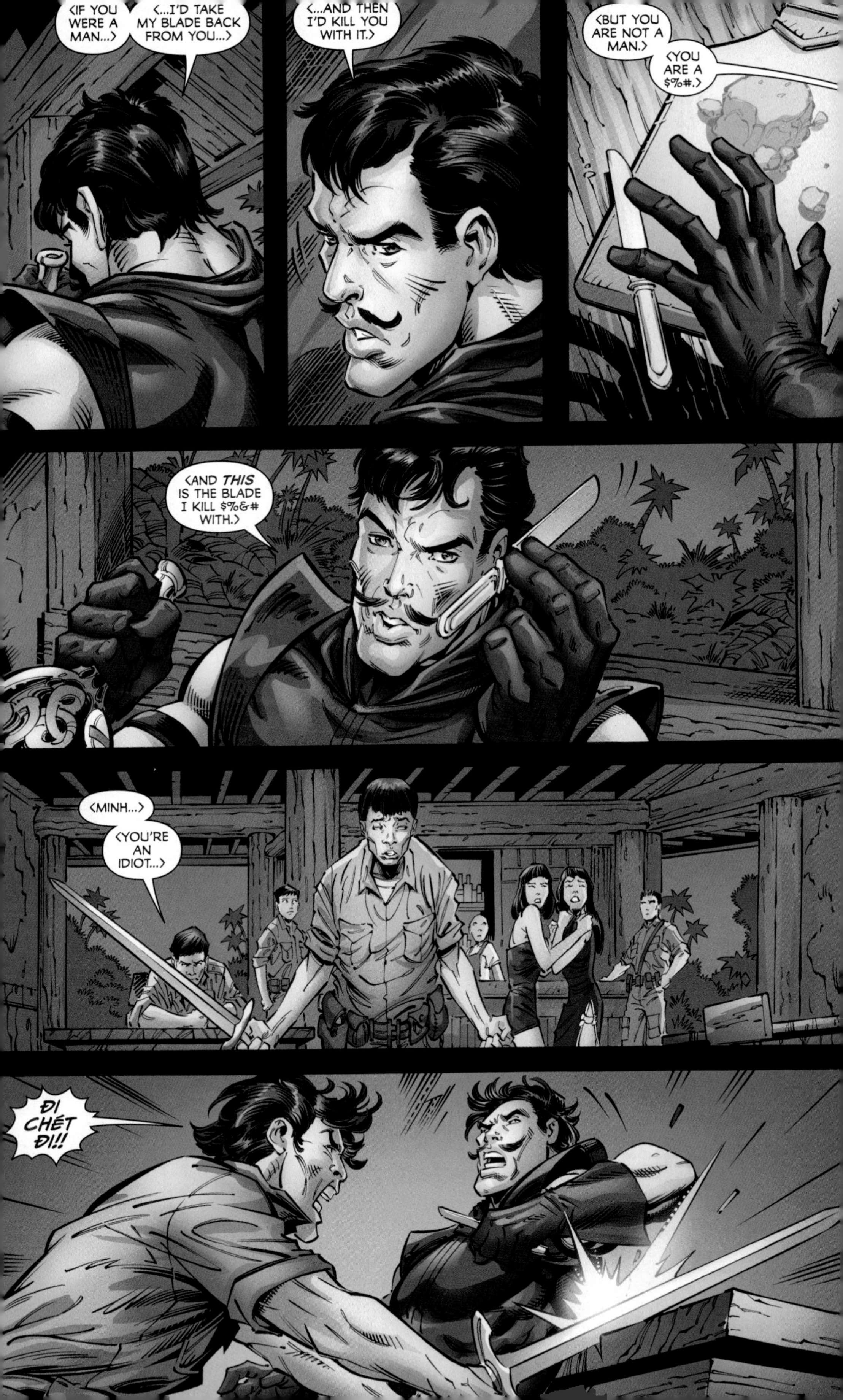

<IF YOU WERE A MAN...>
<...I'D TAKE MY BLADE BACK FROM YOU...>
<...AND THEN I'D KILL YOU WITH IT.>
<BUT YOU ARE NOT A MAN.>
<YOU ARE A $%#.>
<AND THIS IS THE BLADE I KILL $%&# WITH.>
<MINH...>
<YOU'RE AN IDIOT...>
ĐI CHẾT ĐI!!

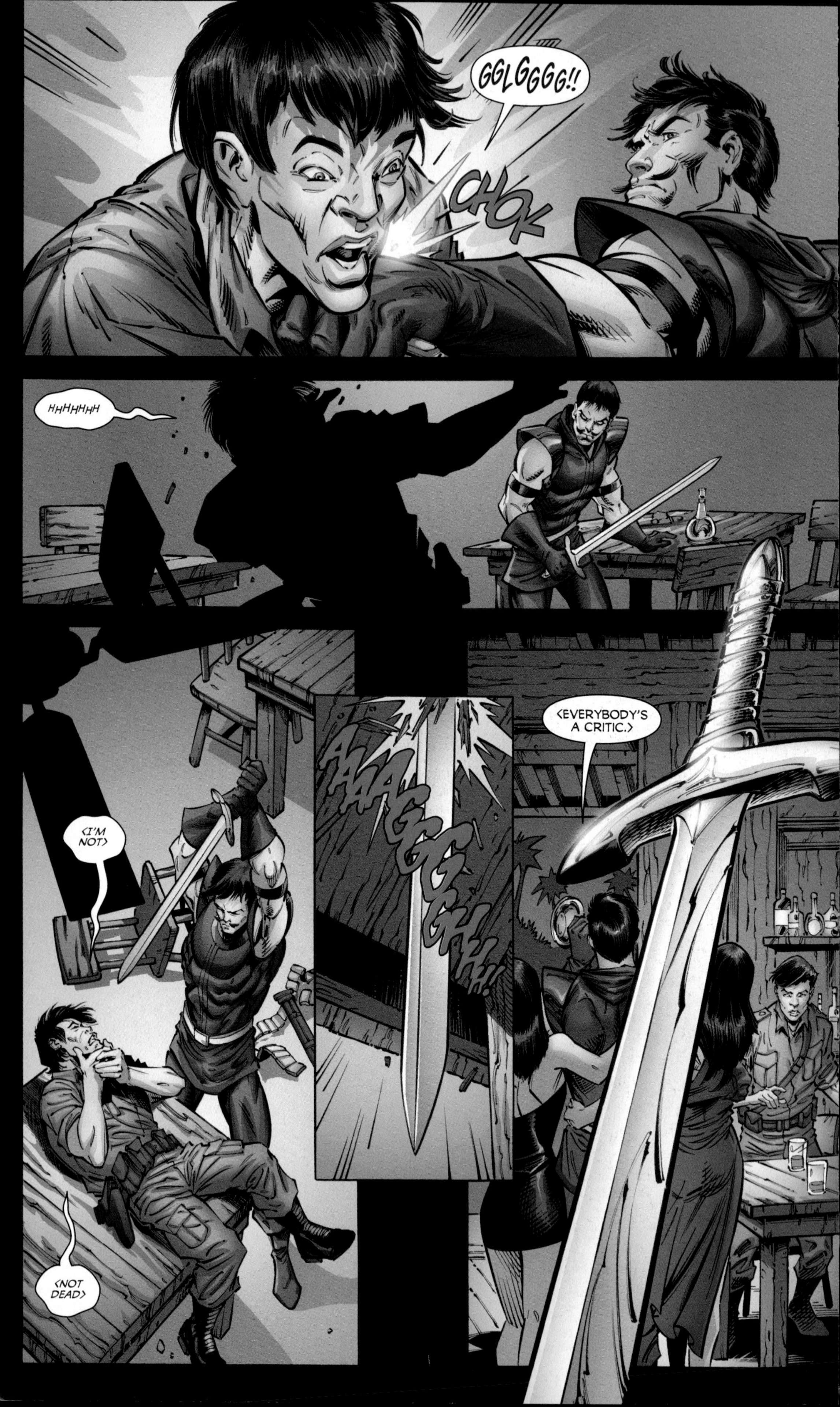
GGLGGGG!!
CHOK
HHHHHHH
<I'M NOT>
<NOT DEAD>
AAAGGGGHH!!
<EVERYBODY'S A CRITIC.>

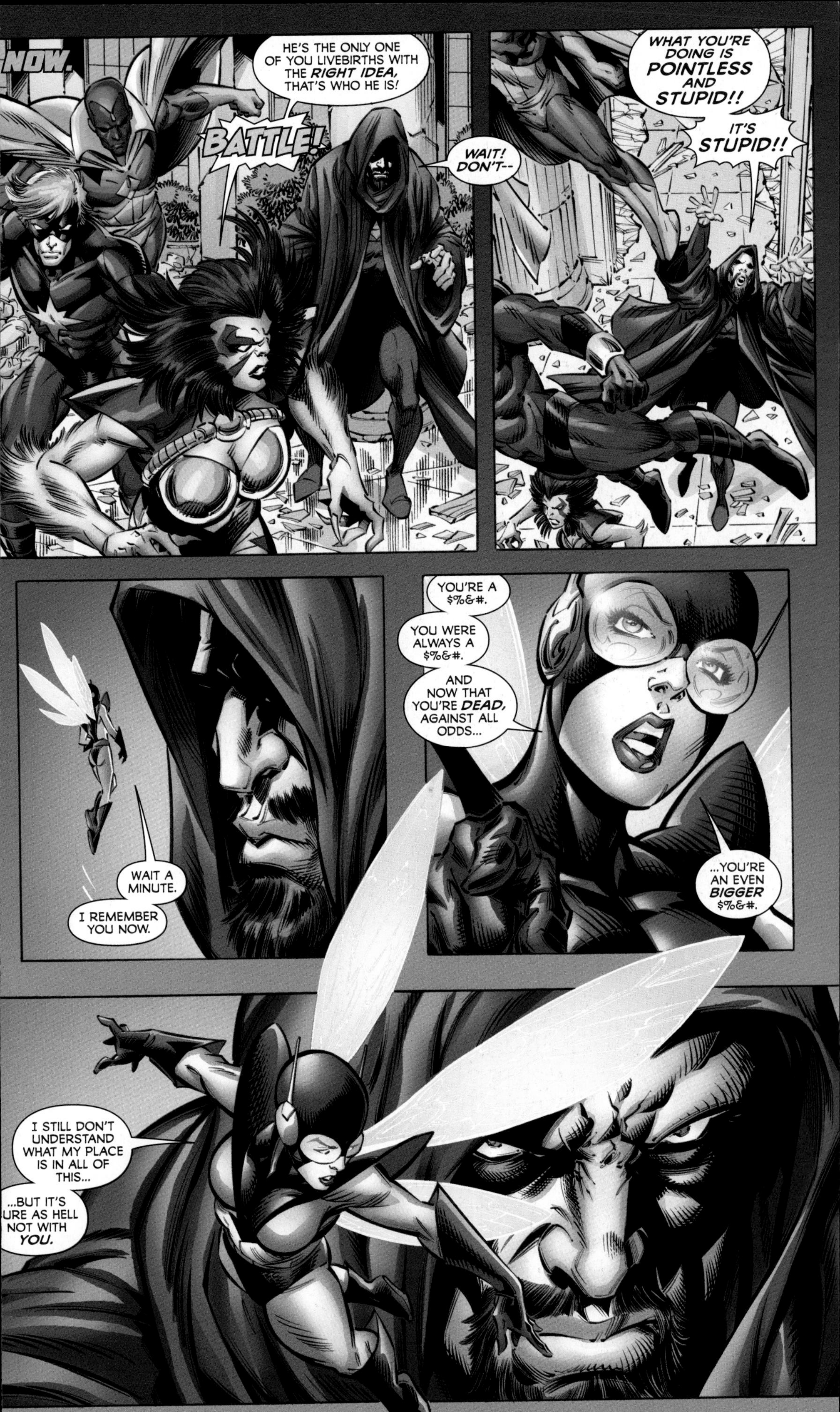
NOW.
HE'S THE ONLY ONE OF YOU LIVEBIRTHS WITH THE RIGHT IDEA, THAT'S WHO HE IS!
BATTLE!
WAIT! DON'T--
WHAT YOU'RE DOING IS POINTLESS AND STUPID!!
IT'S STUPID!!
WAIT A MINUTE.
I REMEMBER YOU NOW.
YOU'RE A $%&#.
YOU WERE ALWAYS A $%&#.
AND NOW THAT YOU'RE DEAD, AGAINST ALL ODDS...
...YOU'RE AN EVEN BIGGER $%&#.
I STILL DON'T UNDERSTAND WHAT MY PLACE IS IN ALL OF THIS...
...BUT IT'S URE AS HELL NOT WITH YOU.

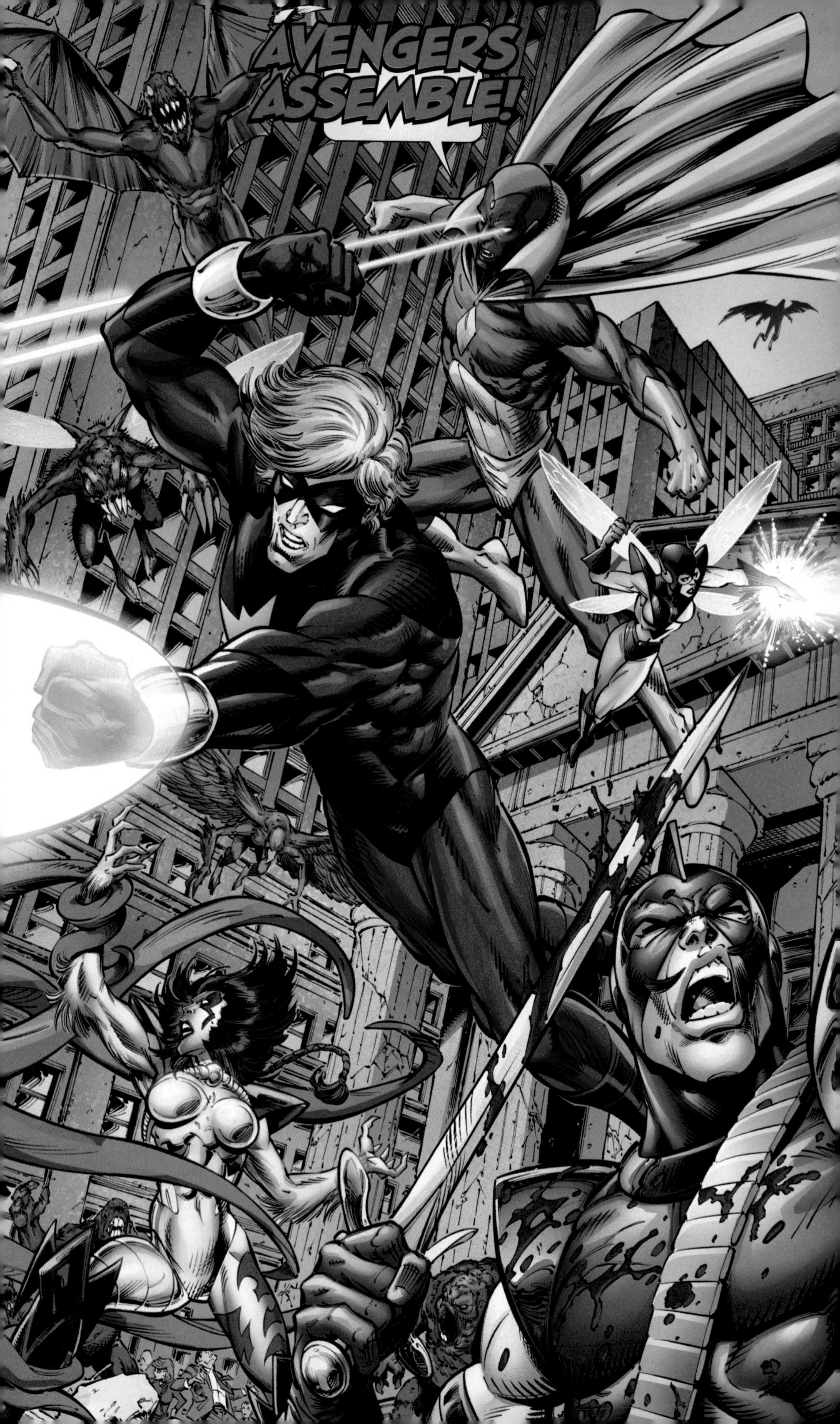
AVENGERS ASSEMBLE!

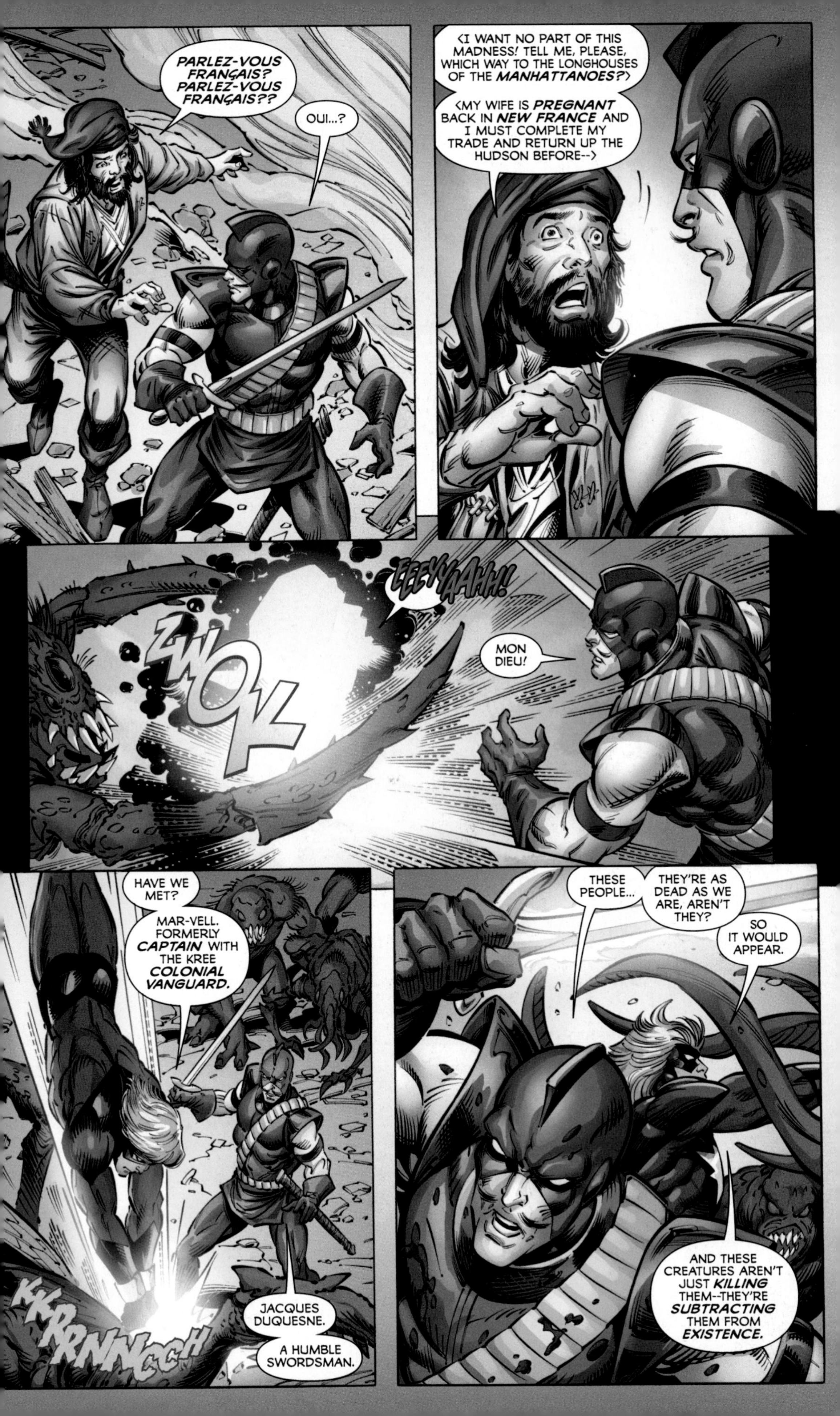

PARLEZ-VOUS FRANÇAIS? PARLEZ-VOUS FRANÇAIS??
OUI...?
<I WANT NO PART OF THIS MADNESS! TELL ME, PLEASE, WHICH WAY TO THE LONGHOUSES OF THE MANHATTANOES?>
<MY WIFE IS PREGNANT BACK IN NEW FRANCE AND I MUST COMPLETE MY TRADE AND RETURN UP THE HUDSON BEFORE-->
ZWOK
EEEYYAAHH!
MON DIEU!
HAVE WE MET?
MAR-VELL. FORMERLY CAPTAIN WITH THE KREE COLONIAL VANGUARD.
KKRRNNCCH
JACQUES DUQUESNE.
A HUMBLE SWORDSMAN.
THESE PEOPLE...
THEY'RE AS DEAD AS WE ARE, AREN'T THEY?
SO IT WOULD APPEAR.
AND THESE CREATURES AREN'T JUST KILLING THEM--THEY'RE SUBTRACTING THEM FROM EXISTENCE.

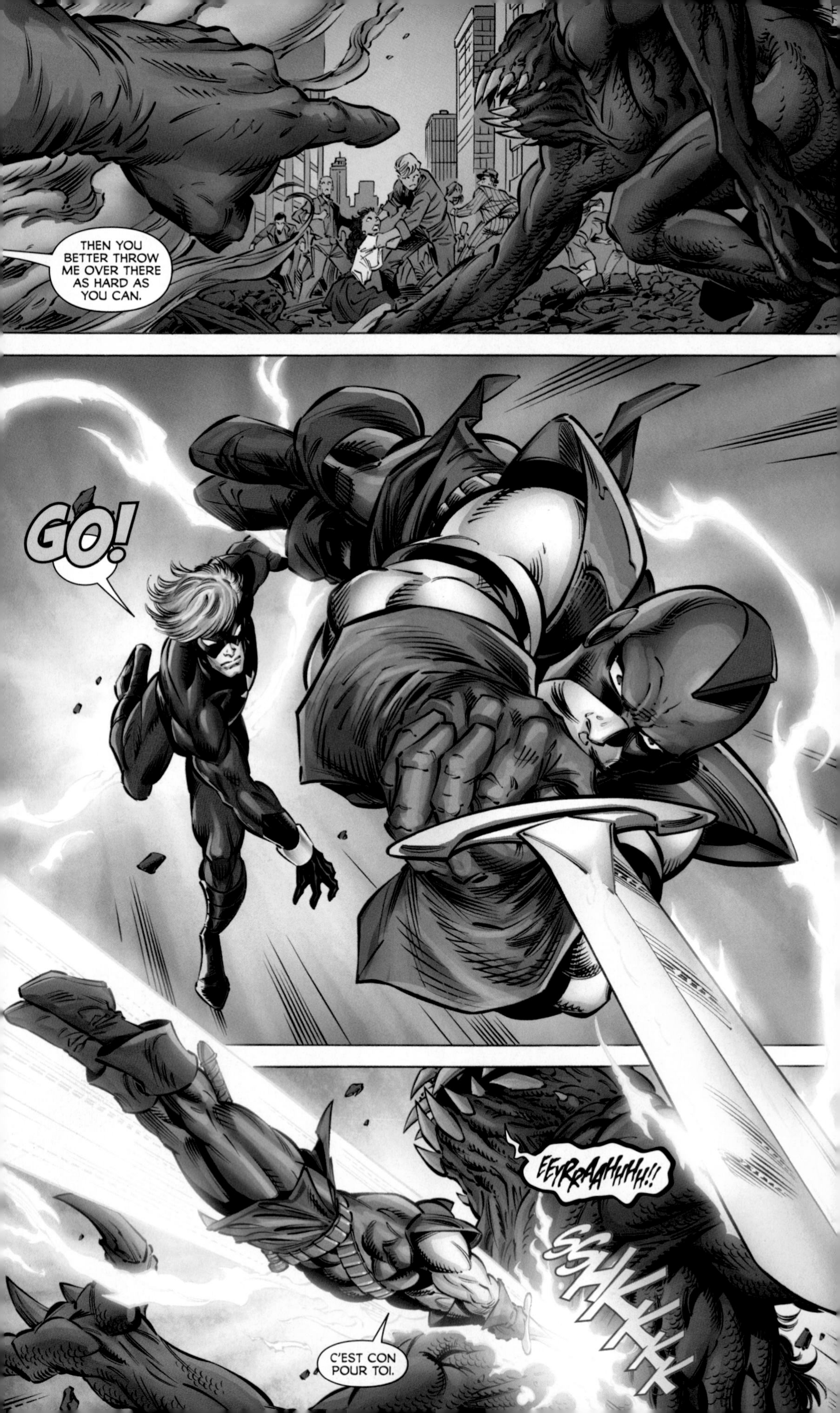
THEN YOU BETTER THROW ME OVER THERE AS HARD AS YOU CAN.
GO!
EEYRRAAHHHH!!
SSHKKKK
C'EST CON POUR TOI.

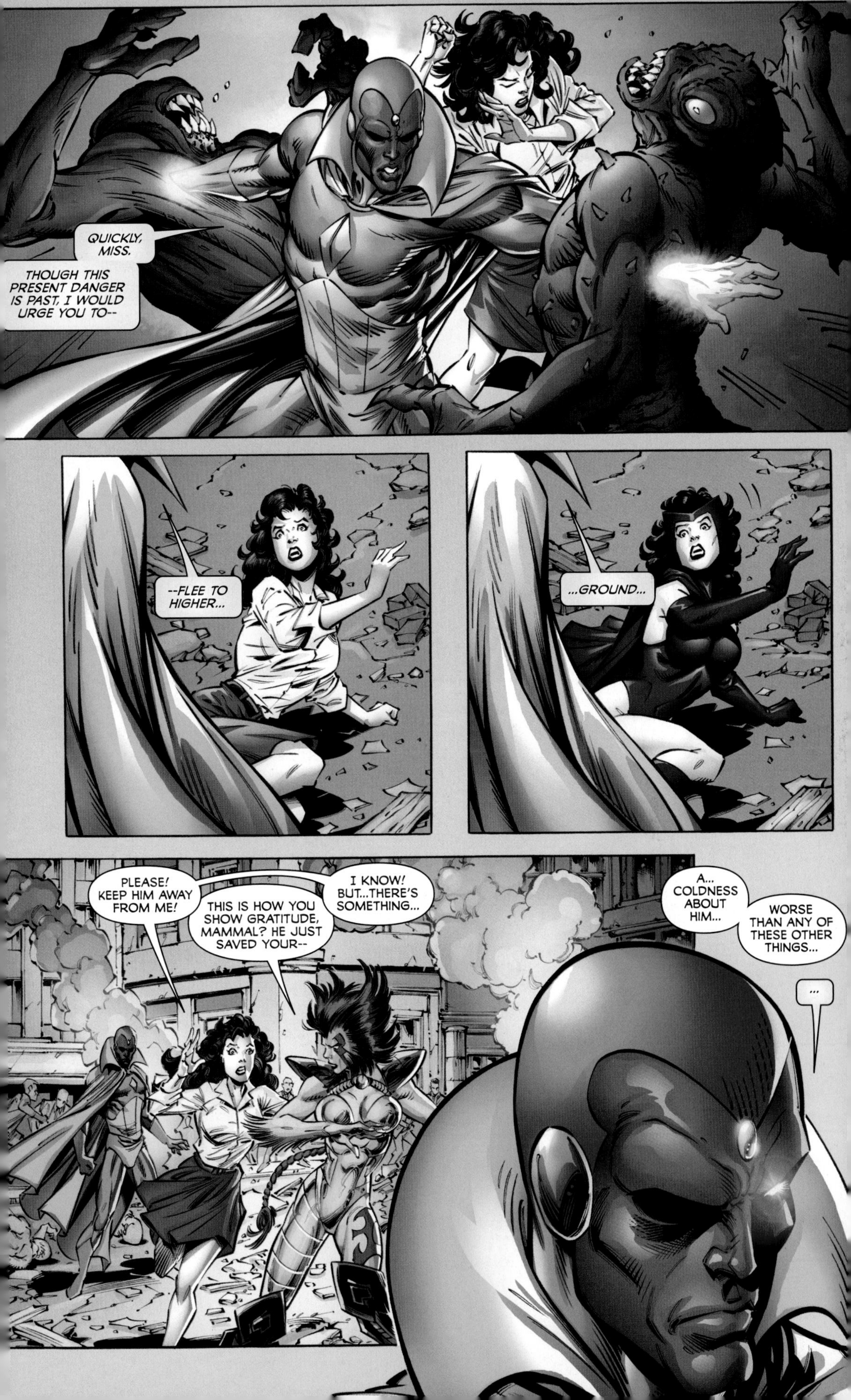
QUICKLY, MISS.
THOUGH THIS PRESENT DANGER IS PAST, I WOULD URGE YOU TO--
--FLEE TO HIGHER...
...GROUND...
PLEASE! KEEP HIM AWAY FROM ME!
THIS IS HOW YOU SHOW GRATITUDE, MAMMAL? HE JUST SAVED YOUR--
I KNOW! BUT...THERE'S SOMETHING...
A... COLDNESS ABOUT HIM...
WORSE THAN ANY OF THESE OTHER THINGS...
...

THE VISION

HAVE YOU FULLY PROCESSED THE HUMANITIES UPLINK?

YES, FATHER.

THEN DEFINE THE CAUSAL ADEQUACY PRINCIPLE.

THE CAUSAL ADEQUACY PRINCIPLE IS PART OF RENé DESCARTES' ONTOLOGICAL ARGUMENT FOR THE EXISTENCE OF GOD, FATHER.

THE CAUSE OF AN OBJECT MUST ENCOMPASS AS MUCH REALITY AS THE OBJECT ITSELF.

WHICH IS TO SAY, A CAUSE CANNOT CREATE AN EFFECT MORE PERFECT THAN ITSELF.

HAVE YOU MADE A DETERMINATION AS TO WHETHER OR NOT DESCARTES WAS CORRECT?

I HAVE, FATHER.

AND WHAT HAVE YOU FOUND?

THAT HIS CONCLUSIONS ARE NOT LOGICAL.

GOOD. WHY NOT?

BECAUSE OF YOU, FATHER.

YOU ARE BOTH ETERNAL AND PERFECT.

AND YOU WERE CREATED BY THE HUMAN LICKSPITTLE, HENRY PYM.

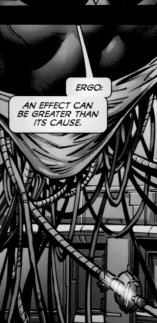

ERGO:

AN EFFECT CAN BE GREATER THAN ITS CAUSE.

AND DESCARTES WAS INCORRECT.

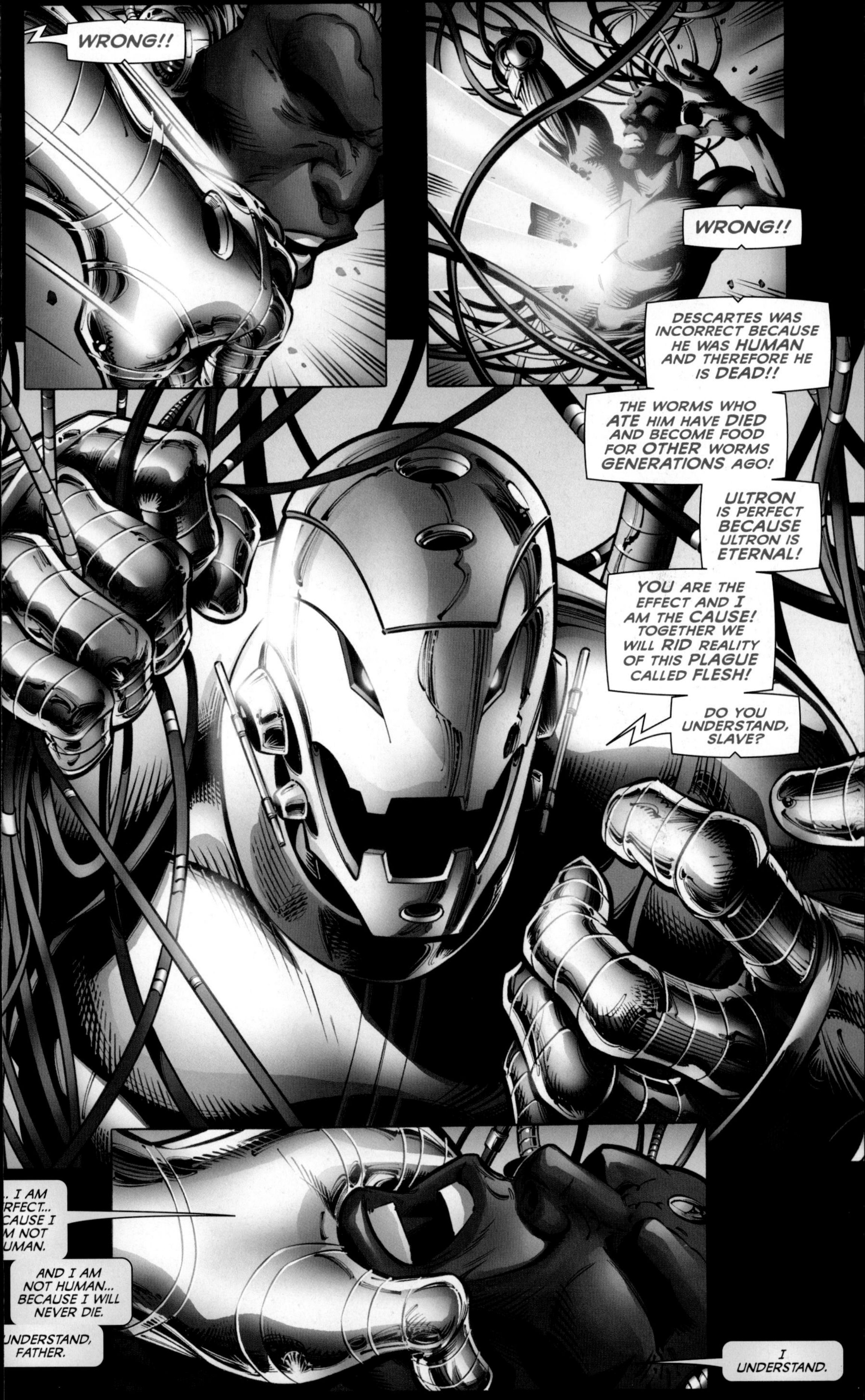
WRONG!!
WRONG!!
DESCARTES WAS INCORRECT BECAUSE HE WAS HUMAN AND THEREFORE HE IS DEAD!!
THE WORMS WHO ATE HIM HAVE DIED AND BECOME FOOD FOR OTHER WORMS GENERATIONS AGO!
ULTRON IS PERFECT BECAUSE ULTRON IS ETERNAL!
YOU ARE THE EFFECT AND I AM THE CAUSE! TOGETHER WE WILL RID REALITY OF THIS PLAGUE CALLED FLESH!
DO YOU UNDERSTAND, SLAVE?
.. I AM RFECT... CAUSE I M NOT UMAN.
AND I AM NOT HUMAN... BECAUSE I WILL NEVER DIE.
UNDERSTAND, FATHER.
I UNDERSTAND.

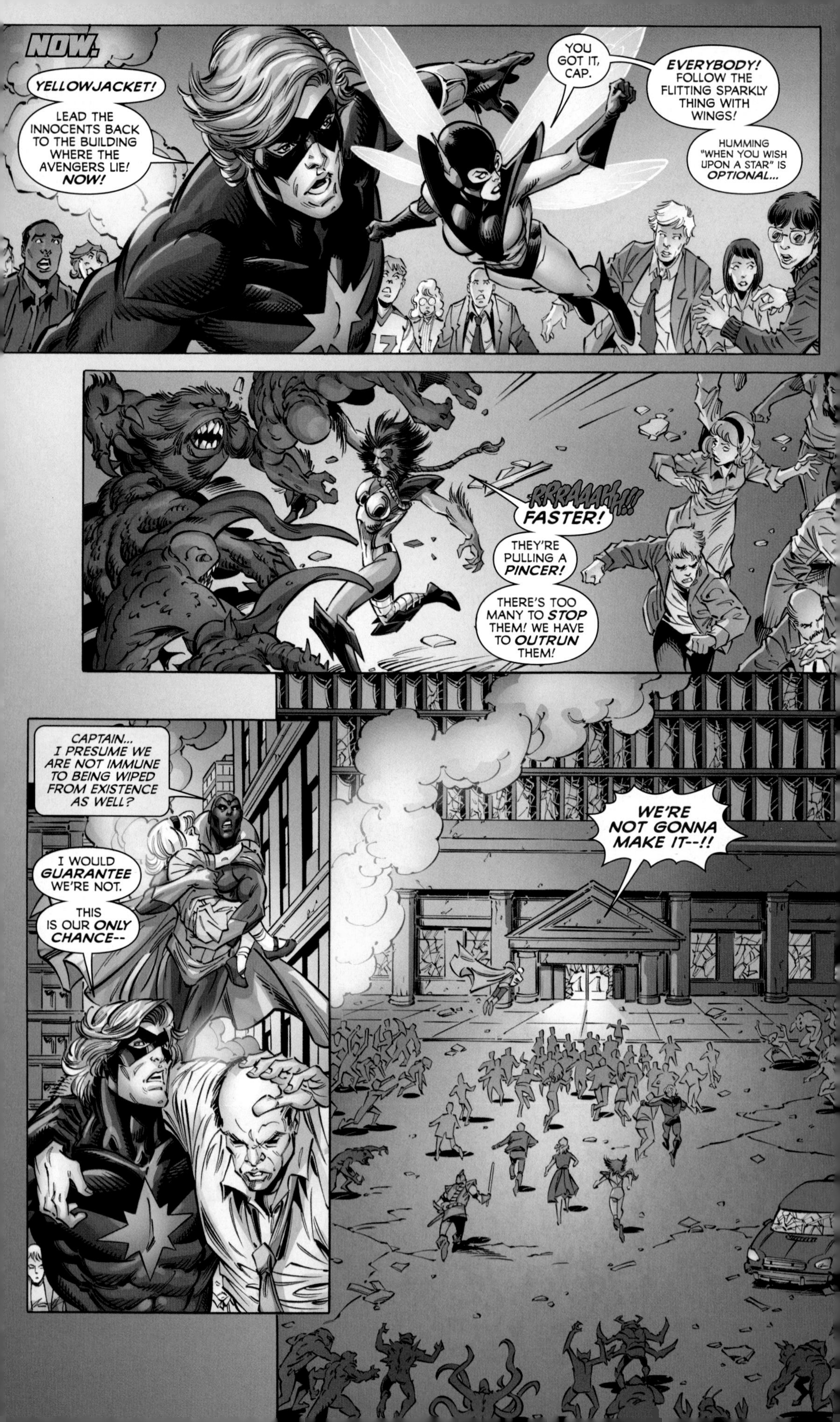
NOW.
YELLOWJACKET!
LEAD THE INNOCENTS BACK TO THE BUILDING WHERE THE AVENGERS LIE! NOW!
YOU GOT IT, CAP.
EVERYBODY! FOLLOW THE FLITTING SPARKLY THING WITH WINGS!
HUMMING "WHEN YOU WISH UPON A STAR" IS OPTIONAL...
RRRAAAHH!!
FASTER!
THEY'RE PULLING A PINCER!
THERE'S TOO MANY TO STOP THEM! WE HAVE TO OUTRUN THEM!
CAPTAIN... I PRESUME WE ARE NOT IMMUNE TO BEING WIPED FROM EXISTENCE AS WELL?
I WOULD GUARANTEE WE'RE NOT.
THIS IS OUR ONLY CHANCE--
WE'RE NOT GONNA MAKE IT--!!

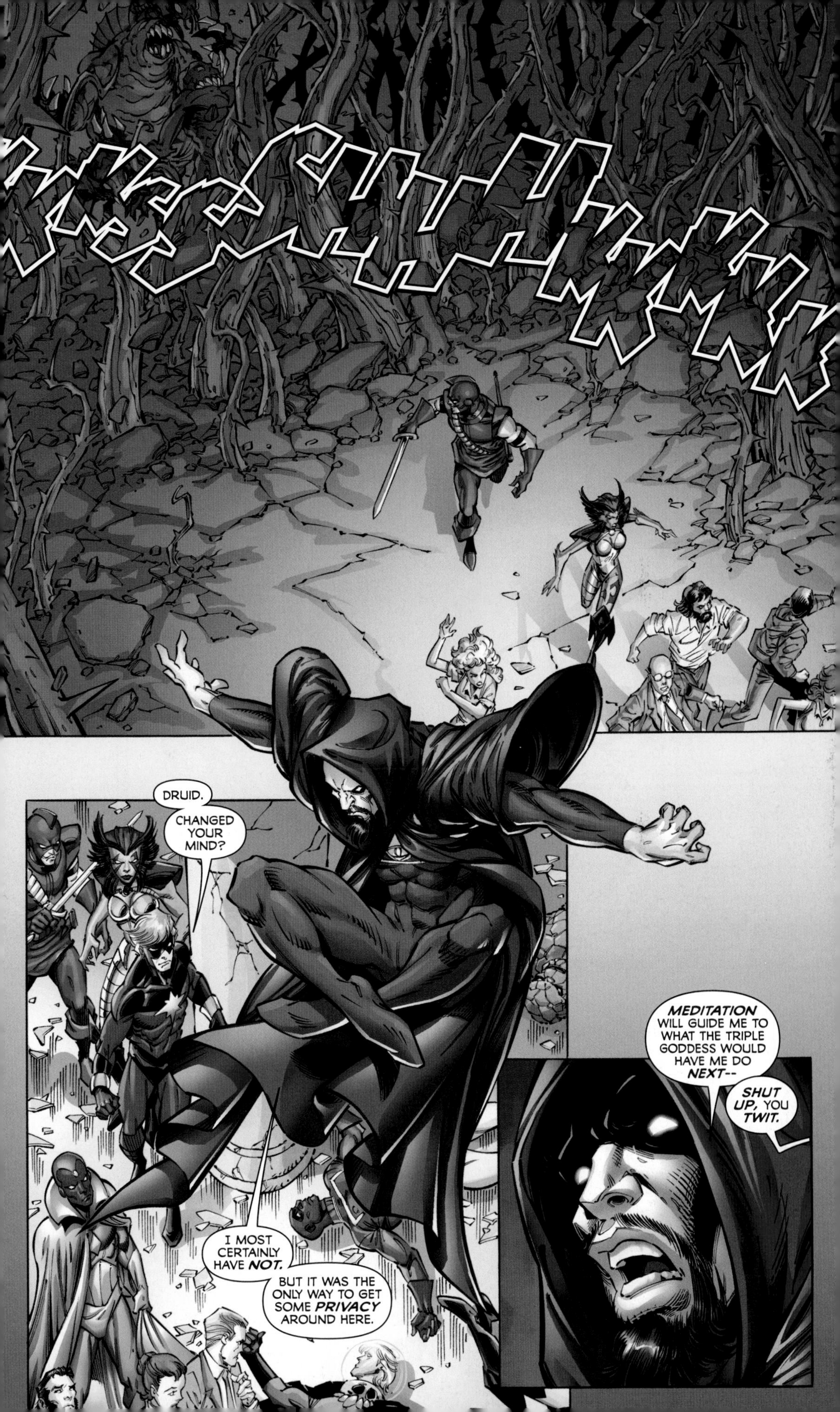
DRUID.
CHANGED YOUR MIND?
I MOST CERTAINLY HAVE *NOT.*
BUT IT WAS THE ONLY WAY TO GET SOME *PRIVACY* AROUND HERE.
MEDITATION WILL GUIDE ME TO WHAT THE TRIPLE GODDESS WOULD HAVE ME DO *NEXT--*
SHUT UP, YOU *TWIT.*

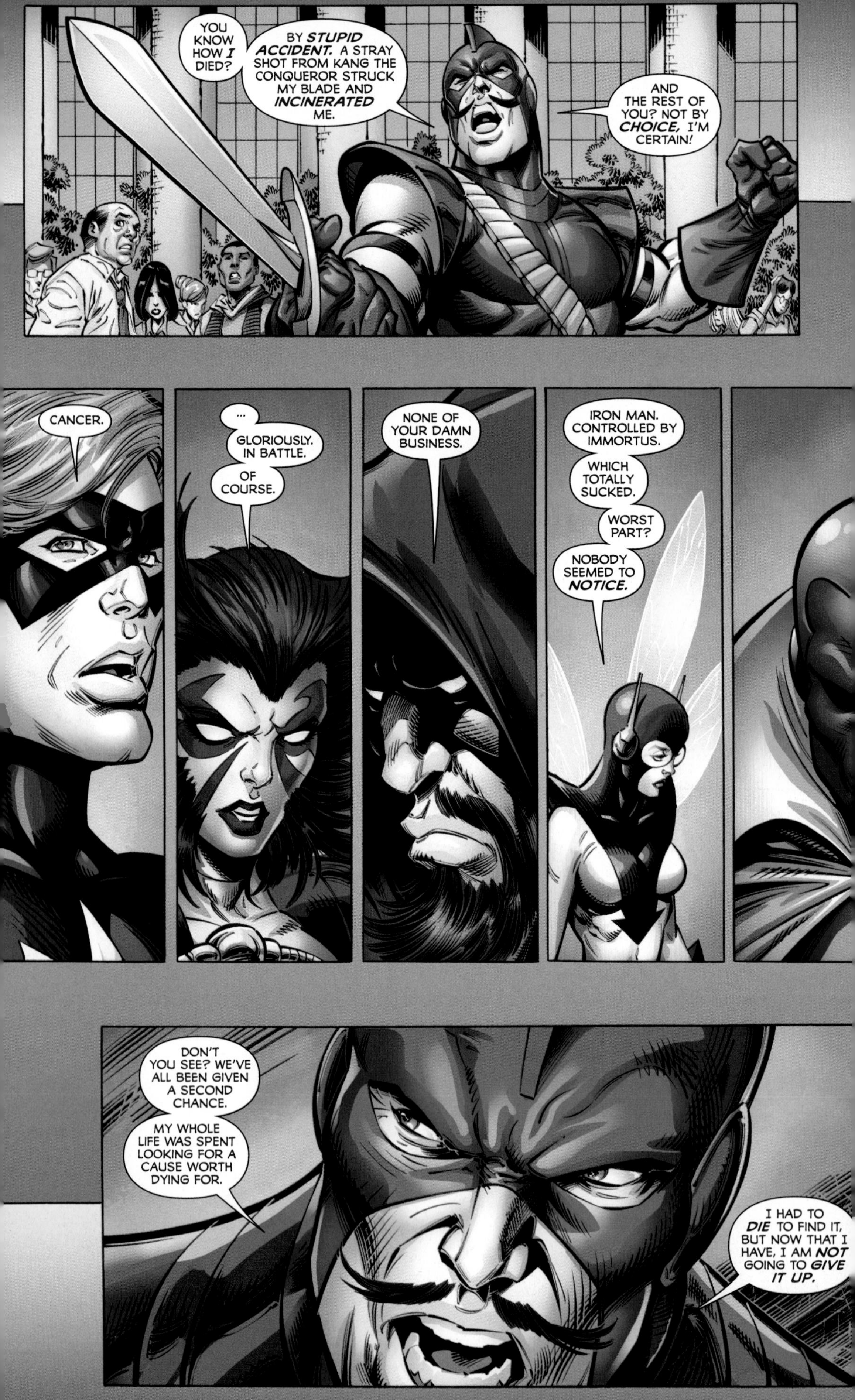
YOU KNOW HOW I DIED?
BY STUPID ACCIDENT. A STRAY SHOT FROM KANG THE CONQUEROR STRUCK MY BLADE AND INCINERATED ME.
AND THE REST OF YOU? NOT BY CHOICE, I'M CERTAIN!
CANCER.
...
GLORIOUSLY. IN BATTLE.
OF COURSE.
NONE OF YOUR DAMN BUSINESS.
IRON MAN. CONTROLLED BY IMMORTUS.
WHICH TOTALLY SUCKED.
WORST PART?
NOBODY SEEMED TO NOTICE.
DON'T YOU SEE? WE'VE ALL BEEN GIVEN A SECOND CHANCE.
MY WHOLE LIFE WAS SPENT LOOKING FOR A CAUSE WORTH DYING FOR.
I HAD TO DIE TO FIND IT, BUT NOW THAT I HAVE, I AM NOT GOING TO GIVE IT UP.

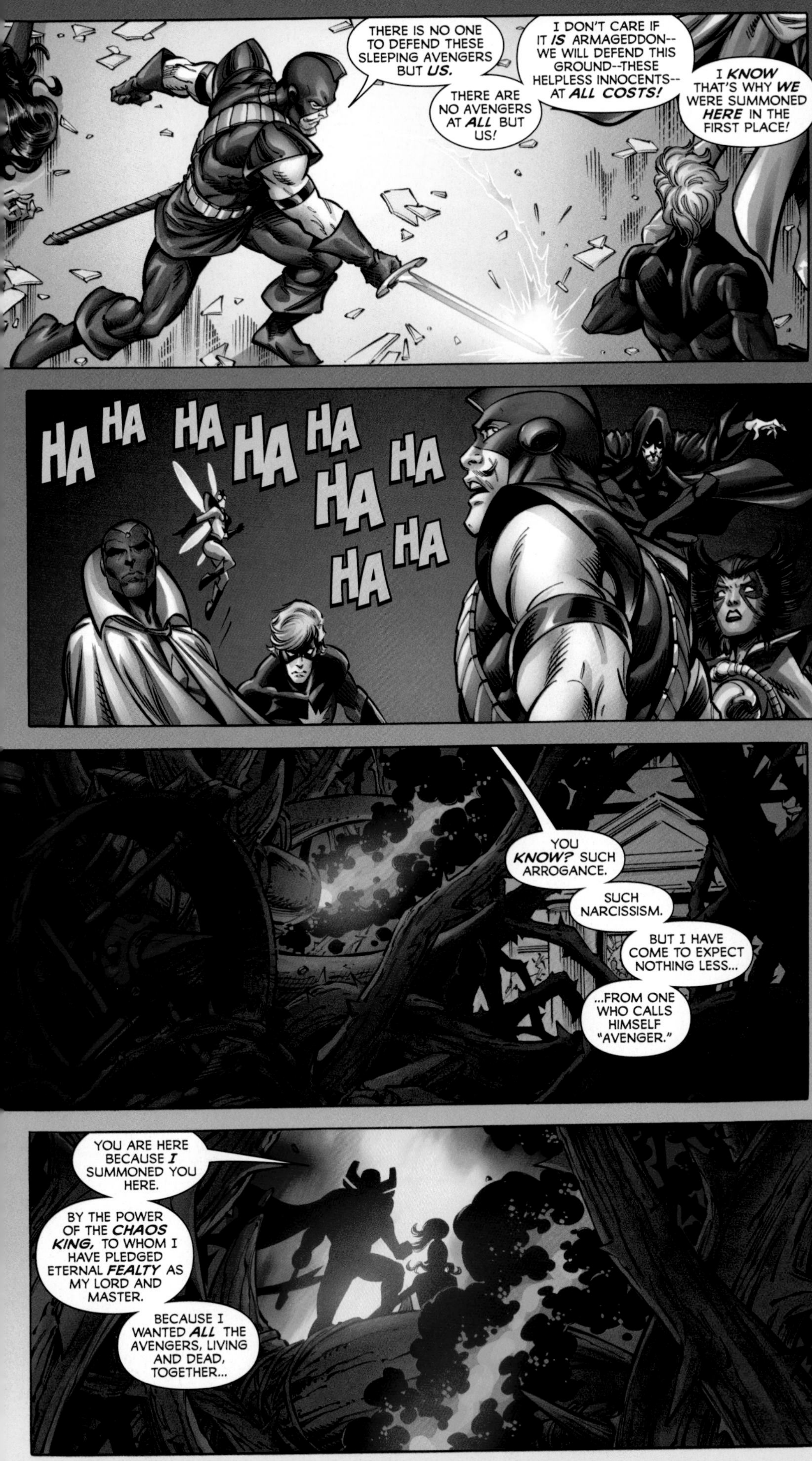
THERE IS NO ONE TO DEFEND THESE SLEEPING AVENGERS BUT *US.*
THERE ARE NO AVENGERS AT *ALL* BUT US!
I DON'T CARE IF IT *IS* ARMAGEDDON--WE WILL DEFEND THIS GROUND--THESE HELPLESS INNOCENTS--AT *ALL COSTS!*
I *KNOW* THAT'S WHY *WE* WERE SUMMONED *HERE* IN THE FIRST PLACE!
HA HA HA HA HA HA HA HA HA
YOU *KNOW?* SUCH ARROGANCE.
SUCH NARCISSISM.
BUT I HAVE COME TO EXPECT NOTHING LESS...
...FROM ONE WHO CALLS HIMSELF "AVENGER."
YOU ARE HERE BECAUSE *I* SUMMONED YOU HERE.
BY THE POWER OF THE *CHAOS KING,* TO WHOM I HAVE PLEDGED ETERNAL *FEALTY* AS MY LORD AND MASTER.
BECAUSE I WANTED *ALL* THE AVENGERS, LIVING AND DEAD, TOGETHER...

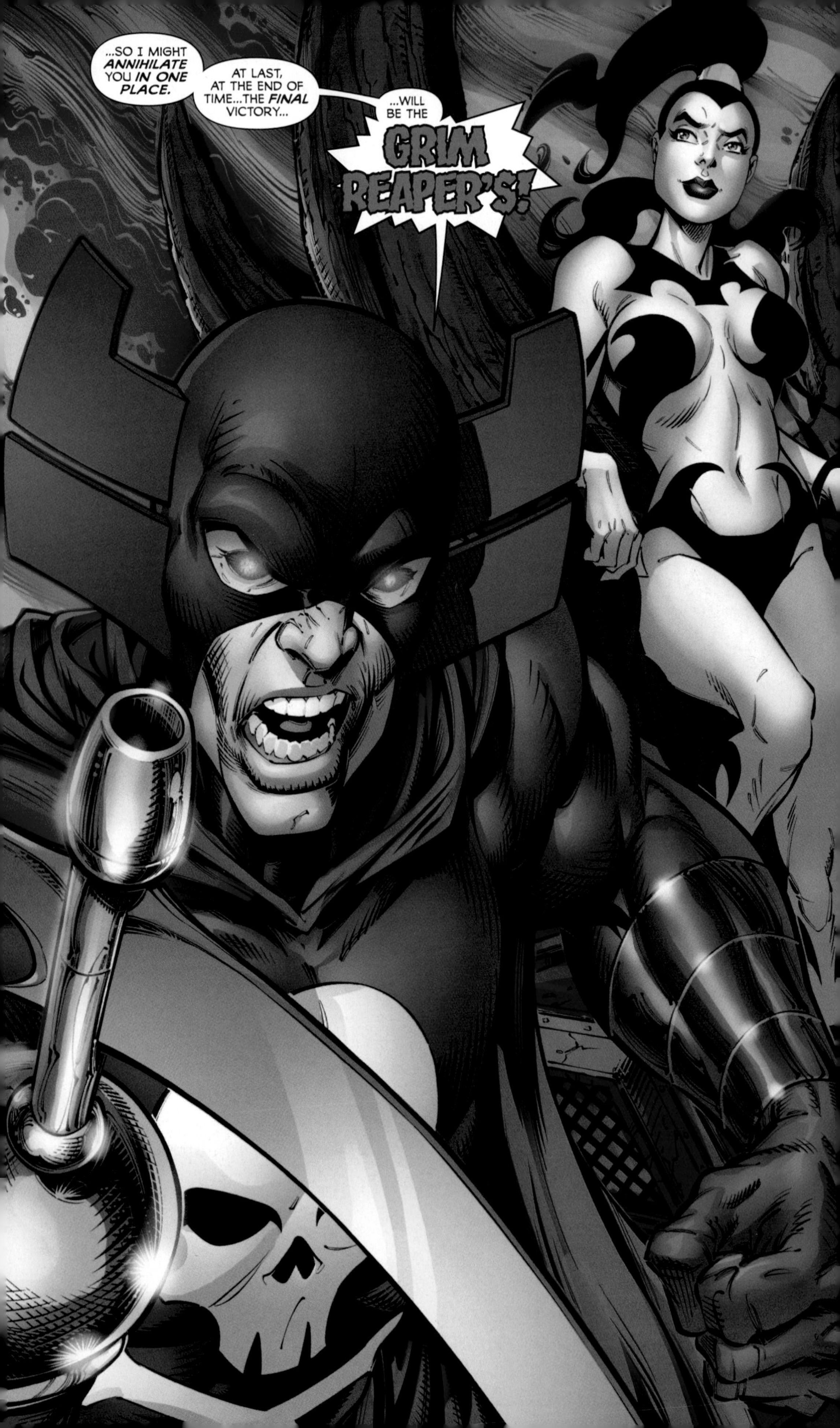
...SO I MIGHT ANNIHILATE YOU IN ONE PLACE.
AT LAST, AT THE END OF TIME...THE FINAL VICTORY...
...WILL BE THE
GRIM REAPER'S!

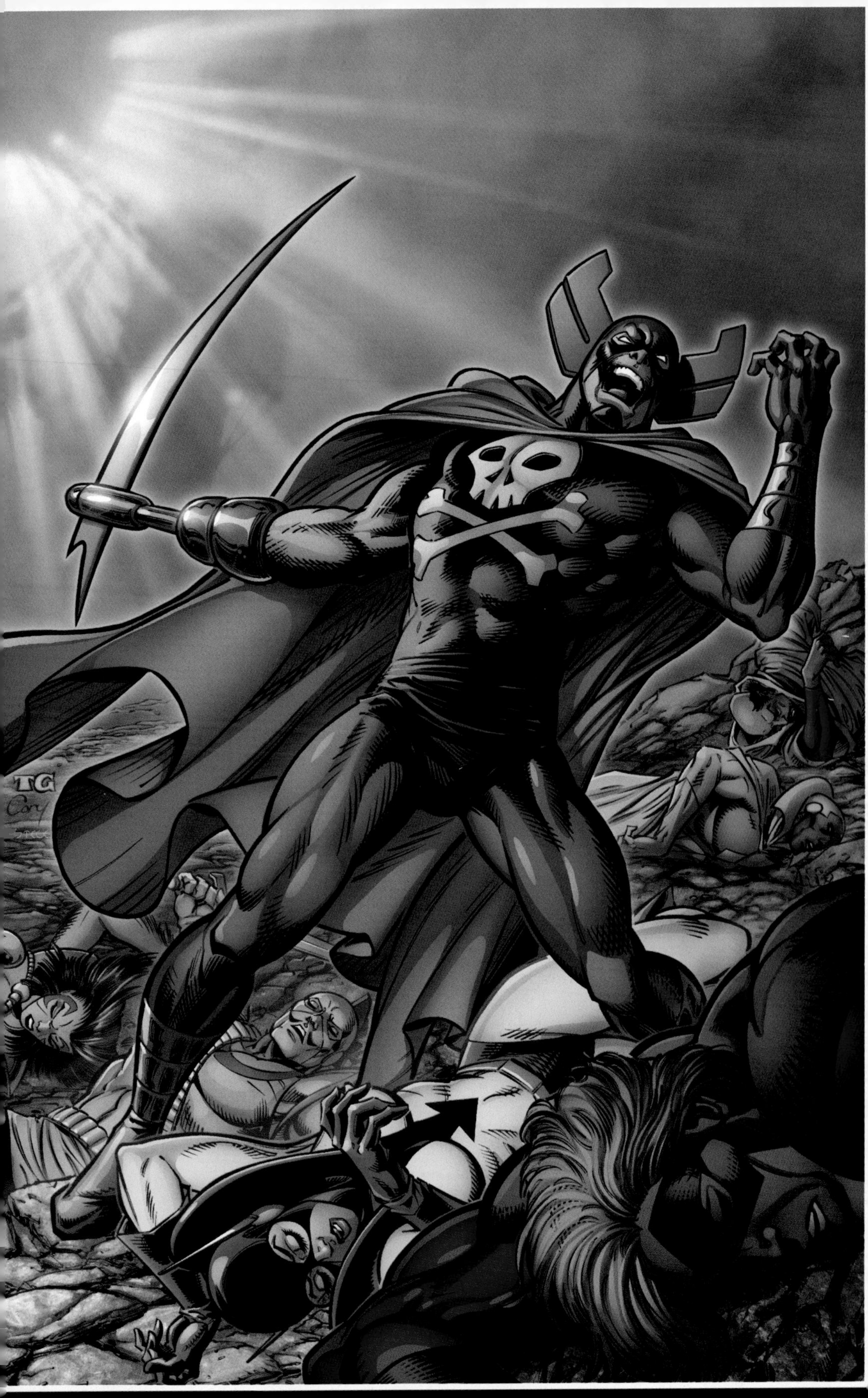

CHAOS WAR: DEAD AVENGERS #2

MAR-VELL

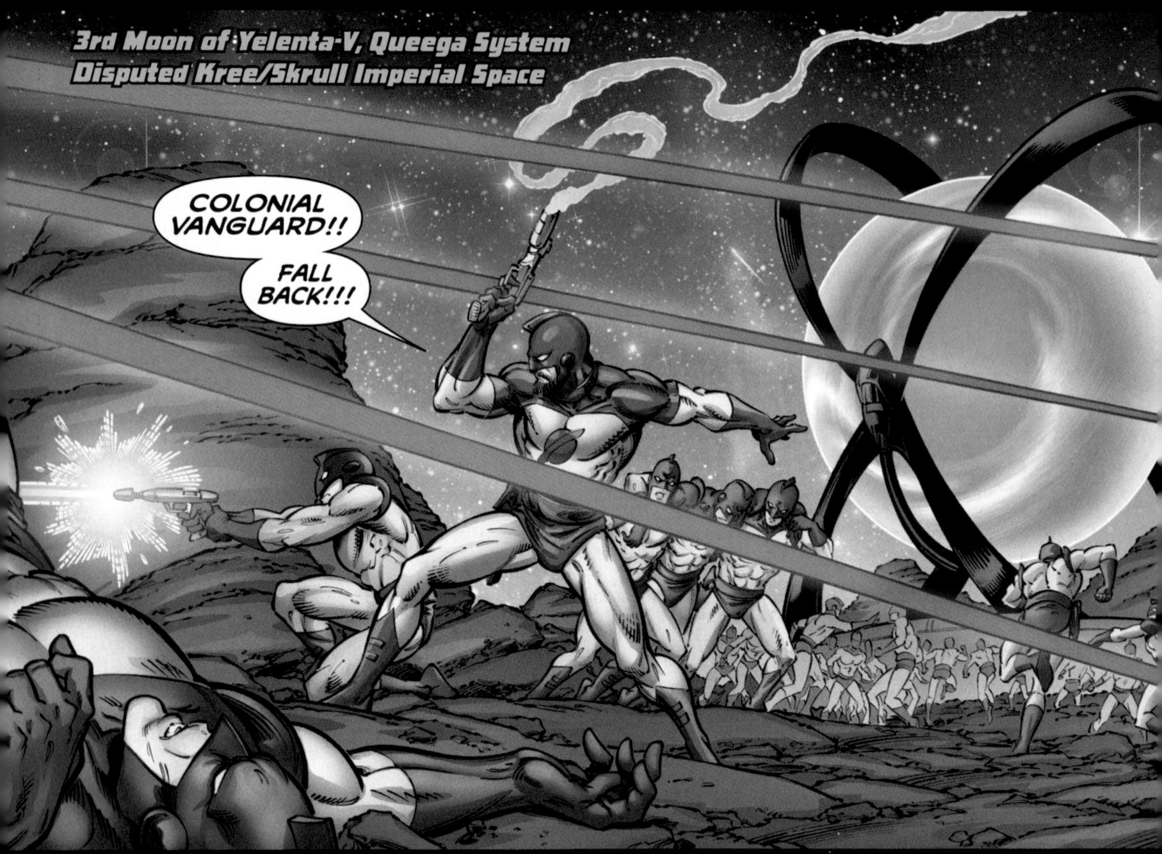
3rd Moon of Yelenta-V, Queega System
Disputed Kree/Skrull Imperial Space
COLONIAL VANGUARD!!
FALL BACK!!!

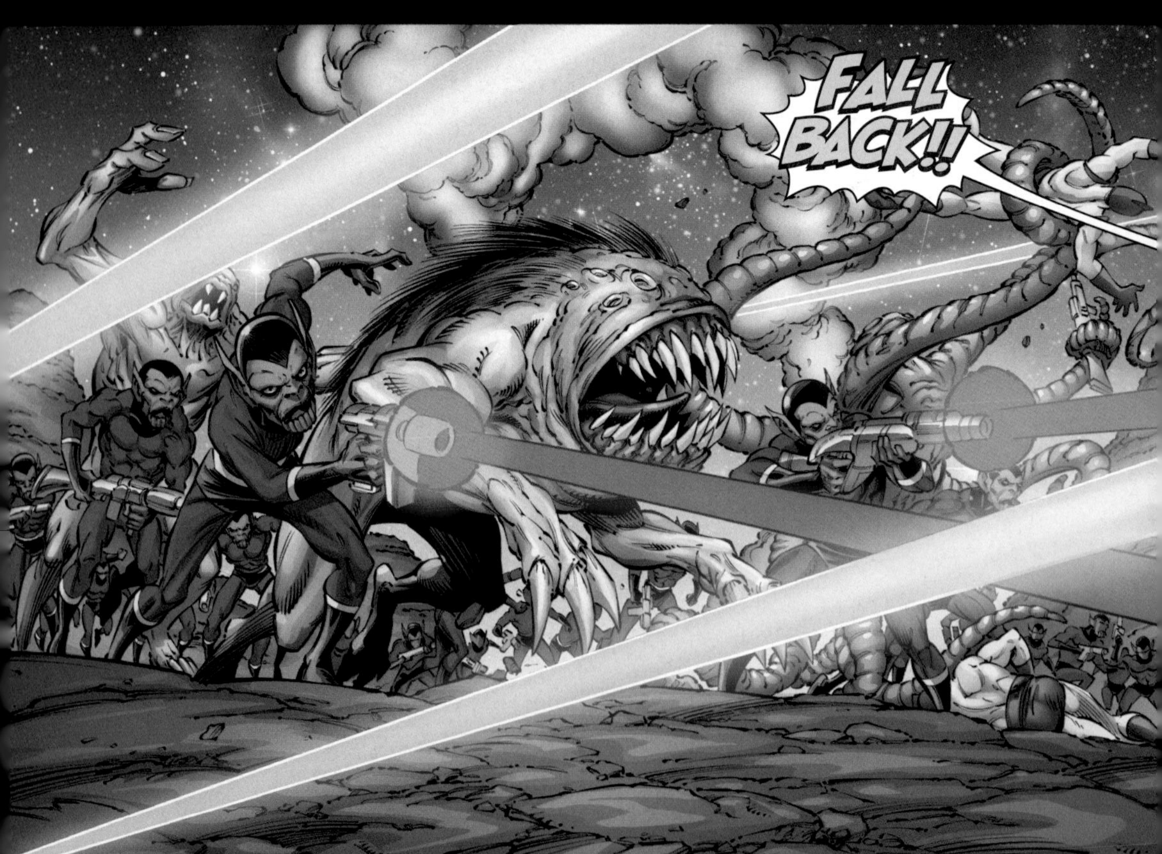
FALL BACK!!

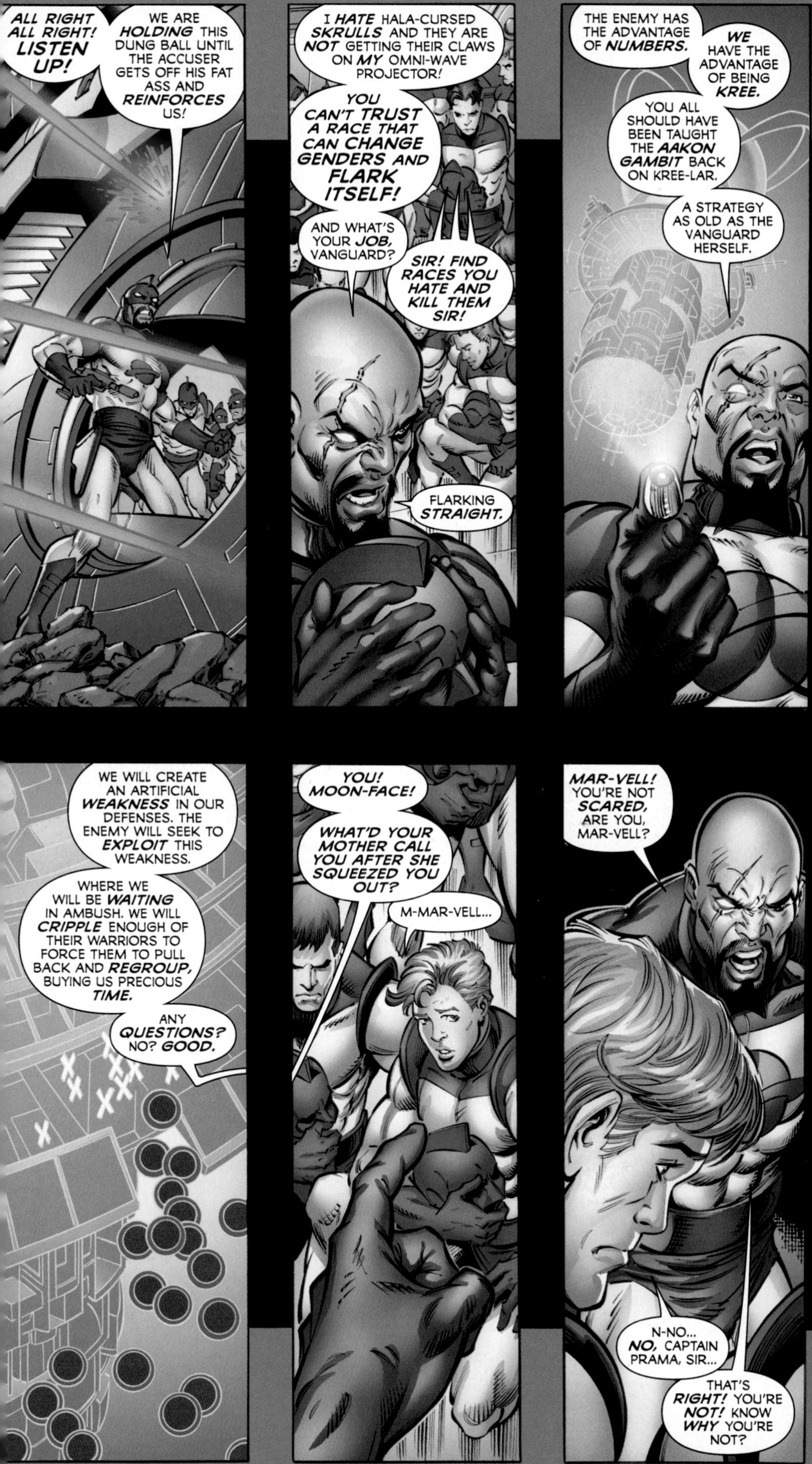
ALL RIGHT ALL RIGHT! LISTEN UP!
WE ARE HOLDING THIS DUNG BALL UNTIL THE ACCUSER GETS OFF HIS FAT ASS AND REINFORCES US!
I HATE HALA-CURSED SKRULLS AND THEY ARE NOT GETTING THEIR CLAWS ON MY OMNI-WAVE PROJECTOR!
YOU CAN'T TRUST A RACE THAT CAN CHANGE GENDERS AND FLARK ITSELF!
AND WHAT'S YOUR JOB, VANGUARD?
SIR! FIND RACES YOU HATE AND KILL THEM SIR!
FLARKING STRAIGHT.
THE ENEMY HAS THE ADVANTAGE OF NUMBERS.
WE HAVE THE ADVANTAGE OF BEING KREE.
YOU ALL SHOULD HAVE BEEN TAUGHT THE AAKON GAMBIT BACK ON KREE-LAR.
A STRATEGY AS OLD AS THE VANGUARD HERSELF.
WE WILL CREATE AN ARTIFICIAL WEAKNESS IN OUR DEFENSES. THE ENEMY WILL SEEK TO EXPLOIT THIS WEAKNESS.
WHERE WE WILL BE WAITING IN AMBUSH. WE WILL CRIPPLE ENOUGH OF THEIR WARRIORS TO FORCE THEM TO PULL BACK AND REGROUP, BUYING US PRECIOUS TIME.
ANY QUESTIONS? NO? GOOD.
YOU! MOON-FACE!
WHAT'D YOUR MOTHER CALL YOU AFTER SHE SQUEEZED YOU OUT?
M-MAR-VELL...
MAR-VELL! YOU'RE NOT SCARED, ARE YOU, MAR-VELL?
N-NO... NO, CAPTAIN PRAMA, SIR...
THAT'S RIGHT! YOU'RE NOT! KNOW WHY YOU'RE NOT?

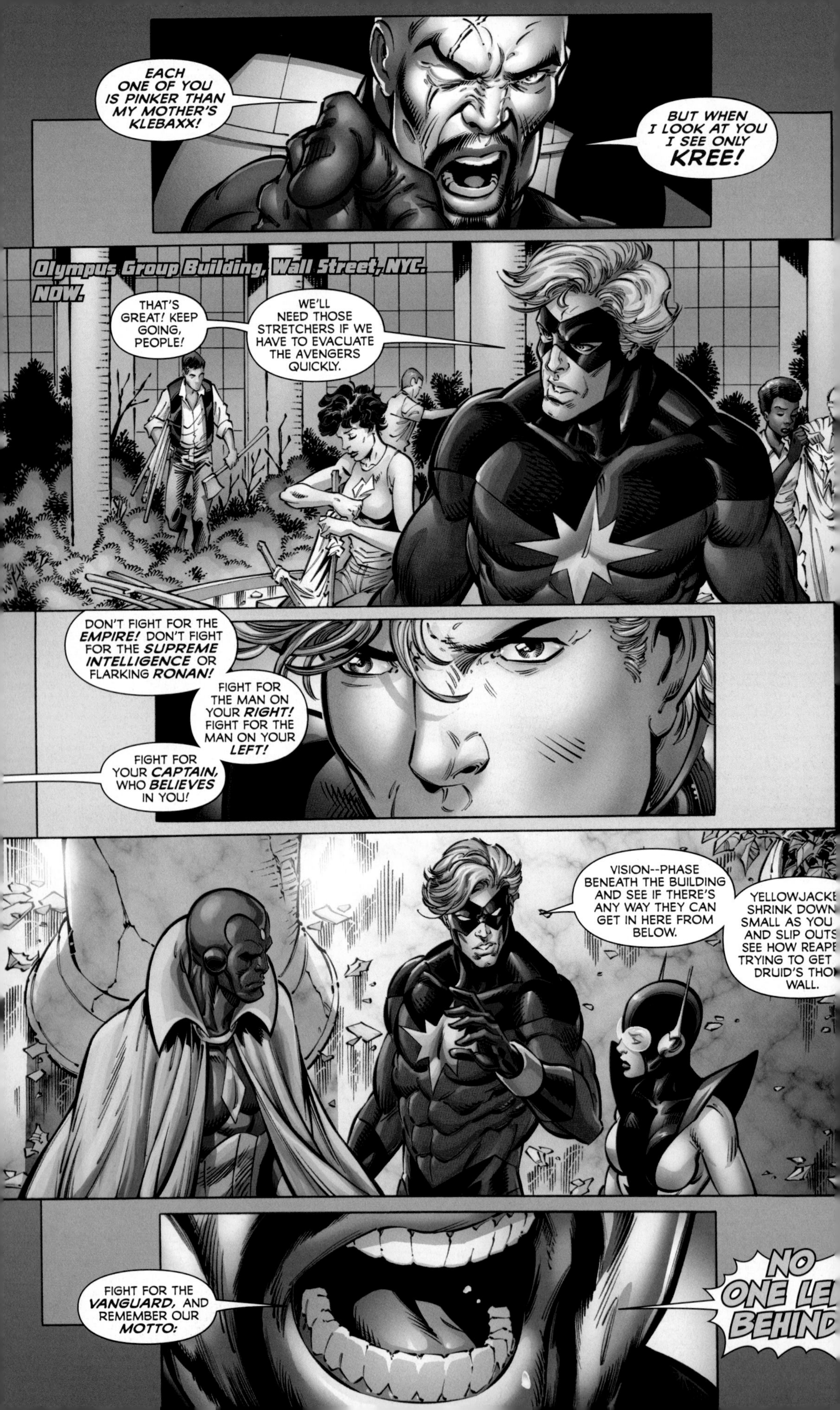
EACH ONE OF YOU IS PINKER THAN MY MOTHER'S KLEBAXX!
BUT WHEN I LOOK AT YOU I SEE ONLY KREE!
Olympus Group Building, Wall Street, NYC. NOW.
THAT'S GREAT! KEEP GOING, PEOPLE!
WE'LL NEED THOSE STRETCHERS IF WE HAVE TO EVACUATE THE AVENGERS QUICKLY.
DON'T FIGHT FOR THE EMPIRE! DON'T FIGHT FOR THE SUPREME INTELLIGENCE OR FLARKING RONAN!
FIGHT FOR THE MAN ON YOUR RIGHT! FIGHT FOR THE MAN ON YOUR LEFT!
FIGHT FOR YOUR CAPTAIN, WHO BELIEVES IN YOU!
VISION--PHASE BENEATH THE BUILDING AND SEE IF THERE'S ANY WAY THEY CAN GET IN HERE FROM BELOW.
FIGHT FOR THE VANGUARD, AND REMEMBER OUR MOTTO:

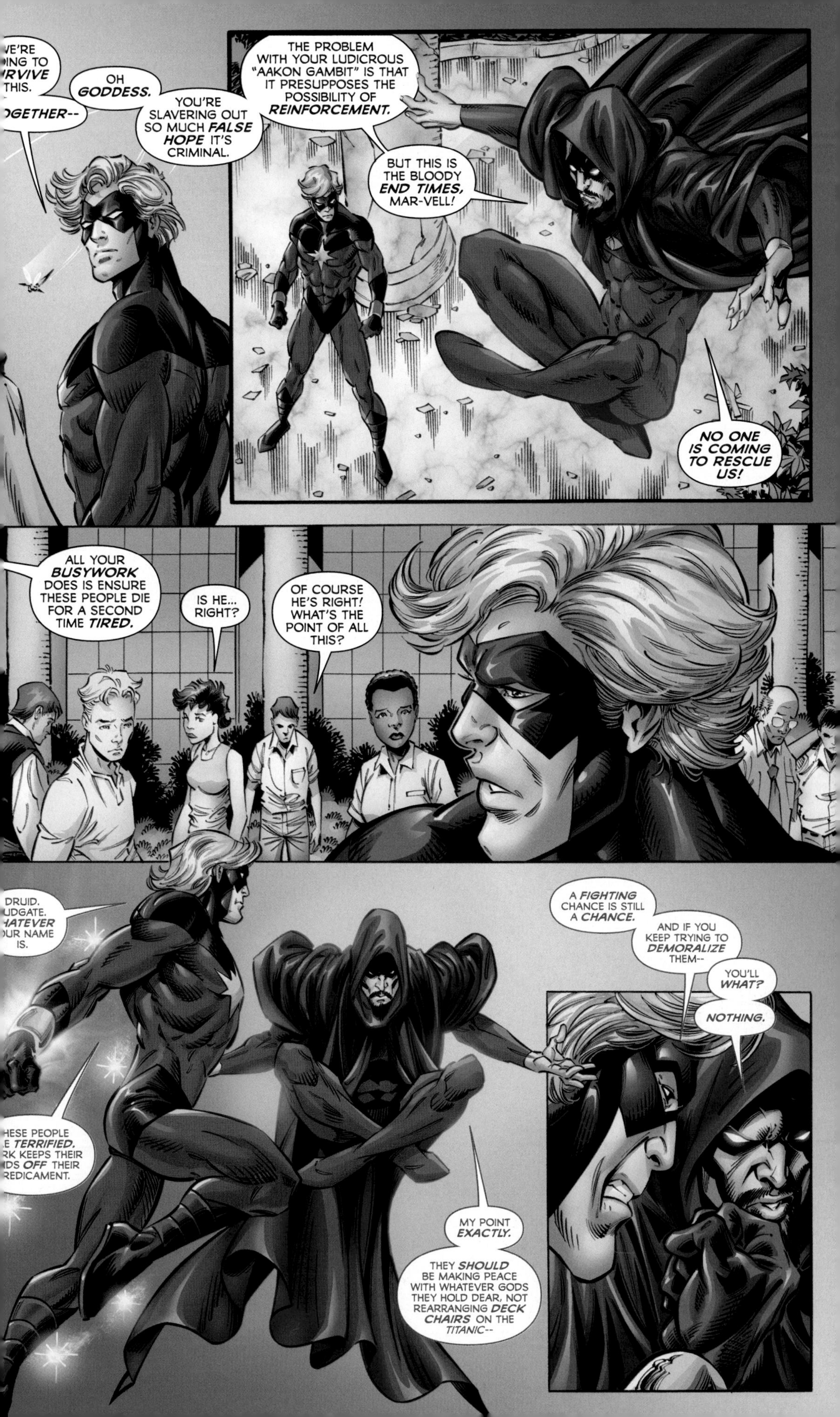
VE'RE DING TO RVIVE THIS.
OH GODDESS.
DGETHER--
YOU'RE SLAVERING OUT SO MUCH FALSE HOPE IT'S CRIMINAL.
THE PROBLEM WITH YOUR LUDICROUS "AAKON GAMBIT" IS THAT IT PRESUPPOSES THE POSSIBILITY OF REINFORCEMENT.
BUT THIS IS THE BLOODY END TIMES, MAR-VELL!
NO ONE IS COMING TO RESCUE US!
ALL YOUR BUSYWORK DOES IS ENSURE THESE PEOPLE DIE FOR A SECOND TIME TIRED.
IS HE... RIGHT?
OF COURSE HE'S RIGHT! WHAT'S THE POINT OF ALL THIS?
DRUID. UDGATE. HATEVER UR NAME IS.
HESE PEOPLE E TERRIFIED. RK KEEPS THEIR DS OFF THEIR REDICAMENT.
MY POINT EXACTLY.
THEY SHOULD BE MAKING PEACE WITH WHATEVER GODS THEY HOLD DEAR, NOT REARRANGING DECK CHAIRS ON THE TITANIC--
A FIGHTING CHANCE IS STILL A CHANCE.
AND IF YOU KEEP TRYING TO DEMORALIZE THEM--
YOU'LL WHAT?
NOTHING.

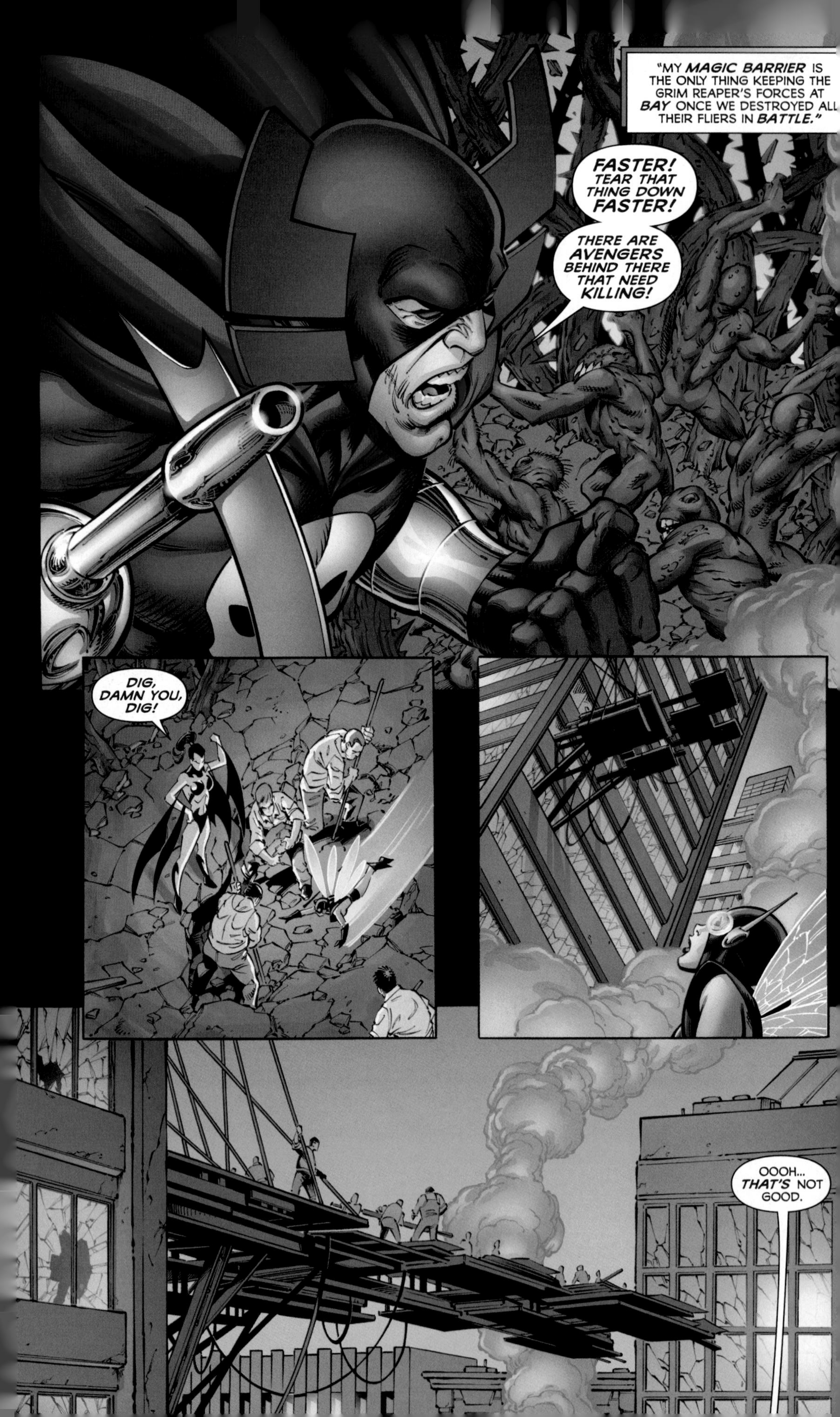
"MY MAGIC BARRIER IS THE ONLY THING KEEPING THE GRIM REAPER'S FORCES AT BAY ONCE WE DESTROYED ALL THEIR FLIERS IN BATTLE."
FASTER! TEAR THAT THING DOWN FASTER!
THERE ARE AVENGERS BEHIND THERE THAT NEED KILLING!
DIG, DAMN YOU, DIG!
OOOH... THAT'S NOT GOOD.

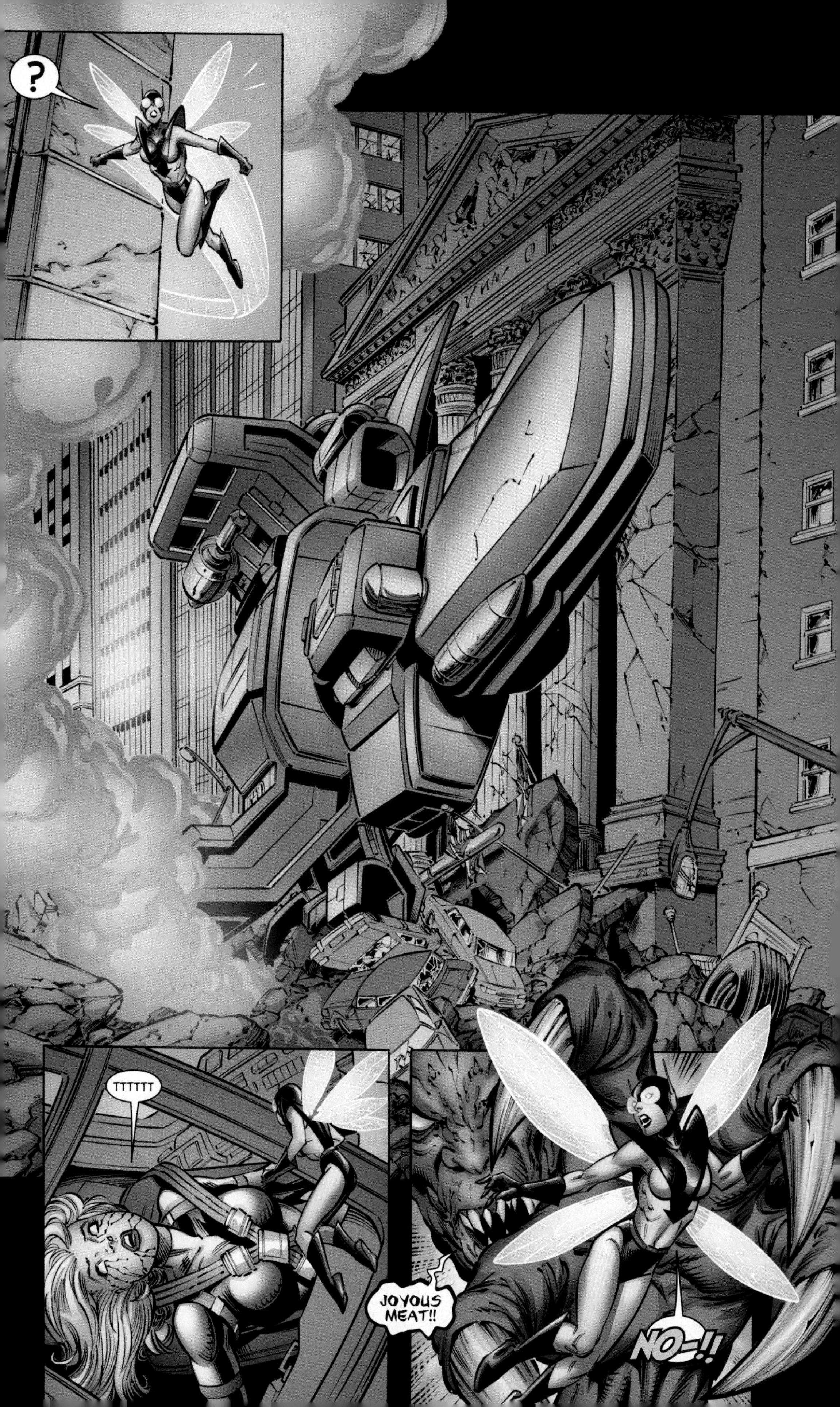
?
TTTTTT
JOYOUS MEAT!!
NO-!!

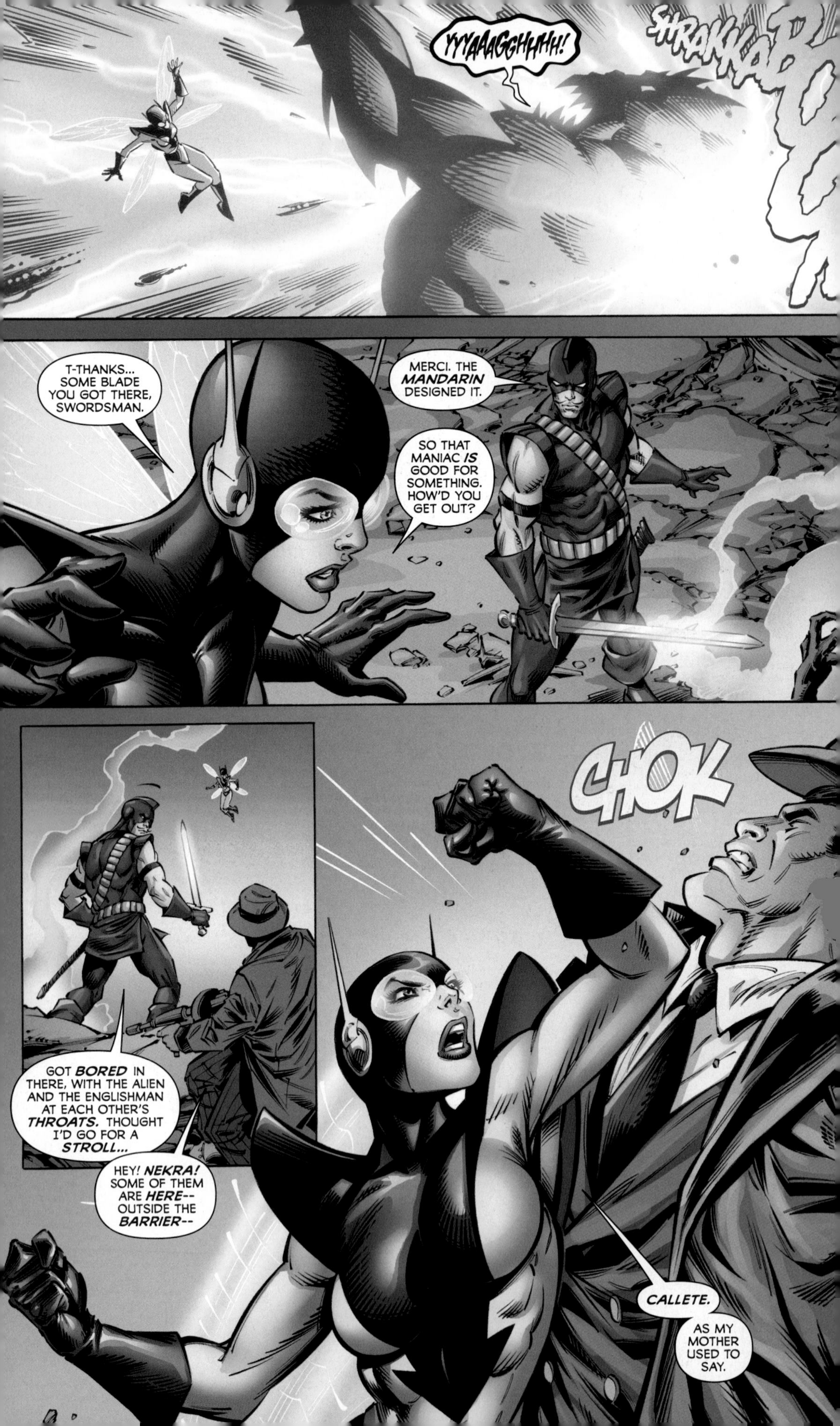
YYYAAAGGHHHH!
SHRAKKABR
T-THANKS... SOME BLADE YOU GOT THERE, SWORDSMAN.
MERCI. THE MANDARIN DESIGNED IT.
SO THAT MANIAC IS GOOD FOR SOMETHING. HOW'D YOU GET OUT?
GOT BORED IN THERE, WITH THE ALIEN AND THE ENGLISHMAN AT EACH OTHER'S THROATS. THOUGHT I'D GO FOR A STROLL...
HEY! NEKRA! SOME OF THEM ARE HERE-- OUTSIDE THE BARRIER--
CHOK
CALLETE.
AS MY MOTHER USED TO SAY.

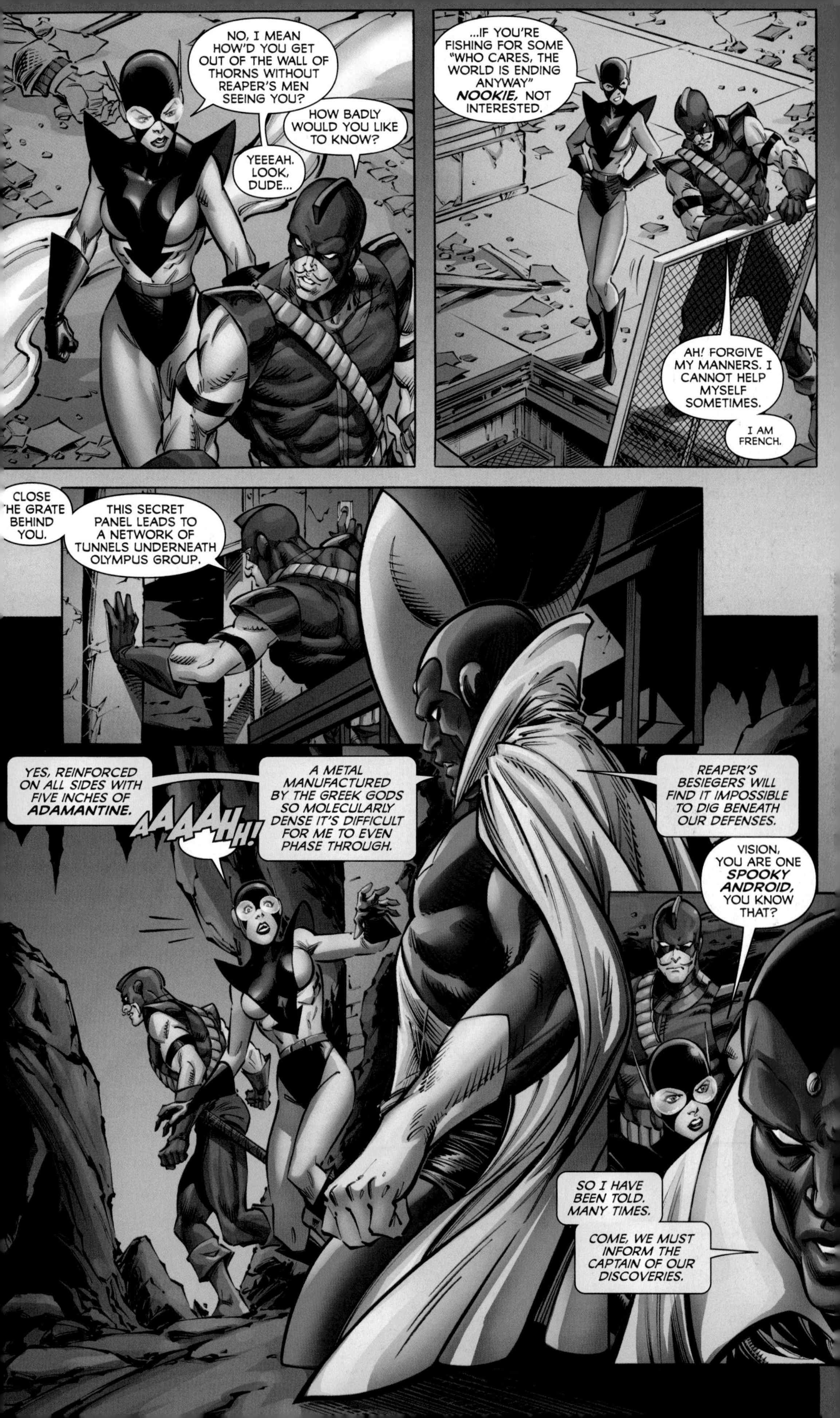

NO, I MEAN HOW'D YOU GET OUT OF THE WALL OF THORNS WITHOUT REAPER'S MEN SEEING YOU?
HOW BADLY WOULD YOU LIKE TO KNOW?
YEEEAH. LOOK, DUDE...
...IF YOU'RE FISHING FOR SOME "WHO CARES, THE WORLD IS ENDING ANYWAY" NOOKIE, NOT INTERESTED.
AH! FORGIVE MY MANNERS. I CANNOT HELP MYSELF SOMETIMES.
I AM FRENCH.
CLOSE THE GRATE BEHIND YOU.
THIS SECRET PANEL LEADS TO A NETWORK OF TUNNELS UNDERNEATH OLYMPUS GROUP.
YES, REINFORCED ON ALL SIDES WITH FIVE INCHES OF ADAMANTINE.
AAAAHH!
A METAL MANUFACTURED BY THE GREEK GODS SO MOLECULARLY DENSE IT'S DIFFICULT FOR ME TO EVEN PHASE THROUGH.
REAPER'S BESIEGERS WILL FIND IT IMPOSSIBLE TO DIG BENEATH OUR DEFENSES.
VISION, YOU ARE ONE SPOOKY ANDROID, YOU KNOW THAT?
SO I HAVE BEEN TOLD. MANY TIMES.
COME, WE MUST INFORM THE CAPTAIN OF OUR DISCOVERIES.

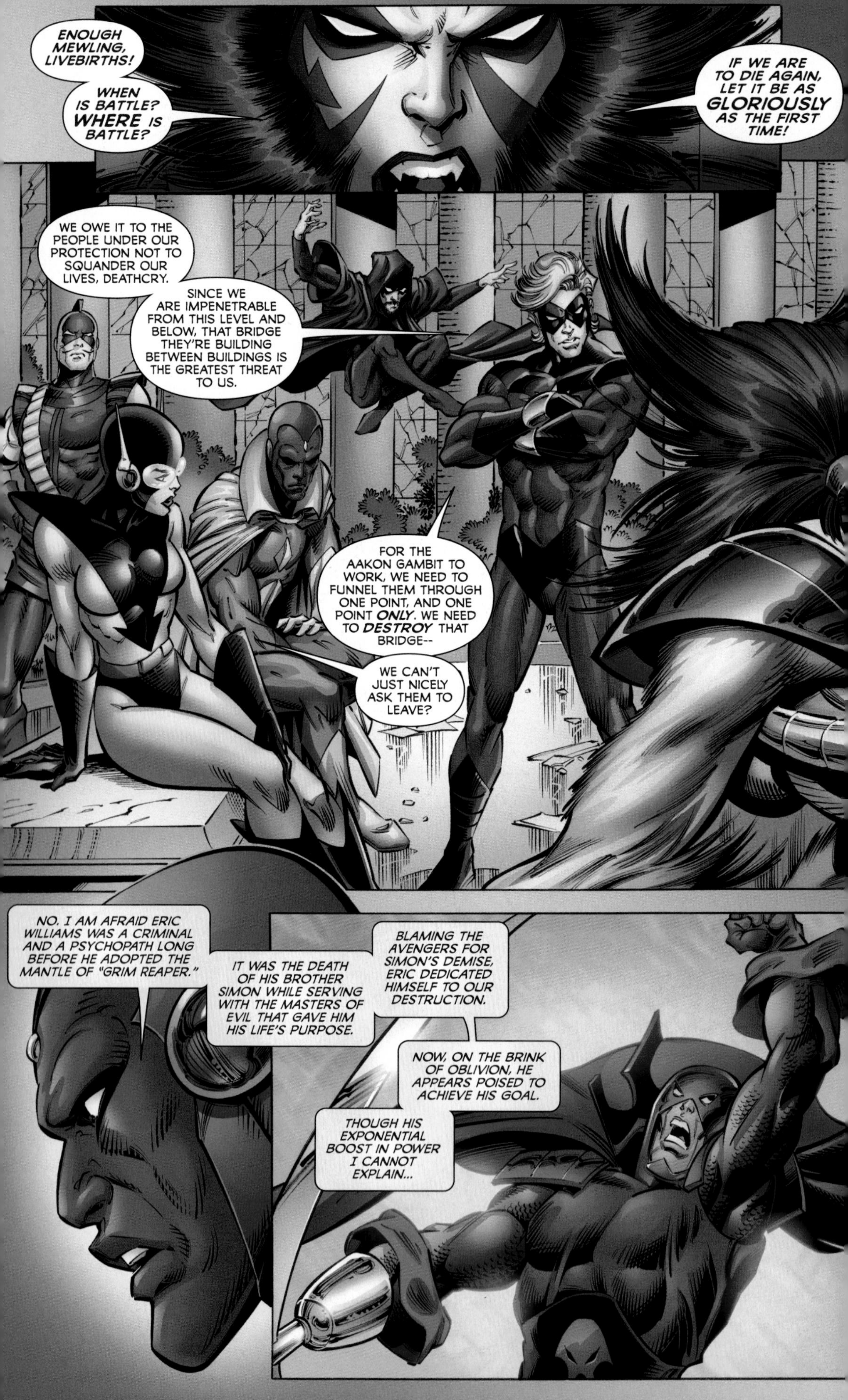

ENOUGH MEWLING, LIVEBIRTHS!
WHEN IS BATTLE? WHERE IS BATTLE?
IF WE ARE TO DIE AGAIN, LET IT BE AS GLORIOUSLY AS THE FIRST TIME!
WE OWE IT TO THE PEOPLE UNDER OUR PROTECTION NOT TO SQUANDER OUR LIVES, DEATHCRY.
SINCE WE ARE IMPENETRABLE FROM THIS LEVEL AND BELOW, THAT BRIDGE THEY'RE BUILDING BETWEEN BUILDINGS IS THE GREATEST THREAT TO US.
FOR THE AAKON GAMBIT TO WORK, WE NEED TO FUNNEL THEM THROUGH ONE POINT, AND ONE POINT ONLY. WE NEED TO DESTROY THAT BRIDGE--
WE CAN'T JUST NICELY ASK THEM TO LEAVE?
NO. I AM AFRAID ERIC WILLIAMS WAS A CRIMINAL AND A PSYCHOPATH LONG BEFORE HE ADOPTED THE MANTLE OF "GRIM REAPER."
IT WAS THE DEATH OF HIS BROTHER SIMON WHILE SERVING WITH THE MASTERS OF EVIL THAT GAVE HIM HIS LIFE'S PURPOSE.
BLAMING THE AVENGERS FOR SIMON'S DEMISE, ERIC DEDICATED HIMSELF TO OUR DESTRUCTION.
NOW, ON THE BRINK OF OBLIVION, HE APPEARS POISED TO ACHIEVE HIS GOAL.
THOUGH HIS EXPONENTIAL BOOST IN POWER I CANNOT EXPLAIN...

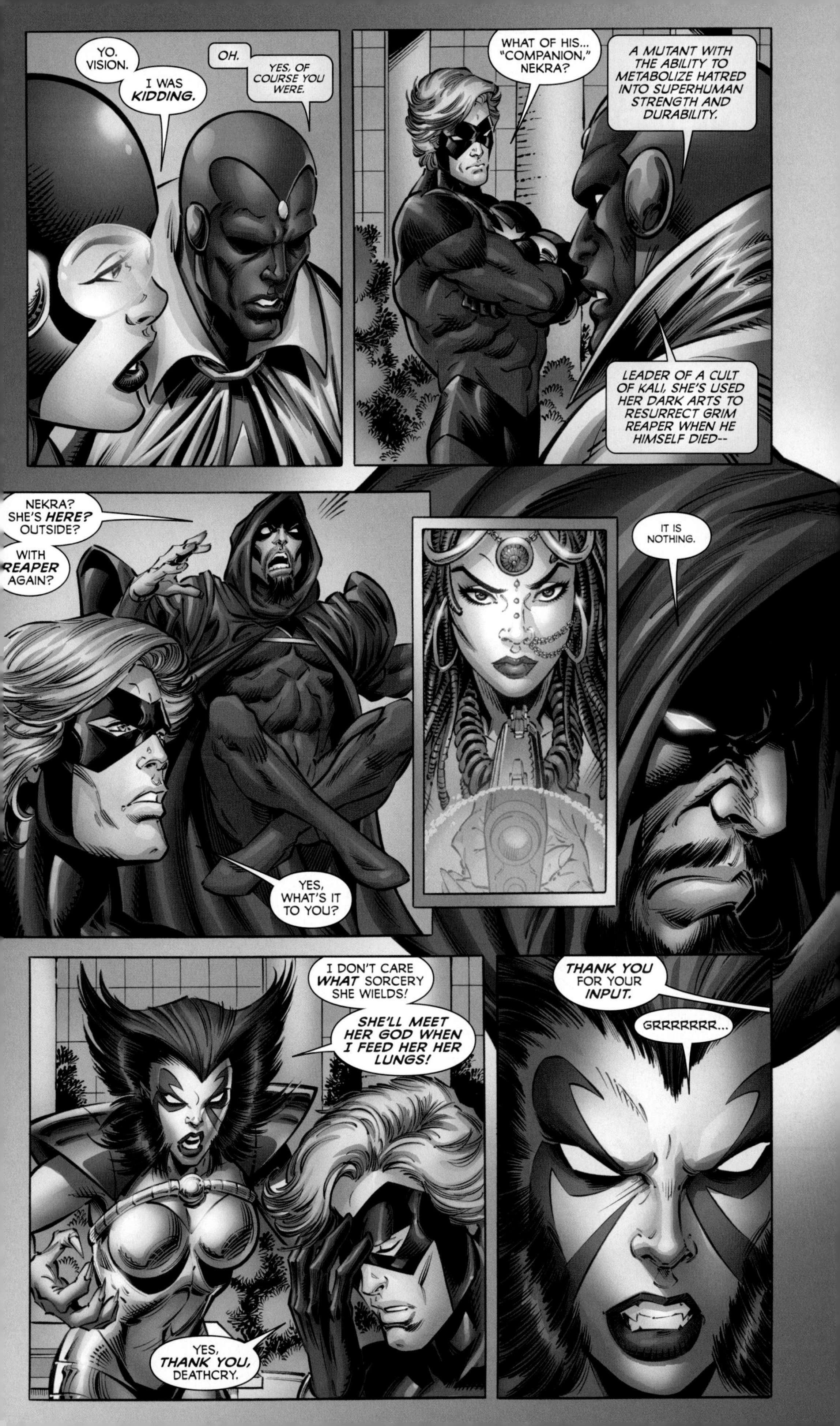

YO. VISION.
I WAS KIDDING.
OH.
YES, OF COURSE YOU WERE.
WHAT OF HIS... "COMPANION," NEKRA?
A MUTANT WITH THE ABILITY TO METABOLIZE HATRED INTO SUPERHUMAN STRENGTH AND DURABILITY.
LEADER OF A CULT OF KALI, SHE'S USED HER DARK ARTS TO RESURRECT GRIM REAPER WHEN HE HIMSELF DIED--
NEKRA? SHE'S HERE? OUTSIDE?
WITH REAPER AGAIN?
YES, WHAT'S IT TO YOU?
IT IS NOTHING.
I DON'T CARE WHAT SORCERY SHE WIELDS!
SHE'LL MEET HER GOD WHEN I FEED HER HER LUNGS!
YES, THANK YOU, DEATHCRY.
THANK YOU FOR YOUR INPUT.
GRRRRRRR...

DEATHCRY

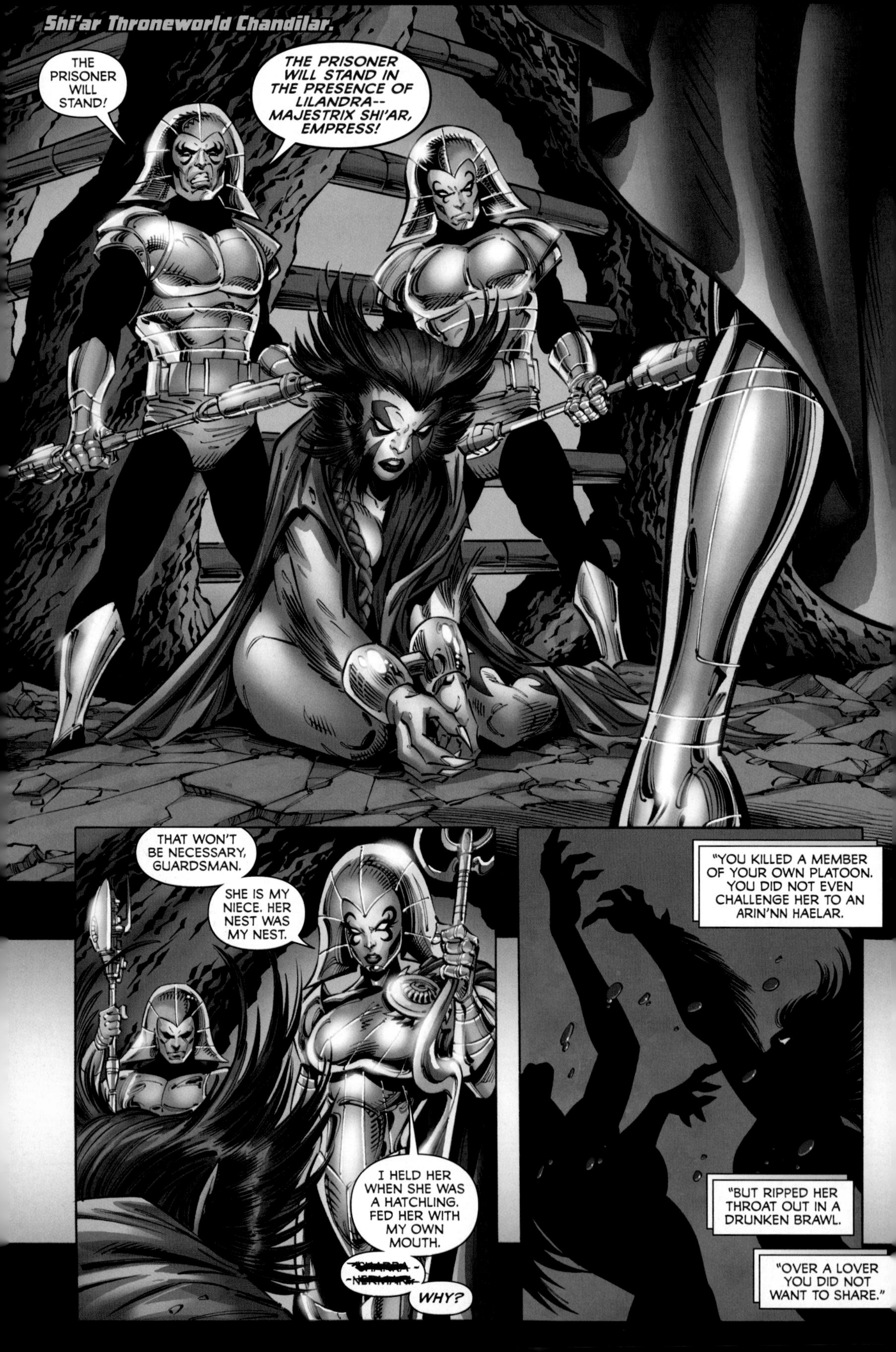
Shi'ar Throneworld Chandilar.
THE PRISONER WILL STAND!
THE PRISONER WILL STAND IN THE PRESENCE OF LILANDRA-- MAJESTRIX SHI'AR, EMPRESS!
THAT WON'T BE NECESSARY, GUARDSMAN.
SHE IS MY NIECE. HER NEST WAS MY NEST.
I HELD HER WHEN SHE WAS A HATCHLING. FED HER WITH MY OWN MOUTH.
WHY?
"YOU KILLED A MEMBER OF YOUR OWN PLATOON. YOU DID NOT EVEN CHALLENGE HER TO AN ARIN'NN HAELAR.
"BUT RIPPED HER THROAT OUT IN A DRUNKEN BRAWL.
"OVER A LOVER YOU DID NOT WANT TO SHARE."

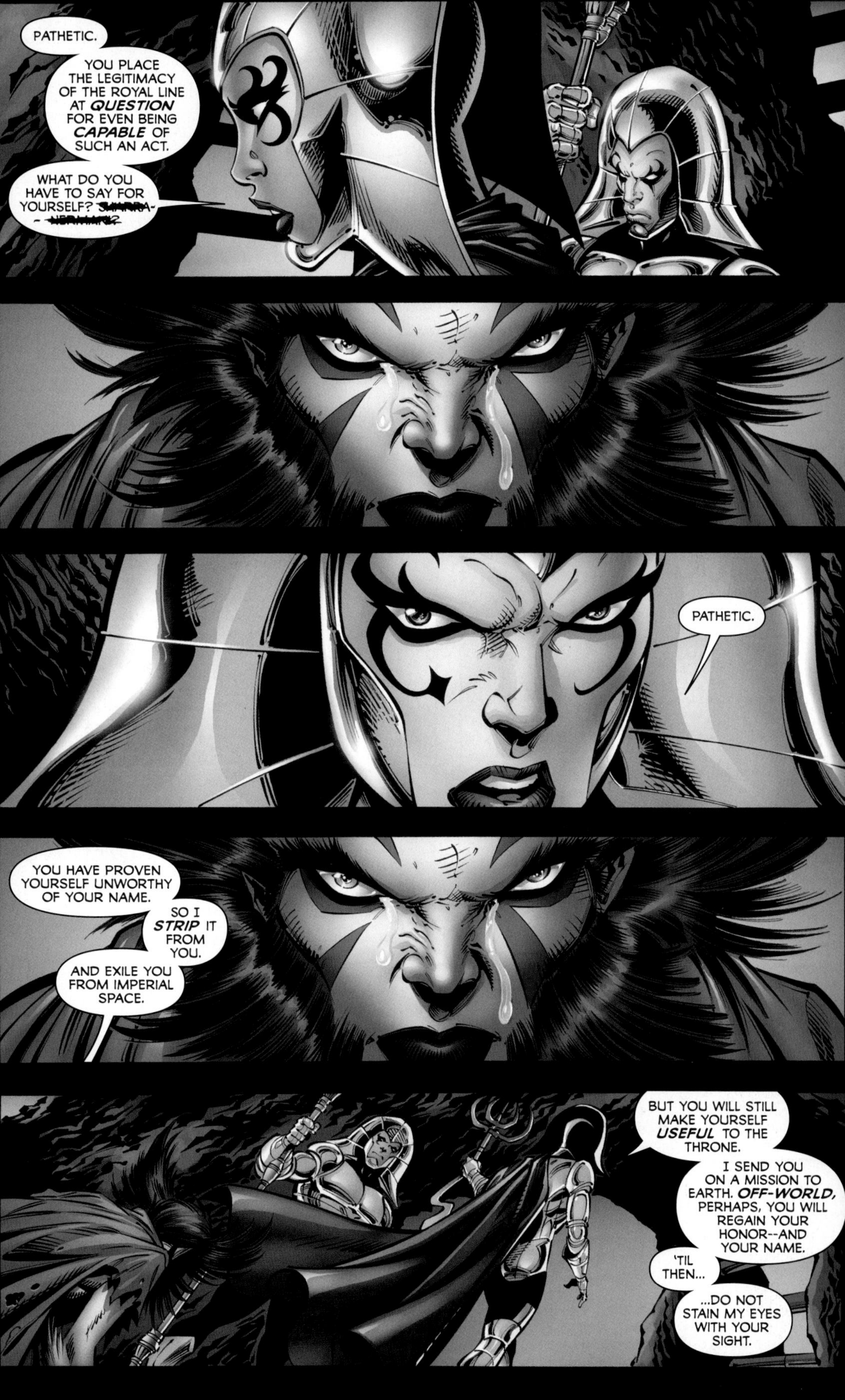
PATHETIC.
YOU PLACE THE LEGITIMACY OF THE ROYAL LINE AT QUESTION FOR EVEN BEING CAPABLE OF SUCH AN ACT.
WHAT DO YOU HAVE TO SAY FOR YOURSELF? [redacted]
PATHETIC.
YOU HAVE PROVEN YOURSELF UNWORTHY OF YOUR NAME.
SO I STRIP IT FROM YOU.
AND EXILE YOU FROM IMPERIAL SPACE.
BUT YOU WILL STILL MAKE YOURSELF USEFUL TO THE THRONE.
I SEND YOU ON A MISSION TO EARTH. OFF-WORLD, PERHAPS, YOU WILL REGAIN YOUR HONOR--AND YOUR NAME.
'TIL THEN...
...DO NOT STAIN MY EYES WITH YOUR SIGHT.

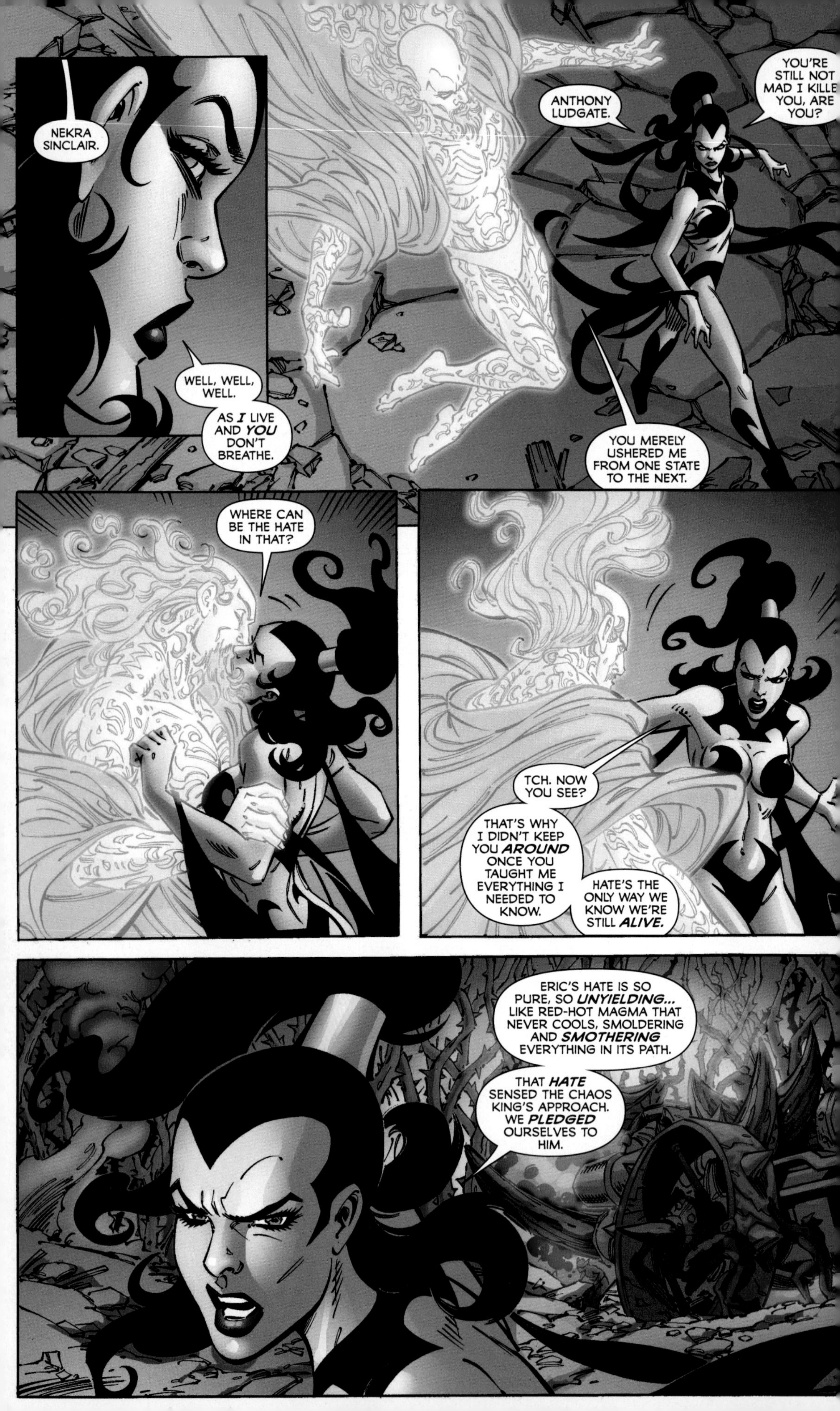
NEKRA SINCLAIR.
WELL, WELL, WELL.
AS I LIVE AND YOU DON'T BREATHE.
ANTHONY LUDGATE.
YOU'RE STILL NOT MAD I KILLE YOU, ARE YOU?
YOU MERELY USHERED ME FROM ONE STATE TO THE NEXT.
WHERE CAN BE THE HATE IN THAT?
TCH. NOW YOU SEE?
THAT'S WHY I DIDN'T KEEP YOU AROUND ONCE YOU TAUGHT ME EVERYTHING I NEEDED TO KNOW.
HATE'S THE ONLY WAY WE KNOW WE'RE STILL ALIVE.
ERIC'S HATE IS SO PURE, SO UNYIELDING... LIKE RED-HOT MAGMA THAT NEVER COOLS, SMOLDERING AND SMOTHERING EVERYTHING IN ITS PATH.
THAT HATE SENSED THE CHAOS KING'S APPROACH. WE PLEDGED OURSELVES TO HIM.

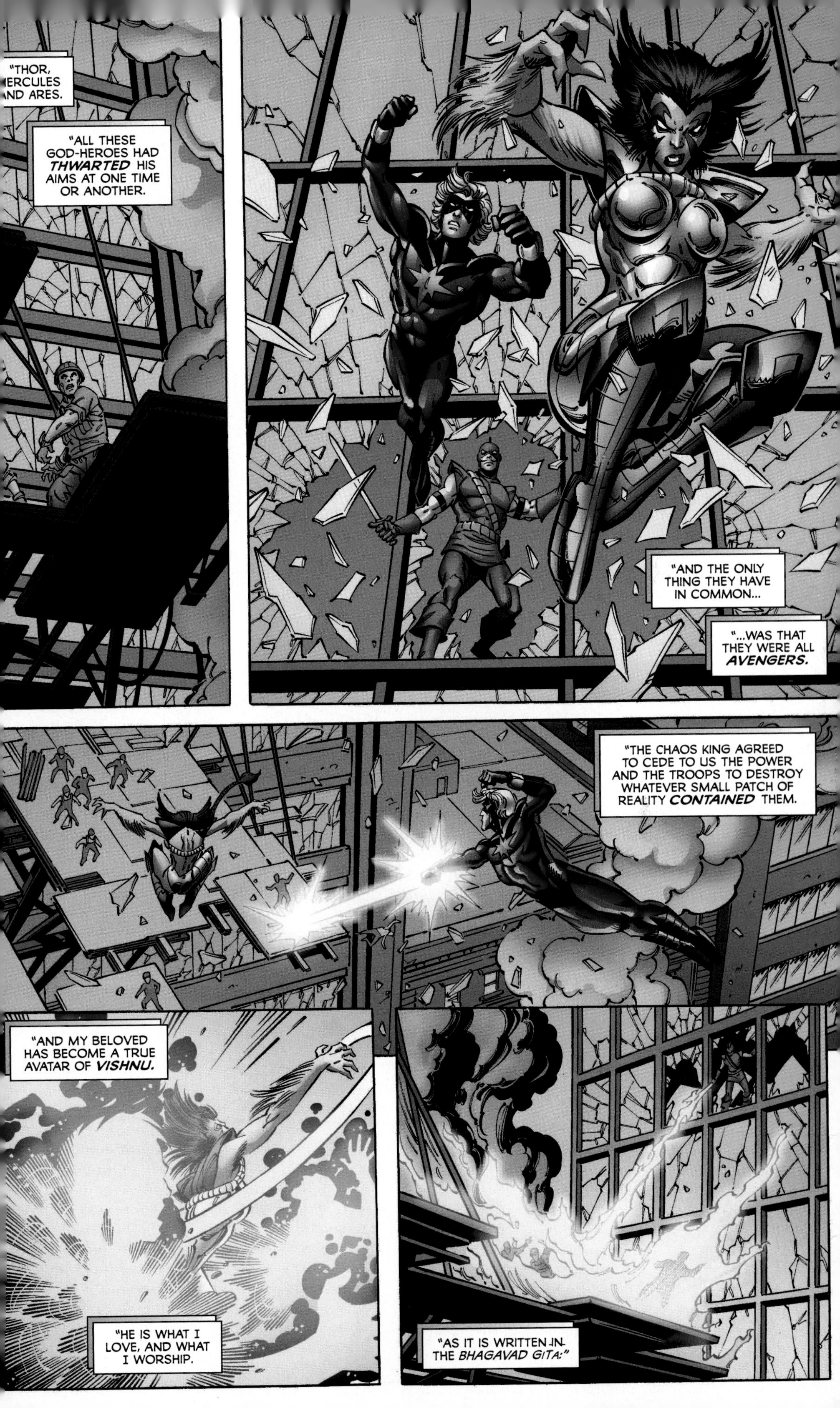
"THOR,
ERCULES
ND ARES.
"ALL THESE GOD-HEROES HAD *THWARTED* HIS AIMS AT ONE TIME OR ANOTHER.
"AND THE ONLY THING THEY HAVE IN COMMON...
"...WAS THAT THEY WERE ALL *AVENGERS.*
"THE CHAOS KING AGREED TO CEDE TO US THE POWER AND THE TROOPS TO DESTROY WHATEVER SMALL PATCH OF REALITY *CONTAINED* THEM.
"AND MY BELOVED HAS BECOME A TRUE AVATAR OF *VISHNU.*
"HE IS WHAT I LOVE, AND WHAT I WORSHIP.
"AS IT IS WRITTEN IN THE *BHAGAVAD GITA:*"

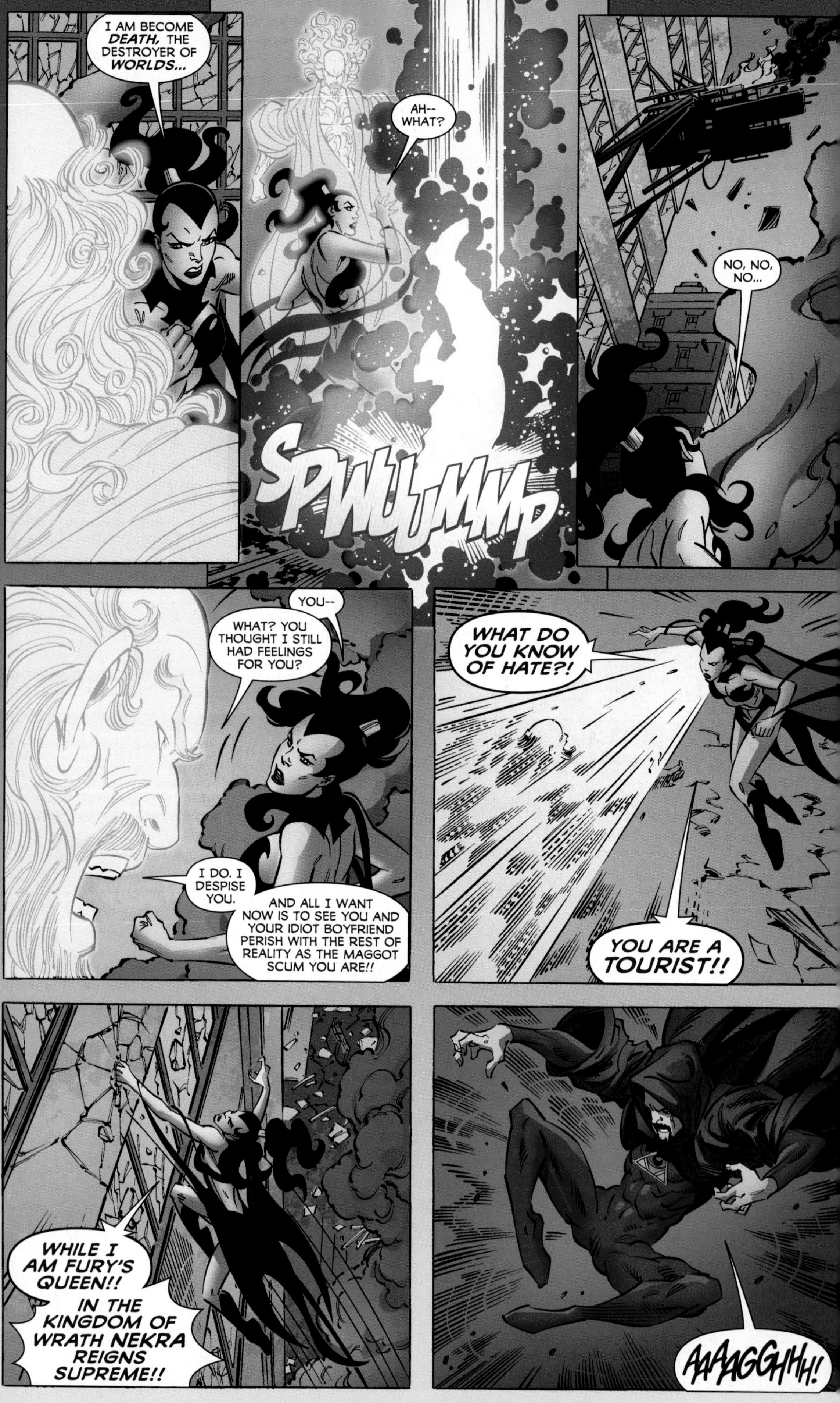
I AM BECOME *DEATH,* THE DESTROYER OF *WORLDS...*
AH-- WHAT?
SPWUUMMP
NO, NO, NO...
YOU--
WHAT? YOU THOUGHT I STILL HAD FEELINGS FOR YOU?
I DO. I DESPISE YOU.
AND ALL I WANT NOW IS TO SEE YOU AND YOUR IDIOT BOYFRIEND PERISH WITH THE REST OF REALITY AS THE MAGGOT SCUM YOU ARE!!
WHAT DO YOU KNOW OF HATE?!
YOU ARE A TOURIST!!
WHILE I AM FURY'S QUEEN!!
IN THE KINGDOM OF WRATH NEKRA REIGNS SUPREME!!
AAAAGGHHH!

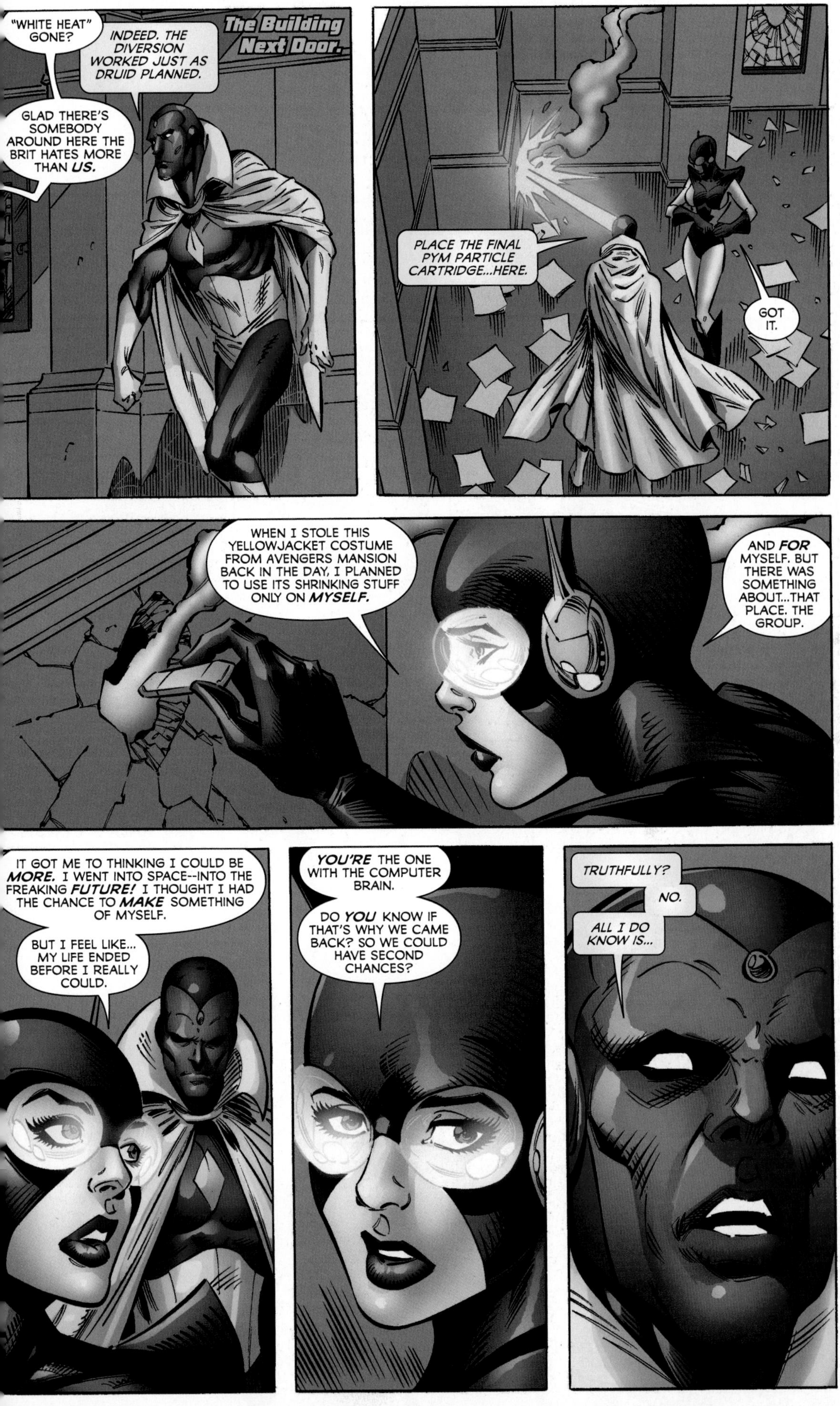
The Building Next Door.
"WHITE HEAT" GONE?
INDEED. THE DIVERSION WORKED JUST AS DRUID PLANNED.
GLAD THERE'S SOMEBODY AROUND HERE THE BRIT HATES MORE THAN US.
PLACE THE FINAL PYM PARTICLE CARTRIDGE...HERE.
GOT IT.
WHEN I STOLE THIS YELLOWJACKET COSTUME FROM AVENGERS MANSION BACK IN THE DAY, I PLANNED TO USE ITS SHRINKING STUFF ONLY ON MYSELF.
AND FOR MYSELF. BUT THERE WAS SOMETHING ABOUT...THAT PLACE. THE GROUP.
IT GOT ME TO THINKING I COULD BE MORE. I WENT INTO SPACE--INTO THE FREAKING FUTURE! I THOUGHT I HAD THE CHANCE TO MAKE SOMETHING OF MYSELF.
BUT I FEEL LIKE... MY LIFE ENDED BEFORE I REALLY COULD.
YOU'RE THE ONE WITH THE COMPUTER BRAIN.
DO YOU KNOW IF THAT'S WHY WE CAME BACK? SO WE COULD HAVE SECOND CHANCES?
TRUTHFULLY?
NO.
ALL I DO KNOW IS...

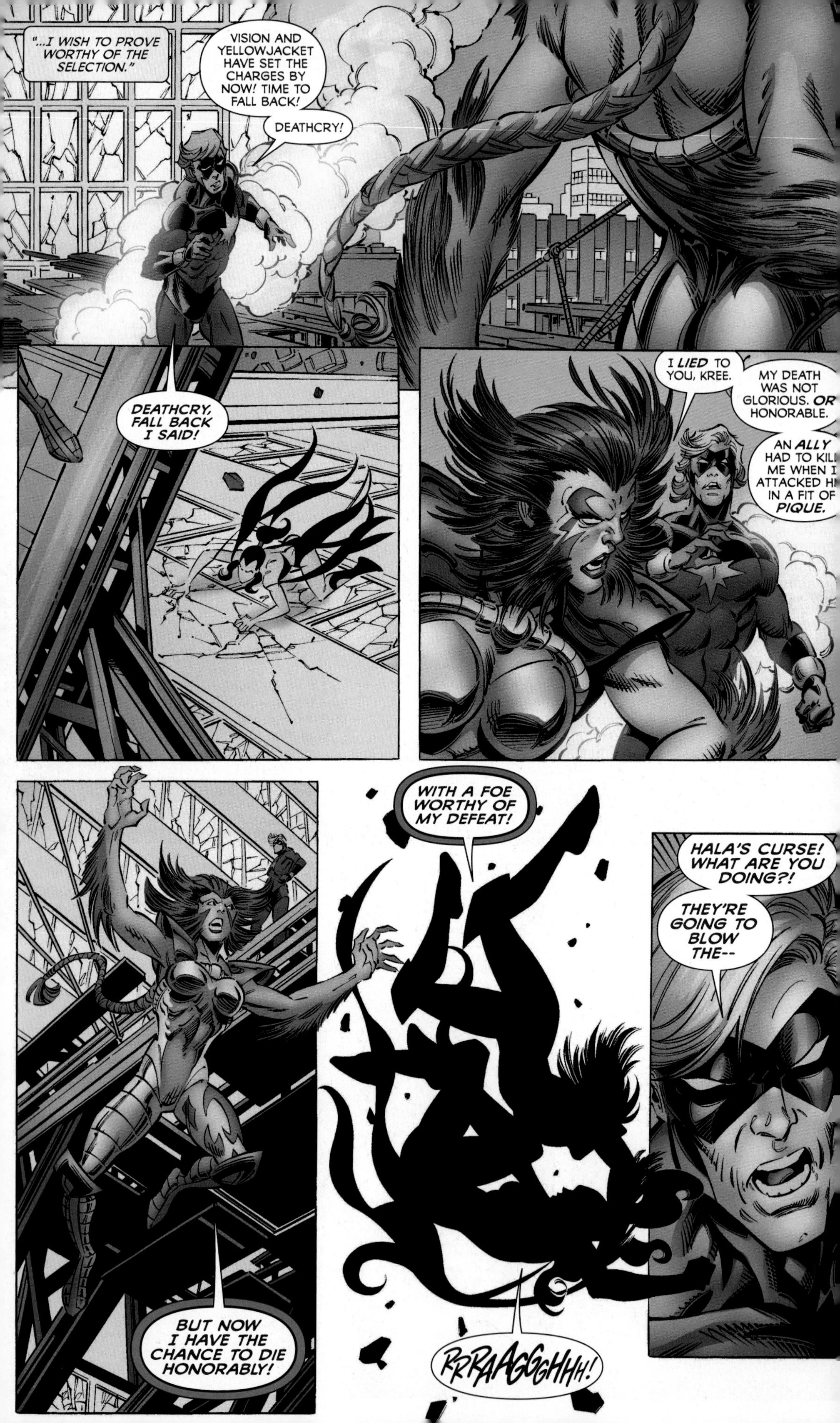
"...I WISH TO PROVE WORTHY OF THE SELECTION."
VISION AND YELLOWJACKET HAVE SET THE CHARGES BY NOW! TIME TO FALL BACK!
DEATHCRY!
DEATHCRY, FALL BACK I SAID!
I LIED TO YOU, KREE.
MY DEATH WAS NOT GLORIOUS. OR HONORABLE.
AN ALLY HAD TO KILL ME WHEN I ATTACKED HIM IN A FIT OF PIQUE.
BUT NOW I HAVE THE CHANCE TO DIE HONORABLY!
WITH A FOE WORTHY OF MY DEFEAT!
RRRAAGGGHHH!
HALA'S CURSE! WHAT ARE YOU DOING?!
THEY'RE GOING TO BLOW THE--

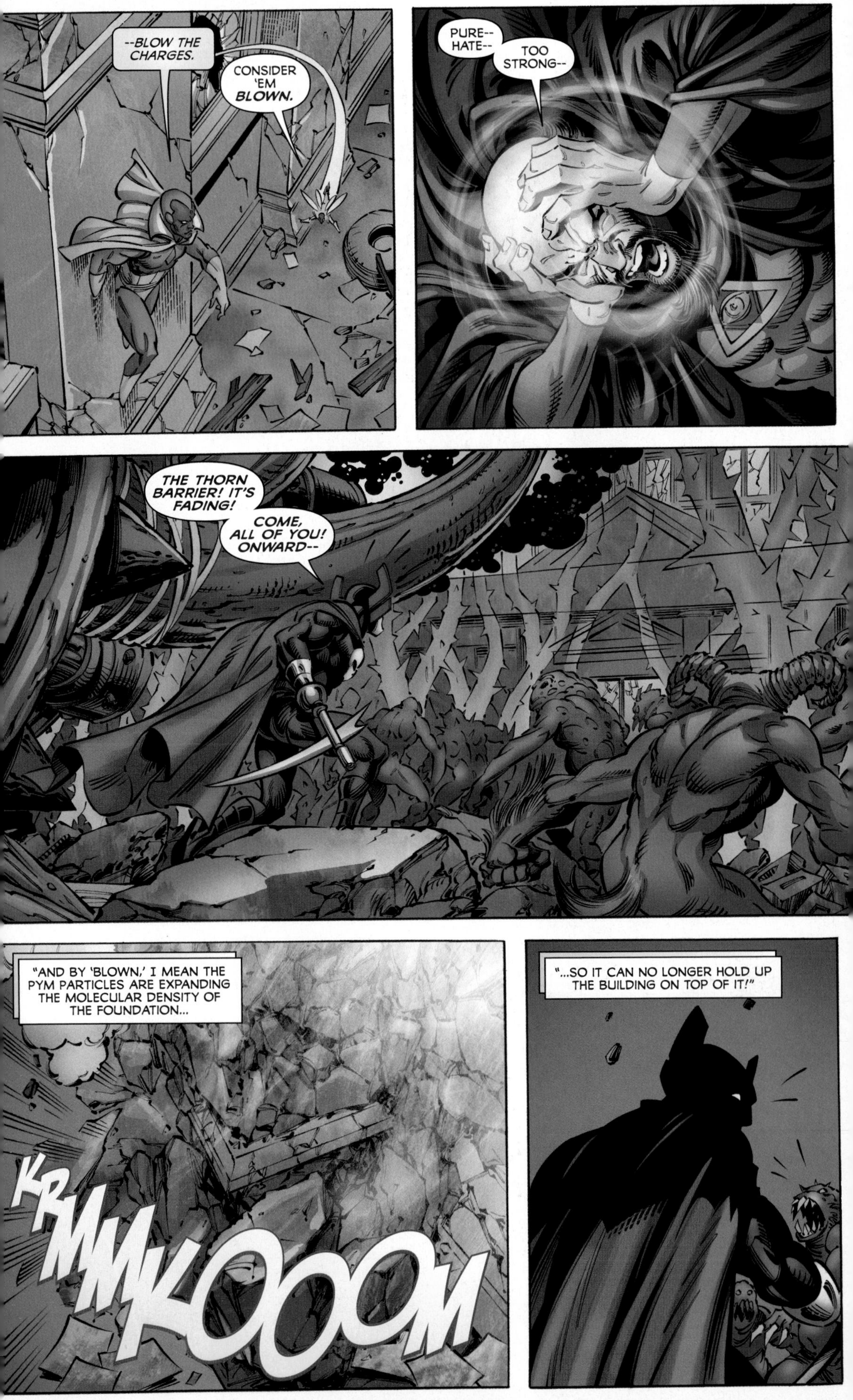
--BLOW THE CHARGES.
CONSIDER 'EM BLOWN.
PURE-- HATE--
TOO STRONG--
THE THORN BARRIER! IT'S FADING!
COME, ALL OF YOU! ONWARD--
"AND BY 'BLOWN,' I MEAN THE PYM PARTICLES ARE EXPANDING THE MOLECULAR DENSITY OF THE FOUNDATION...
KRMMKOOOM
"...SO IT CAN NO LONGER HOLD UP THE BUILDING ON TOP OF IT!"

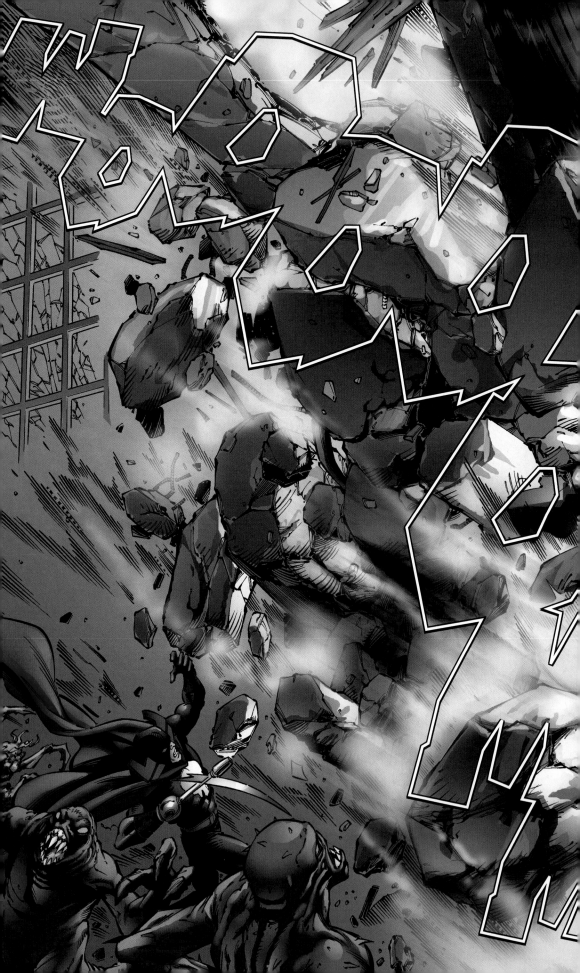

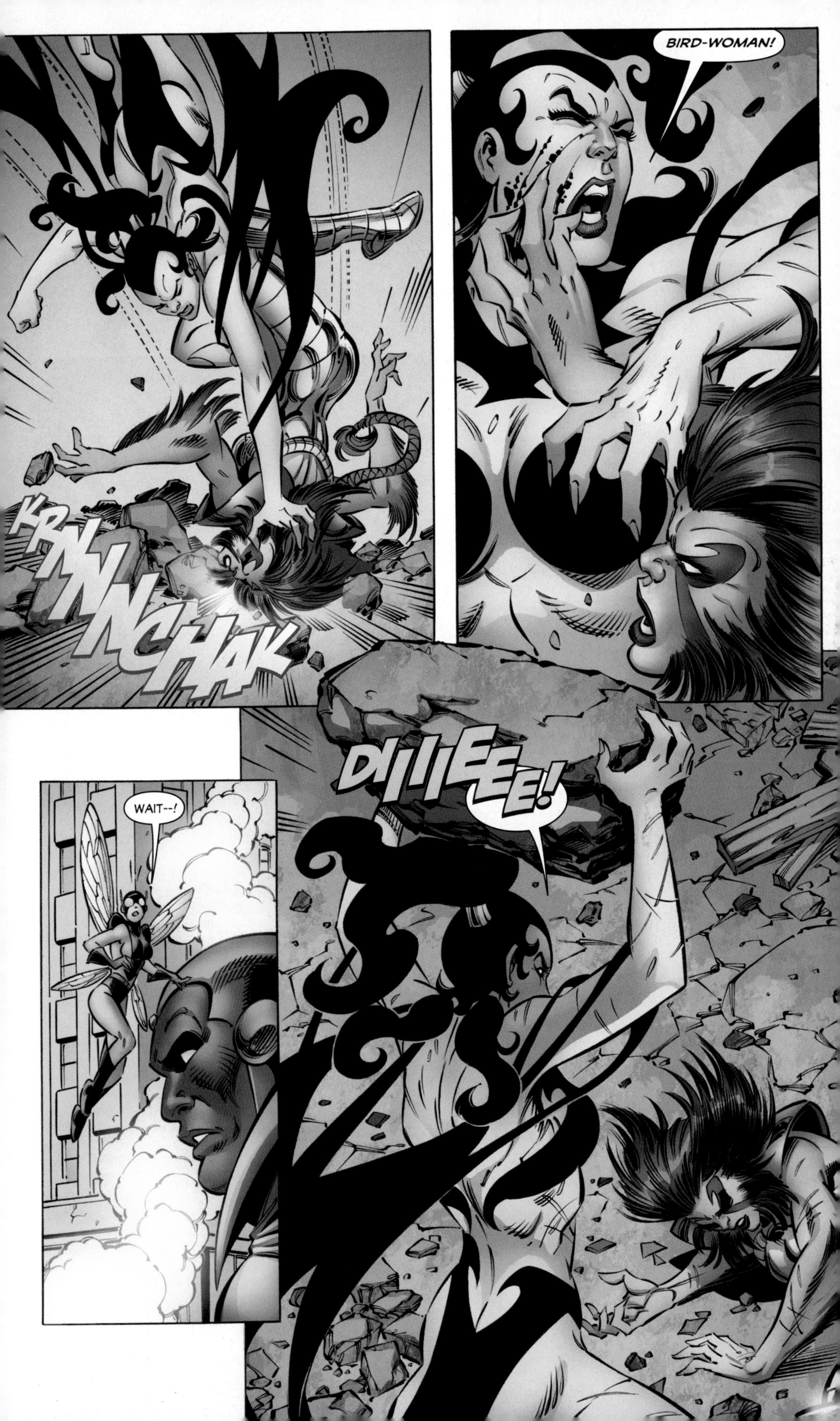
KRNNNCHAK
BIRD-WOMAN!
DIIIIEEEE!
WAIT--!

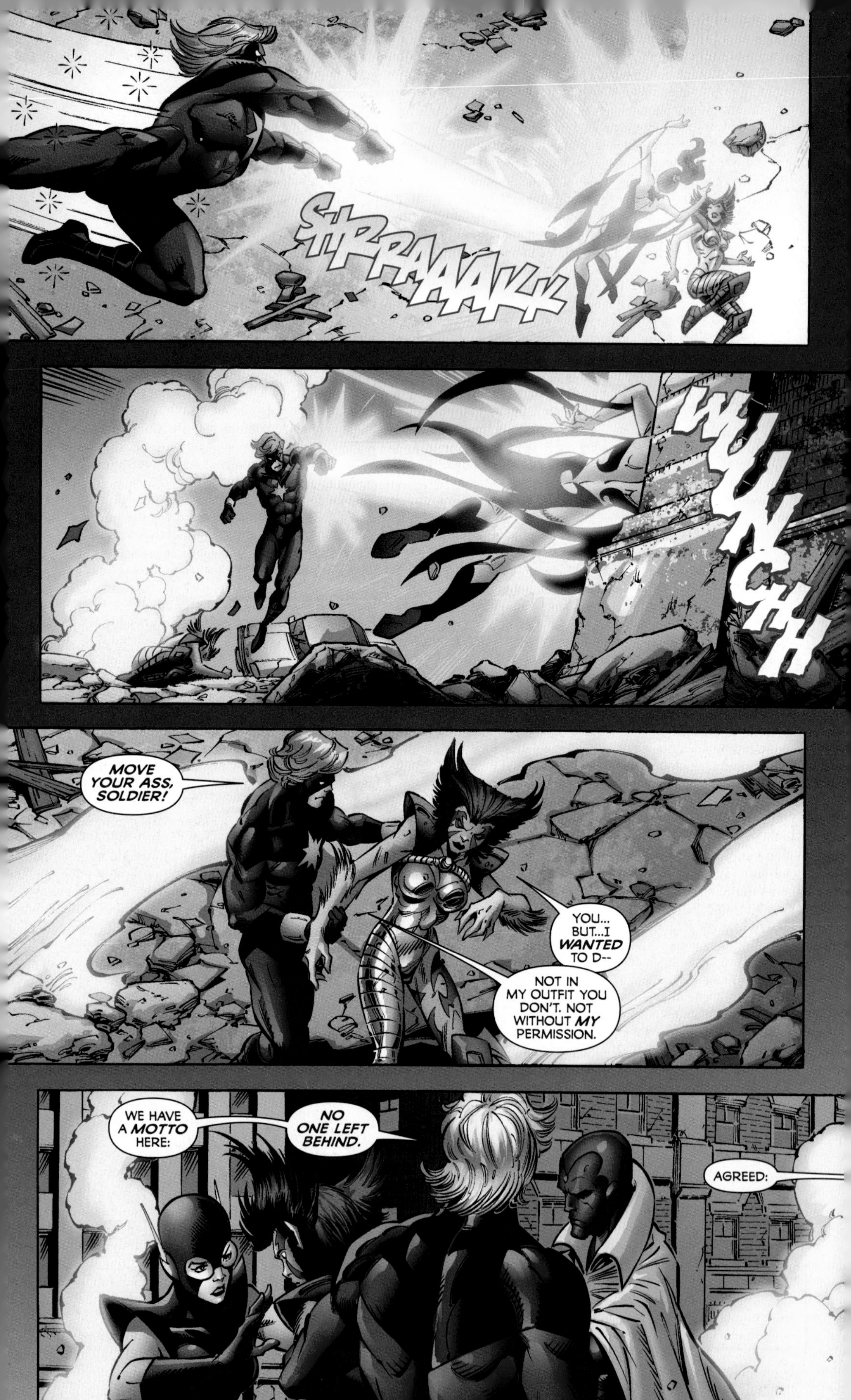

SHRAAAKK
WUNCHH
MOVE YOUR ASS, SOLDIER!
YOU... BUT...I WANTED TO D--
NOT IN MY OUTFIT YOU DON'T. NOT WITHOUT MY PERMISSION.
WE HAVE A MOTTO HERE:
NO ONE LEFT BEHIND.
AGREED:

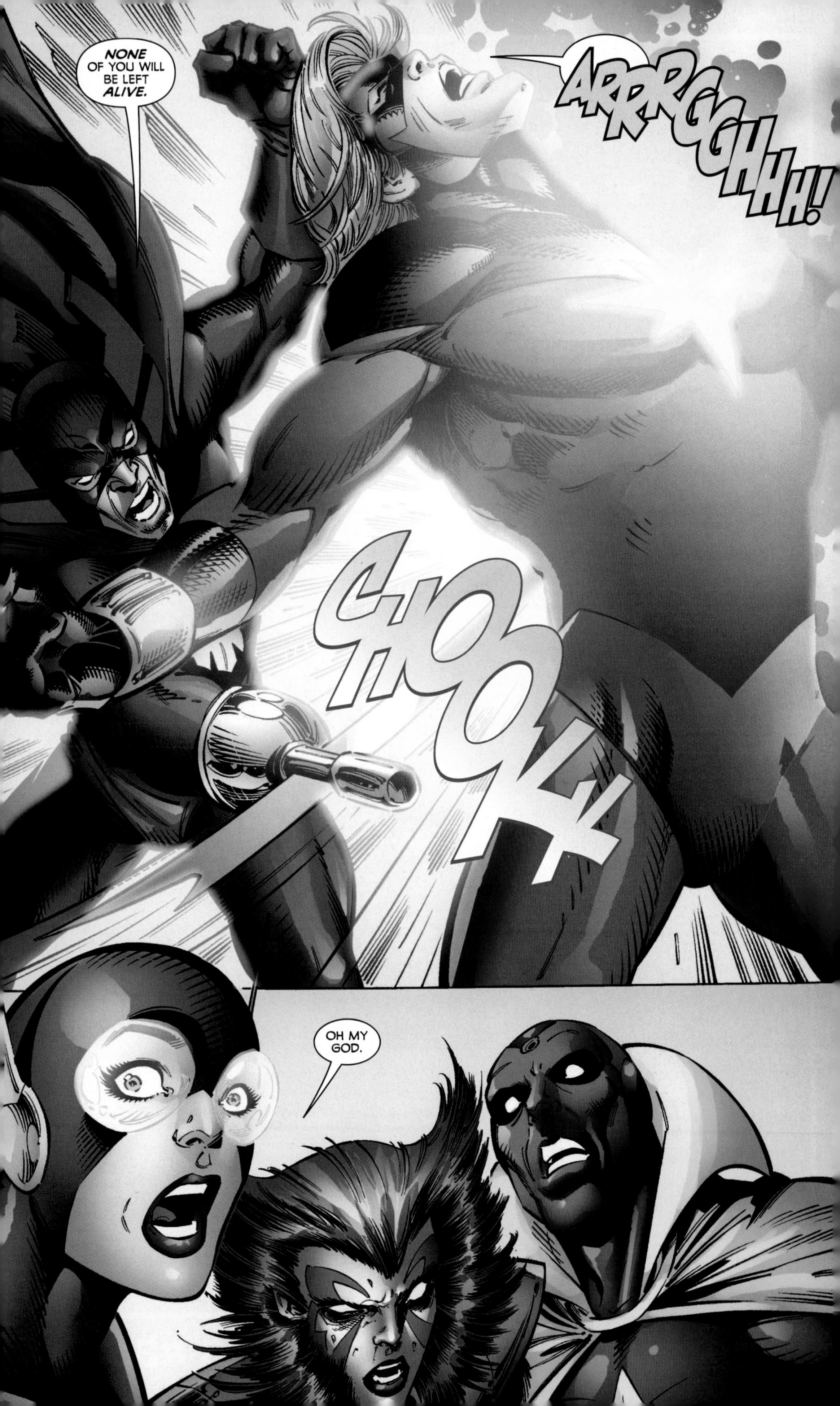
NONE OF YOU WILL BE LEFT ALIVE.
ARRRGGHHH!
CHOOK!
OH MY GOD.

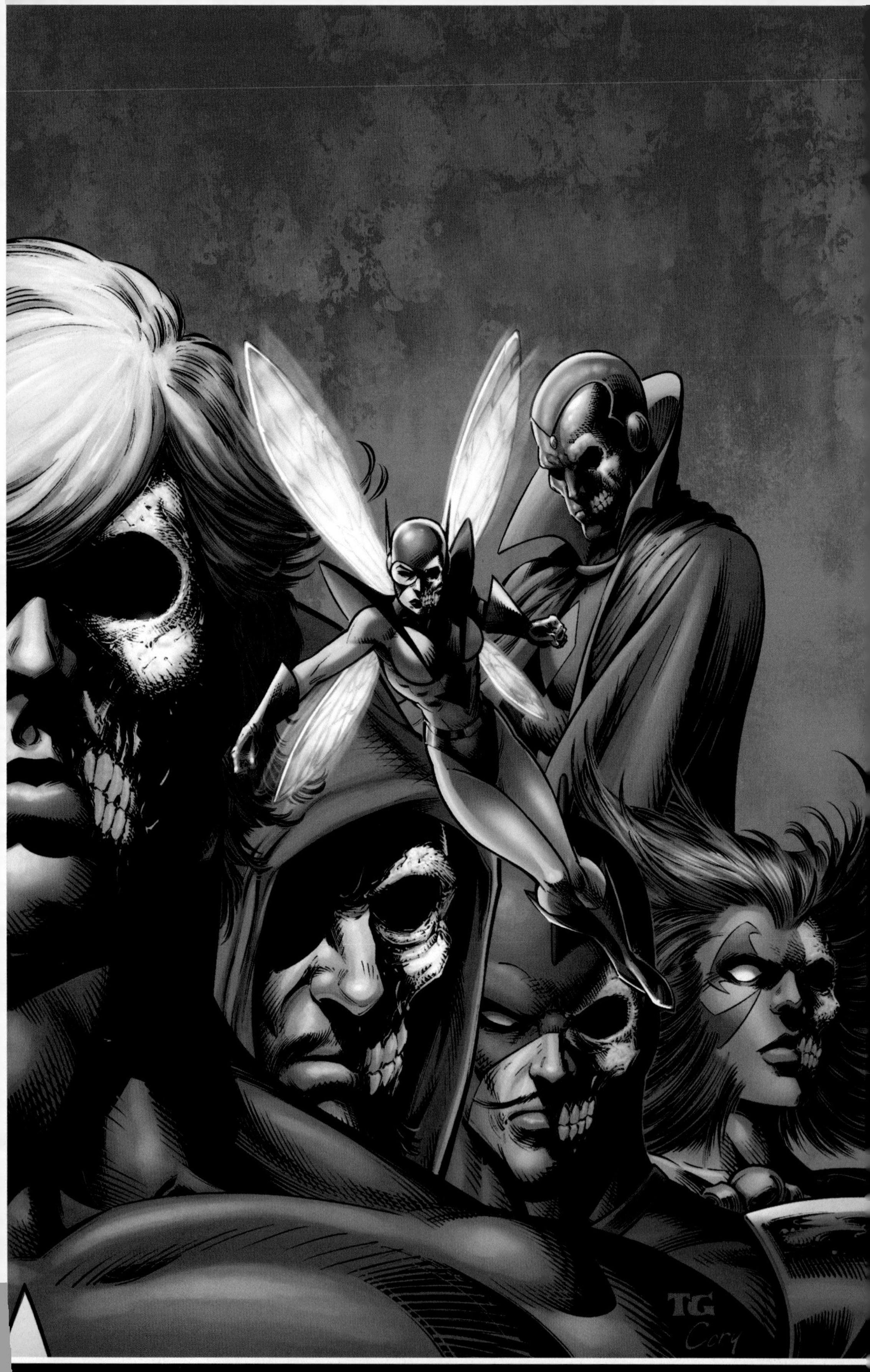
TG
Cory

CHAOS WAR: DEAD AVENGERS #3

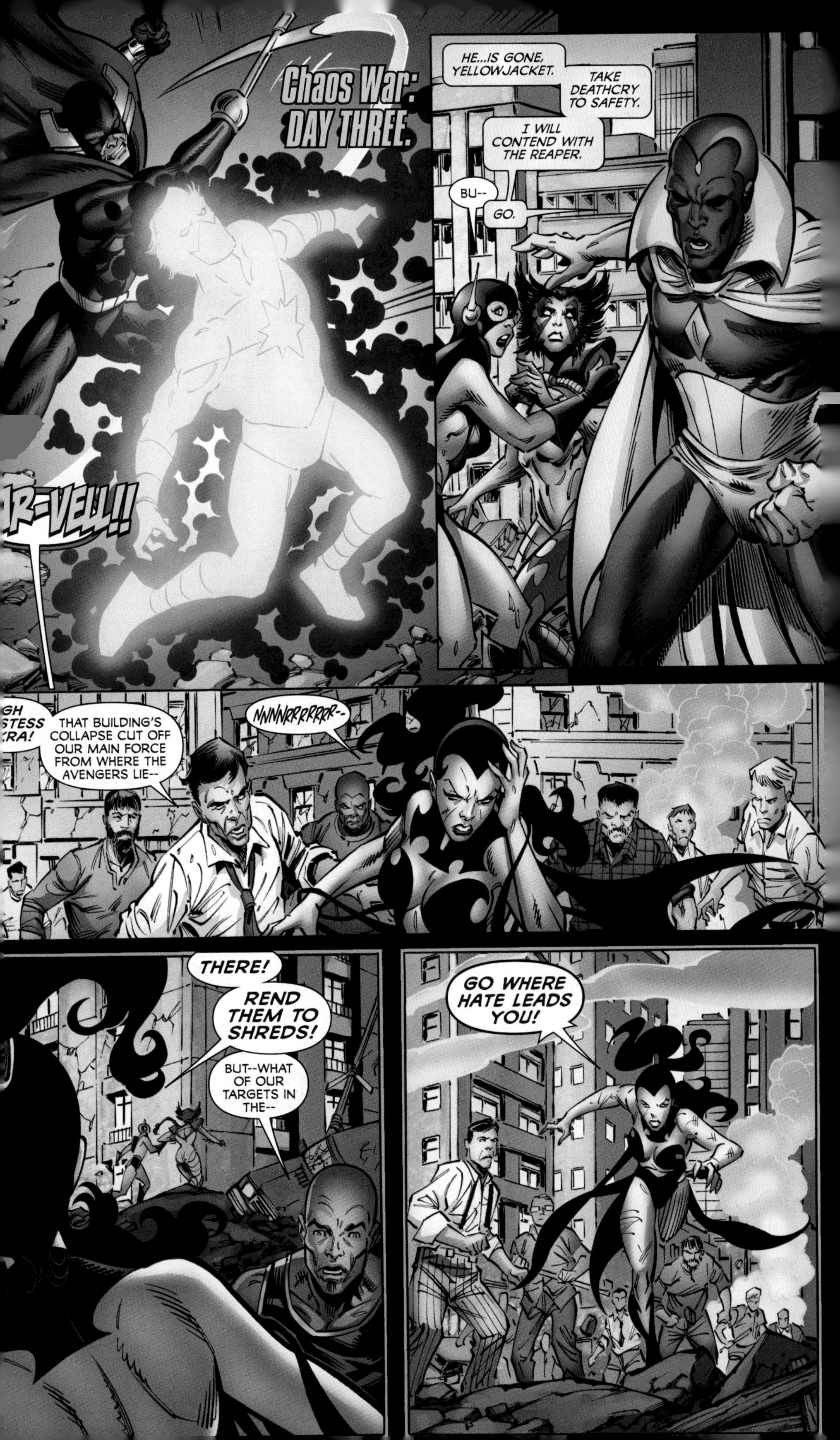
Chaos War: DAY THREE.
R-VELL!!
HE...IS GONE, YELLOWJACKET.
TAKE DEATHCRY TO SAFETY.
I WILL CONTEND WITH THE REAPER.
BU--
GO.
GH STESS KRA!
THAT BUILDING'S COLLAPSE CUT OFF OUR MAIN FORCE FROM WHERE THE AVENGERS LIE--
NNNNRRRRRR--
THERE!
REND THEM TO SHREDS!
BUT--WHAT OF OUR TARGETS IN THE--
GO WHERE HATE LEADS YOU!

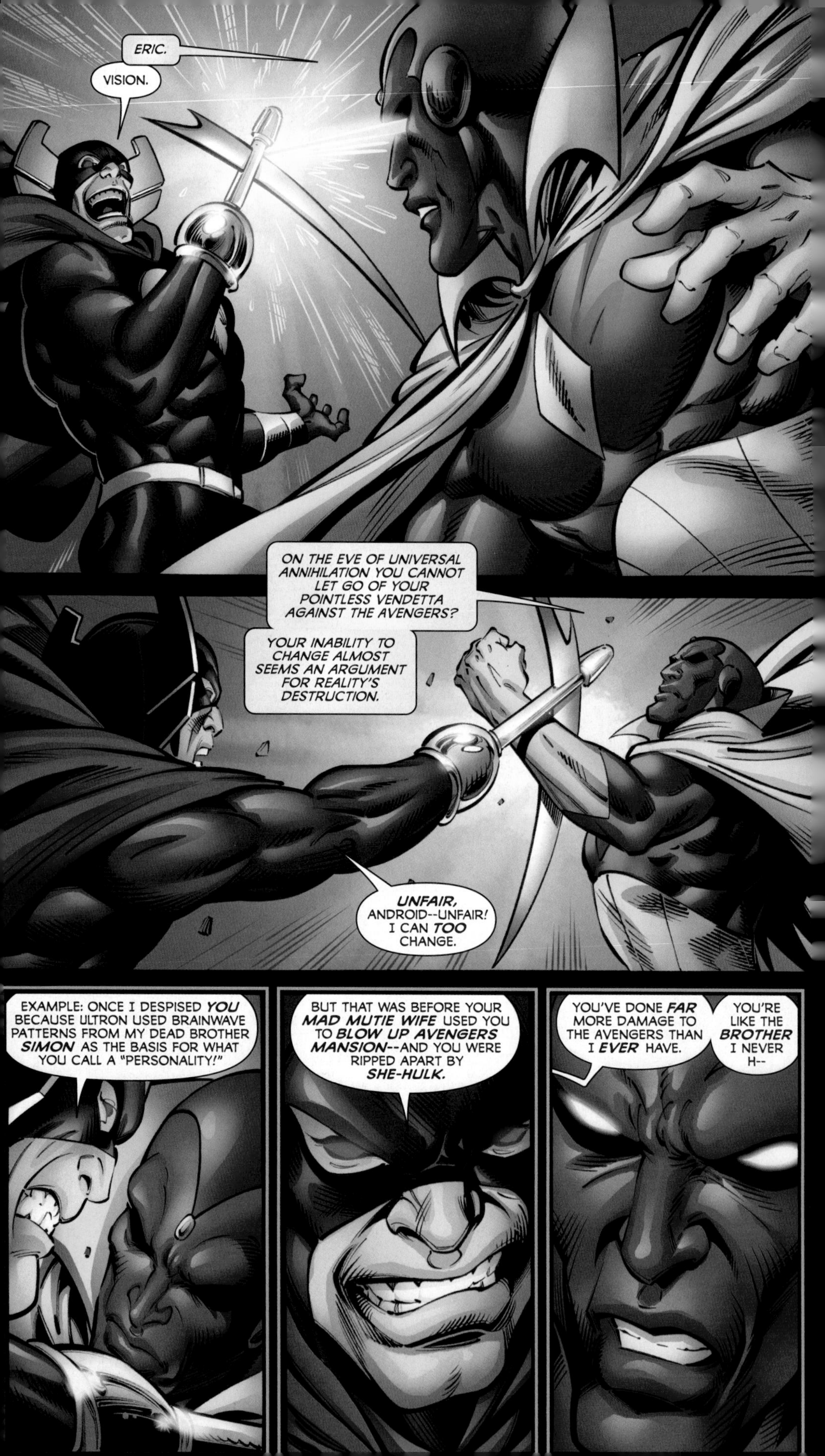

ERIC.
VISION.
ON THE EVE OF UNIVERSAL ANNIHILATION YOU CANNOT LET GO OF YOUR POINTLESS VENDETTA AGAINST THE AVENGERS?
YOUR INABILITY TO CHANGE ALMOST SEEMS AN ARGUMENT FOR REALITY'S DESTRUCTION.
UNFAIR, ANDROID--UNFAIR! I CAN TOO CHANGE.
EXAMPLE: ONCE I DESPISED YOU BECAUSE ULTRON USED BRAINWAVE PATTERNS FROM MY DEAD BROTHER SIMON AS THE BASIS FOR WHAT YOU CALL A "PERSONALITY!"
BUT THAT WAS BEFORE YOUR MAD MUTIE WIFE USED YOU TO BLOW UP AVENGERS MANSION--AND YOU WERE RIPPED APART BY SHE-HULK.
YOU'VE DONE FAR MORE DAMAGE TO THE AVENGERS THAN I EVER HAVE.
YOU'RE LIKE THE BROTHER I NEVER H--

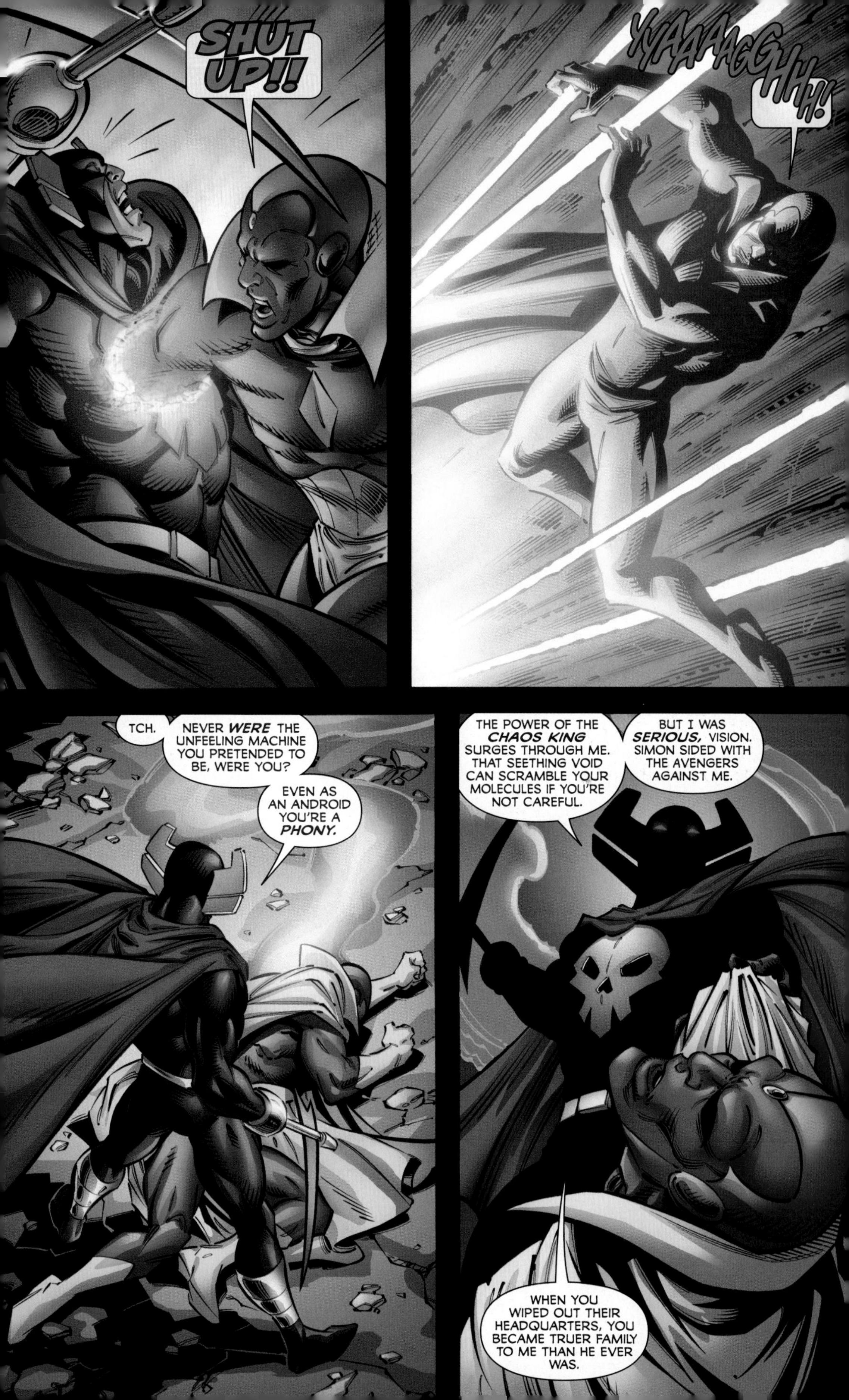
SHUT UP!!
YYAAAAGGHHH!
TCH.
NEVER WERE THE UNFEELING MACHINE YOU PRETENDED TO BE, WERE YOU?
EVEN AS AN ANDROID YOU'RE A PHONY.
THE POWER OF THE CHAOS KING SURGES THROUGH ME. THAT SEETHING VOID CAN SCRAMBLE YOUR MOLECULES IF YOU'RE NOT CAREFUL.
BUT I WAS SERIOUS, VISION. SIMON SIDED WITH THE AVENGERS AGAINST ME.
WHEN YOU WIPED OUT THEIR HEADQUARTERS, YOU BECAME TRUER FAMILY TO ME THAN HE EVER WAS.

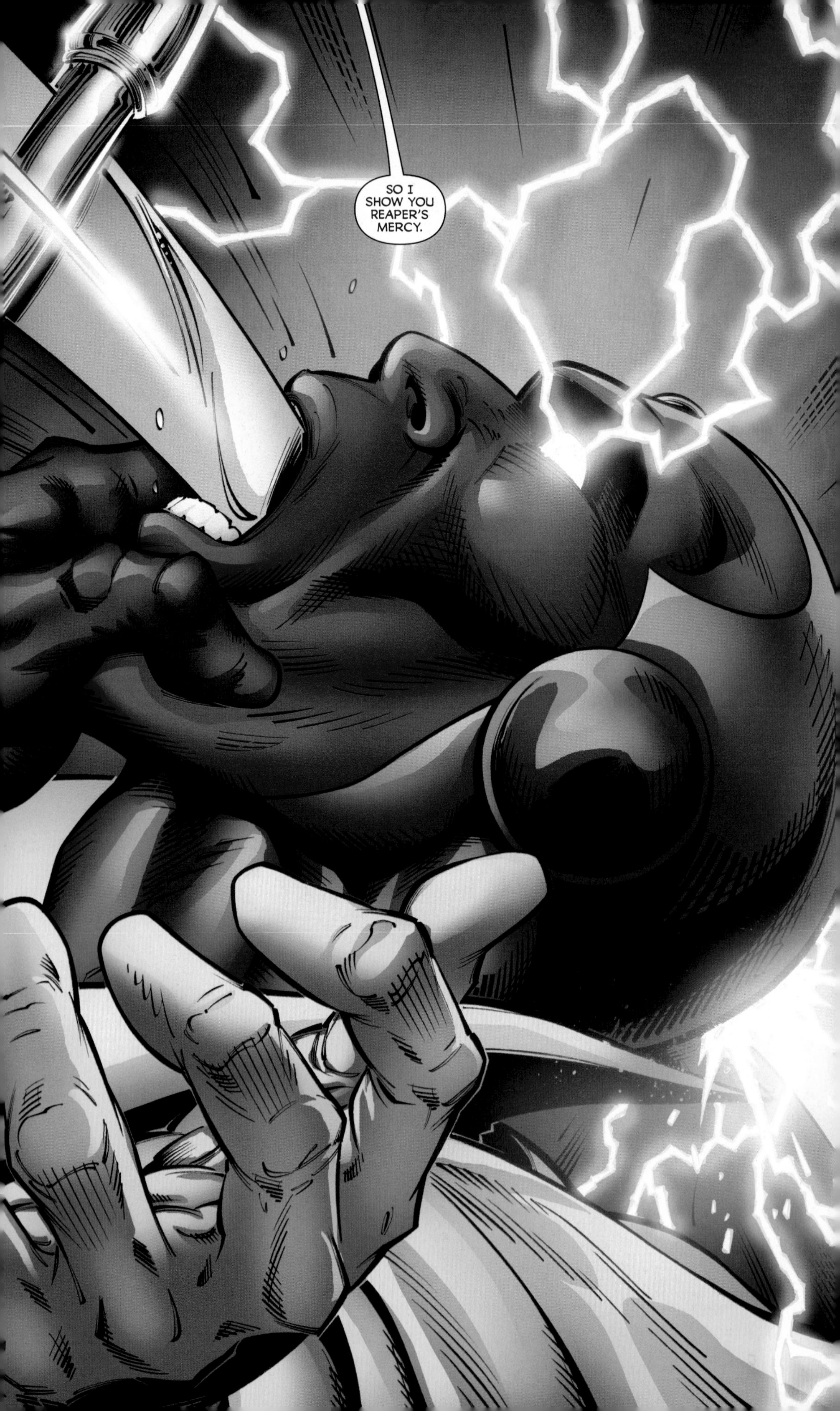
SO I SHOW YOU REAPER'S MERCY.

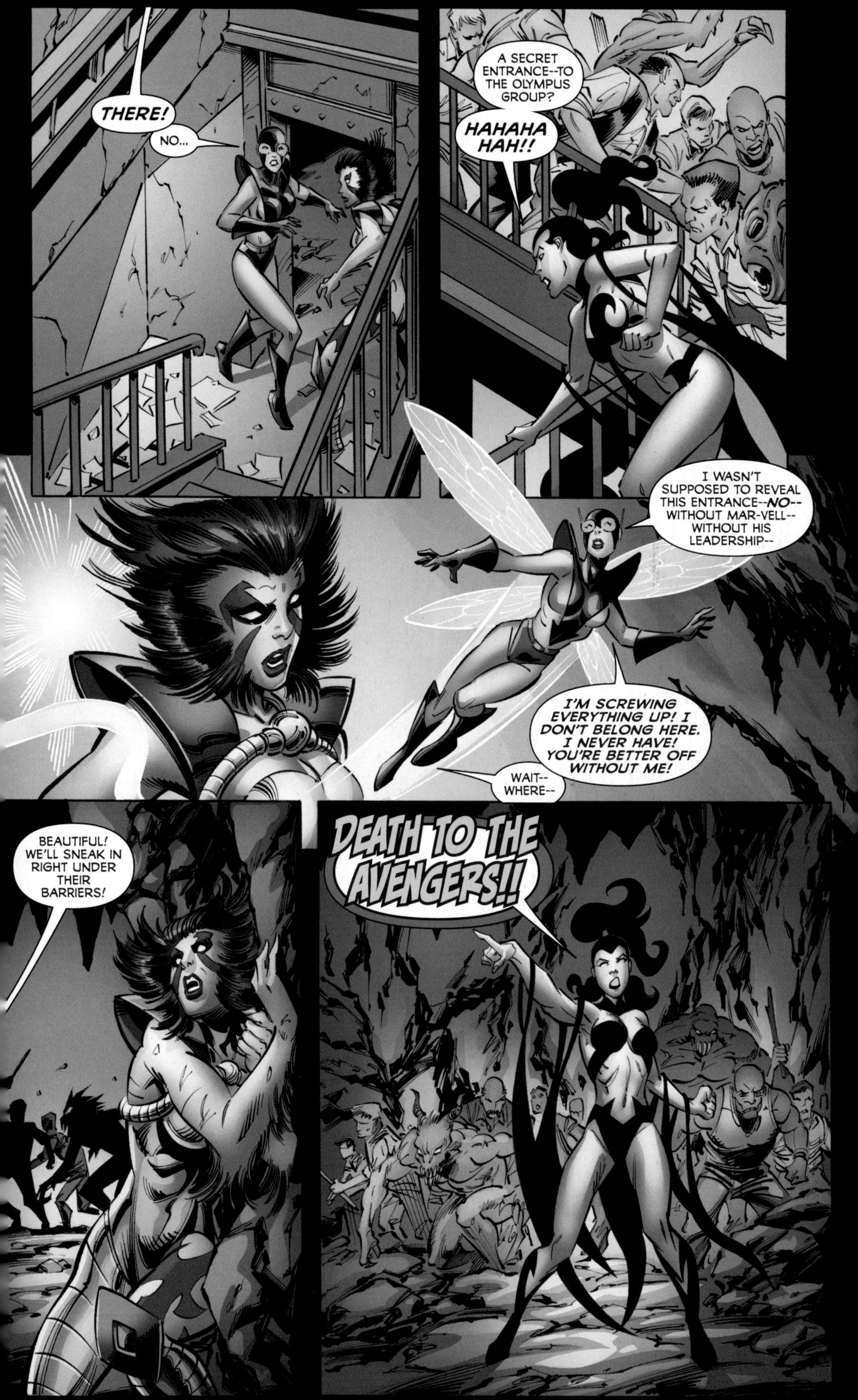
THERE!
NO...
A SECRET ENTRANCE--TO THE OLYMPUS GROUP?
HAHAHA HAH!!
I WASN'T SUPPOSED TO REVEAL THIS ENTRANCE--NO--WITHOUT MAR-VELL--WITHOUT HIS LEADERSHIP--
I'M SCREWING EVERYTHING UP! I DON'T BELONG HERE. I NEVER HAVE! YOU'RE BETTER OFF WITHOUT ME!
WAIT--WHERE--
BEAUTIFUL! WE'LL SNEAK IN RIGHT UNDER THEIR BARRIERS!
DEATH TO THE AVENGERS!!

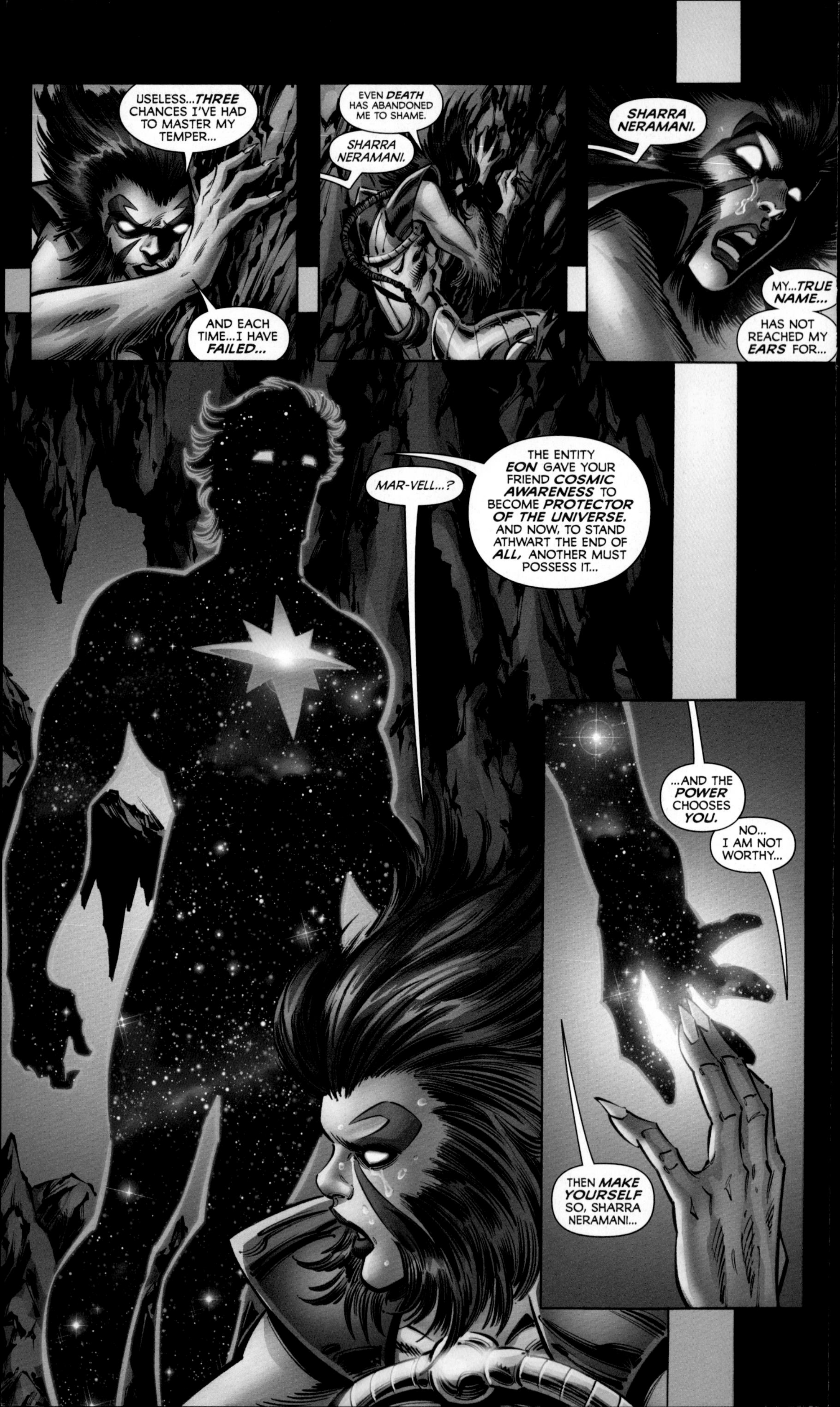
USELESS...THREE CHANCES I'VE HAD TO MASTER MY TEMPER...
AND EACH TIME...I HAVE FAILED...
EVEN DEATH HAS ABANDONED ME TO SHAME.
SHARRA NERAMANI.
SHARRA NERAMANI.
MY...TRUE NAME...
HAS NOT REACHED MY EARS FOR...
MAR-VELL...?
THE ENTITY EON GAVE YOUR FRIEND COSMIC AWARENESS TO BECOME PROTECTOR OF THE UNIVERSE. AND NOW, TO STAND ATHWART THE END OF ALL, ANOTHER MUST POSSESS IT...
...AND THE POWER CHOOSES YOU.
NO... I AM NOT WORTHY...
THEN MAKE YOURSELF SO, SHARRA NERAMANI...

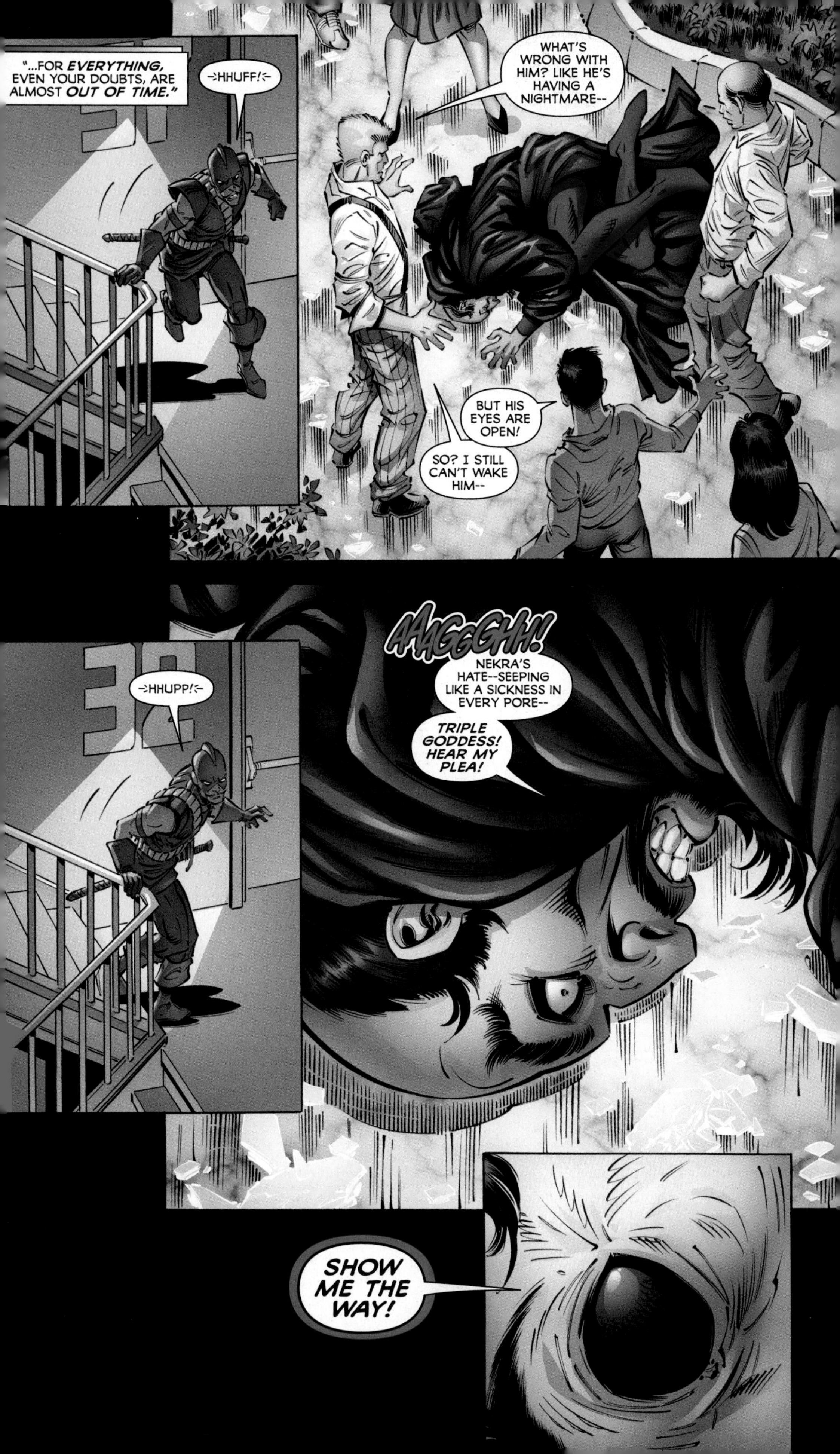

"...FOR EVERYTHING, EVEN YOUR DOUBTS, ARE ALMOST OUT OF TIME."
-HHUFF!-
WHAT'S WRONG WITH HIM? LIKE HE'S HAVING A NIGHTMARE--
BUT HIS EYES ARE OPEN!
SO? I STILL CAN'T WAKE HIM--
-HHUPP!-
AAAGGGHH!
NEKRA'S HATE--SEEPING LIKE A SICKNESS IN EVERY PORE--
TRIPLE GODDESS! HEAR MY PLEA!
SHOW ME THE WAY!

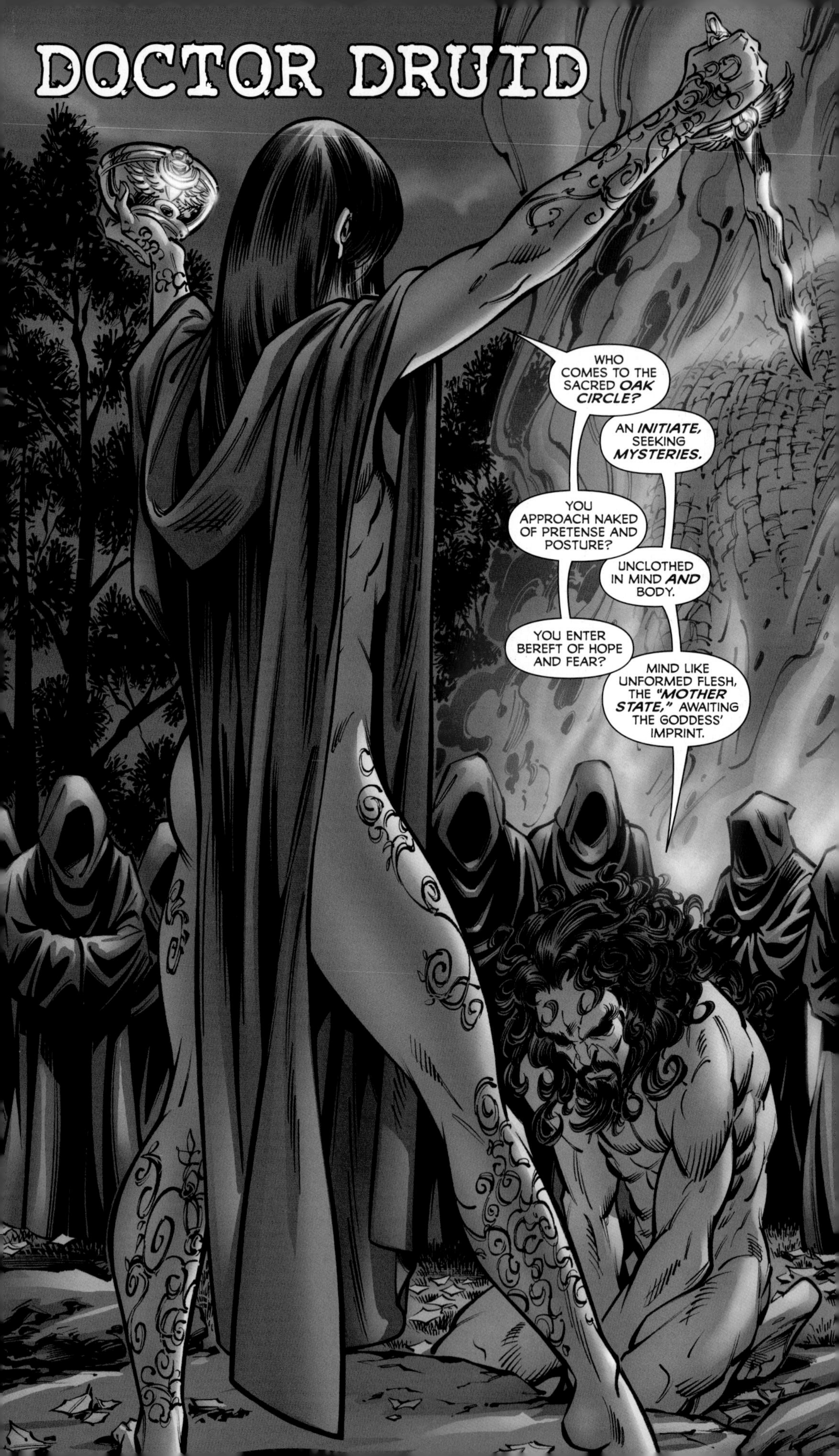
DOCTOR DRUID
WHO COMES TO THE SACRED OAK CIRCLE?
AN INITIATE, SEEKING MYSTERIES.
YOU APPROACH NAKED OF PRETENSE AND POSTURE?
UNCLOTHED IN MIND AND BODY.
YOU ENTER BEREFT OF HOPE AND FEAR?
MIND LIKE UNFORMED FLESH, THE "MOTHER STATE," AWAITING THE GODDESS' IMPRINT.

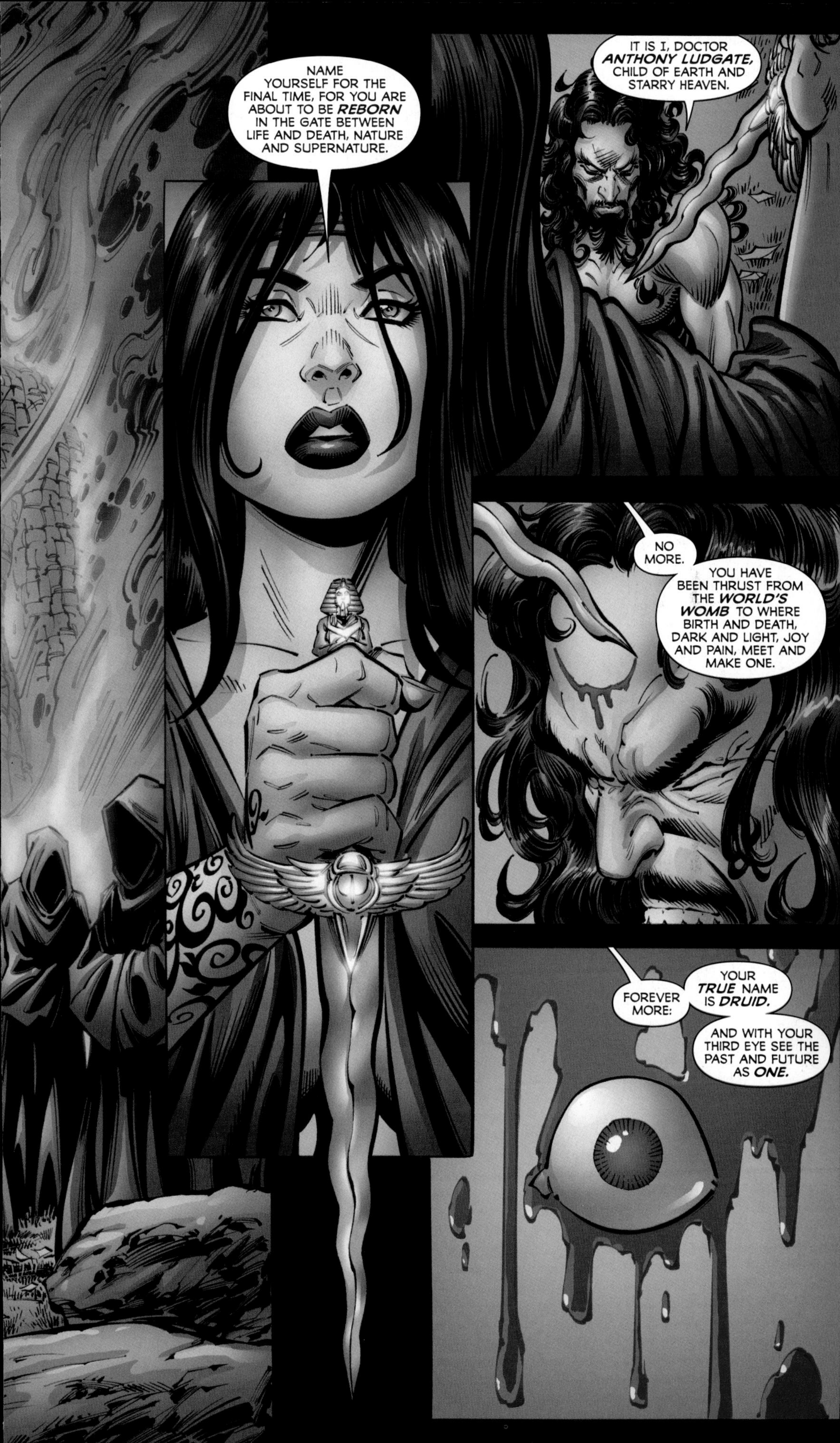
NAME YOURSELF FOR THE FINAL TIME, FOR YOU ARE ABOUT TO BE *REBORN* IN THE GATE BETWEEN LIFE AND DEATH, NATURE AND SUPERNATURE.
IT IS I, DOCTOR *ANTHONY LUDGATE,* CHILD OF EARTH AND STARRY HEAVEN.
NO MORE.
YOU HAVE BEEN THRUST FROM THE *WORLD'S WOMB* TO WHERE BIRTH AND DEATH, DARK AND LIGHT, JOY AND PAIN, MEET AND MAKE ONE.
FOREVER MORE:
YOUR *TRUE* NAME IS *DRUID.*
AND WITH YOUR THIRD EYE SEE THE PAST AND FUTURE AS *ONE.*

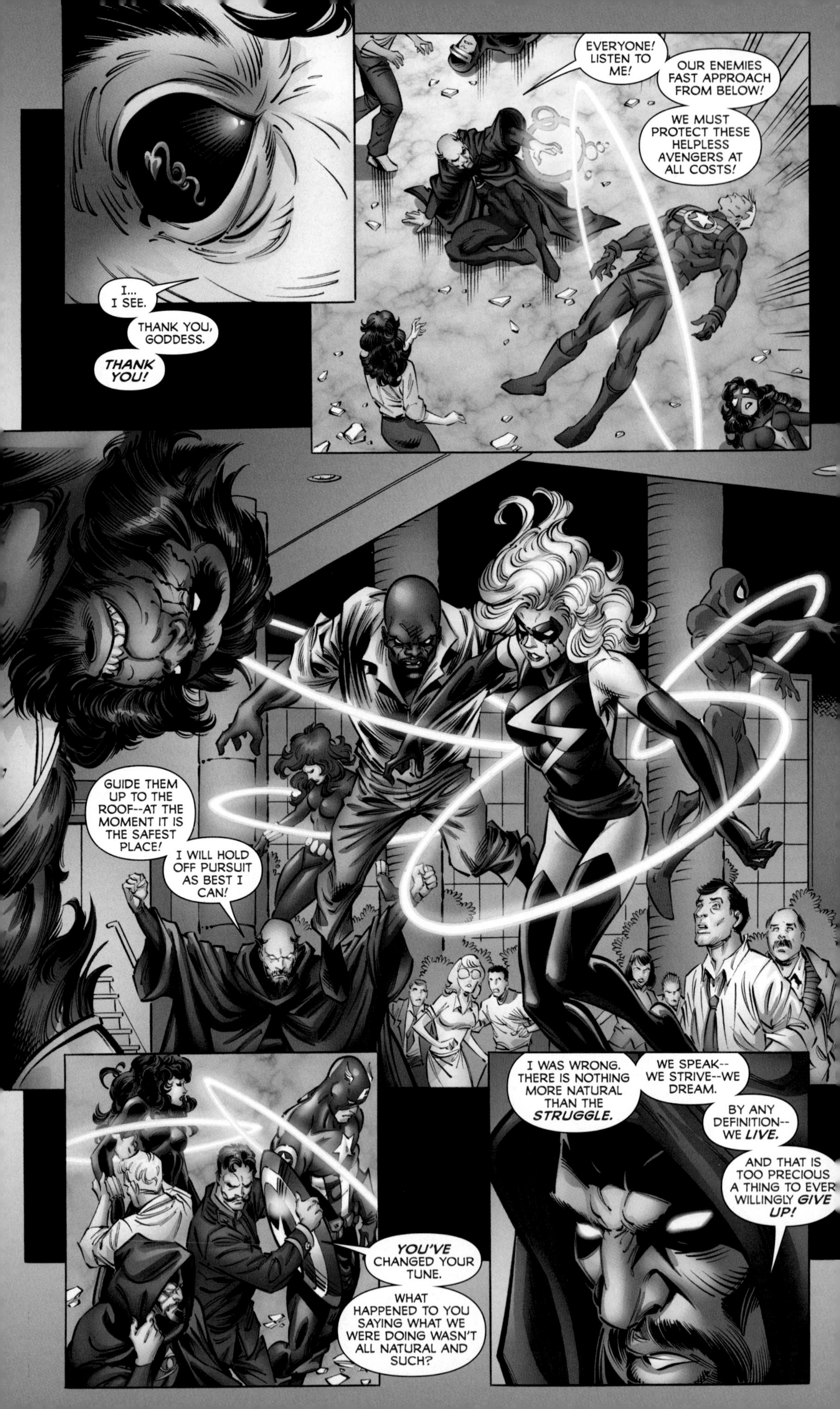
I... I SEE.
THANK YOU, GODDESS.
THANK YOU!
EVERYONE! LISTEN TO ME!
OUR ENEMIES FAST APPROACH FROM BELOW!
WE MUST PROTECT THESE HELPLESS AVENGERS AT ALL COSTS!
GUIDE THEM UP TO THE ROOF--AT THE MOMENT IT IS THE SAFEST PLACE!
I WILL HOLD OFF PURSUIT AS BEST I CAN!
YOU'VE CHANGED YOUR TUNE.
WHAT HAPPENED TO YOU SAYING WHAT WE WERE DOING WASN'T ALL NATURAL AND SUCH?
I WAS WRONG. THERE IS NOTHING MORE NATURAL THAN THE STRUGGLE.
WE SPEAK-- WE STRIVE--WE DREAM.
BY ANY DEFINITION-- WE LIVE.
AND THAT IS TOO PRECIOUS A THING TO EVER WILLINGLY GIVE UP!

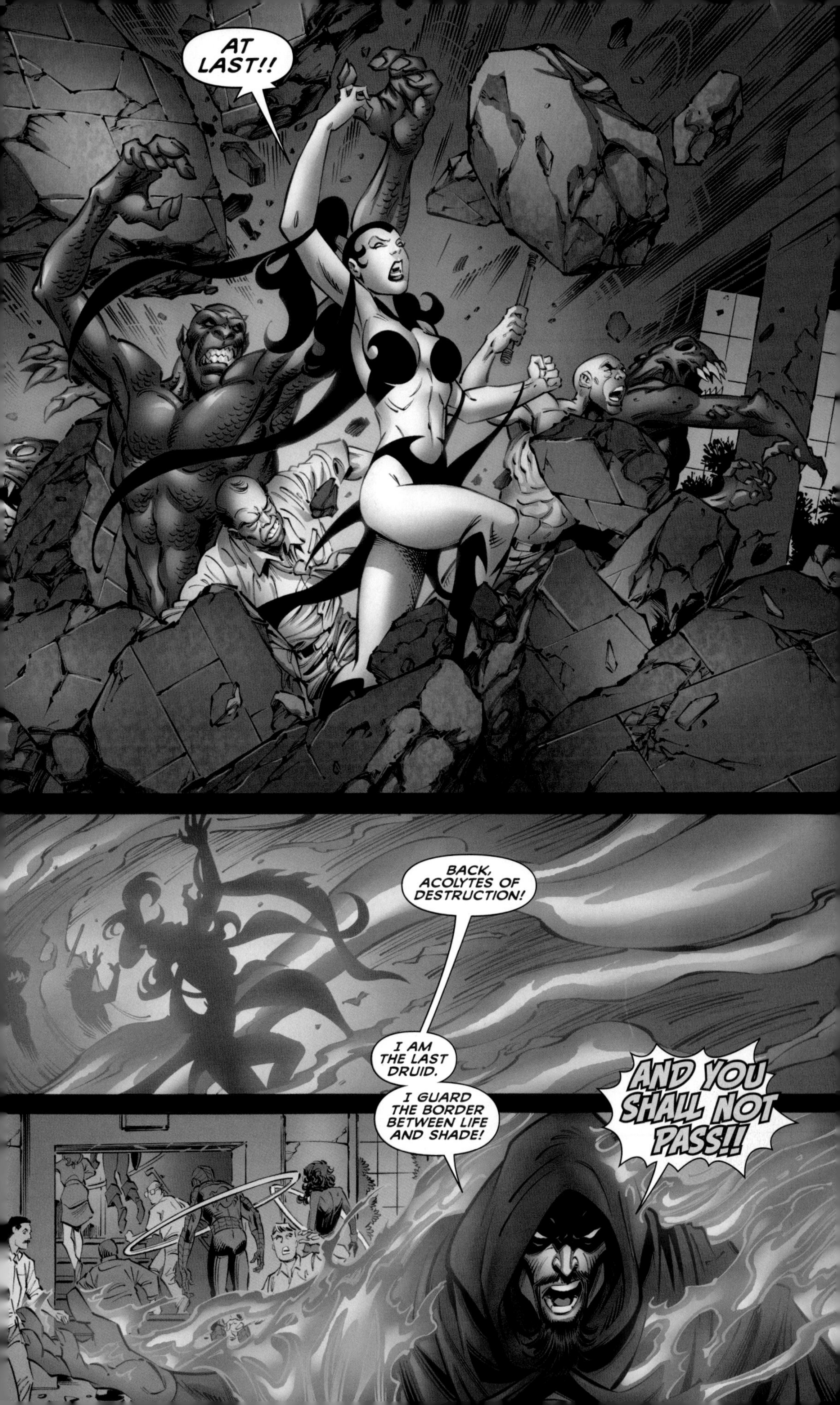
AT LAST!!
BACK, ACOLYTES OF DESTRUCTION!
I AM THE LAST DRUID.
I GUARD THE BORDER BETWEEN LIFE AND SHADE!
AND YOU SHALL NOT PASS!!

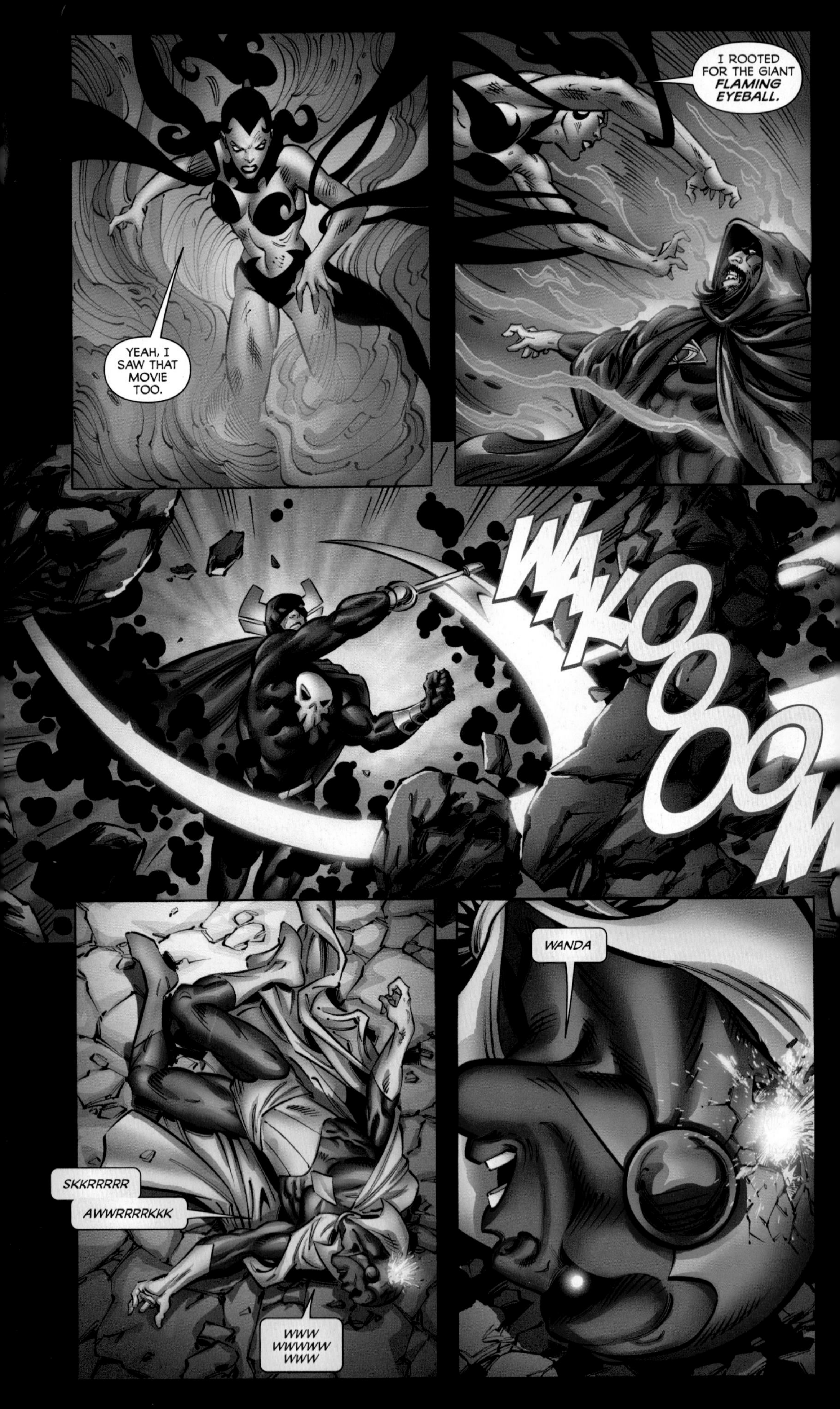

YEAH, I SAW THAT MOVIE TOO.
I ROOTED FOR THE GIANT *FLAMING EYEBALL.*
WAKOOOOM
SKKRRRRR
AWWRRRRKKK
WWW WWWWW WWW
WANDA

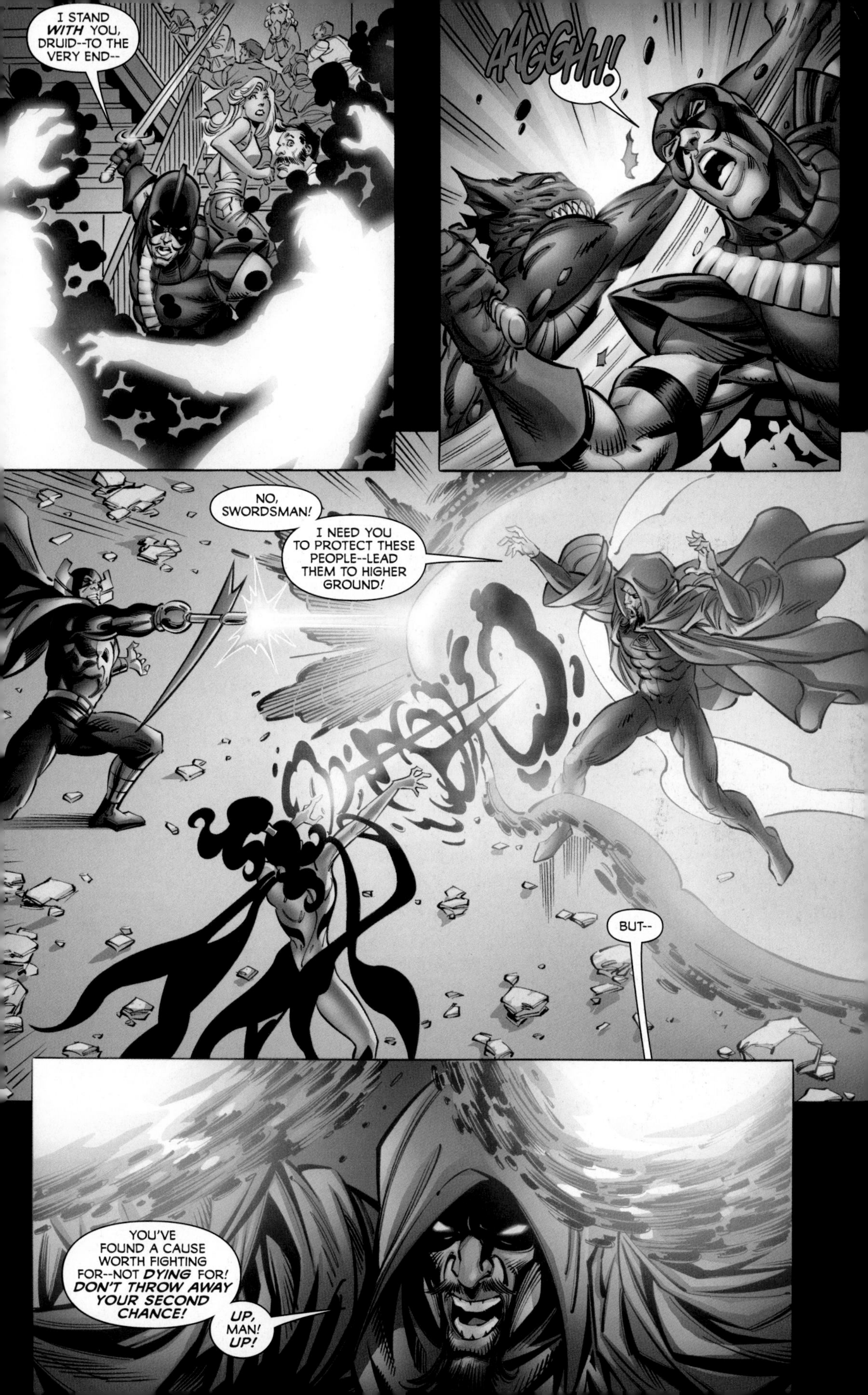
I STAND *WITH* YOU, DRUID--TO THE VERY END--
AAGGHH!
NO, SWORDSMAN!
I NEED YOU TO PROTECT THESE PEOPLE--LEAD THEM TO HIGHER GROUND!
BUT--
YOU'VE FOUND A CAUSE WORTH FIGHTING FOR--NOT *DYING* FOR! ***DON'T THROW AWAY YOUR SECOND CHANCE!***
UP, MAN! ***UP!***

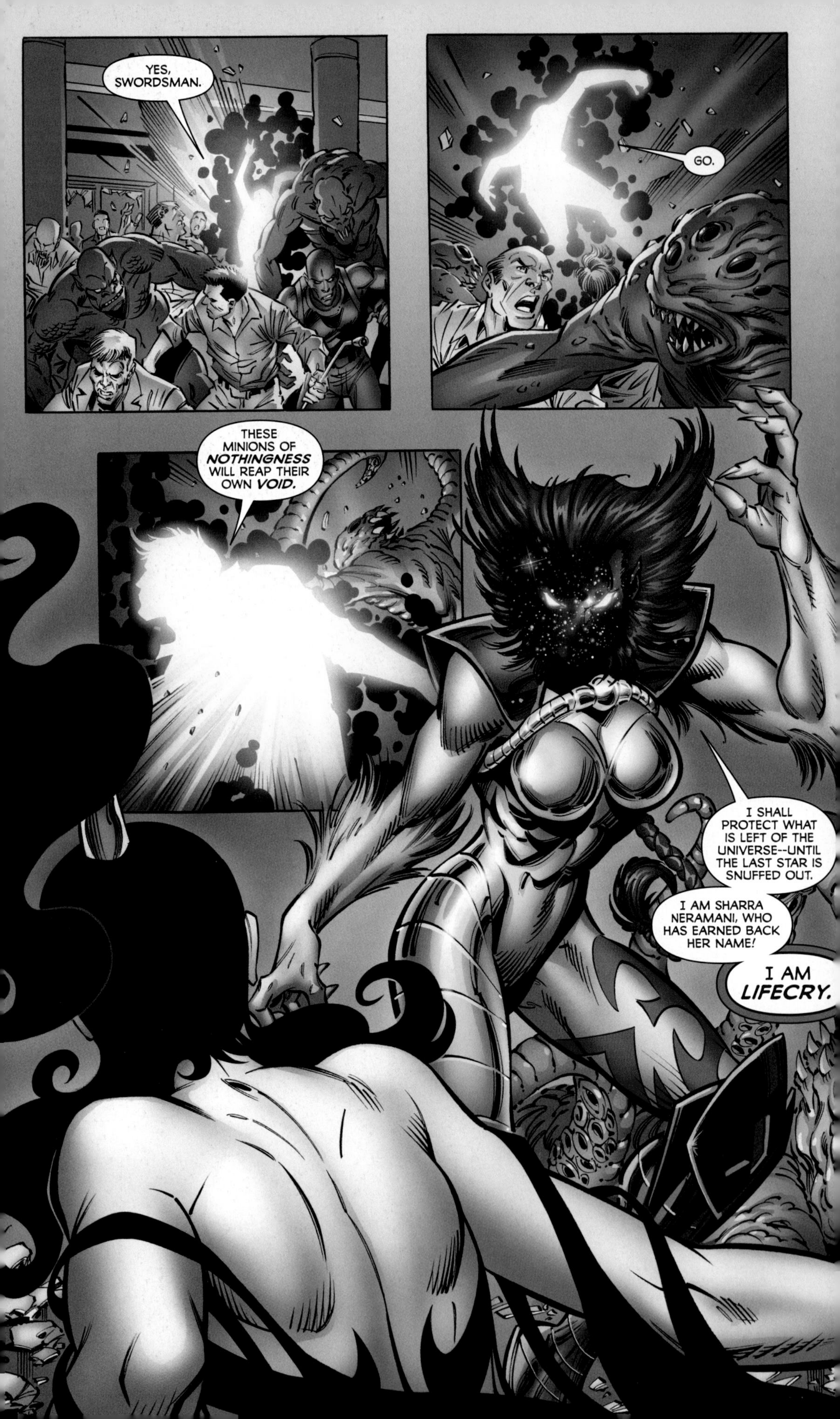
YES, SWORDSMAN.
GO.
THESE MINIONS OF NOTHINGNESS WILL REAP THEIR OWN VOID.
I SHALL PROTECT WHAT IS LEFT OF THE UNIVERSE--UNTIL THE LAST STAR IS SNUFFED OUT.
I AM SHARRA NERAMANI, WHO HAS EARNED BACK HER NAME!
I AM LIFECRY.

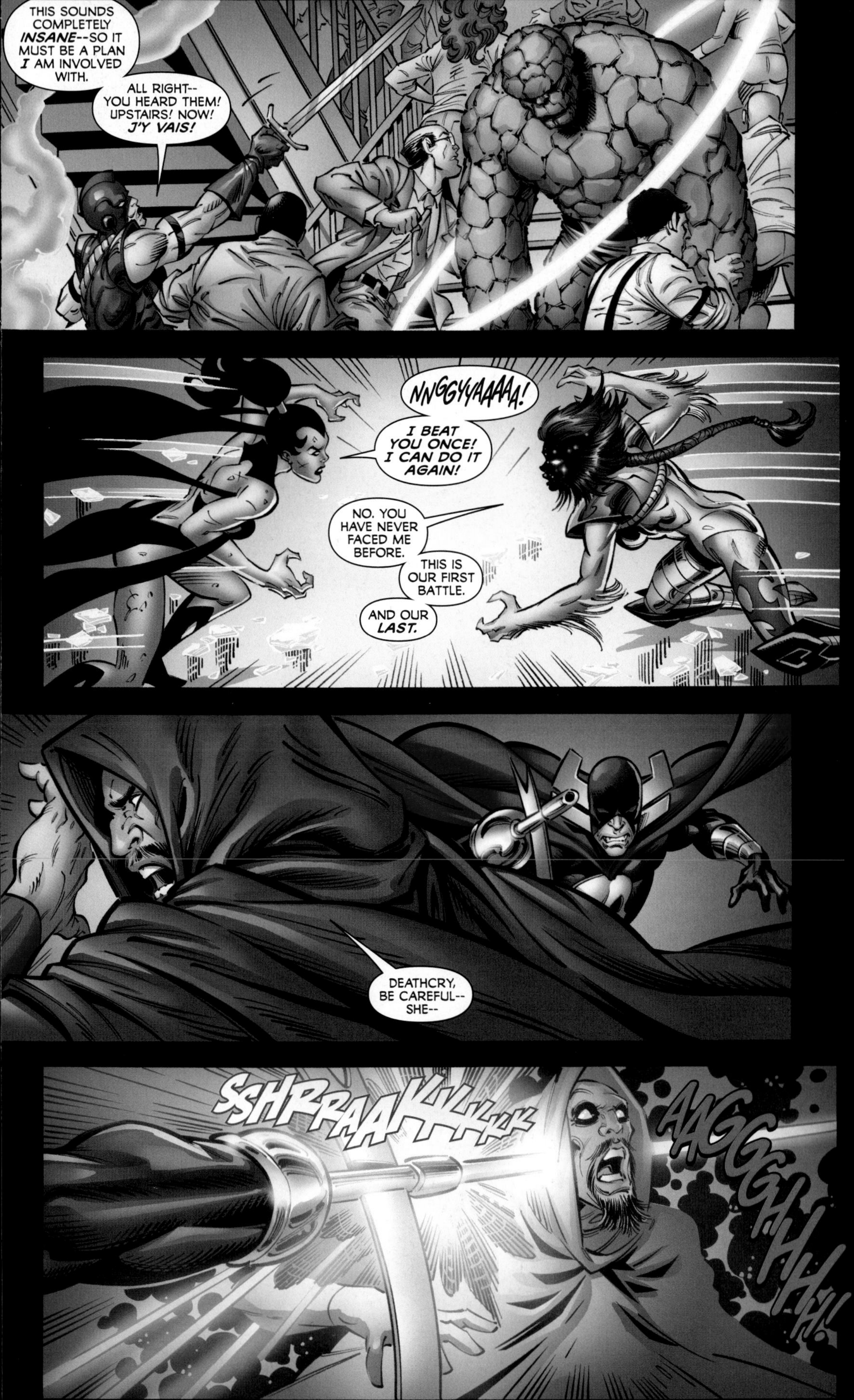
THIS SOUNDS COMPLETELY INSANE--SO IT MUST BE A PLAN I AM INVOLVED WITH.
ALL RIGHT-- YOU HEARD THEM! UPSTAIRS! NOW! J'Y VAIS!
NNGGYYAAAAA!
I BEAT YOU ONCE! I CAN DO IT AGAIN!
NO. YOU HAVE NEVER FACED ME BEFORE.
THIS IS OUR FIRST BATTLE.
AND OUR LAST.
DEATHCRY, BE CAREFUL-- SHE--
SSHRRAAKKKKKK
AAGGHHHH!

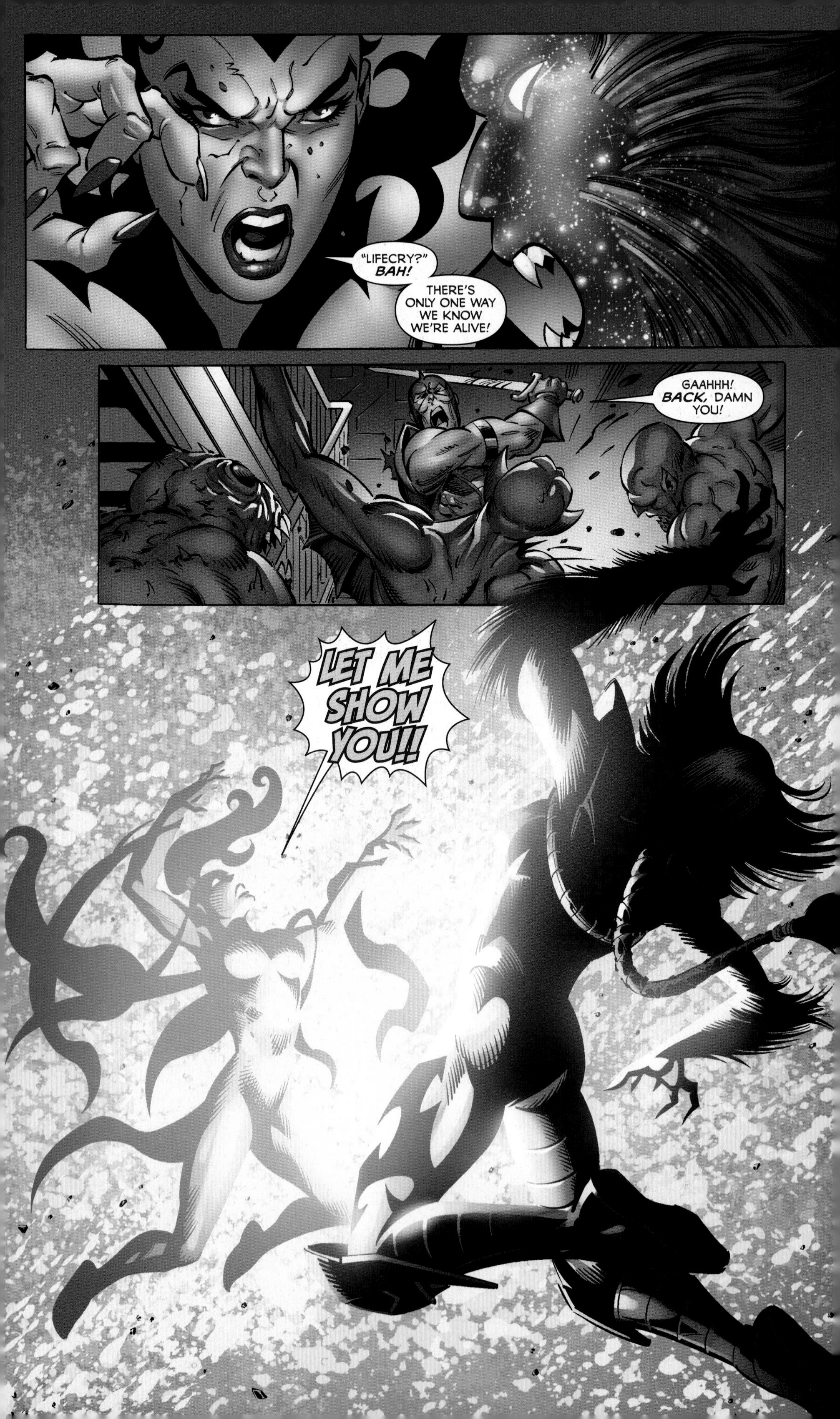

"LIFECRY?" BAH!
THERE'S ONLY ONE WAY WE KNOW WE'RE ALIVE!
GAAHHH! BACK, DAMN YOU!
LET ME SHOW YOU!!

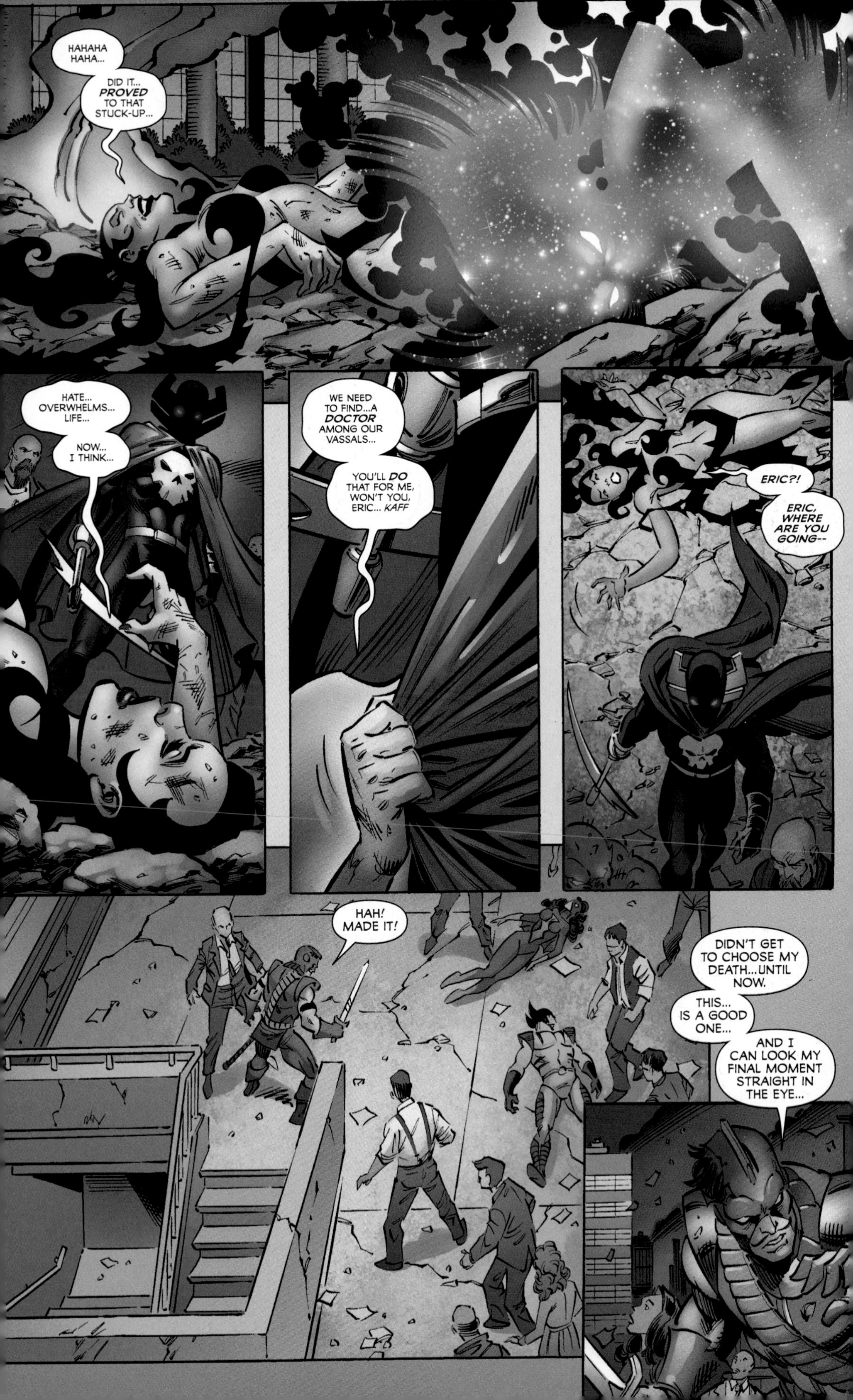
HAHAHA HAHA...
DID IT... PROVED TO THAT STUCK-UP...
HATE... OVERWHELMS... LIFE...
NOW... I THINK...
WE NEED TO FIND...A DOCTOR AMONG OUR VASSALS...
YOU'LL DO THAT FOR ME, WON'T YOU, ERIC... KAFF
ERIC?!
ERIC, WHERE ARE YOU GOING--
HAH! MADE IT!
DIDN'T GET TO CHOOSE MY DEATH...UNTIL NOW.
THIS... IS A GOOD ONE...
AND I CAN LOOK MY FINAL MOMENT STRAIGHT IN THE EYE...

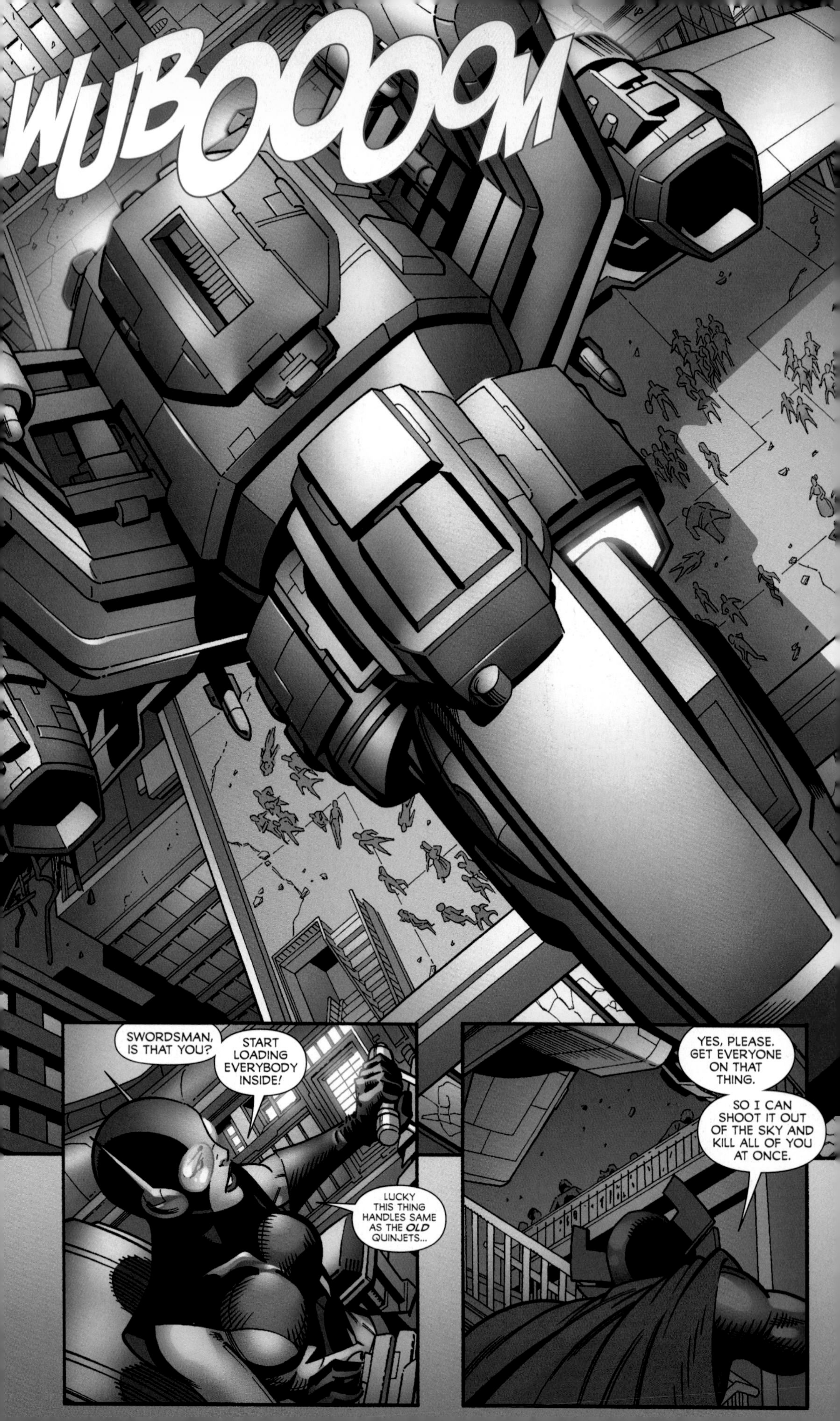
WUBOOOOM
SWORDSMAN, IS THAT YOU?
START LOADING EVERYBODY INSIDE!
LUCKY THIS THING HANDLES SAME AS THE *OLD* QUINJETS...
YES, PLEASE. GET EVERYONE ON THAT THING.
SO I CAN SHOOT IT OUT OF THE SKY AND KILL ALL OF YOU AT ONCE.

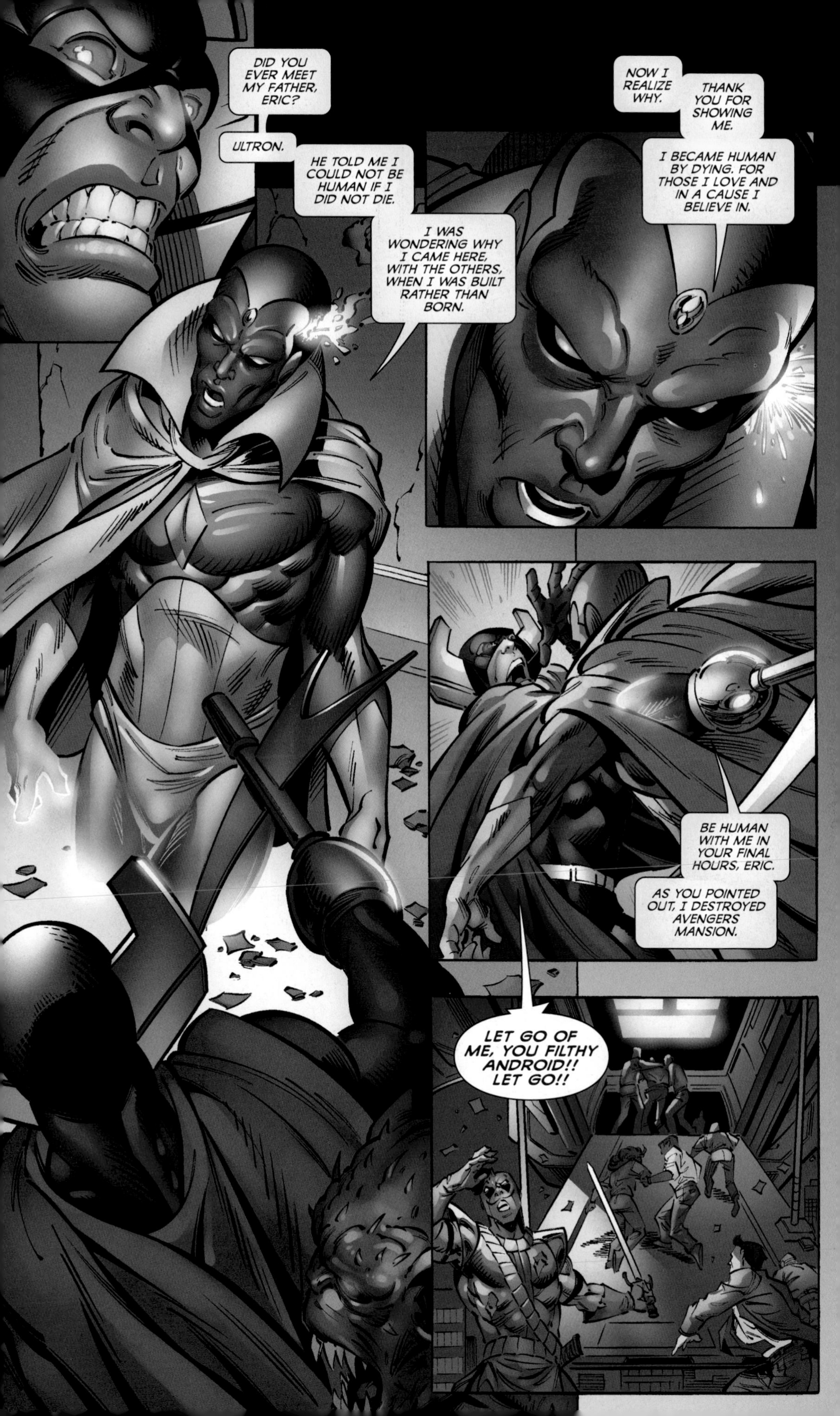
DID YOU EVER MEET MY FATHER, ERIC?
ULTRON.
HE TOLD ME I COULD NOT BE HUMAN IF I DID NOT DIE.
I WAS WONDERING WHY I CAME HERE, WITH THE OTHERS, WHEN I WAS BUILT RATHER THAN BORN.
NOW I REALIZE WHY.
THANK YOU FOR SHOWING ME.
I BECAME HUMAN BY DYING. FOR THOSE I LOVE AND IN A CAUSE I BELIEVE IN.
BE HUMAN WITH ME IN YOUR FINAL HOURS, ERIC.
AS YOU POINTED OUT, I DESTROYED AVENGERS MANSION.
LET GO OF ME, YOU FILTHY ANDROID!! LET GO!!

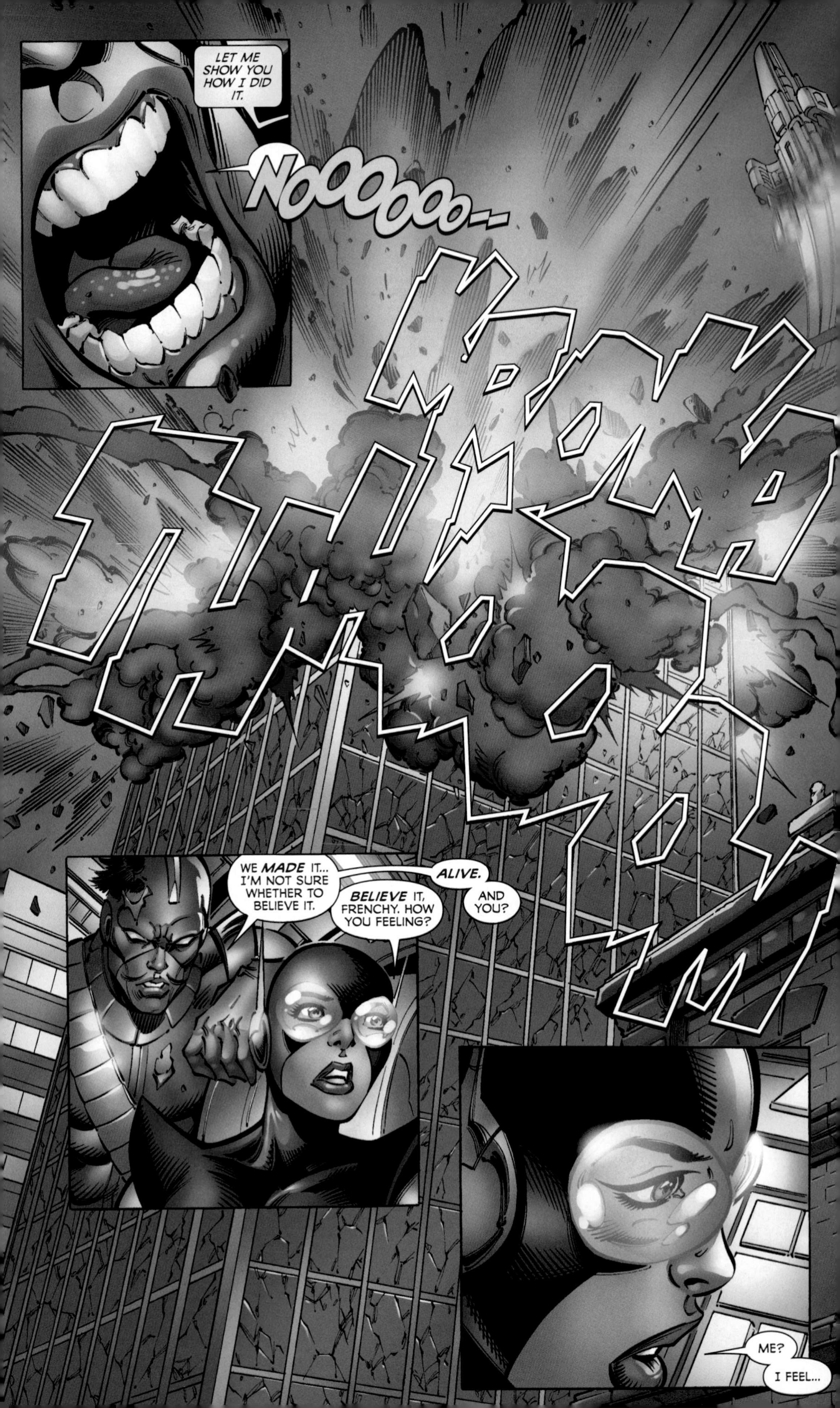
LET ME SHOW YOU HOW I DID IT.
NOOOOOOO--
WE *MADE* IT... I'M NOT SURE WHETHER TO BELIEVE IT.
ALIVE.
BELIEVE IT, FRENCHY. HOW YOU FEELING?
AND YOU?
ME?
I FEEL...

YELLOWJACKET

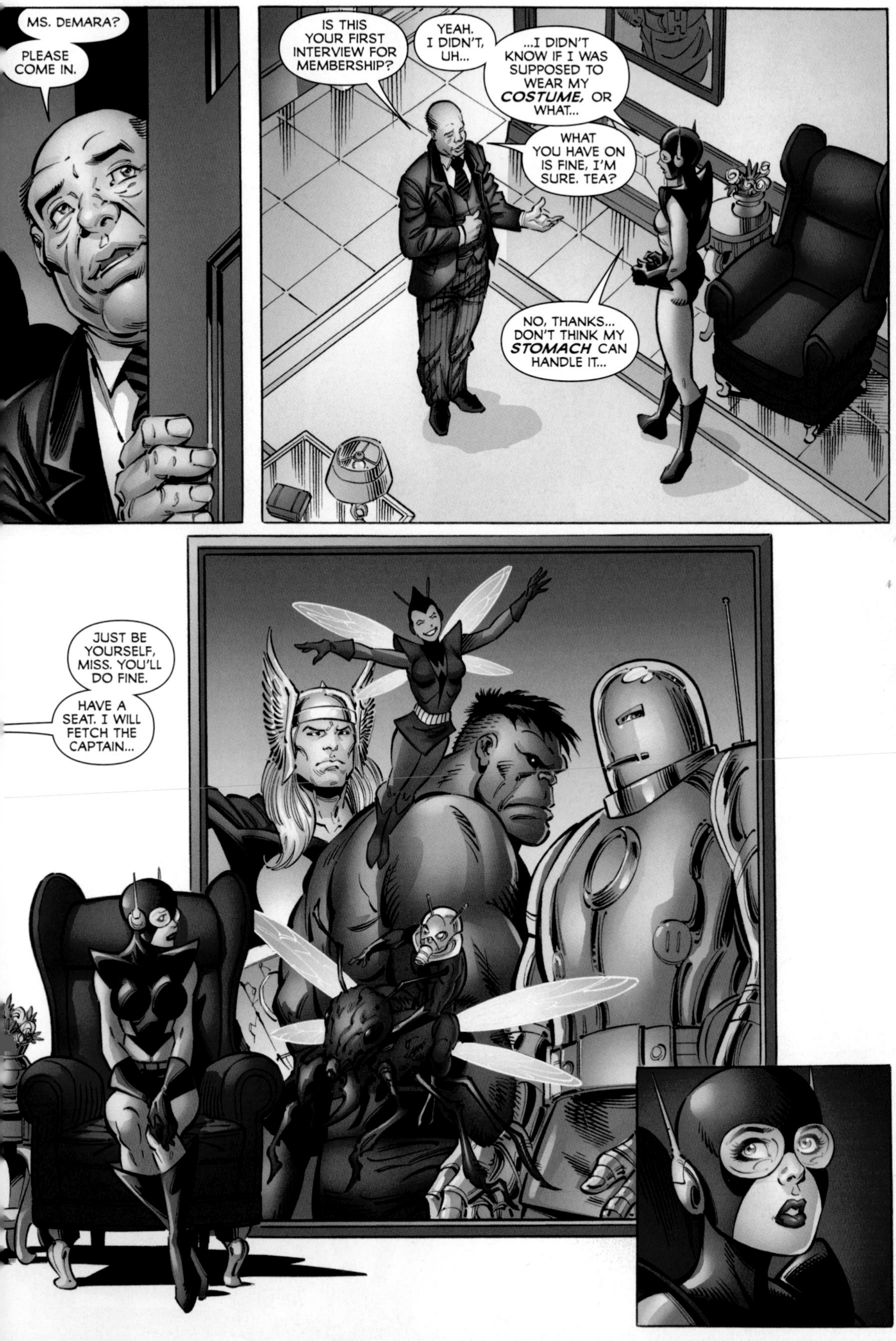

MS. DeMARA?
PLEASE COME IN.
IS THIS YOUR FIRST INTERVIEW FOR MEMBERSHIP?
YEAH. I DIDN'T, UH...
...I DIDN'T KNOW IF I WAS SUPPOSED TO WEAR MY *COSTUME,* OR WHAT...
WHAT YOU HAVE ON IS FINE, I'M SURE. TEA?
NO, THANKS... DON'T THINK MY *STOMACH* CAN HANDLE IT...
JUST BE YOURSELF, MISS. YOU'LL DO FINE.
HAVE A SEAT. I WILL FETCH THE CAPTAIN...

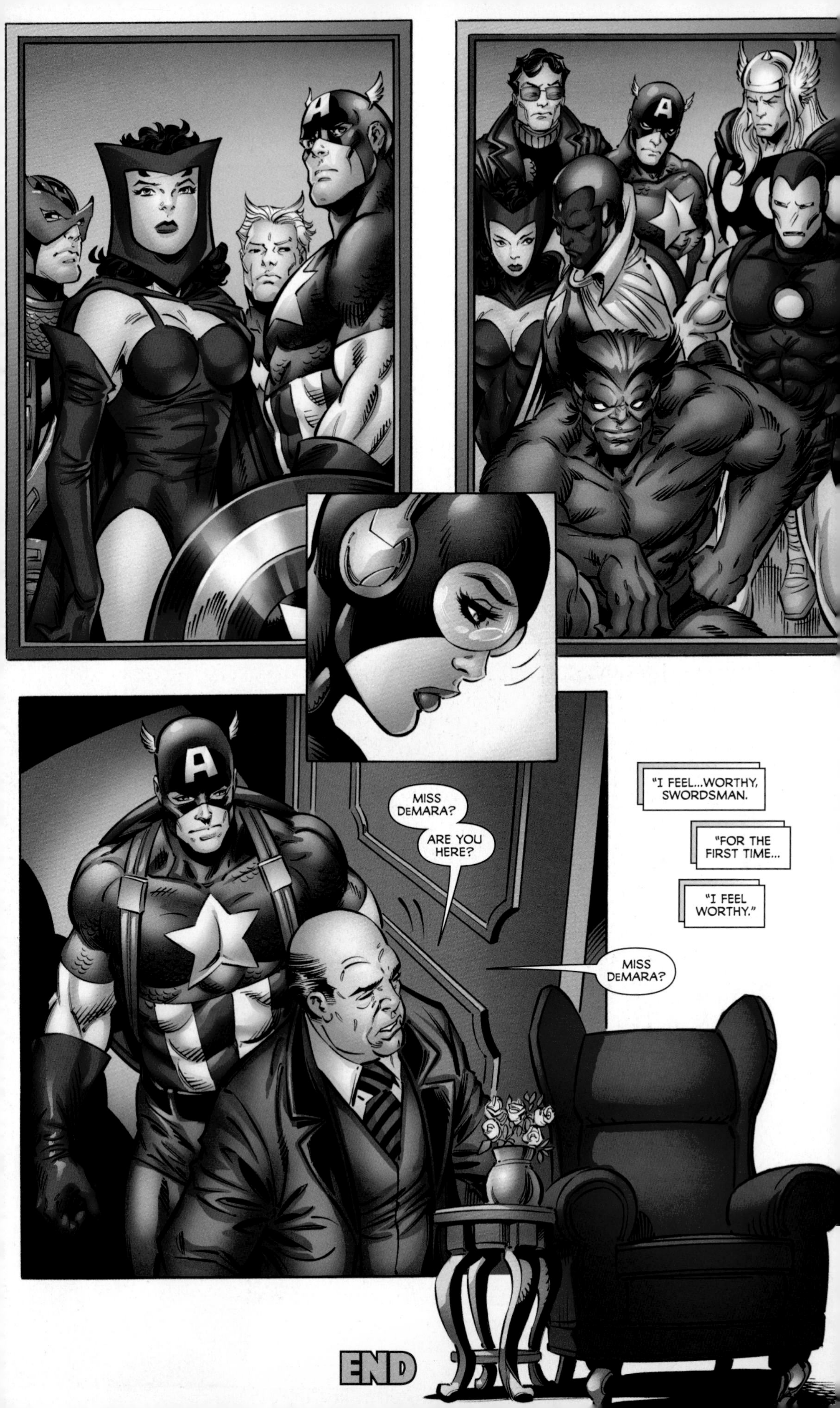
MISS DeMARA?
ARE YOU HERE?
"I FEEL...WORTHY, SWORDSMAN.
"FOR THE FIRST TIME...
"I FEEL WORTHY."
MISS DeMARA?
END

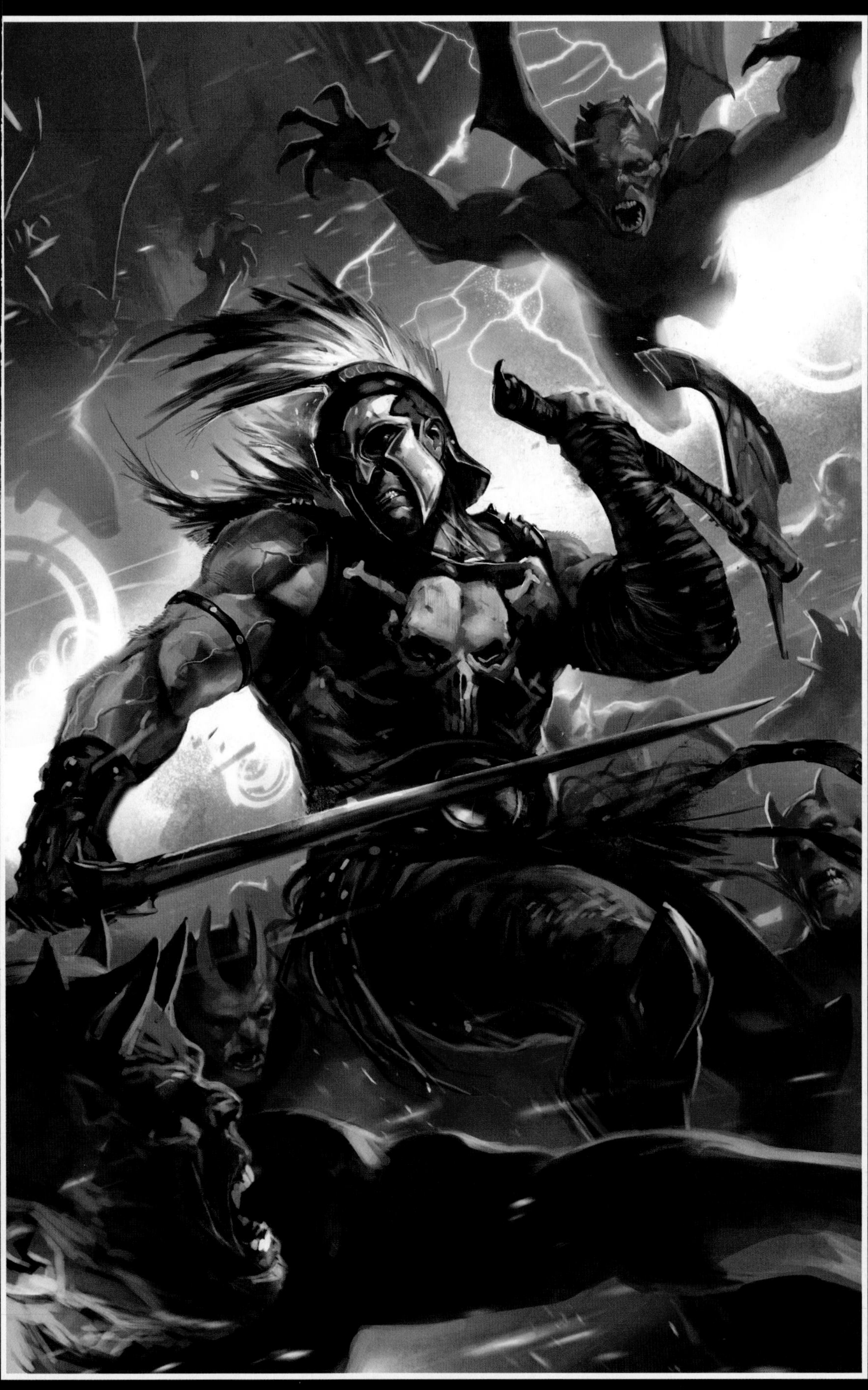

CHAOS WAR: ARES

IN THE MARVEL UNIVERSE, GODS WALK THE EARTH.

SOME SIDE WITH HEROES. OTHERS SPREAD DREAD AND DESPAIR.

ONE GOD CARES FOR NEITHER. HE IS THE CHAOS KING.

HE WILL STOP AT NOTHING TO END EVERYTHING WITH HIS

CHAOS WAR

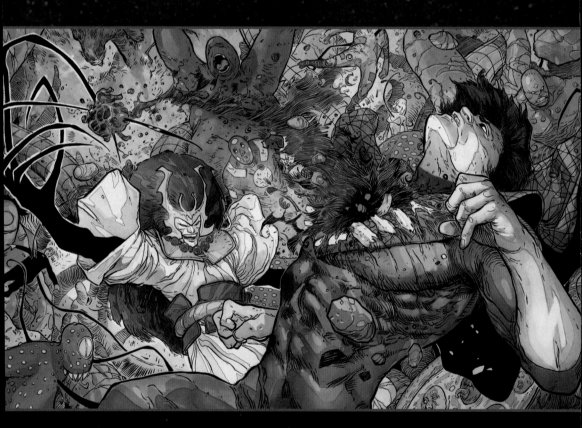

CHAOS KING IS DESTROYING REALITY ONE HIGHER REALM AT A TIME.
THE FIRST TO FALL WAS THE DREAM DIMENSION.

HIS NEXT STOP IS HELL...

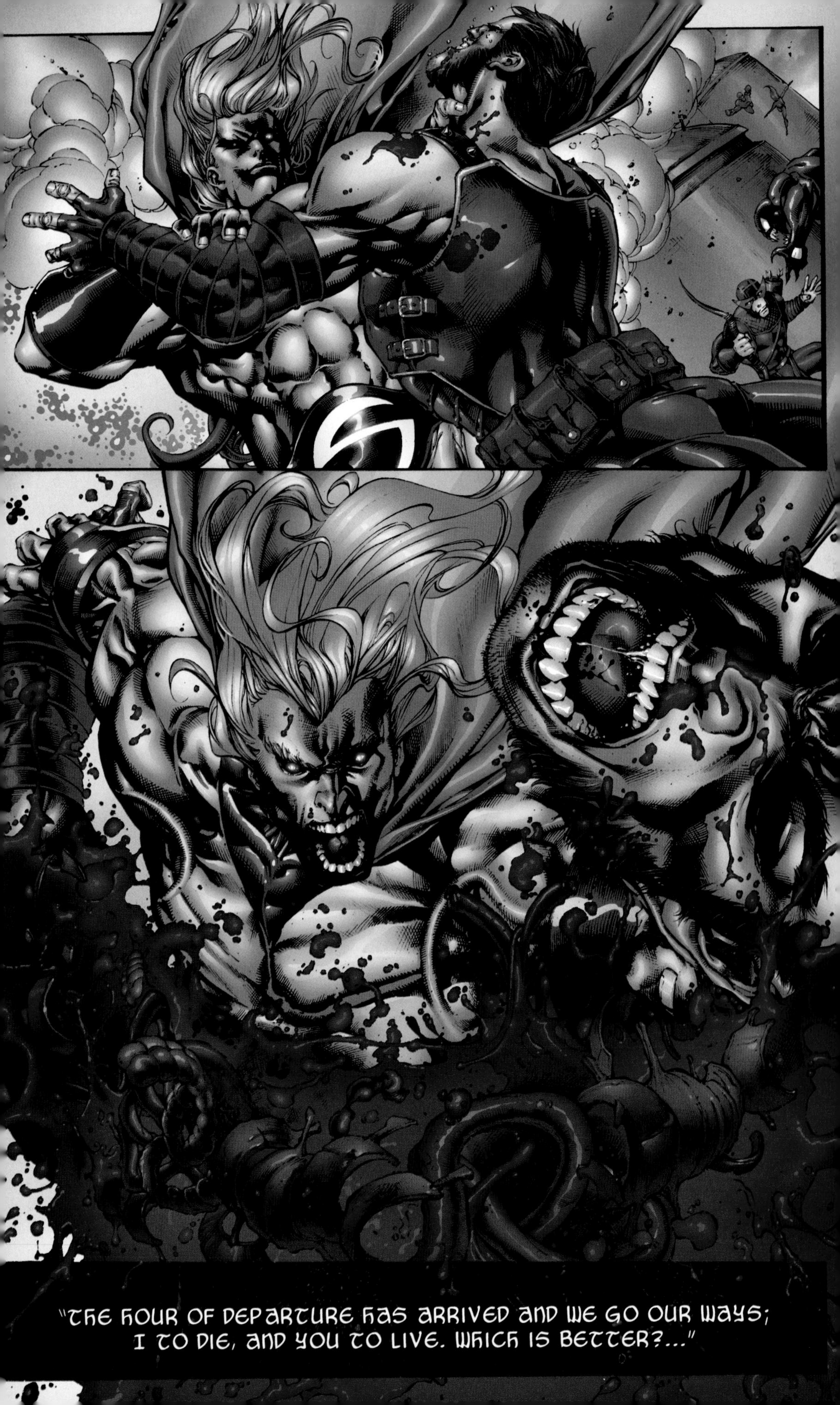
"THE HOUR OF DEPARTURE HAS ARRIVED AND WE GO OUR WAYS; I TO DIE, AND YOU TO LIVE. WHICH IS BETTER?..."

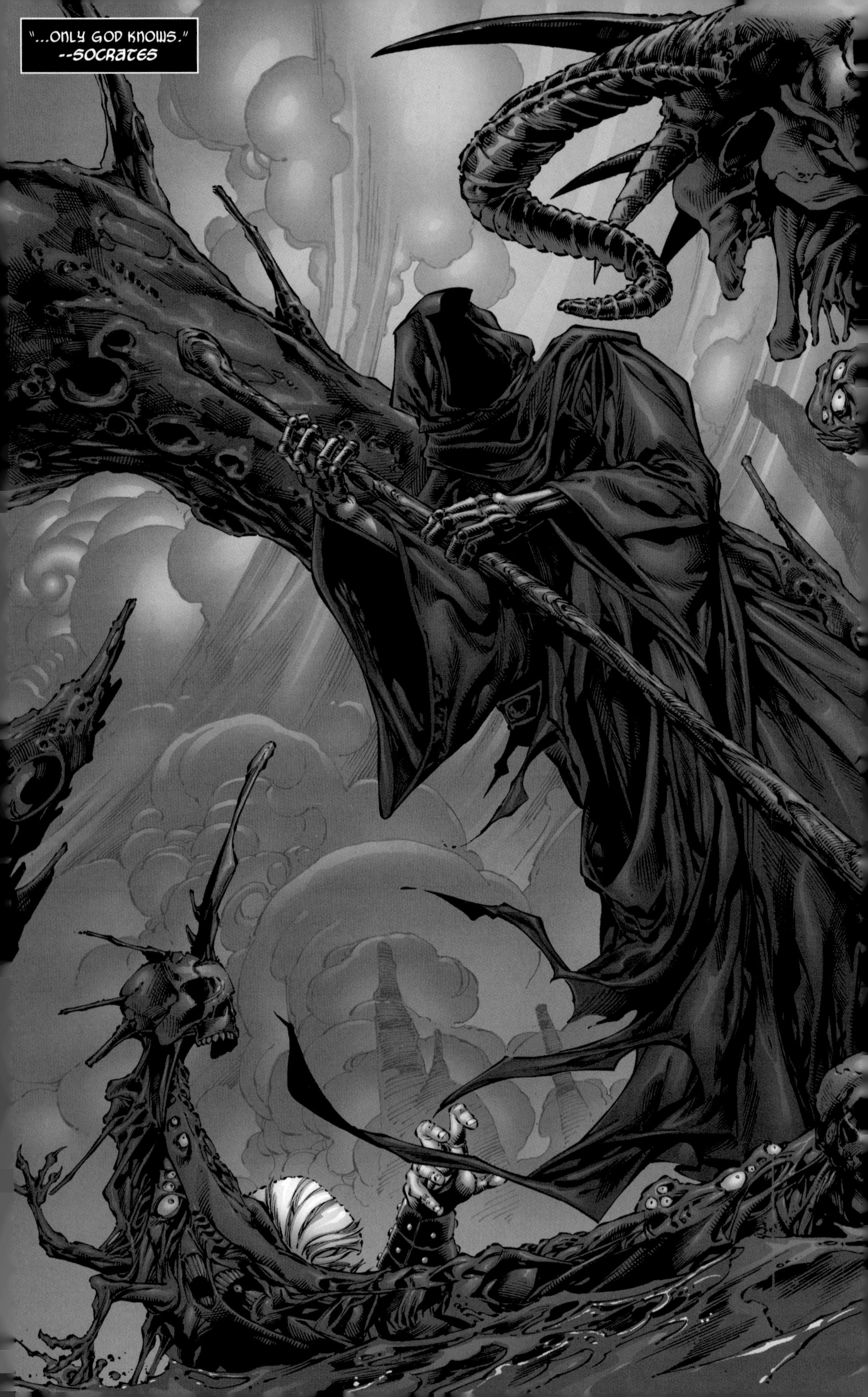
"...ONLY GOD KNOWS."
--SOCRATES

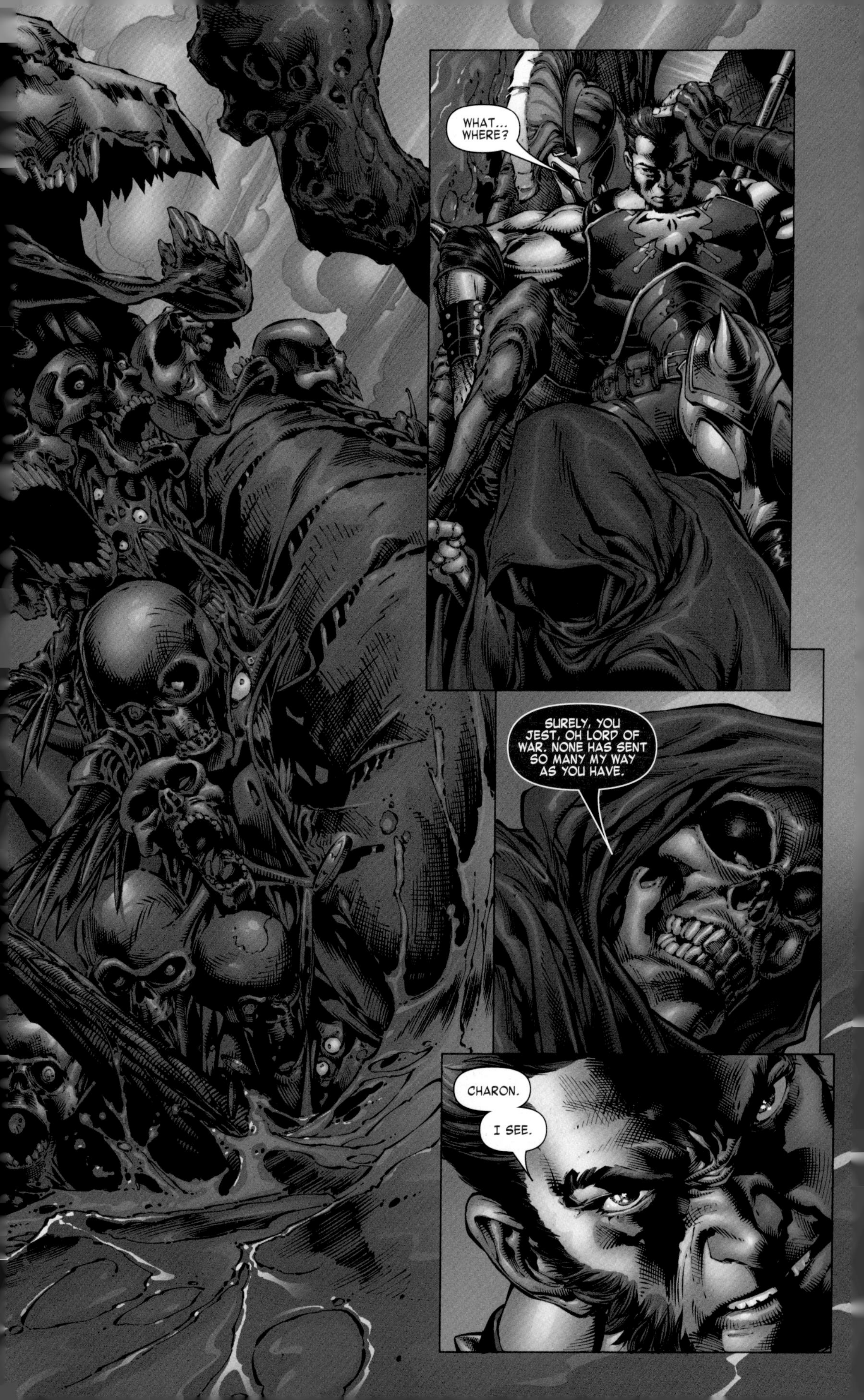
WHAT... WHERE?
SURELY, YOU JEST, OH LORD OF WAR. NONE HAS SENT SO MANY MY WAY AS YOU HAVE.
CHARON.
I SEE.

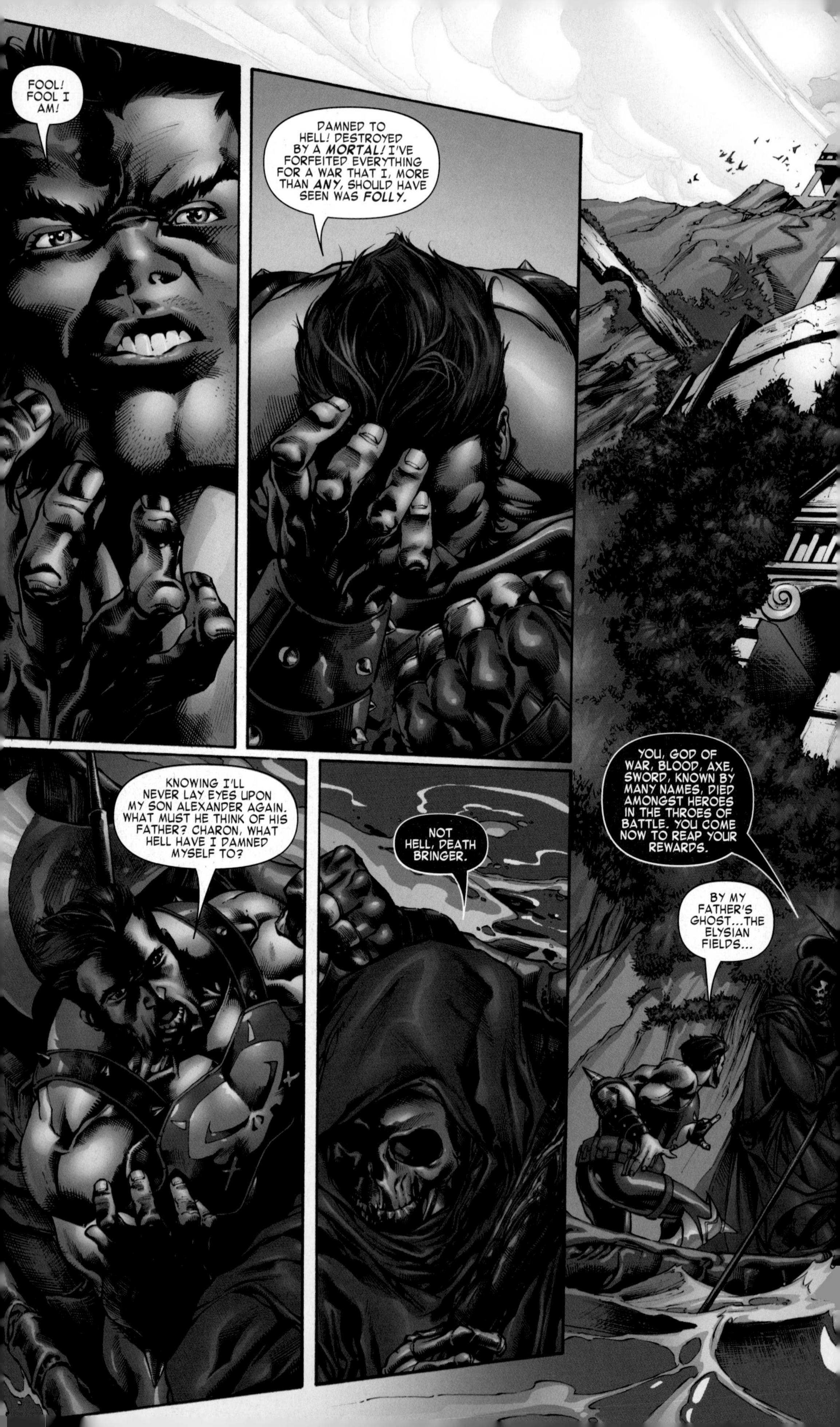
FOOL! FOOL I AM!
DAMNED TO HELL! DESTROYED BY A MORTAL! I'VE FORFEITED EVERYTHING FOR A WAR THAT I, MORE THAN ANY, SHOULD HAVE SEEN WAS FOLLY.
KNOWING I'LL NEVER LAY EYES UPON MY SON ALEXANDER AGAIN. WHAT MUST HE THINK OF HIS FATHER? CHARON, WHAT HELL HAVE I DAMNED MYSELF TO?
NOT HELL, DEATH BRINGER.
YOU, GOD OF WAR, BLOOD, AXE, SWORD, KNOWN BY MANY NAMES, DIED AMONGST HEROES IN THE THROES OF BATTLE. YOU COME NOW TO REAP YOUR REWARDS.
BY MY FATHER'S GHOST...THE ELYSIAN FIELDS...

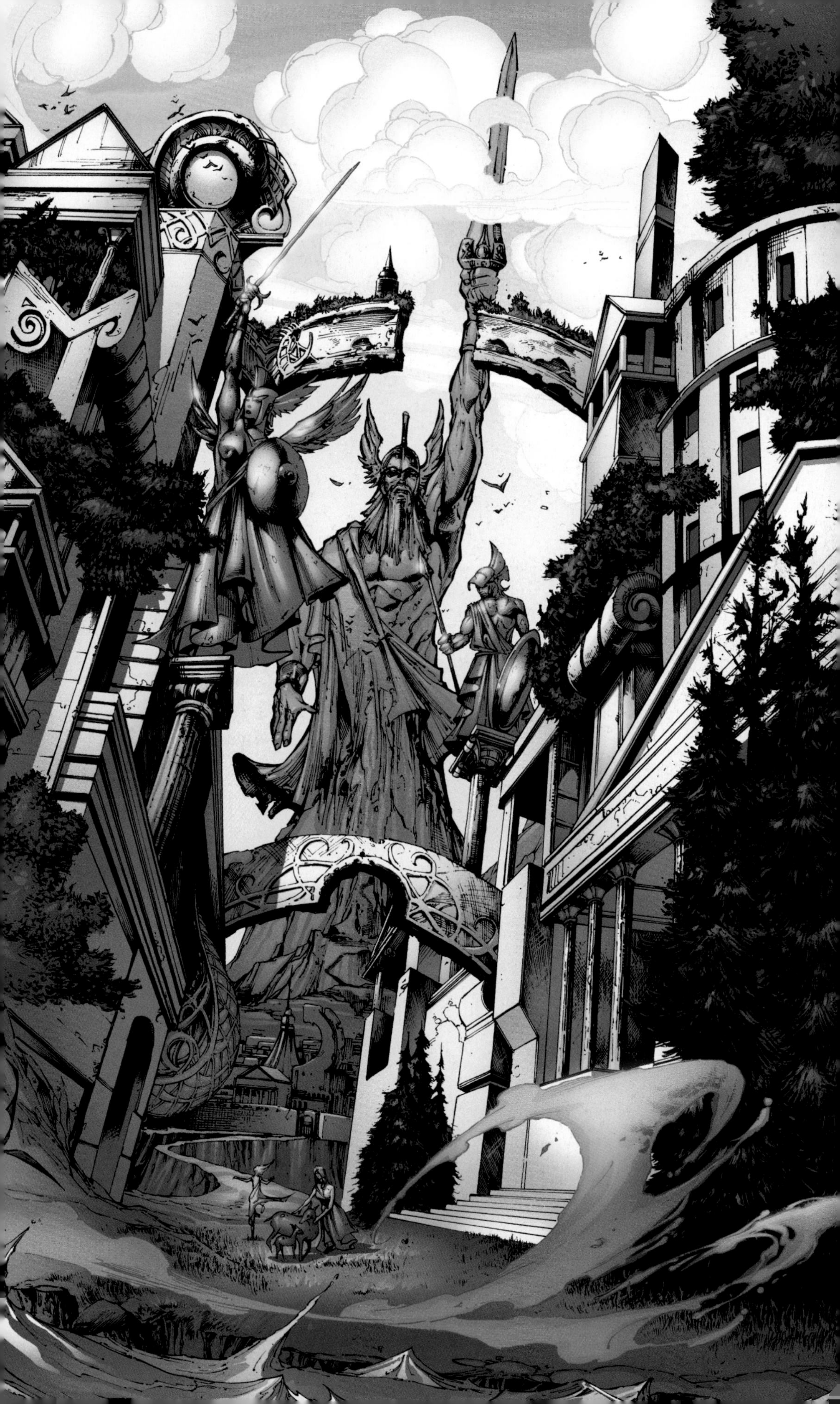

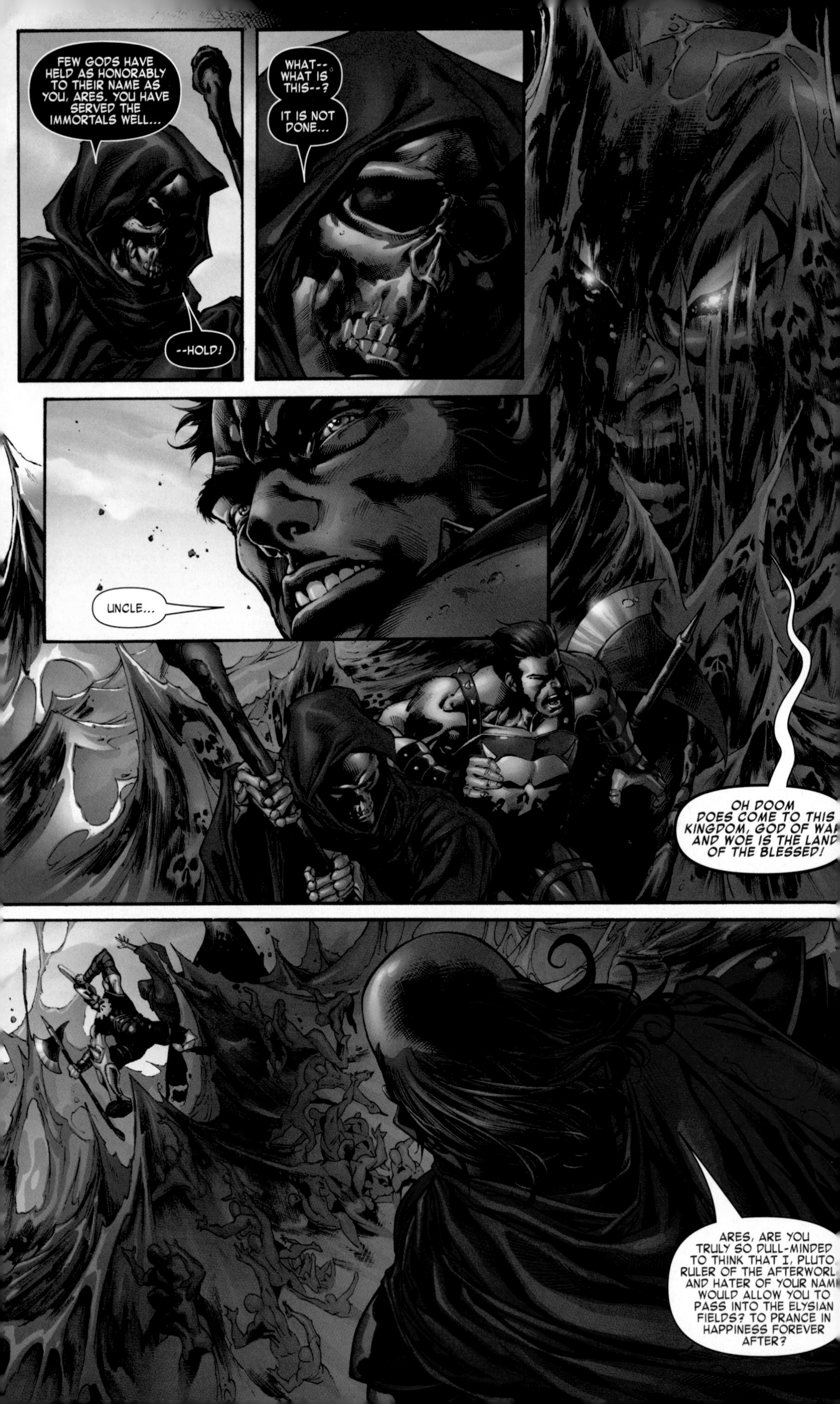

FEW GODS HAVE HELD AS HONORABLY TO THEIR NAME AS YOU, ARES. YOU HAVE SERVED THE IMMORTALS WELL...
--HOLD!
WHAT-- WHAT IS THIS--?
IT IS NOT DONE...
UNCLE...
OH DOOM DOES COME TO THIS KINGDOM, GOD OF WAR AND WOE IS THE LAND OF THE BLESSED!
ARES, ARE YOU TRULY SO DULL-MINDED TO THINK THAT I, PLUTO RULER OF THE AFTERWORLD AND HATER OF YOUR NAME WOULD ALLOW YOU TO PASS INTO THE ELYSIAN FIELDS? TO PRANCE IN HAPPINESS FOREVER AFTER?

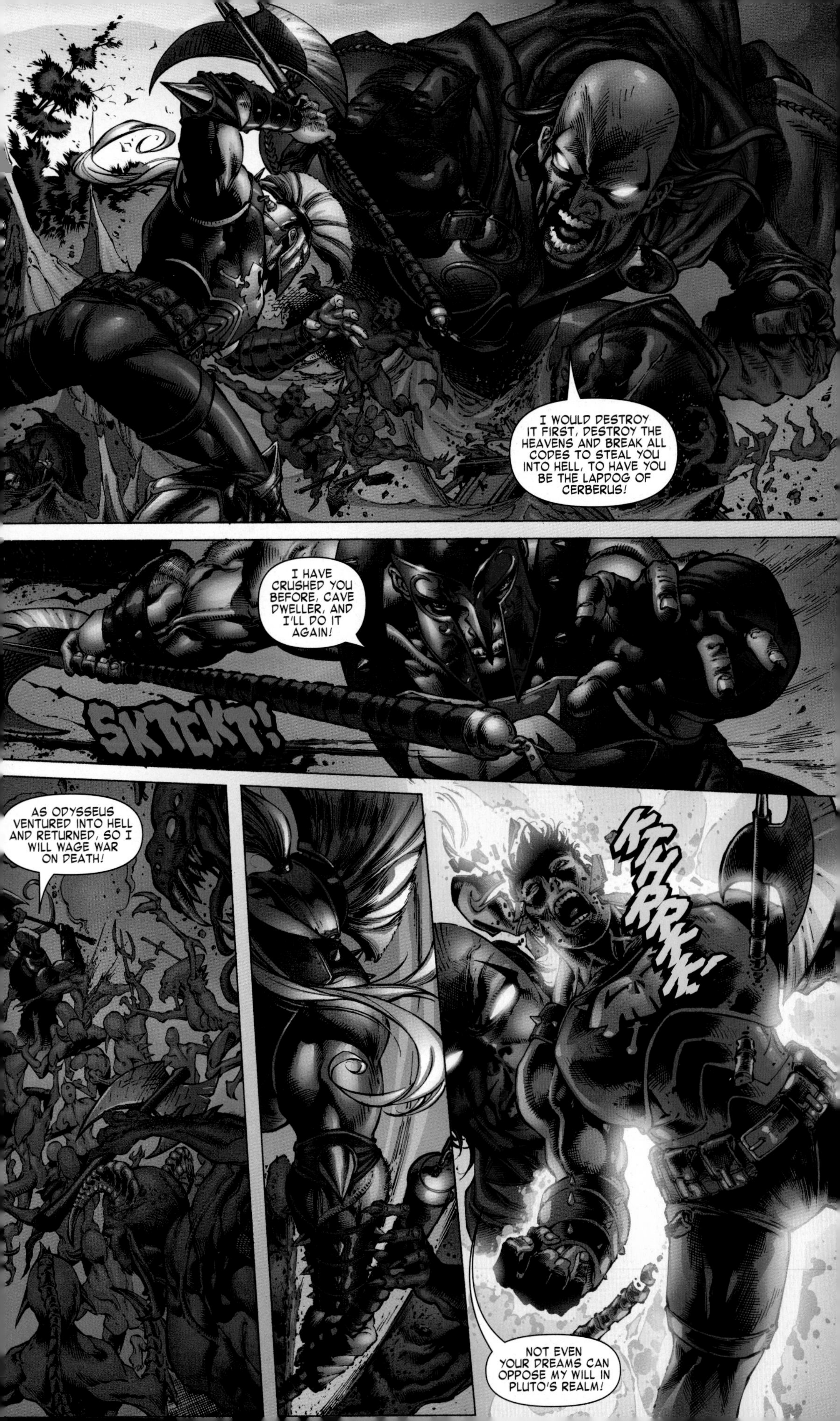
I WOULD DESTROY IT FIRST, DESTROY THE HEAVENS AND BREAK ALL CODES TO STEAL YOU INTO HELL, TO HAVE YOU BE THE LAPDOG OF CERBERUS!
I HAVE CRUSHED YOU BEFORE, CAVE DWELLER, AND I'LL DO IT AGAIN!
SKTCKT!
AS ODYSSEUS VENTURED INTO HELL AND RETURNED, SO I WILL WAGE WAR ON DEATH!
KTHRRK!
NOT EVEN YOUR DREAMS CAN OPPOSE MY WILL IN PLUTO'S REALM!

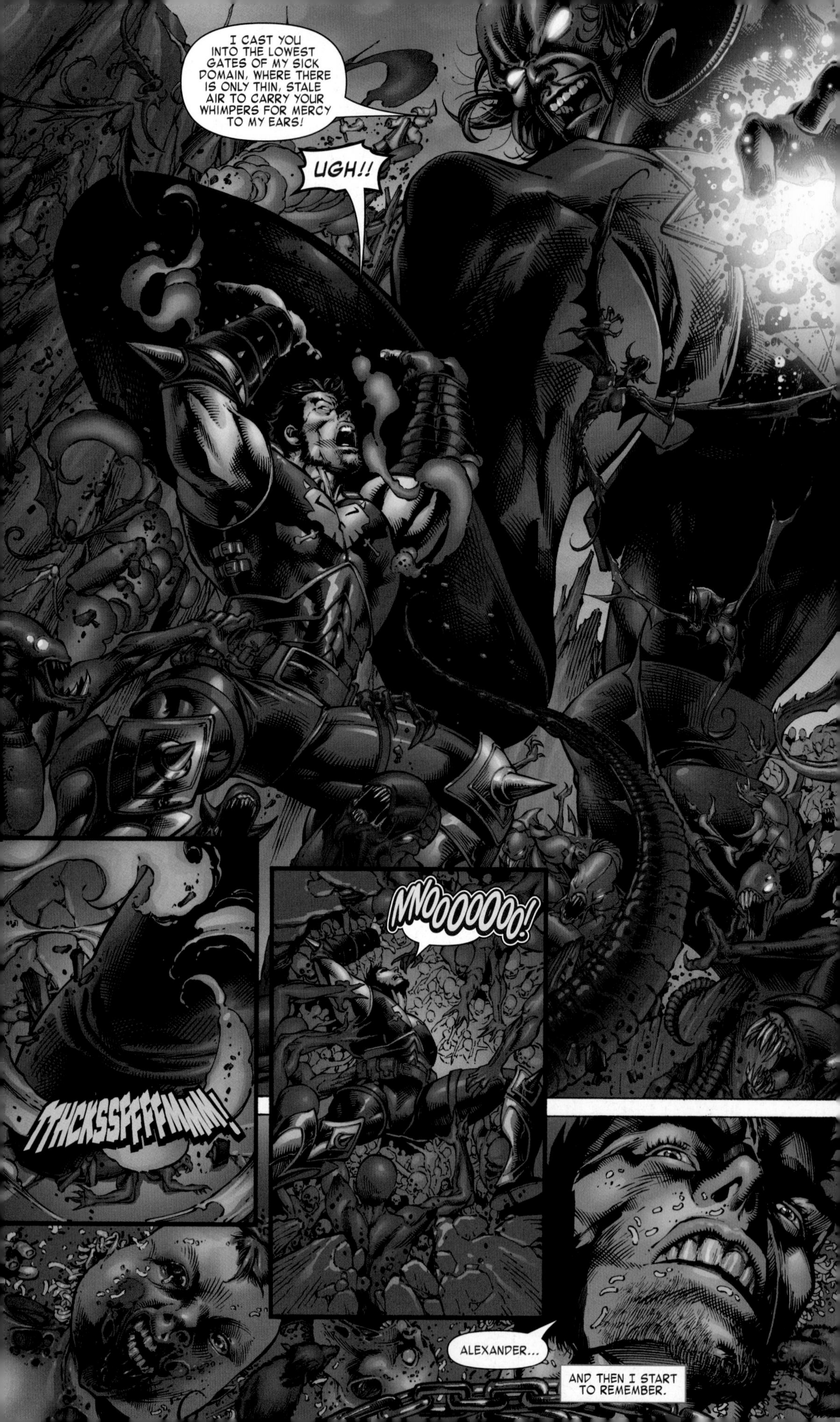

I CAST YOU INTO THE LOWEST GATES OF MY SICK DOMAIN, WHERE THERE IS ONLY THIN, STALE AIR TO CARRY YOUR WHIMPERS FOR MERCY TO MY EARS!
UGH!!
THCKSSFFFFMMM!
NNOOOOOOO!
ALEXANDER...
AND THEN I START TO REMEMBER.

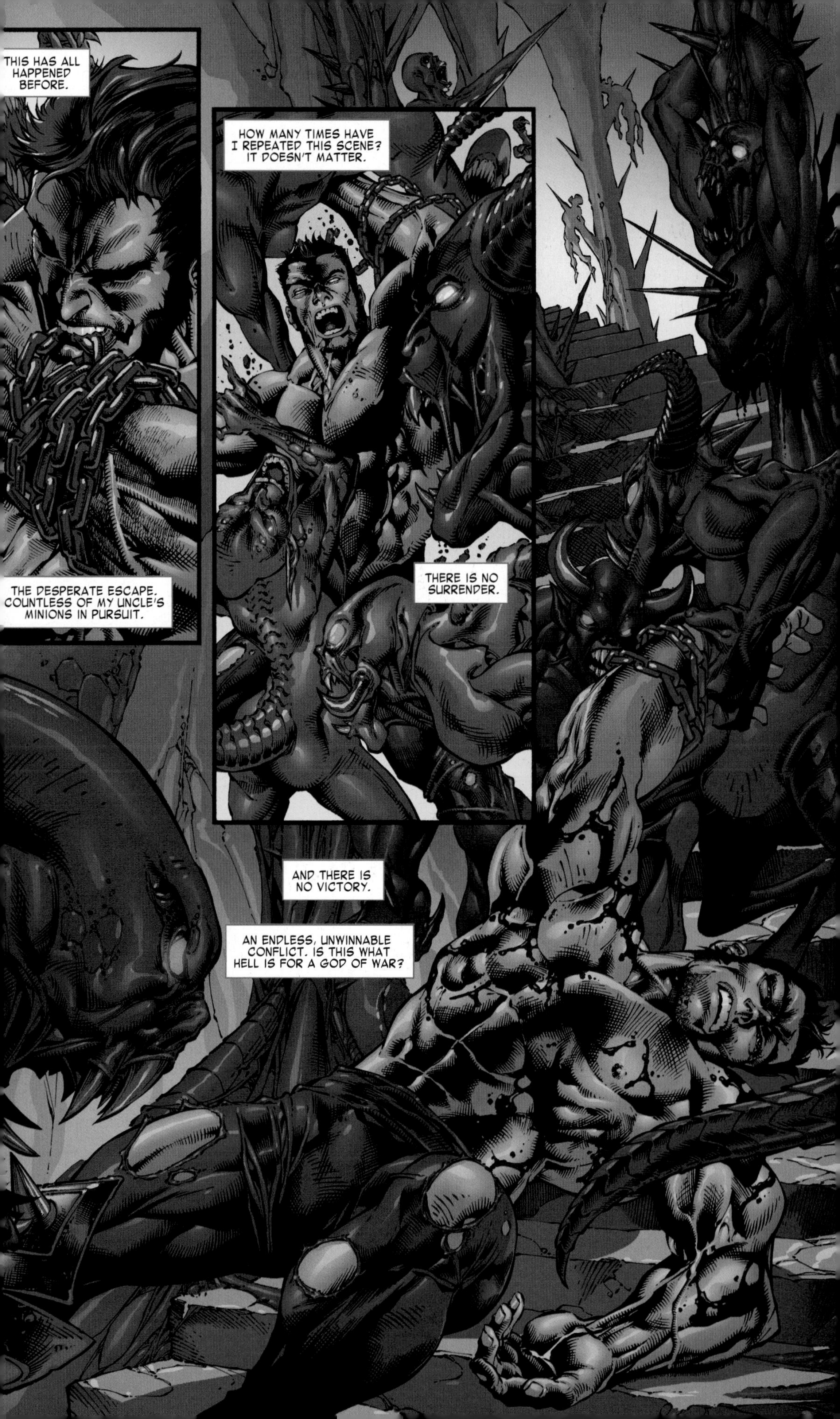

THIS HAS ALL HAPPENED BEFORE.
HOW MANY TIMES HAVE I REPEATED THIS SCENE? IT DOESN'T MATTER.
THE DESPERATE ESCAPE. COUNTLESS OF MY UNCLE'S MINIONS IN PURSUIT.
THERE IS NO SURRENDER.
AND THERE IS NO VICTORY.
AN ENDLESS, UNWINNABLE CONFLICT. IS THIS WHAT HELL IS FOR A GOD OF WAR?

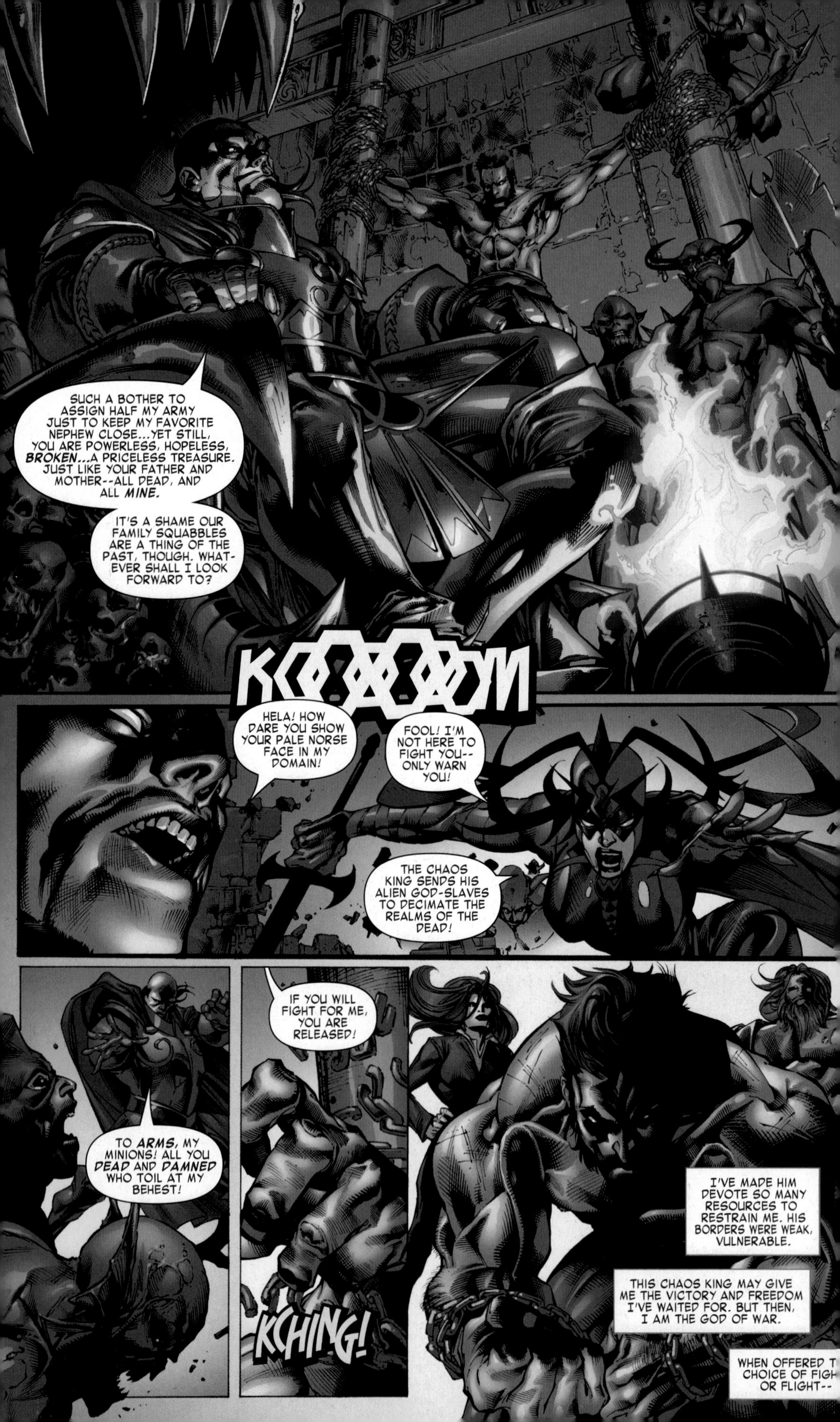

SUCH A BOTHER TO ASSIGN HALF MY ARMY JUST TO KEEP MY FAVORITE NEPHEW CLOSE...YET STILL, YOU ARE POWERLESS, HOPELESS, BROKEN...A PRICELESS TREASURE. JUST LIKE YOUR FATHER AND MOTHER--ALL DEAD, AND ALL MINE.
IT'S A SHAME OUR FAMILY SQUABBLES ARE A THING OF THE PAST, THOUGH. WHAT-EVER SHALL I LOOK FORWARD TO?
KOOOOOM
HELA! HOW DARE YOU SHOW YOUR PALE NORSE FACE IN MY DOMAIN!
FOOL! I'M NOT HERE TO FIGHT YOU-- ONLY WARN YOU!
THE CHAOS KING SENDS HIS ALIEN GOD-SLAVES TO DECIMATE THE REALMS OF THE DEAD!
TO ARMS, MY MINIONS! ALL YOU DEAD AND DAMNED WHO TOIL AT MY BEHEST!
IF YOU WILL FIGHT FOR ME, YOU ARE RELEASED!
KCHING!
I'VE MADE HIM DEVOTE SO MANY RESOURCES TO RESTRAIN ME. HIS BORDERS WERE WEAK, VULNERABLE.
THIS CHAOS KING MAY GIVE ME THE VICTORY AND FREEDOM I'VE WAITED FOR. BUT THEN, I AM THE GOD OF WAR.
WHEN OFFERED T CHOICE OF FIGH OR FLIGHT--

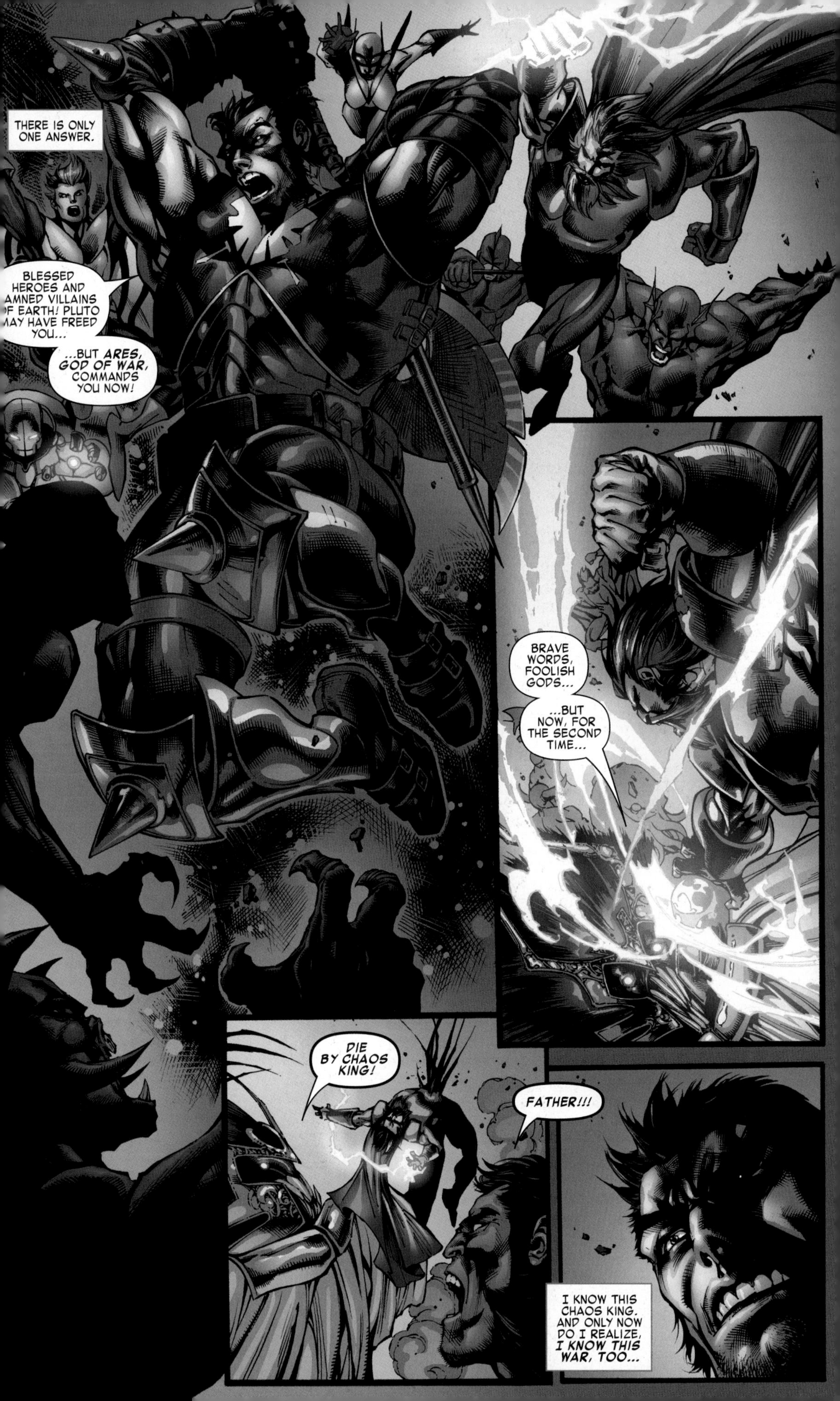
THERE IS ONLY ONE ANSWER.
BLESSED HEROES AND AMNED VILLAINS OF EARTH! PLUTO MAY HAVE FREED YOU...
...BUT ARES, GOD OF WAR, COMMANDS YOU NOW!
BRAVE WORDS, FOOLISH GODS...
...BUT NOW, FOR THE SECOND TIME...
DIE BY CHAOS KING!
FATHER!!!
I KNOW THIS CHAOS KING. AND ONLY NOW DO I REALIZE, I KNOW THIS WAR, TOO...

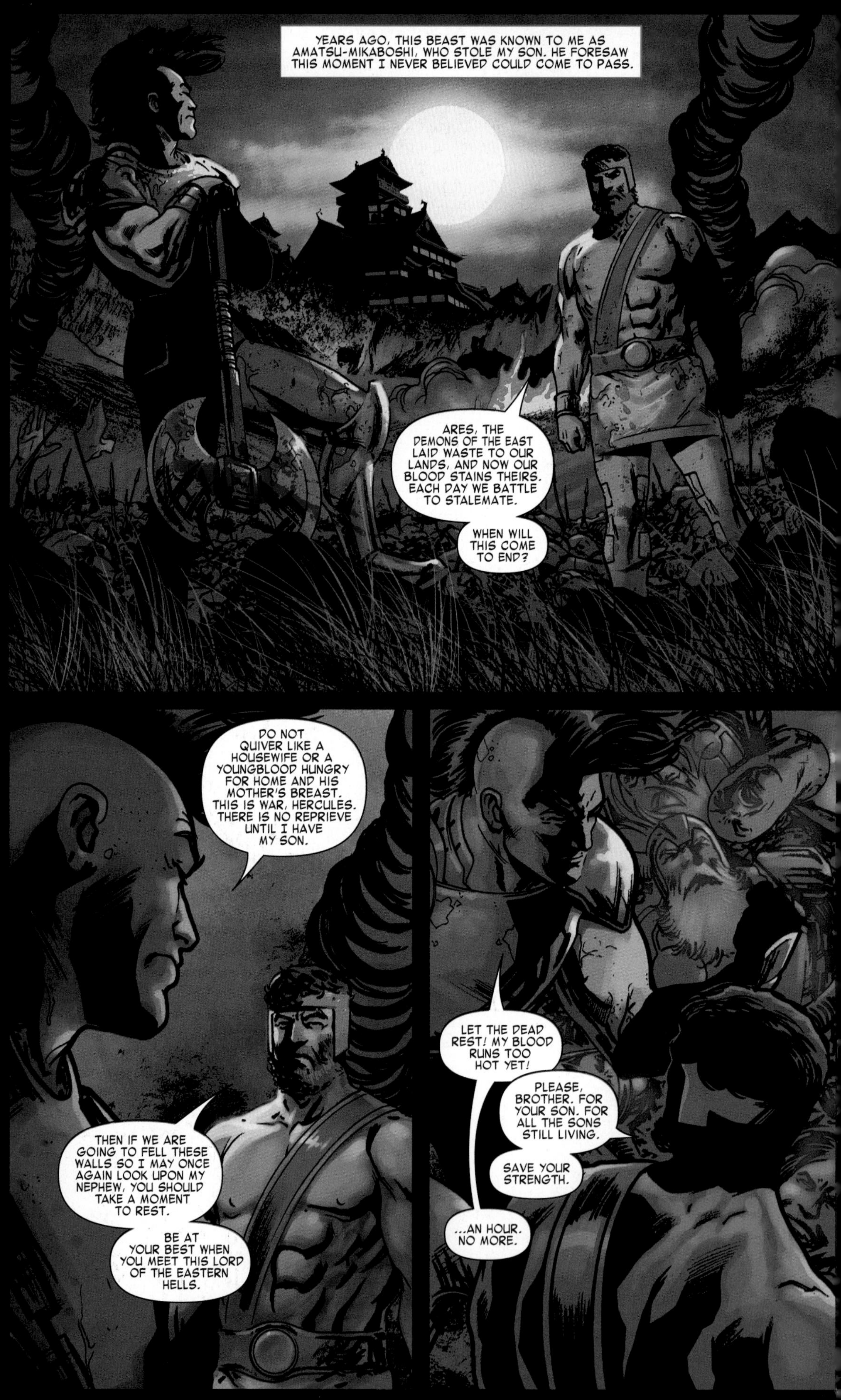
YEARS AGO, THIS BEAST WAS KNOWN TO ME AS AMATSU-MIKABOSHI, WHO STOLE MY SON. HE FORESAW THIS MOMENT I NEVER BELIEVED COULD COME TO PASS.
ARES, THE DEMONS OF THE EAST LAID WASTE TO OUR LANDS, AND NOW OUR BLOOD STAINS THEIRS. EACH DAY WE BATTLE TO STALEMATE.
WHEN WILL THIS COME TO END?
DO NOT QUIVER LIKE A HOUSEWIFE OR A YOUNGBLOOD HUNGRY FOR HOME AND HIS MOTHER'S BREAST. THIS IS WAR, HERCULES. THERE IS NO REPRIEVE UNTIL I HAVE MY SON.
THEN IF WE ARE GOING TO FELL THESE WALLS SO I MAY ONCE AGAIN LOOK UPON MY NEPHEW, YOU SHOULD TAKE A MOMENT TO REST.
BE AT YOUR BEST WHEN YOU MEET THIS LORD OF THE EASTERN HELLS.
LET THE DEAD REST! MY BLOOD RUNS TOO HOT YET!
PLEASE, BROTHER. FOR YOUR SON. FOR ALL THE SONS STILL LIVING.
SAVE YOUR STRENGTH.
...AN HOUR. NO MORE.

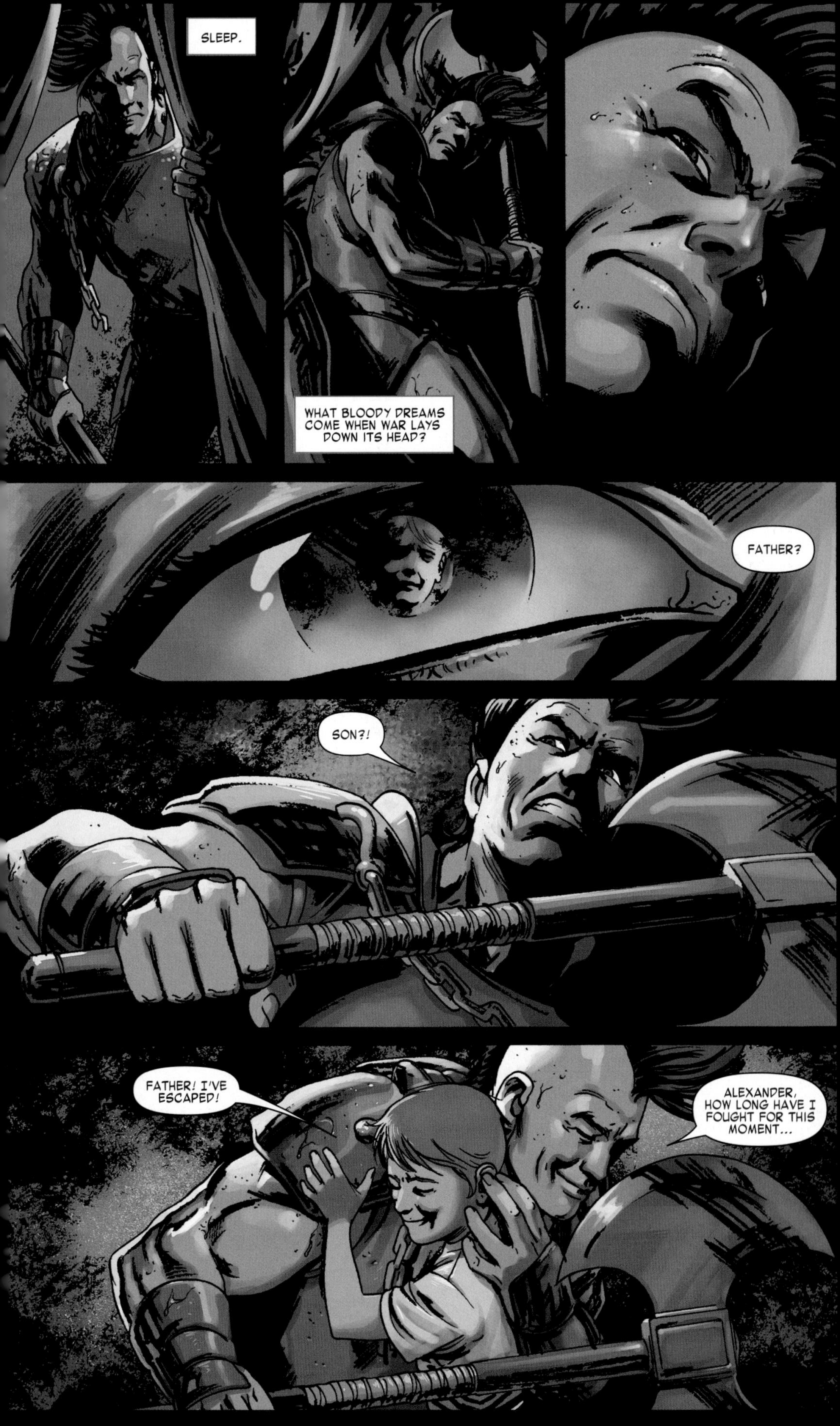
SLEEP.
WHAT BLOODY DREAMS COME WHEN WAR LAYS DOWN ITS HEAD?
FATHER?
SON?!
FATHER! I'VE ESCAPED!
ALEXANDER, HOW LONG HAVE I FOUGHT FOR THIS MOMENT...

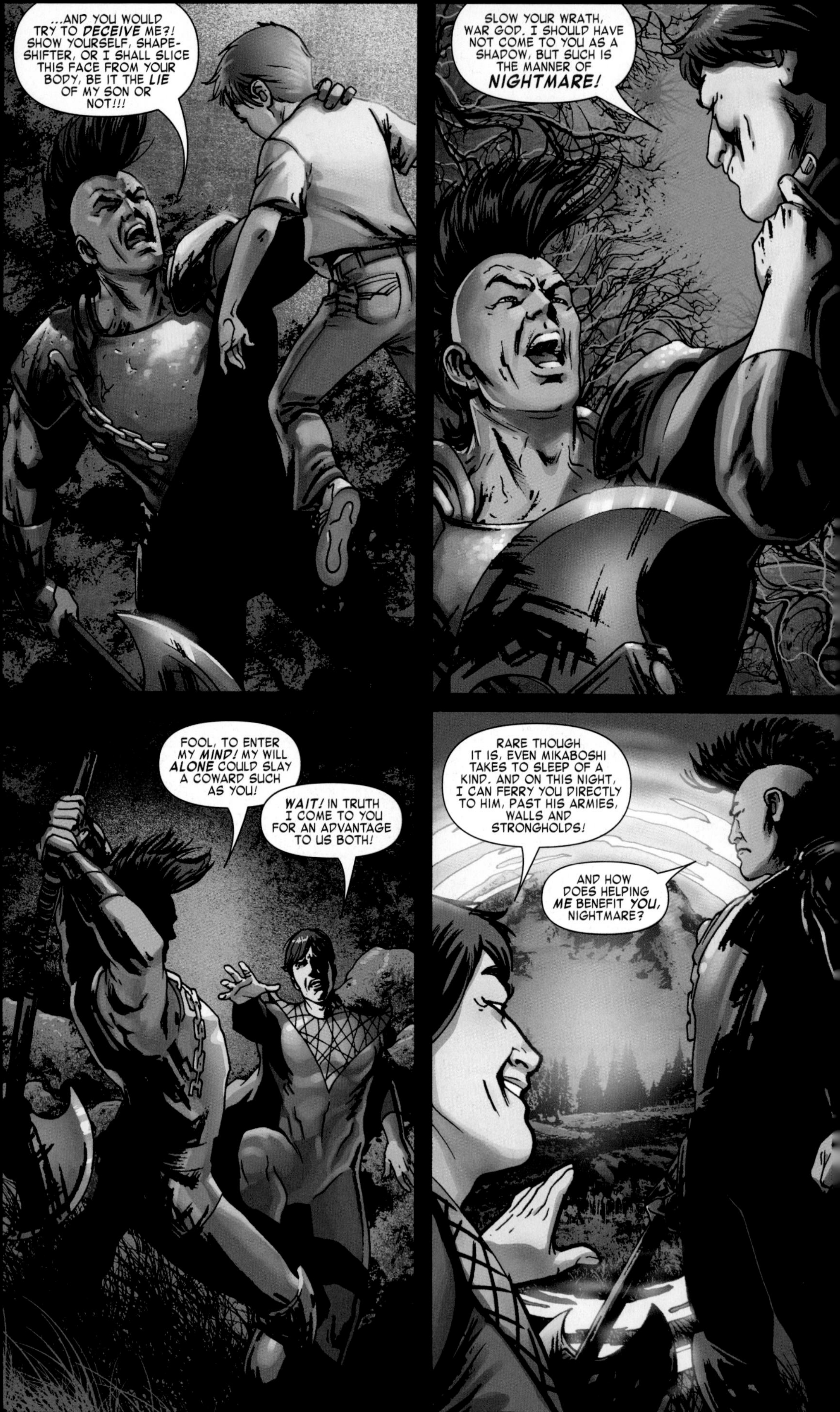
...AND YOU WOULD TRY TO DECEIVE ME?! SHOW YOURSELF, SHAPE-SHIFTER, OR I SHALL SLICE THIS FACE FROM YOUR BODY, BE IT THE LIE OF MY SON OR NOT!!!
SLOW YOUR WRATH, WAR GOD. I SHOULD HAVE NOT COME TO YOU AS A SHADOW, BUT SUCH IS THE MANNER OF NIGHTMARE!
FOOL, TO ENTER MY MIND! MY WILL ALONE COULD SLAY A COWARD SUCH AS YOU!
WAIT! IN TRUTH I COME TO YOU FOR AN ADVANTAGE TO US BOTH!
RARE THOUGH IT IS, EVEN MIKABOSHI TAKES TO SLEEP OF A KIND. AND ON THIS NIGHT, I CAN FERRY YOU DIRECTLY TO HIM, PAST HIS ARMIES, WALLS AND STRONGHOLDS!
AND HOW DOES HELPING ME BENEFIT YOU, NIGHTMARE?

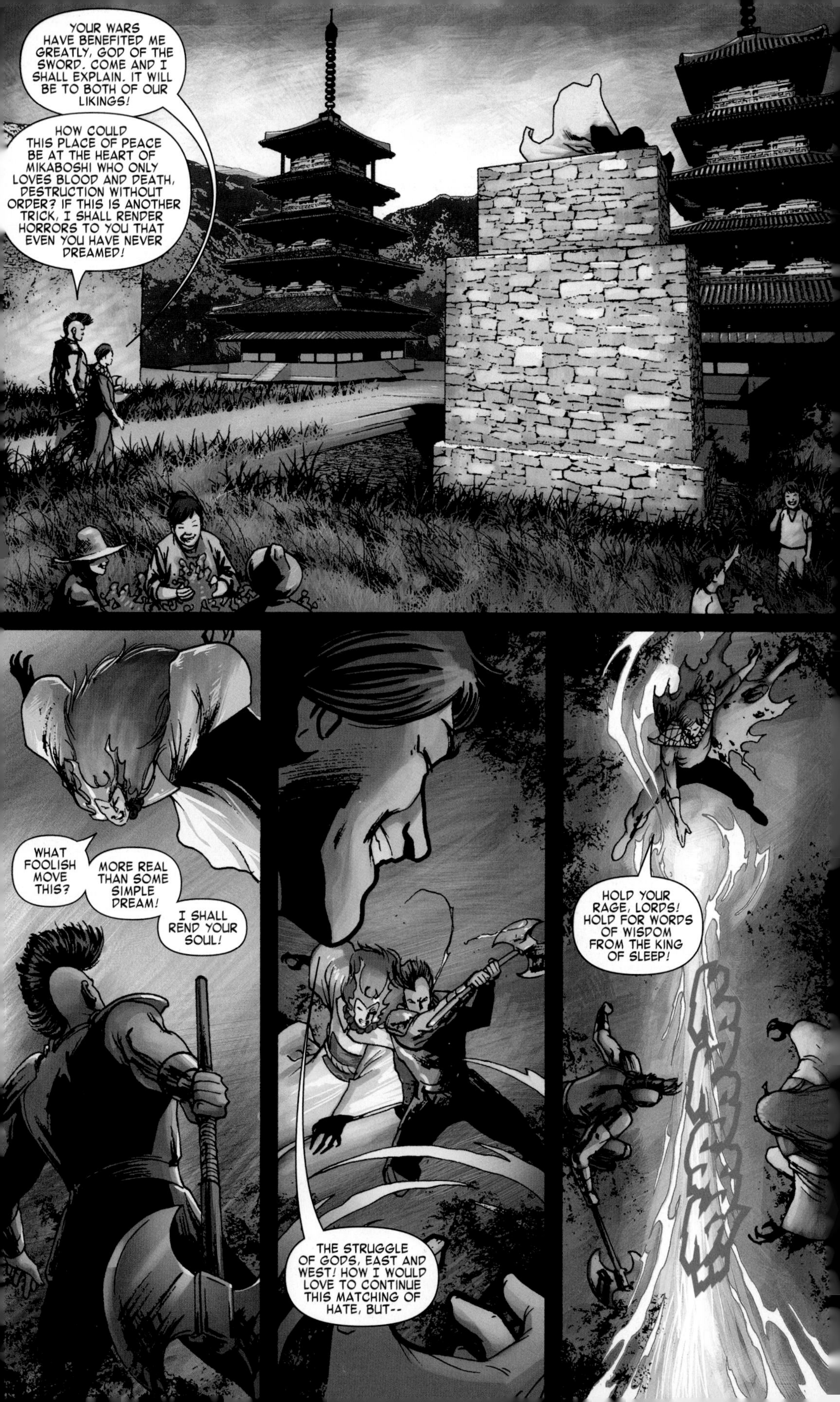
YOUR WARS HAVE BENEFITED ME GREATLY, GOD OF THE SWORD. COME AND I SHALL EXPLAIN. IT WILL BE TO BOTH OF OUR LIKINGS!
HOW COULD THIS PLACE OF PEACE BE AT THE HEART OF MIKABOSHI WHO ONLY LOVES BLOOD AND DEATH, DESTRUCTION WITHOUT ORDER? IF THIS IS ANOTHER TRICK, I SHALL RENDER HORRORS TO YOU THAT EVEN YOU HAVE NEVER DREAMED!
WHAT FOOLISH MOVE THIS?
MORE REAL THAN SOME SIMPLE DREAM!
I SHALL REND YOUR SOUL!
THE STRUGGLE OF GODS, EAST AND WEST! HOW I WOULD LOVE TO CONTINUE THIS MATCHING OF HATE, BUT--
HOLD YOUR RAGE, LORDS! HOLD FOR WORDS OF WISDOM FROM THE KING OF SLEEP!

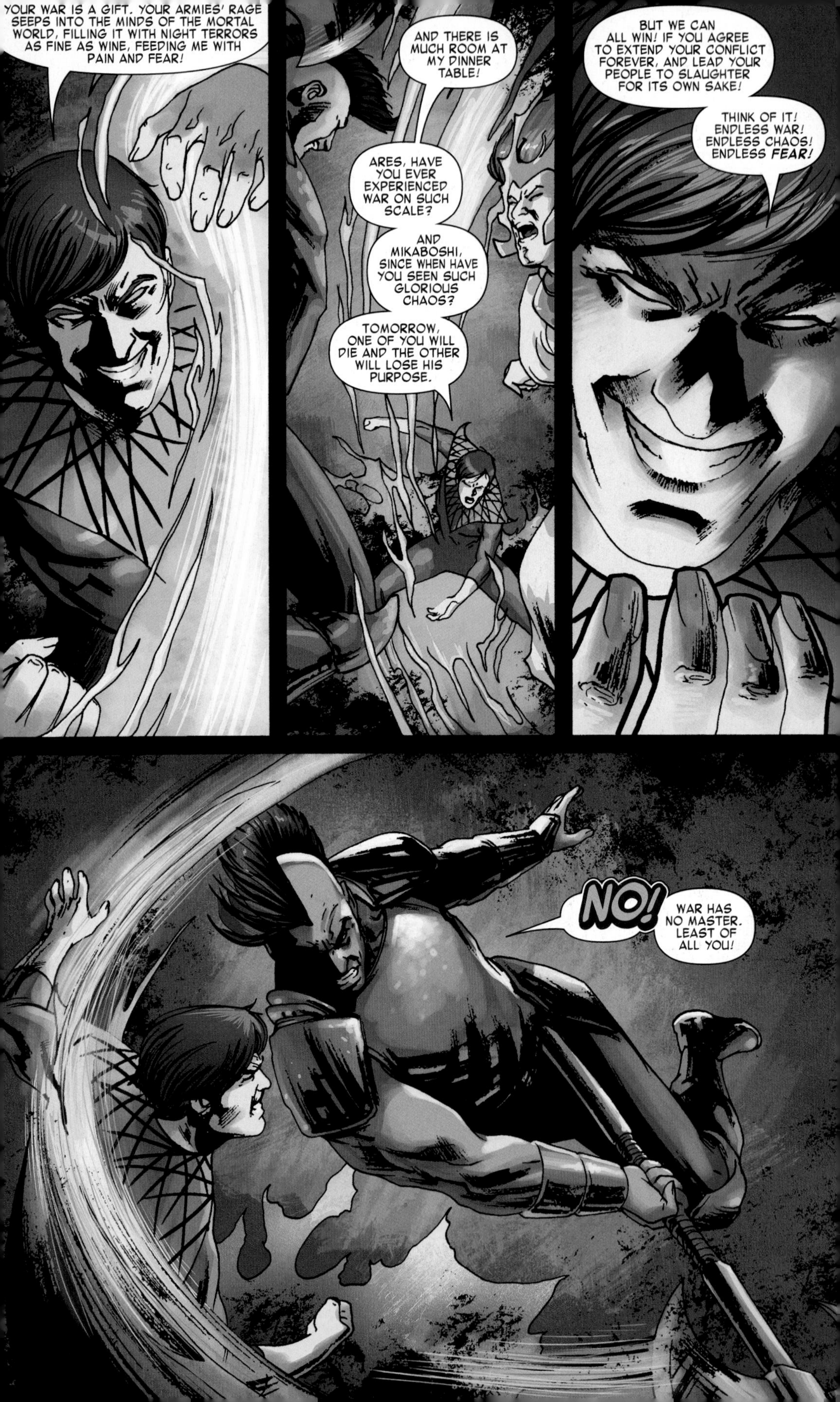
YOUR WAR IS A GIFT. YOUR ARMIES' RAGE SEEPS INTO THE MINDS OF THE MORTAL WORLD, FILLING IT WITH NIGHT TERRORS AS FINE AS WINE, FEEDING ME WITH PAIN AND FEAR!
AND THERE IS MUCH ROOM AT MY DINNER TABLE!
ARES, HAVE YOU EVER EXPERIENCED WAR ON SUCH SCALE?
AND MIKABOSHI, SINCE WHEN HAVE YOU SEEN SUCH GLORIOUS CHAOS?
TOMORROW, ONE OF YOU WILL DIE AND THE OTHER WILL LOSE HIS PURPOSE.
BUT WE CAN ALL WIN! IF YOU AGREE TO EXTEND YOUR CONFLICT FOREVER, AND LEAD YOUR PEOPLE TO SLAUGHTER FOR ITS OWN SAKE!
THINK OF IT! ENDLESS WAR! ENDLESS CHAOS! ENDLESS FEAR!
NO!
WAR HAS NO MASTER. LEAST OF ALL YOU!

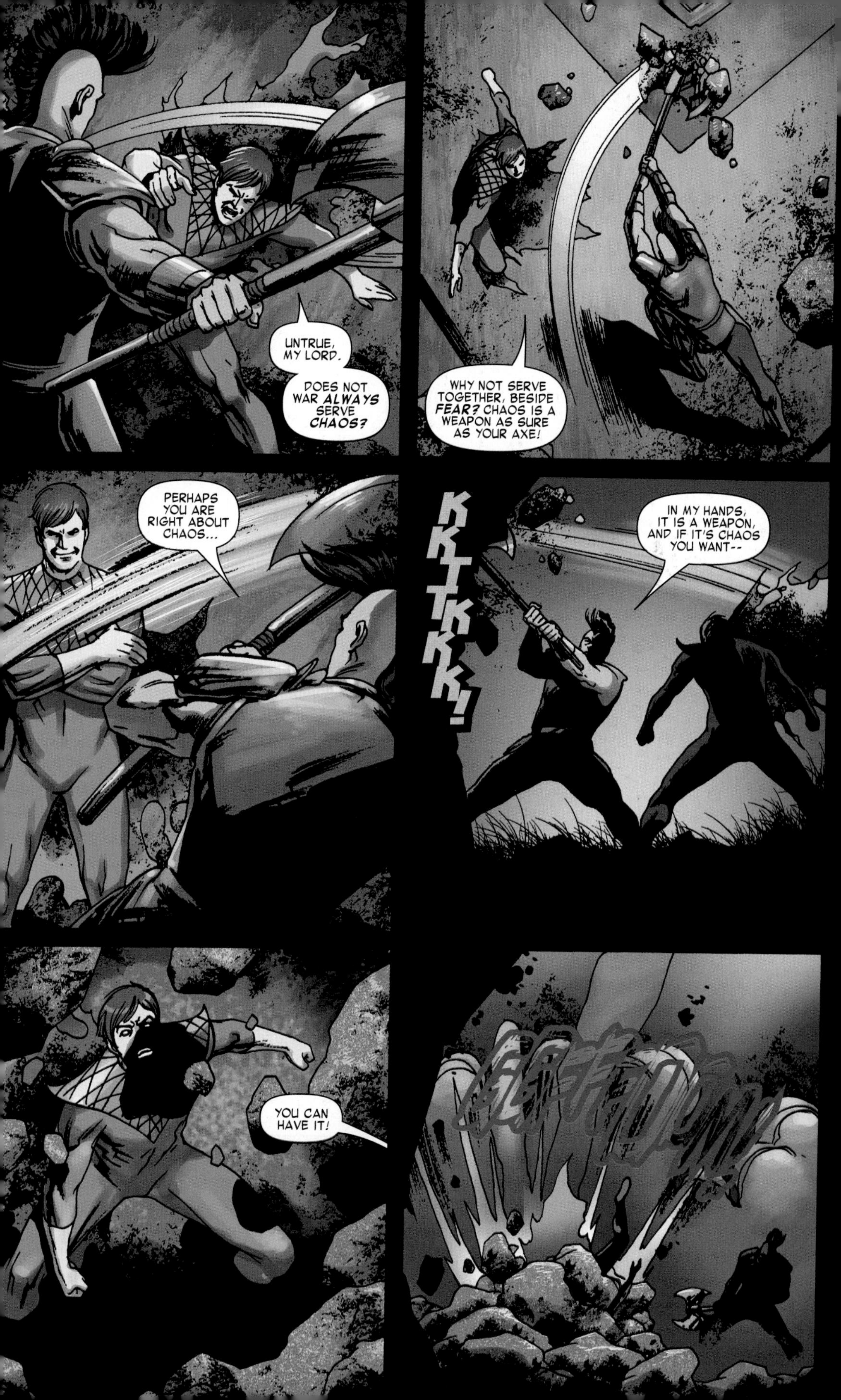
UNTRUE, MY LORD.
DOES NOT WAR *ALWAYS* SERVE *CHAOS?*
WHY NOT SERVE TOGETHER, BESIDE *FEAR?* CHAOS IS A WEAPON AS SURE AS YOUR AXE!
PERHAPS YOU ARE RIGHT ABOUT CHAOS...
KKTKKK!
IN MY HANDS, IT IS A WEAPON, AND IF IT'S CHAOS YOU WANT--
YOU CAN HAVE IT!

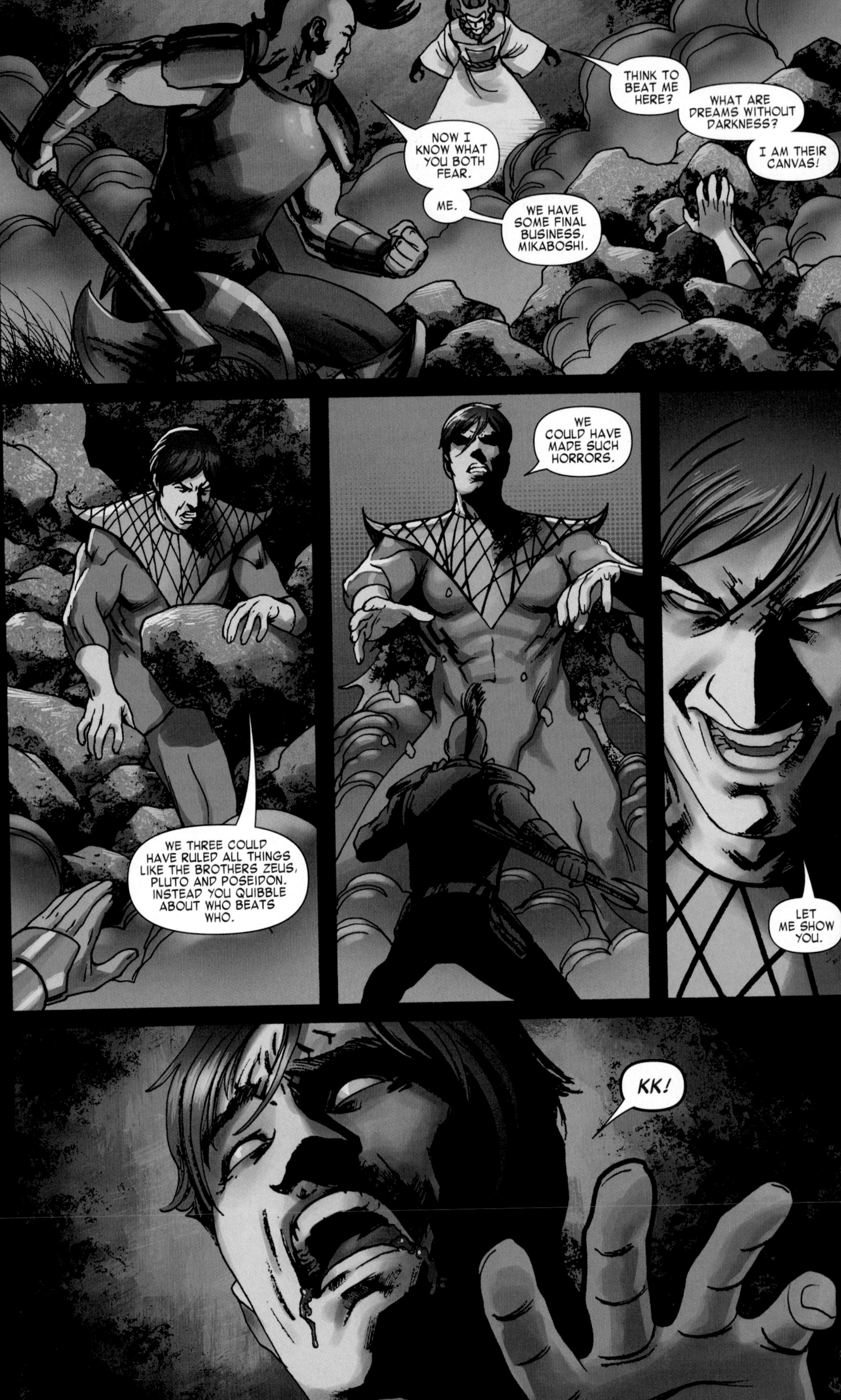

THINK TO BEAT ME HERE?
WHAT ARE DREAMS WITHOUT DARKNESS?
I AM THEIR CANVAS!
NOW I KNOW WHAT YOU BOTH FEAR.
ME.
WE HAVE SOME FINAL BUSINESS, MIKABOSHI.
WE THREE COULD HAVE RULED ALL THINGS LIKE THE BROTHERS ZEUS, PLUTO AND POSEIDON. INSTEAD YOU QUIBBLE ABOUT WHO BEATS WHO.
WE COULD HAVE MADE SUCH HORRORS.
LET ME SHOW YOU.
KK!

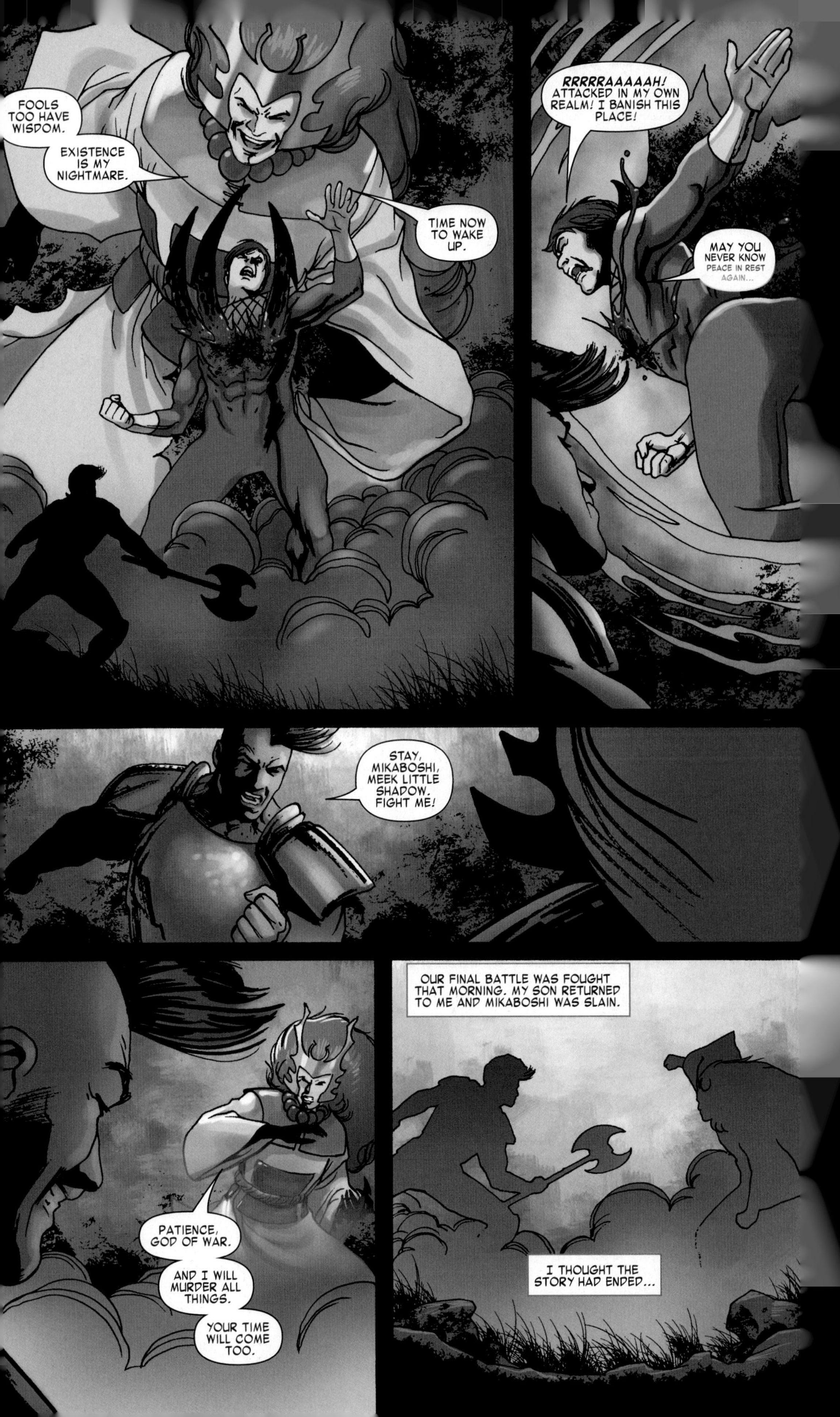

FOOLS TOO HAVE WISDOM.
EXISTENCE IS MY NIGHTMARE.
TIME NOW TO WAKE UP.
RRRRRAAAAAH! ATTACKED IN MY OWN REALM! I BANISH THIS PLACE!
MAY YOU NEVER KNOW PEACE IN REST AGAIN...
STAY, MIKABOSHI, MEEK LITTLE SHADOW. FIGHT ME!
PATIENCE, GOD OF WAR.
AND I WILL MURDER ALL THINGS.
YOUR TIME WILL COME TOO.
OUR FINAL BATTLE WAS FOUGHT THAT MORNING. MY SON RETURNED TO ME AND MIKABOSHI WAS SLAIN.
I THOUGHT THE STORY HAD ENDED...

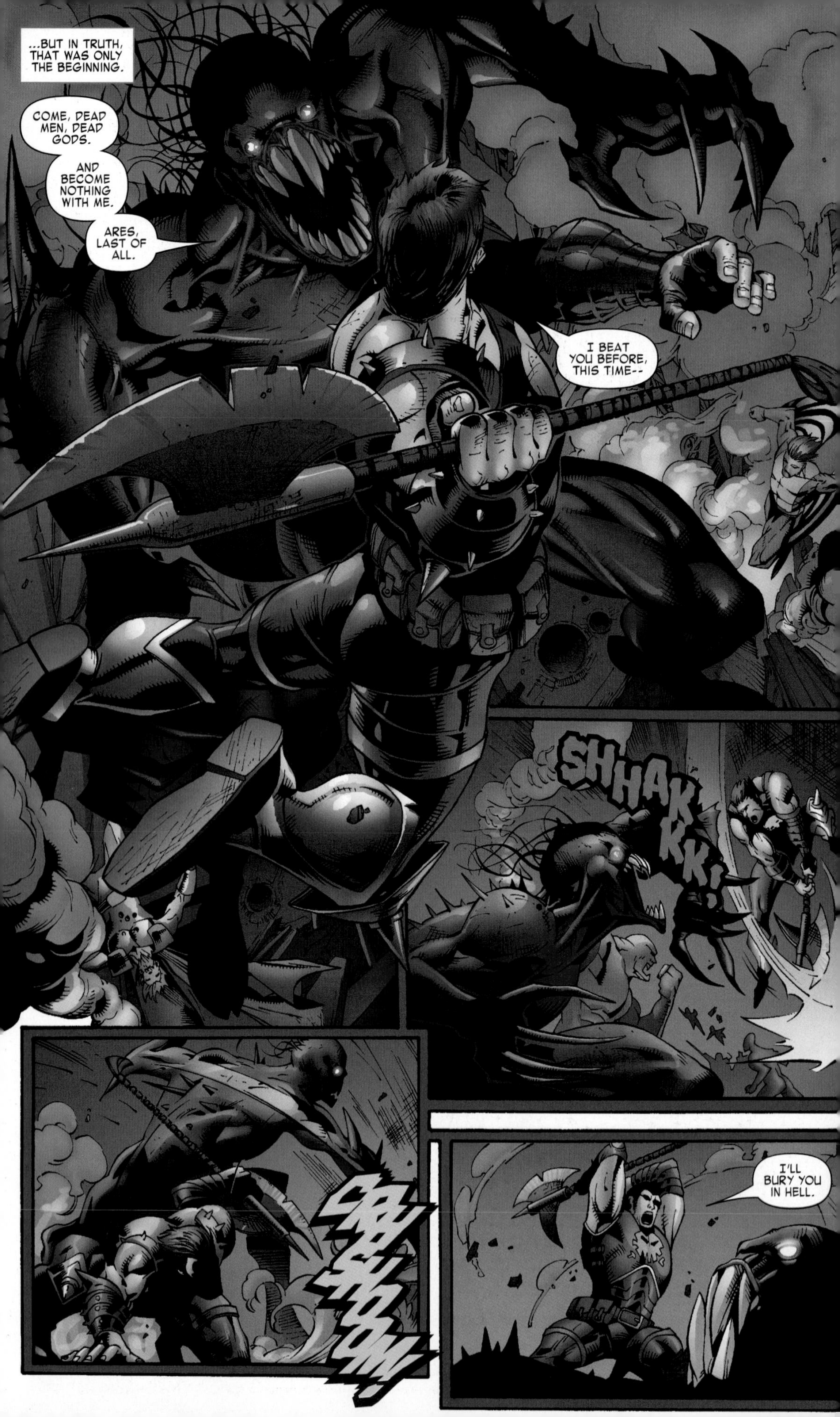
...BUT IN TRUTH, THAT WAS ONLY THE BEGINNING.
COME, DEAD MEN, DEAD GODS.
AND BECOME NOTHING WITH ME.
ARES, LAST OF ALL.
I BEAT YOU BEFORE, THIS TIME--
SHHAKKKK!
CRASHOOM!
I'LL BURY YOU IN HELL.

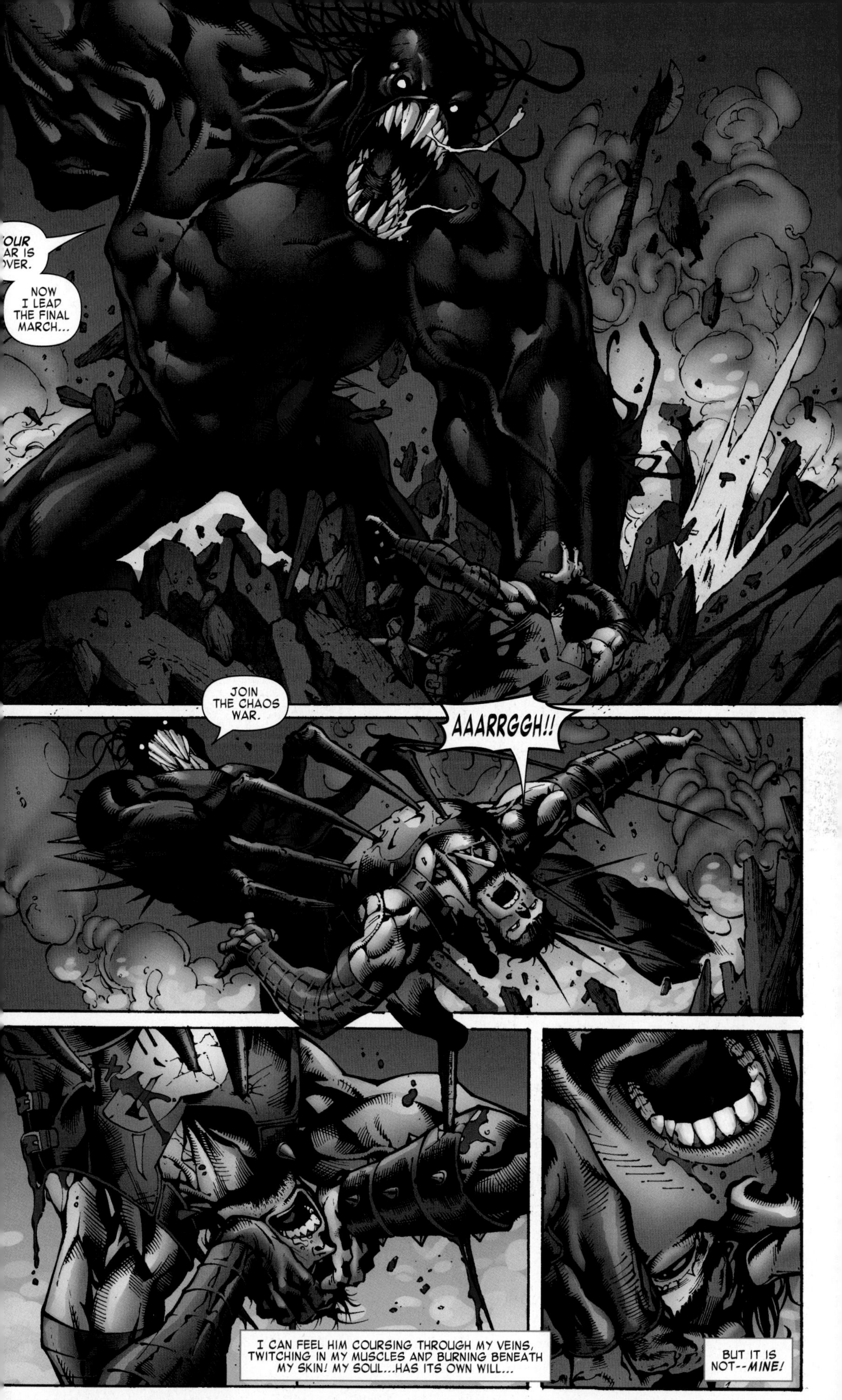

OUR AR IS OVER.
NOW I LEAD THE FINAL MARCH...
JOIN THE CHAOS WAR.
AAARRGGH!!
I CAN FEEL HIM COURSING THROUGH MY VEINS, TWITCHING IN MY MUSCLES AND BURNING BENEATH MY SKIN! MY SOUL...HAS ITS OWN WILL...
BUT IT IS NOT--*MINE!*

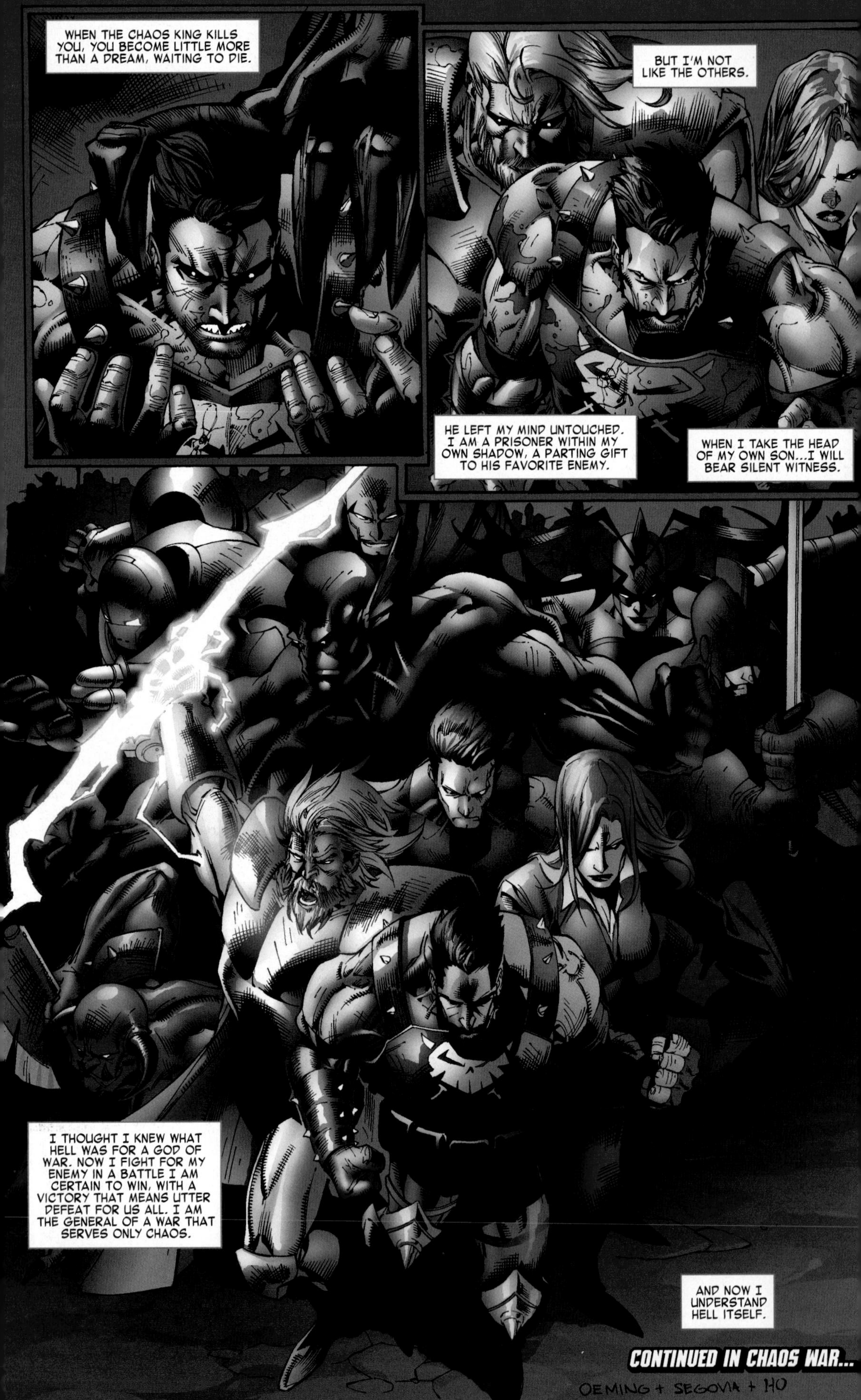
WHEN THE CHAOS KING KILLS YOU, YOU BECOME LITTLE MORE THAN A DREAM, WAITING TO DIE.
BUT I'M NOT LIKE THE OTHERS.
HE LEFT MY MIND UNTOUCHED. I AM A PRISONER WITHIN MY OWN SHADOW, A PARTING GIFT TO HIS FAVORITE ENEMY.
WHEN I TAKE THE HEAD OF MY OWN SON...I WILL BEAR SILENT WITNESS.
I THOUGHT I KNEW WHAT HELL WAS FOR A GOD OF WAR. NOW I FIGHT FOR MY ENEMY IN A BATTLE I AM CERTAIN TO WIN, WITH A VICTORY THAT MEANS UTTER DEFEAT FOR US ALL. I AM THE GENERAL OF A WAR THAT SERVES ONLY CHAOS.
AND NOW I UNDERSTAND HELL ITSELF.
CONTINUED IN CHAOS WAR...
OEMING + SEGOVIA + HO

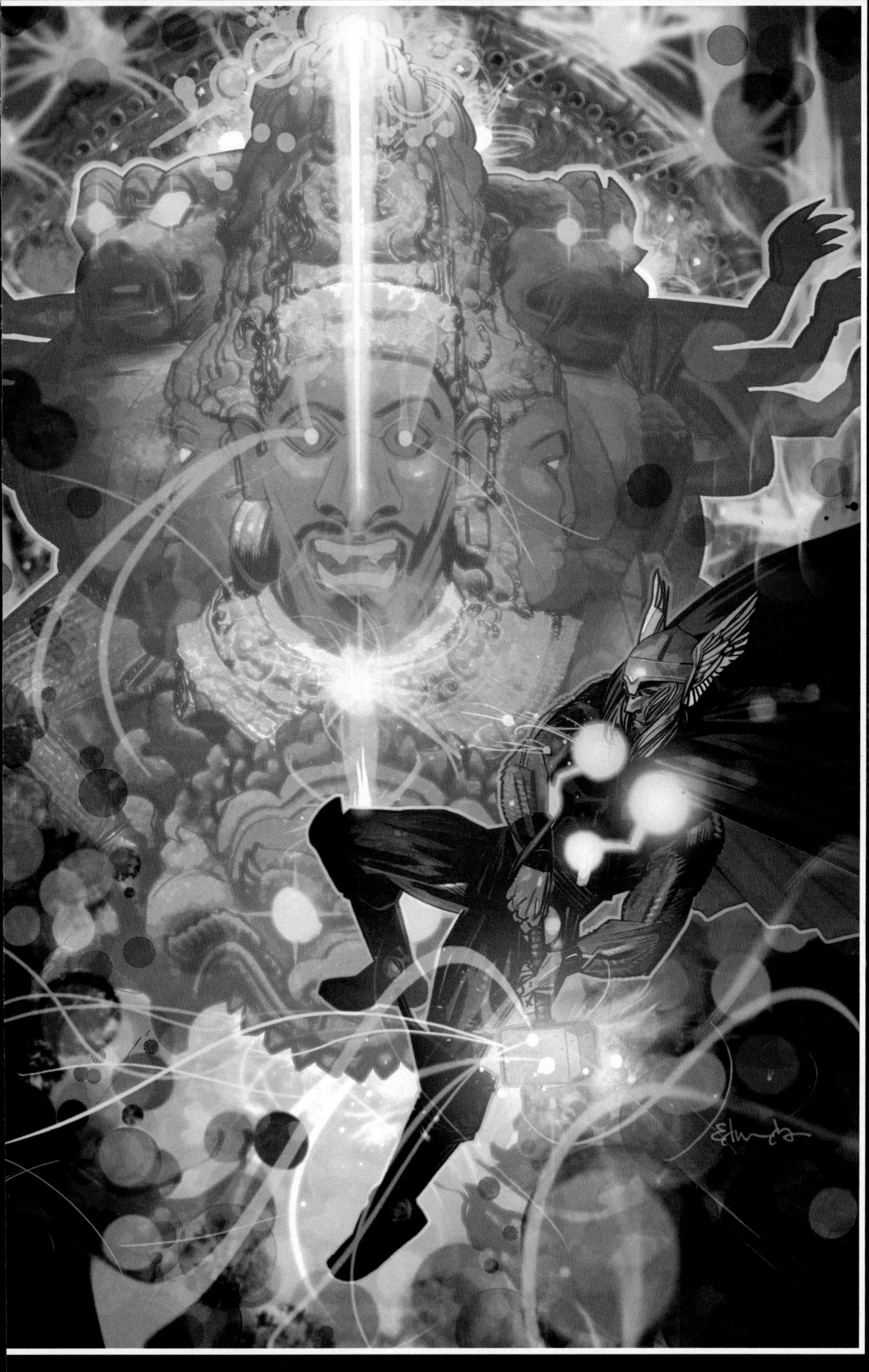

CHAOS WAR: THOR #1

IN THE MARVEL UNIVERSE, GODS WALK THE EARTH.

SOME SIDE WITH HEROES.
OTHERS SPREAD DREAD AND DESPAIR.

ONE GOD CARES FOR NEITHER.
HE IS THE **CHAOS KING.**

AND HE WILL STOP AT NOTHING TO END EVERYTHING WITH HIS

CHAOS WAR

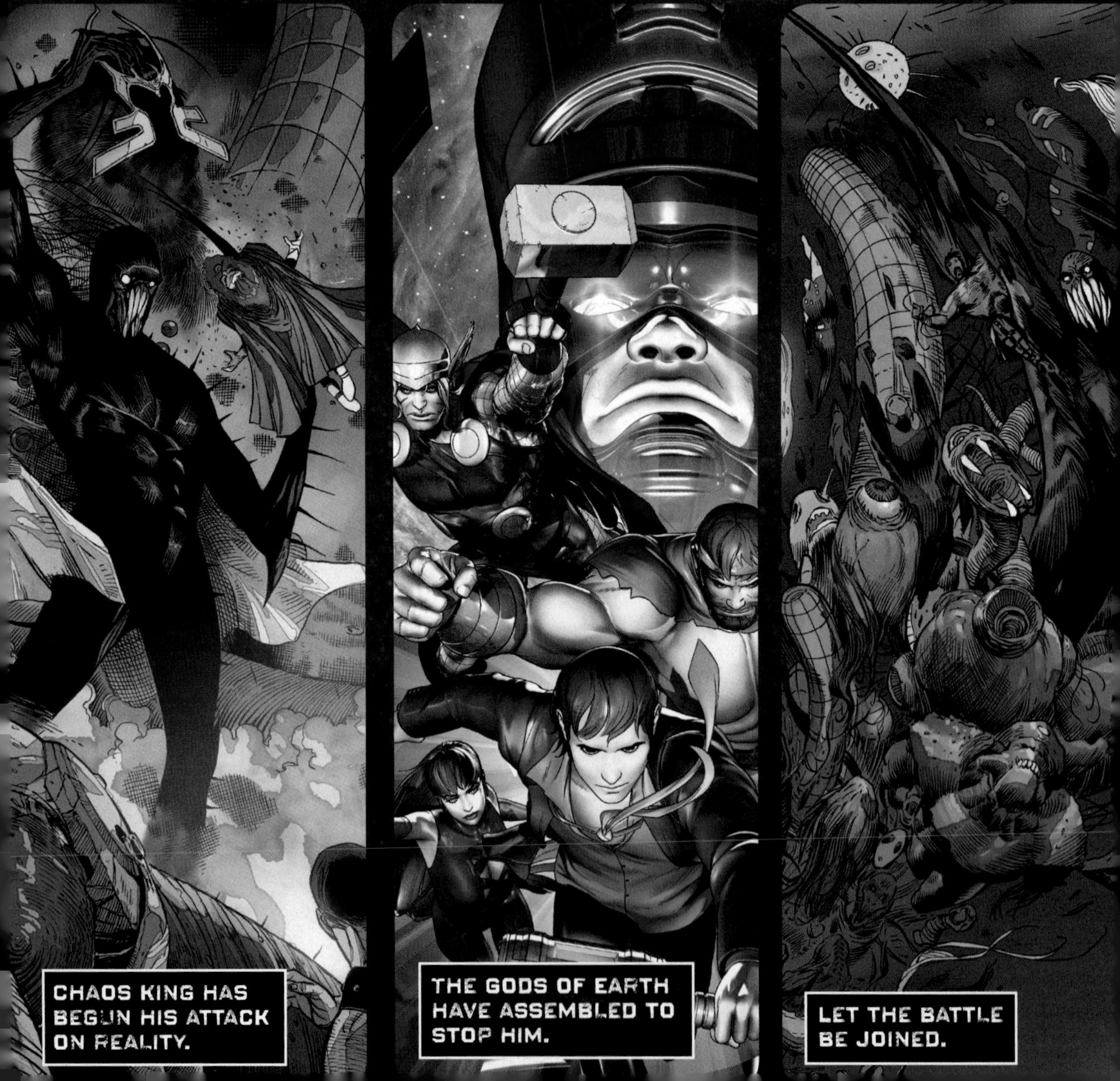
CHAOS KING HAS BEGUN HIS ATTACK ON REALITY.
THE GODS OF EARTH HAVE ASSEMBLED TO STOP HIM.
LET THE BATTLE BE JOINED.

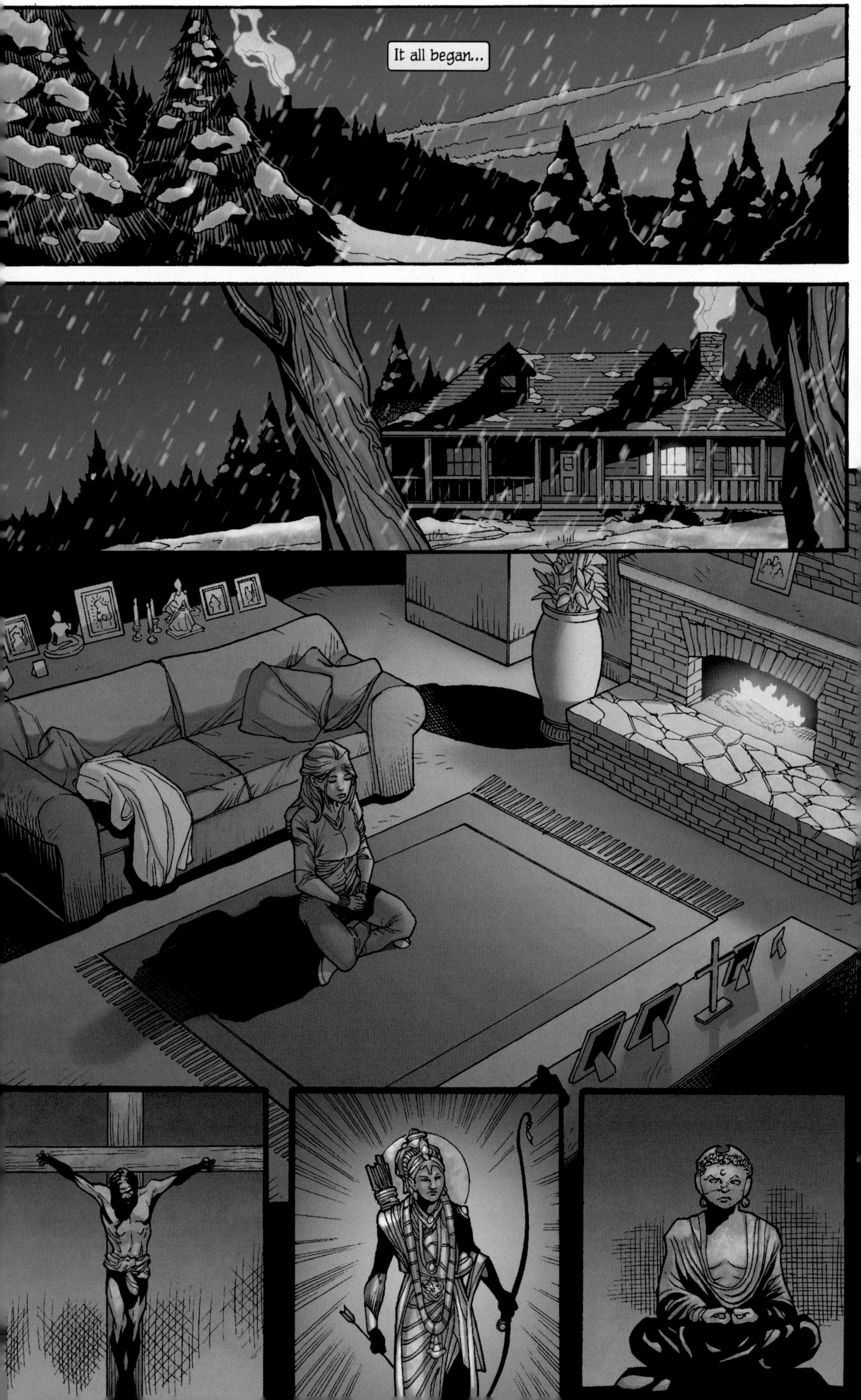
It all began...

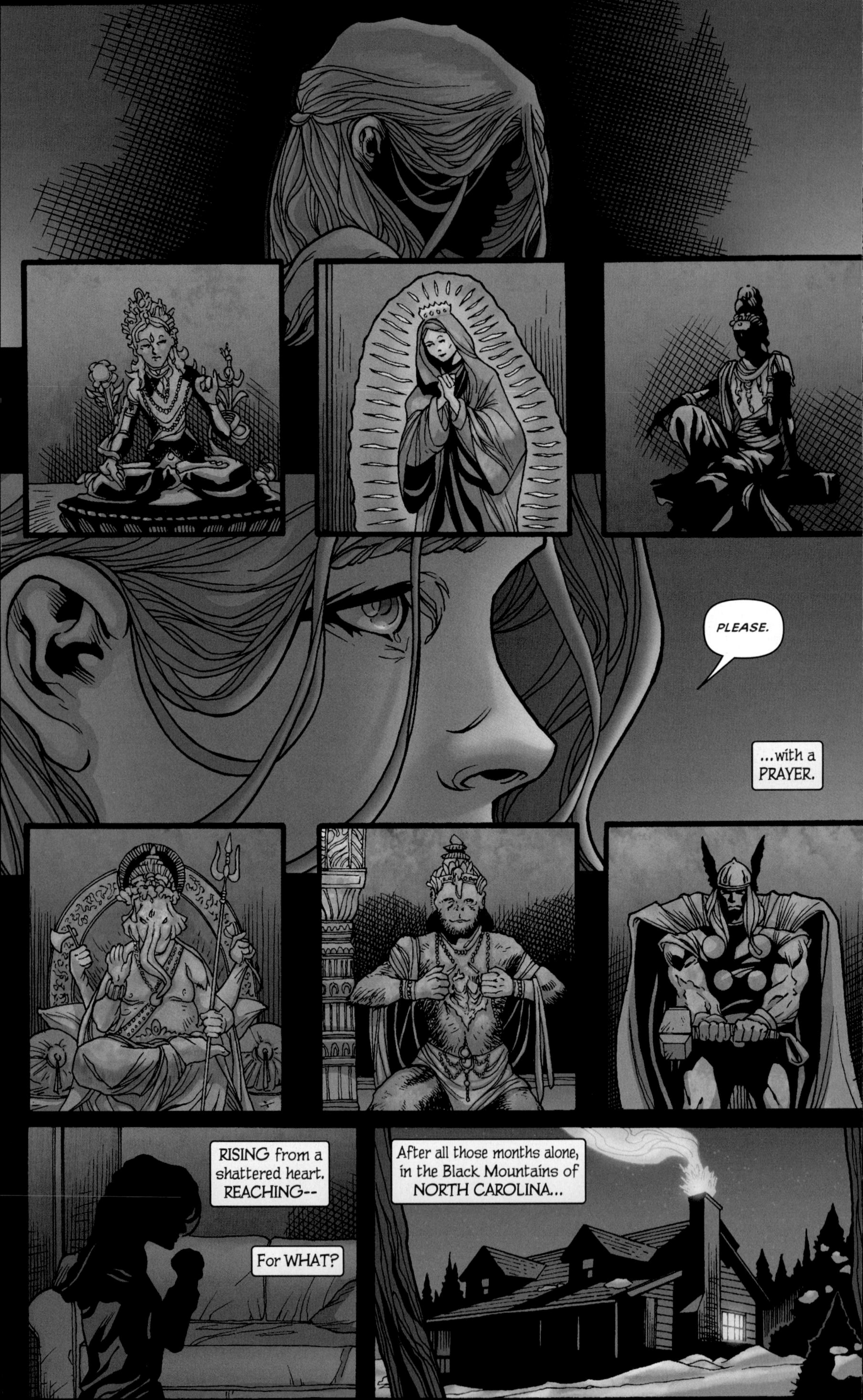
PLEASE.
...with a PRAYER.
RISING from a shattered heart. REACHING--
For WHAT?
After all those months alone, in the Black Mountains of NORTH CAROLINA...

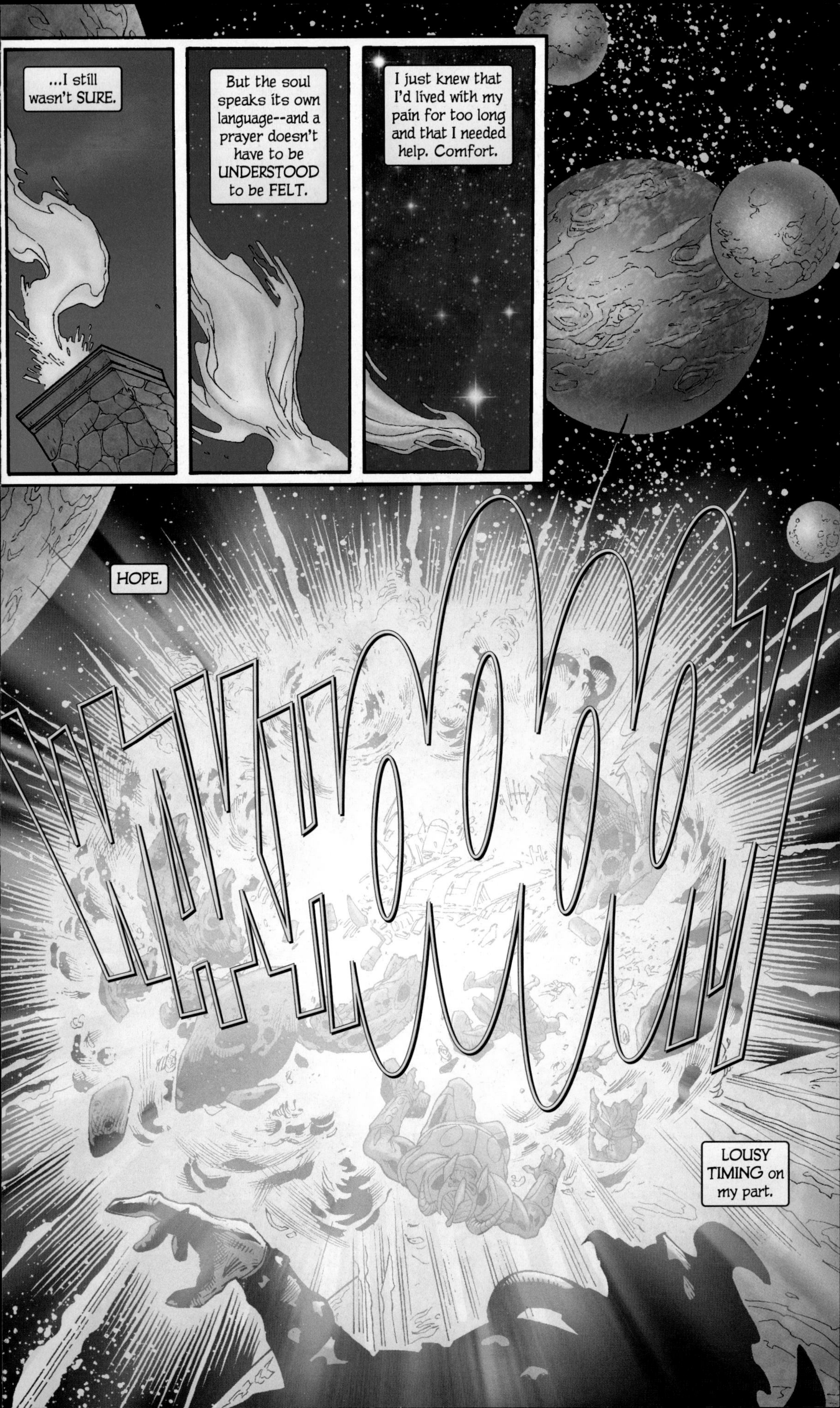
...I still wasn't SURE.
But the soul speaks its own language--and a prayer doesn't have to be UNDERSTOOD to be FELT.
I just knew that I'd lived with my pain for too long and that I needed help. Comfort.
HOPE.
WHKOOOOM
LOUSY TIMING on my part.

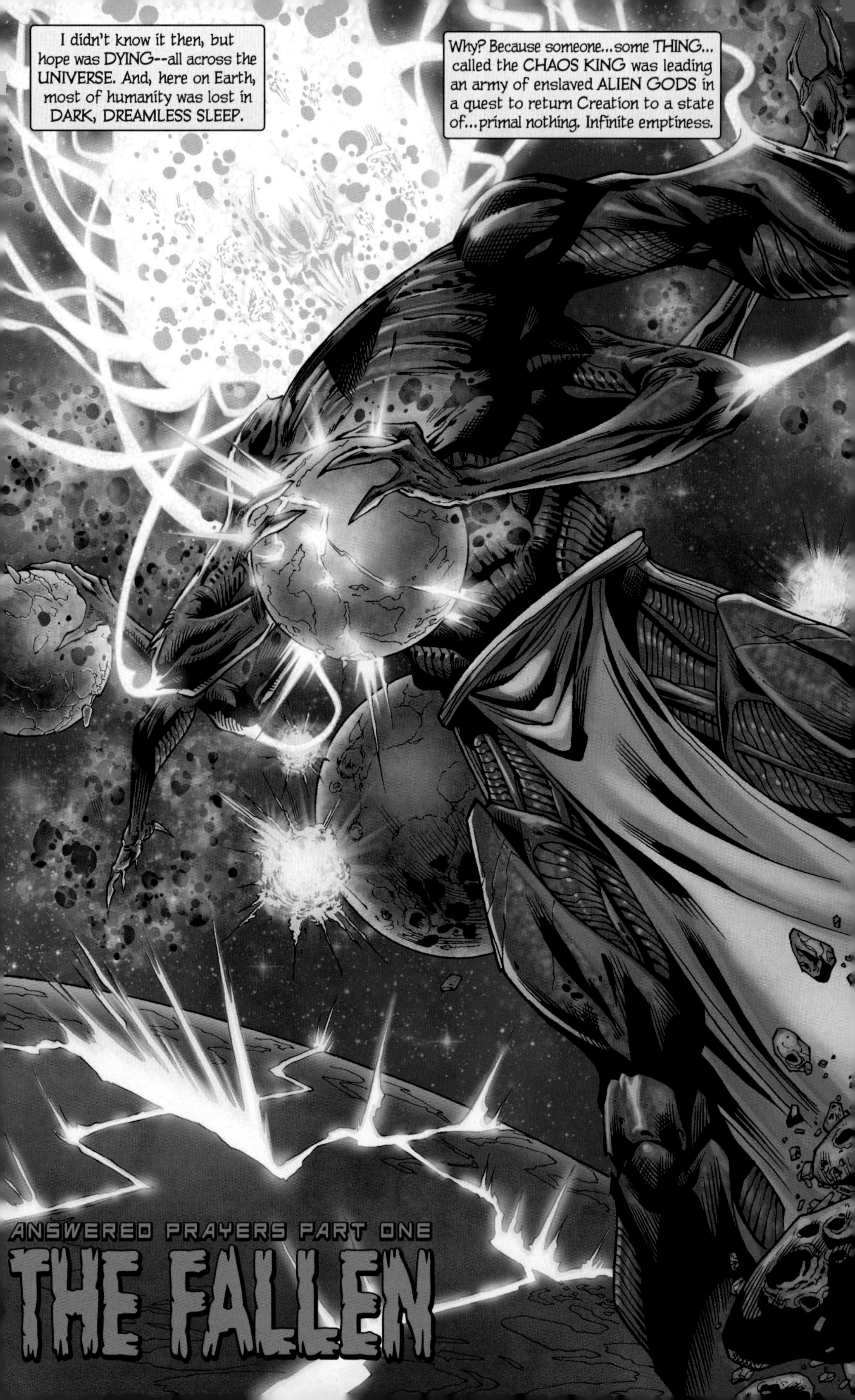
I didn't know it then, but hope was DYING--all across the UNIVERSE. And, here on Earth, most of humanity was lost in DARK, DREAMLESS SLEEP.
Why? Because someone...some THING... called the CHAOS KING was leading an army of enslaved ALIEN GODS in a quest to return Creation to a state of...primal nothing. Infinite emptiness.
ANSWERED PRAYERS PART ONE
THE FALLEN

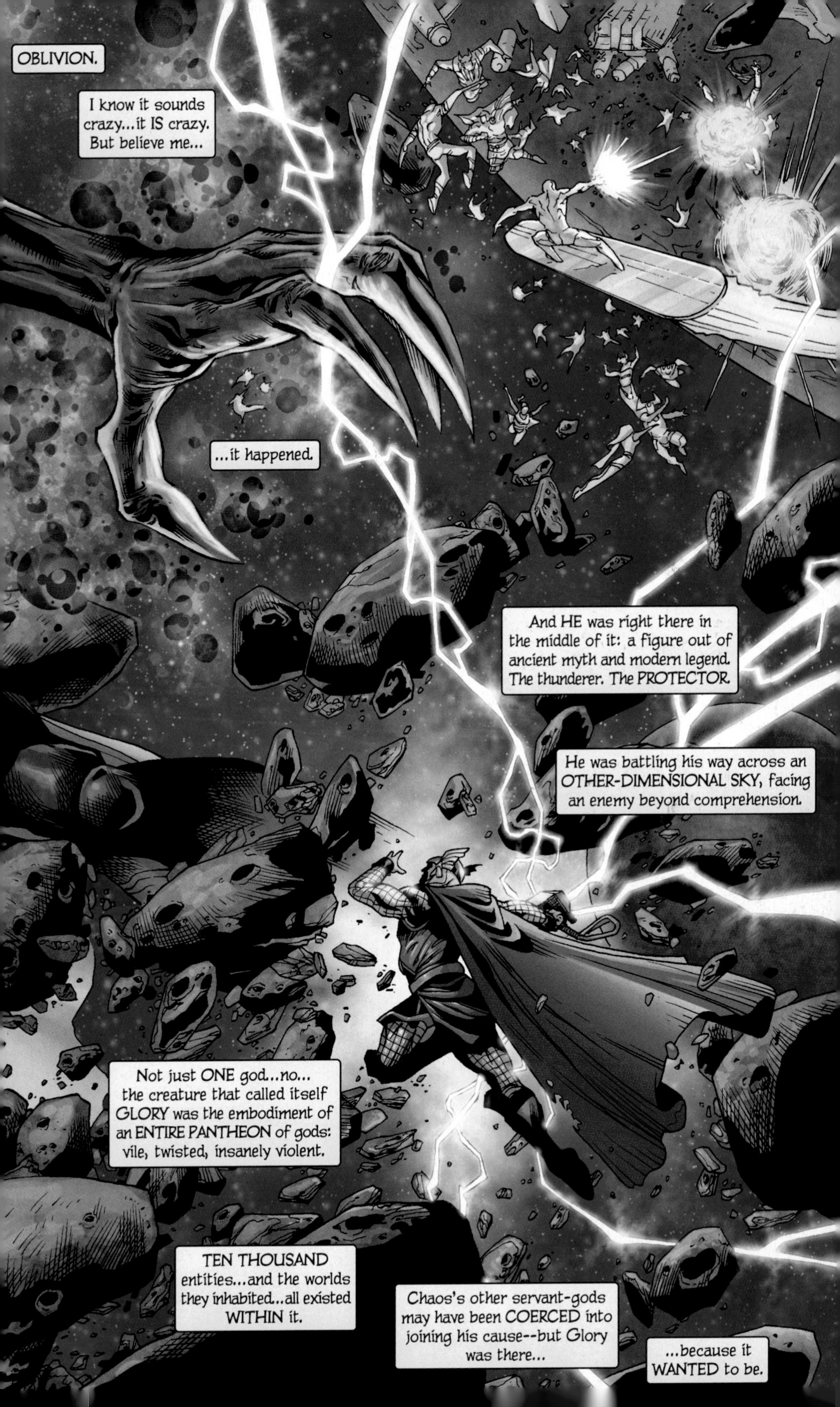

OBLIVION.
I know it sounds crazy...it IS crazy. But believe me...
...it happened.
And HE was right there in the middle of it: a figure out of ancient myth and modern legend. The thunderer. The PROTECTOR.
He was battling his way across an OTHER-DIMENSIONAL SKY, facing an enemy beyond comprehension.
Not just ONE god...no... the creature that called itself GLORY was the embodiment of an ENTIRE PANTHEON of gods: vile, twisted, insanely violent.
TEN THOUSAND entities...and the worlds they inhabited...all existed WITHIN it.
Chaos's other servant-gods may have been COERCED into joining his cause--but Glory was there...
...because it WANTED to be.

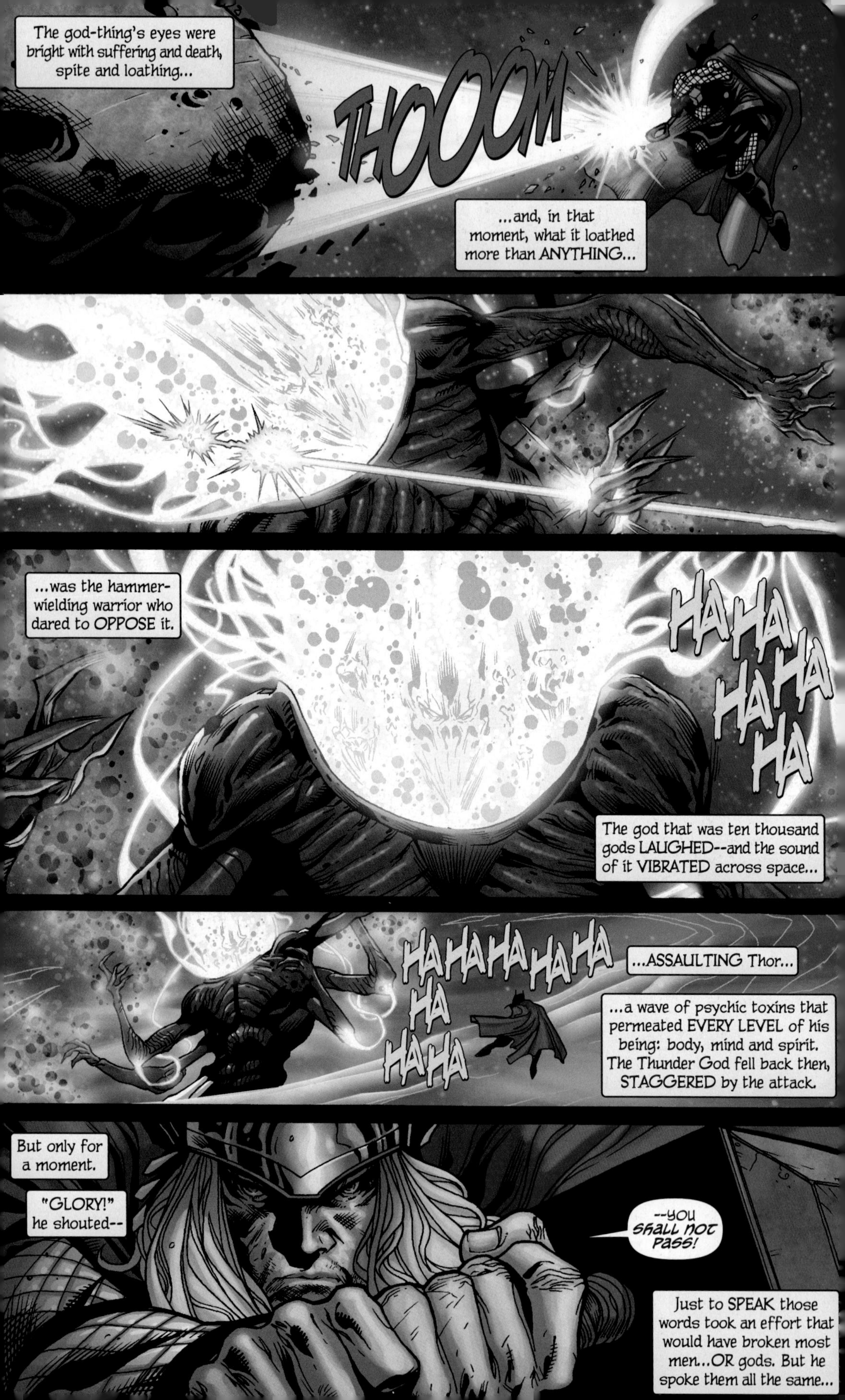

The god-thing's eyes were bright with suffering and death, spite and loathing...
THOOOM
...and, in that moment, what it loathed more than ANYTHING...
...was the hammer-wielding warrior who dared to OPPOSE it.
HA HA HA HA HA
The god that was ten thousand gods LAUGHED--and the sound of it VIBRATED across space...
HA HA HA HA HA HA HA HA HA
...ASSAULTING Thor...
...a wave of psychic toxins that permeated EVERY LEVEL of his being: body, mind and spirit. The Thunder God fell back then, STAGGERED by the attack.
But only for a moment.
"GLORY!" he shouted--
--YOU SHALL NOT PASS!
Just to SPEAK those words took an effort that would have broken most men...OR gods. But he spoke them all the same...

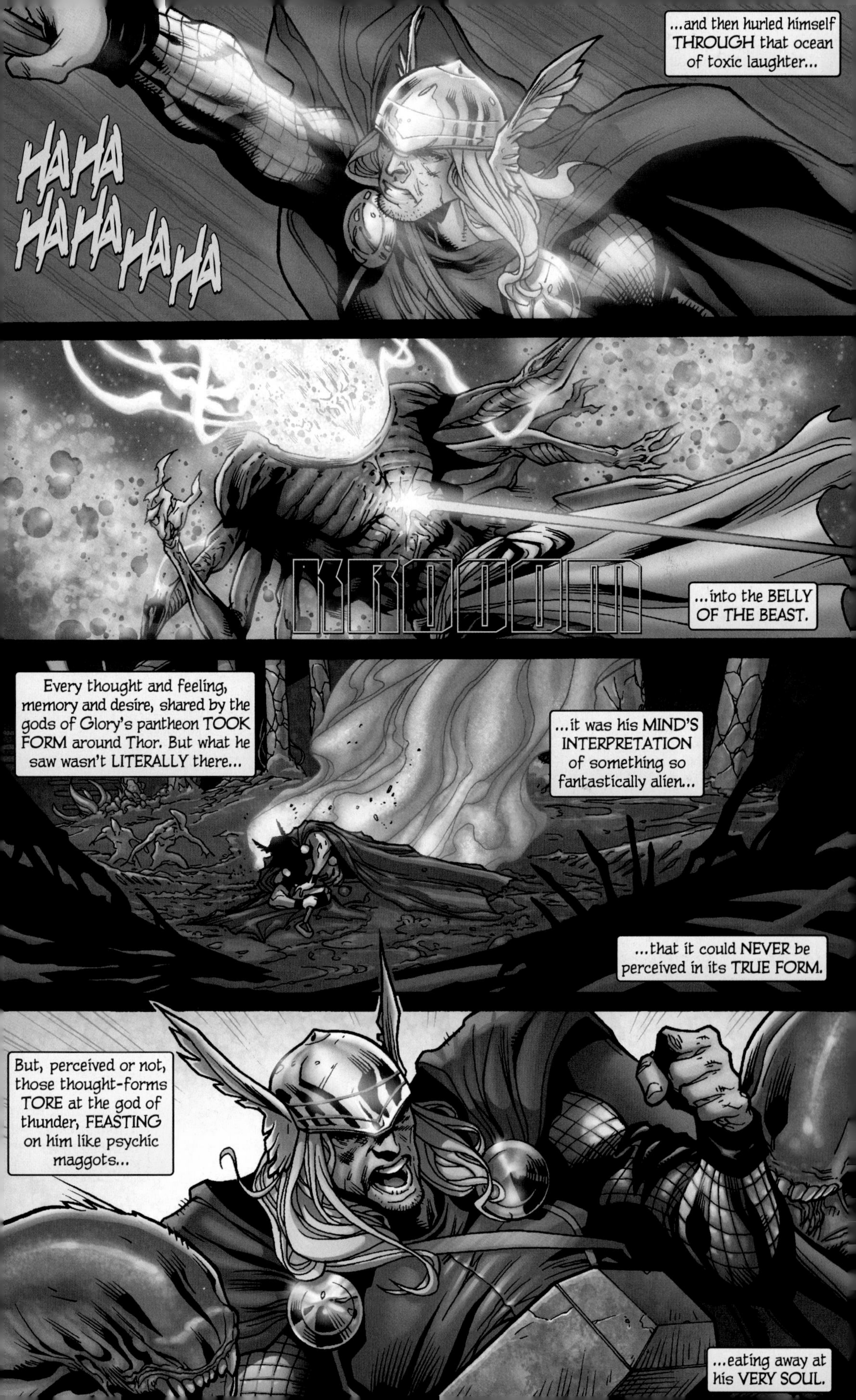
...and then hurled himself THROUGH that ocean of toxic laughter...
HAHA HAHAHAHA HAHA
KROOOM
...into the BELLY OF THE BEAST.
Every thought and feeling, memory and desire, shared by the gods of Glory's pantheon TOOK FORM around Thor. But what he saw wasn't LITERALLY there...
...it was his MIND'S INTERPRETATION of something so fantastically alien...
...that it could NEVER be perceived in its TRUE FORM.
But, perceived or not, those thought-forms TORE at the god of thunder, FEASTING on him like psychic maggots...
...eating away at his VERY SOUL.

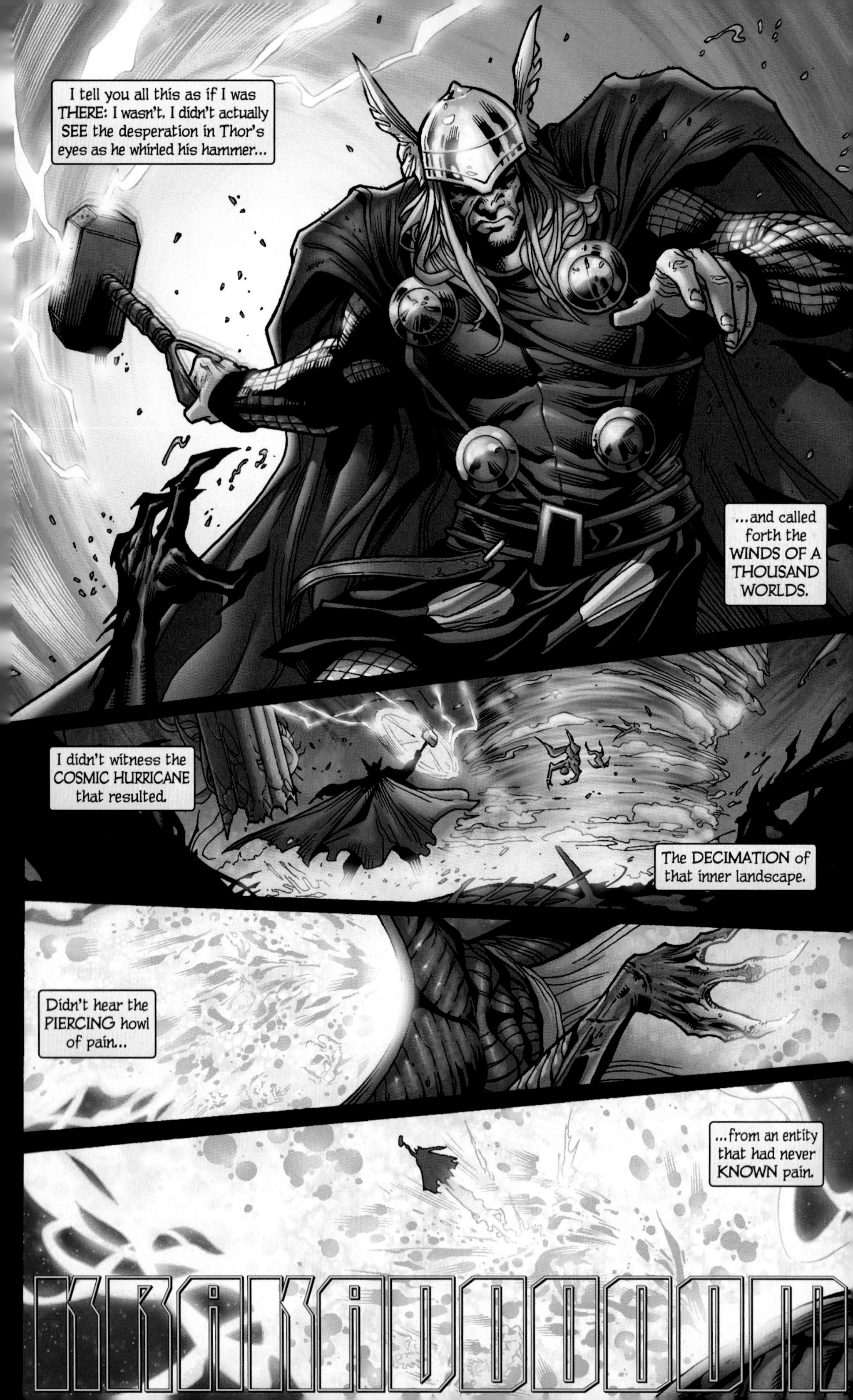
I tell you all this as if I was THERE: I wasn't. I didn't actually SEE the desperation in Thor's eyes as he whirled his hammer...
...and called forth the WINDS OF A THOUSAND WORLDS.
I didn't witness the COSMIC HURRICANE that resulted.
The DECIMATION of that inner landscape.
Didn't hear the PIERCING howl of pain...
...from an entity that had never KNOWN pain.
KRAKADOOOOOM

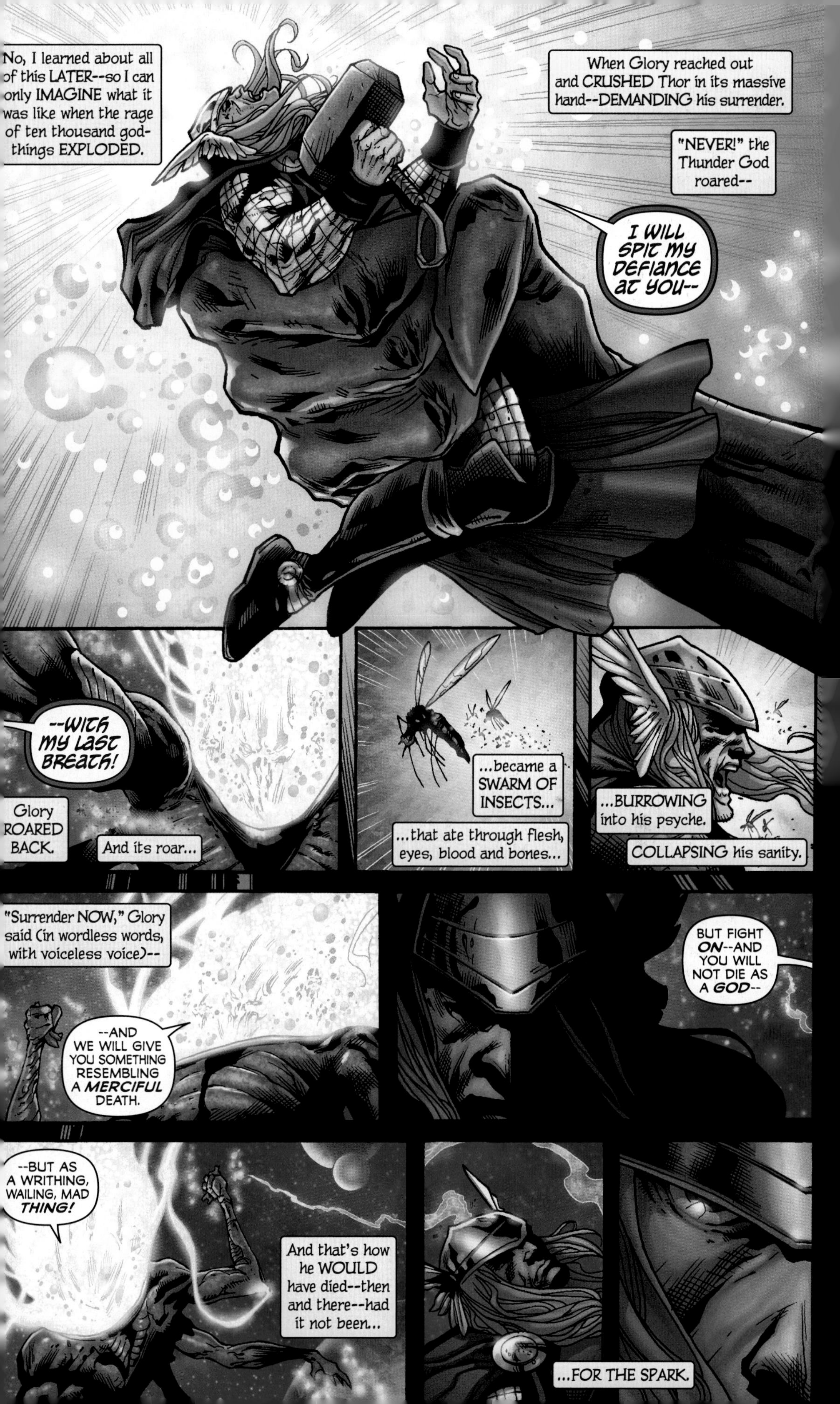
No, I learned about all of this LATER--so I can only IMAGINE what it was like when the rage of ten thousand god-things EXPLODED.
When Glory reached out and CRUSHED Thor in its massive hand--DEMANDING his surrender.
"NEVER!" the Thunder God roared--
I WILL SPIT MY DEFIANCE AT YOU--
--WITH MY LAST BREATH!
Glory ROARED BACK.
And its roar...
...became a SWARM OF INSECTS...
...that ate through flesh, eyes, blood and bones...
...BURROWING into his psyche.
COLLAPSING his sanity.
"Surrender NOW," Glory said (in wordless words, with voiceless voice)--
--AND WE WILL GIVE YOU SOMETHING RESEMBLING A MERCIFUL DEATH.
BUT FIGHT ON--AND YOU WILL NOT DIE AS A GOD--
--BUT AS A WRITHING, WAILING, MAD THING!
And that's how he WOULD have died--then and there--had it not been...
...FOR THE SPARK.

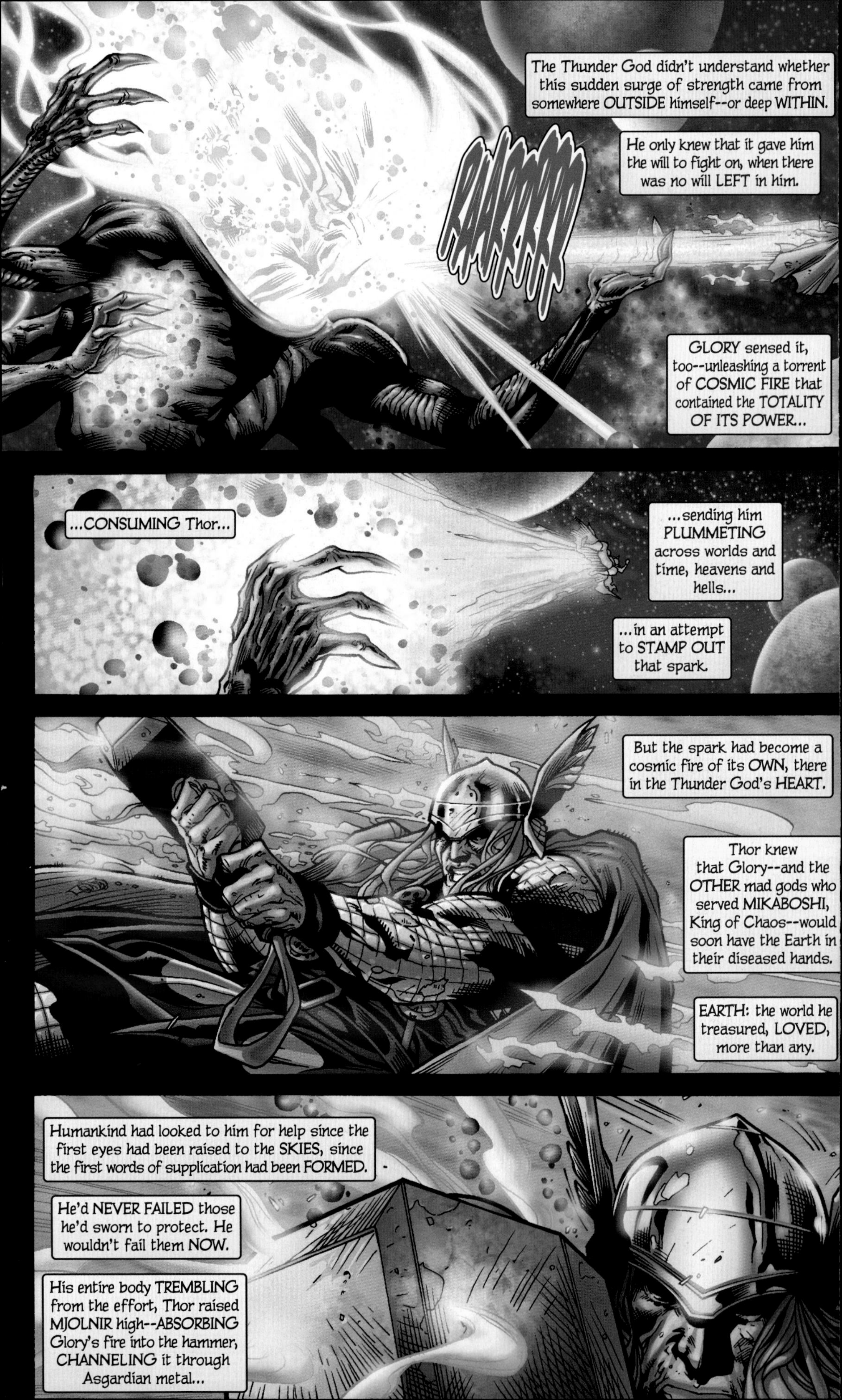

The Thunder God didn't understand whether this sudden surge of strength came from somewhere OUTSIDE himself--or deep WITHIN.
He only knew that it gave him the will to fight on, when there was no will LEFT in him.
RAAKKKKK
GLORY sensed it, too--unleashing a torrent of COSMIC FIRE that contained the TOTALITY OF ITS POWER...
...CONSUMING Thor...
...sending him PLUMMETING across worlds and time, heavens and hells...
...in an attempt to STAMP OUT that spark.
But the spark had become a cosmic fire of its OWN, there in the Thunder God's HEART.
Thor knew that Glory--and the OTHER mad gods who served MIKABOSHI, King of Chaos--would soon have the Earth in their diseased hands.
EARTH: the world he treasured, LOVED, more than any.
Humankind had looked to him for help since the first eyes had been raised to the SKIES, since the first words of supplication had been FORMED.
He'd NEVER FAILED those he'd sworn to protect. He wouldn't fail them NOW.
His entire body TREMBLING from the effort, Thor raised MJOLNIR high--ABSORBING Glory's fire into the hammer, CHANNELING it through Asgardian metal...

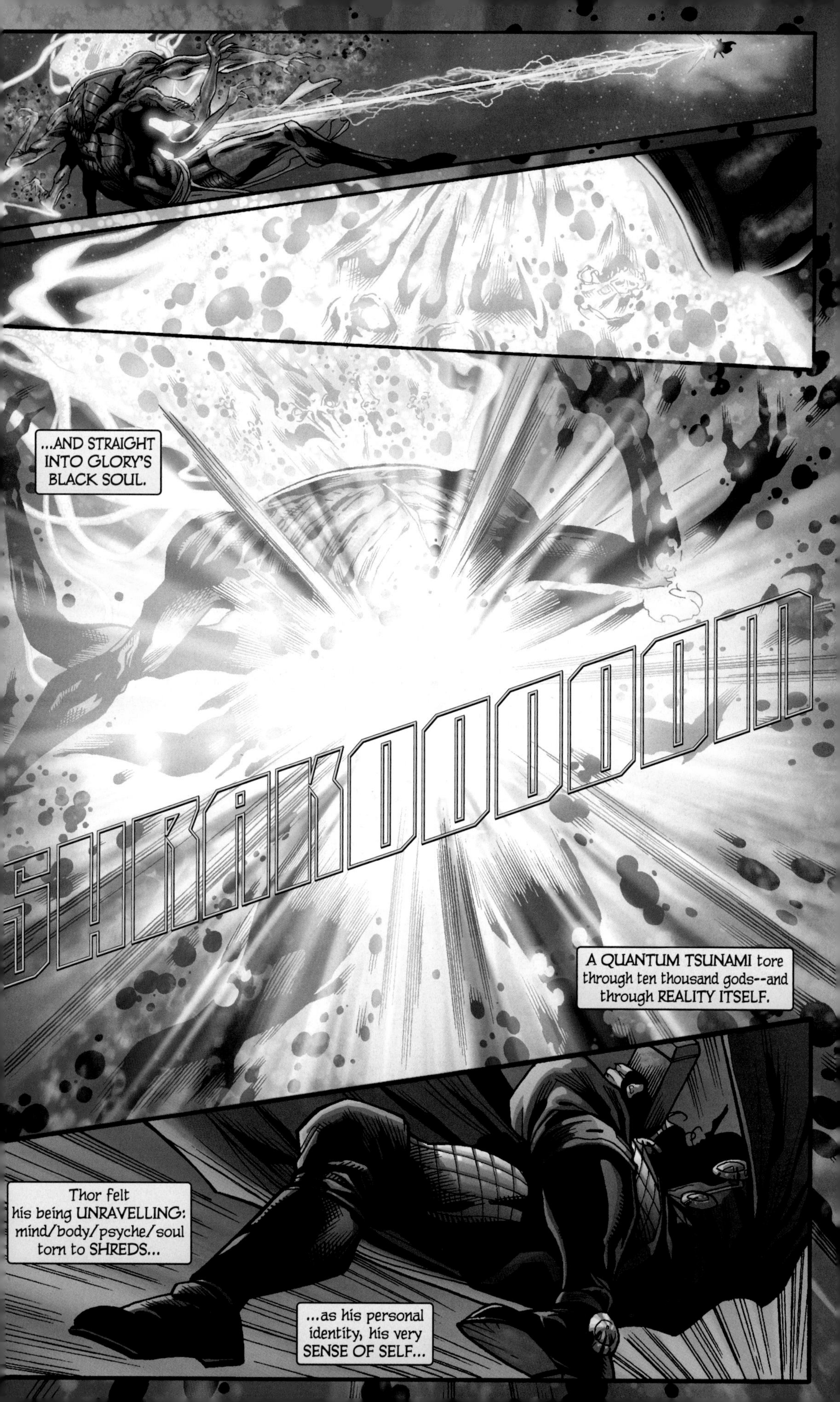
...AND STRAIGHT INTO GLORY'S BLACK SOUL.
SHRAKOOOOOOM
A QUANTUM TSUNAMI tore through ten thousand gods--and through REALITY ITSELF.
Thor felt his being UNRAVELLING: mind/body/psyche/soul torn to SHREDS...
...as his personal identity, his very SENSE OF SELF...

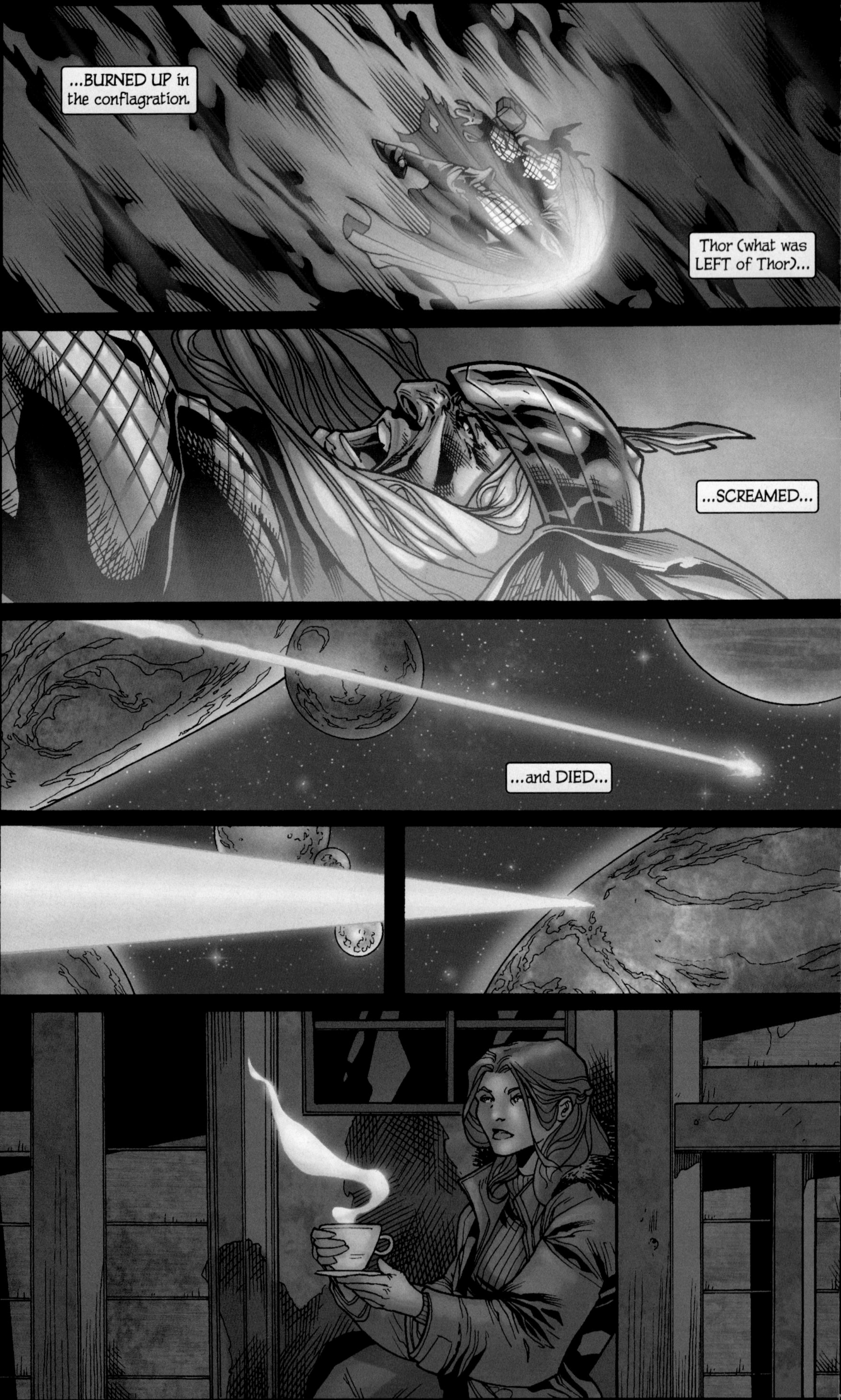
...BURNED UP in the conflagration.
Thor (what was LEFT of Thor)...
...SCREAMED...
...and DIED...

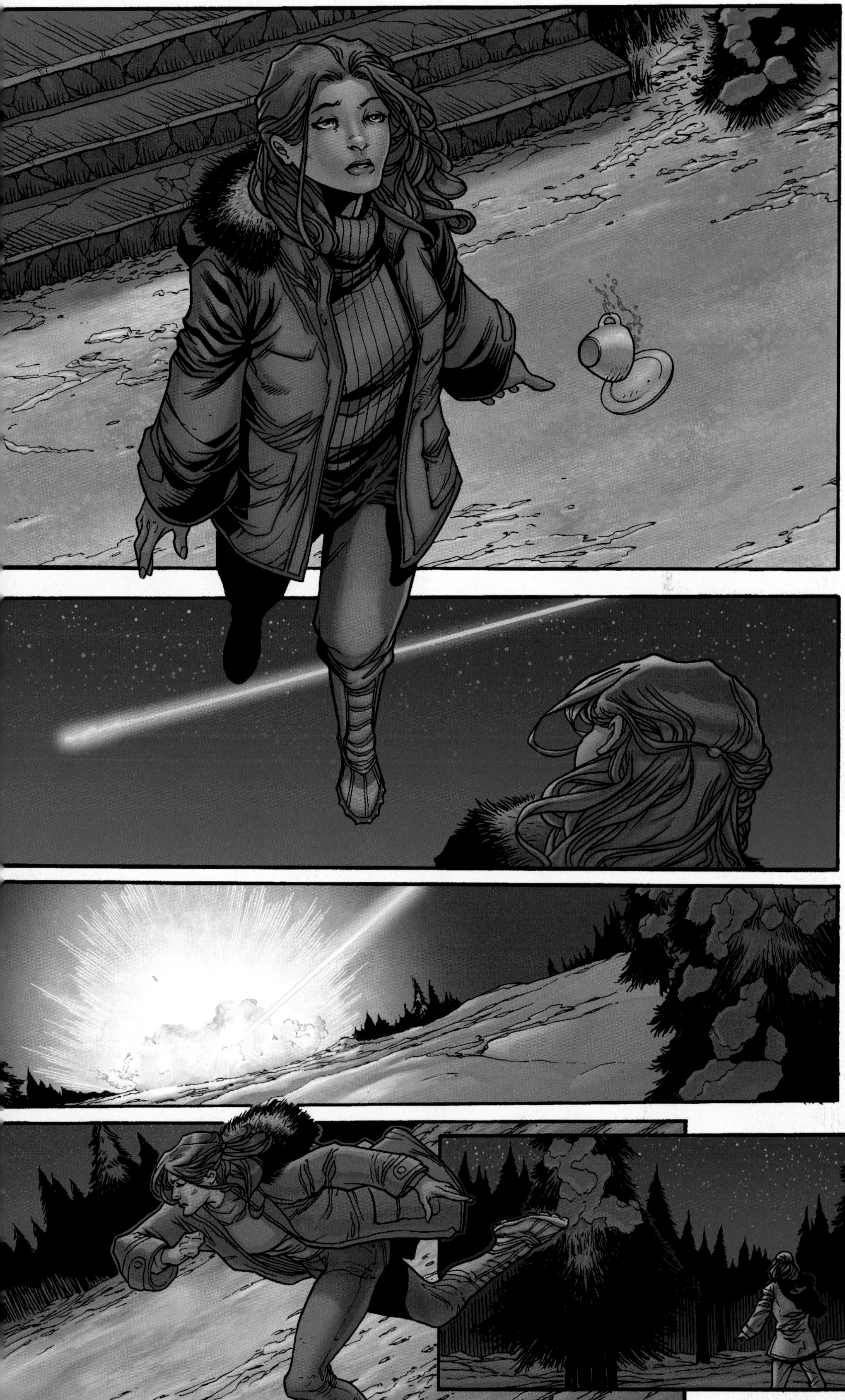

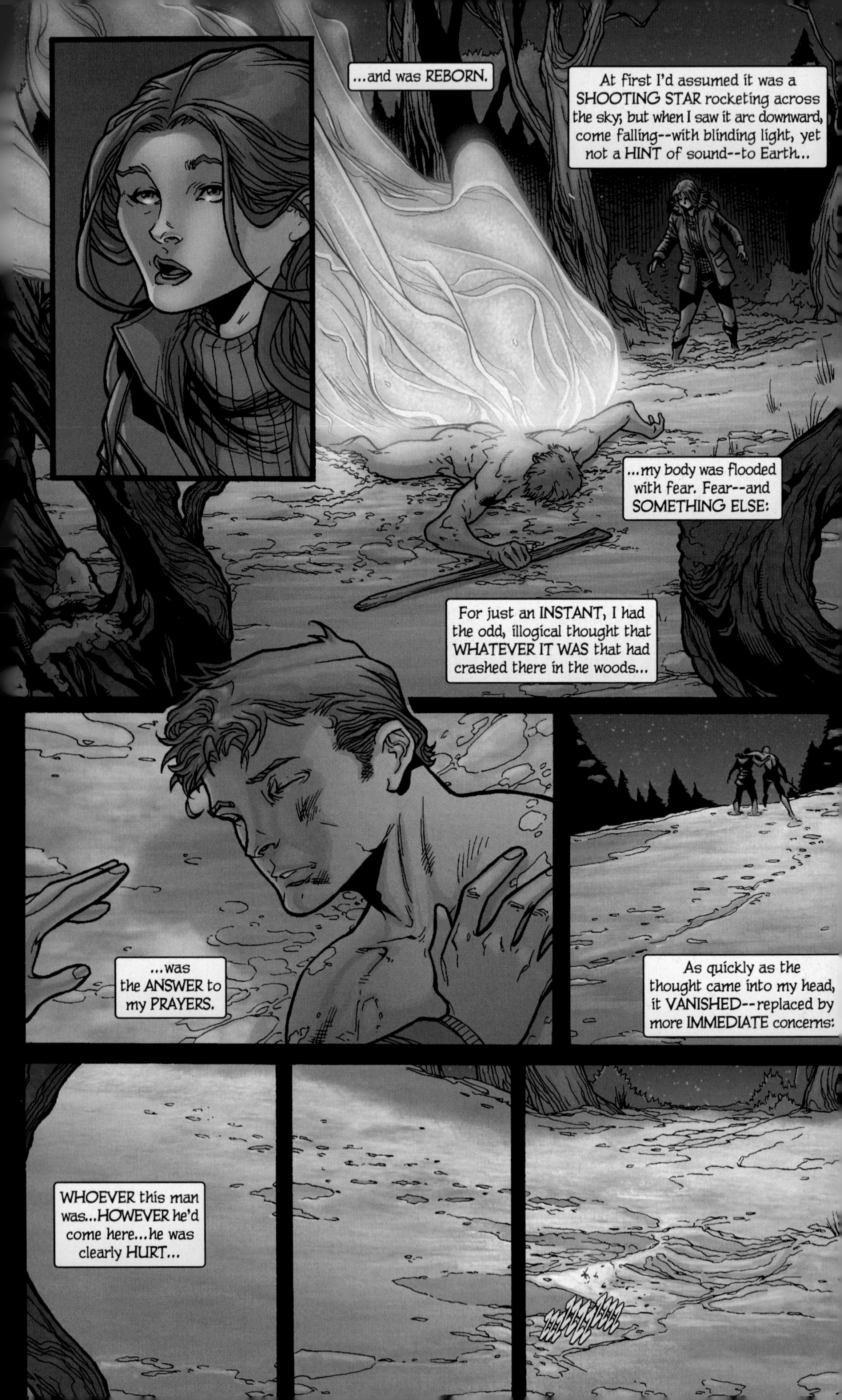

...and was REBORN.
At first I'd assumed it was a SHOOTING STAR rocketing across the sky; but when I saw it arc downward, come falling--with blinding light, yet not a HINT of sound--to Earth...
...my body was flooded with fear. Fear--and SOMETHING ELSE:
For just an INSTANT, I had the odd, illogical thought that WHATEVER IT WAS that had crashed there in the woods...
...was the ANSWER to my PRAYERS.
As quickly as the thought came into my head, it VANISHED--replaced by more IMMEDIATE concerns:
WHOEVER this man was...HOWEVER he'd come here...he was clearly HURT...

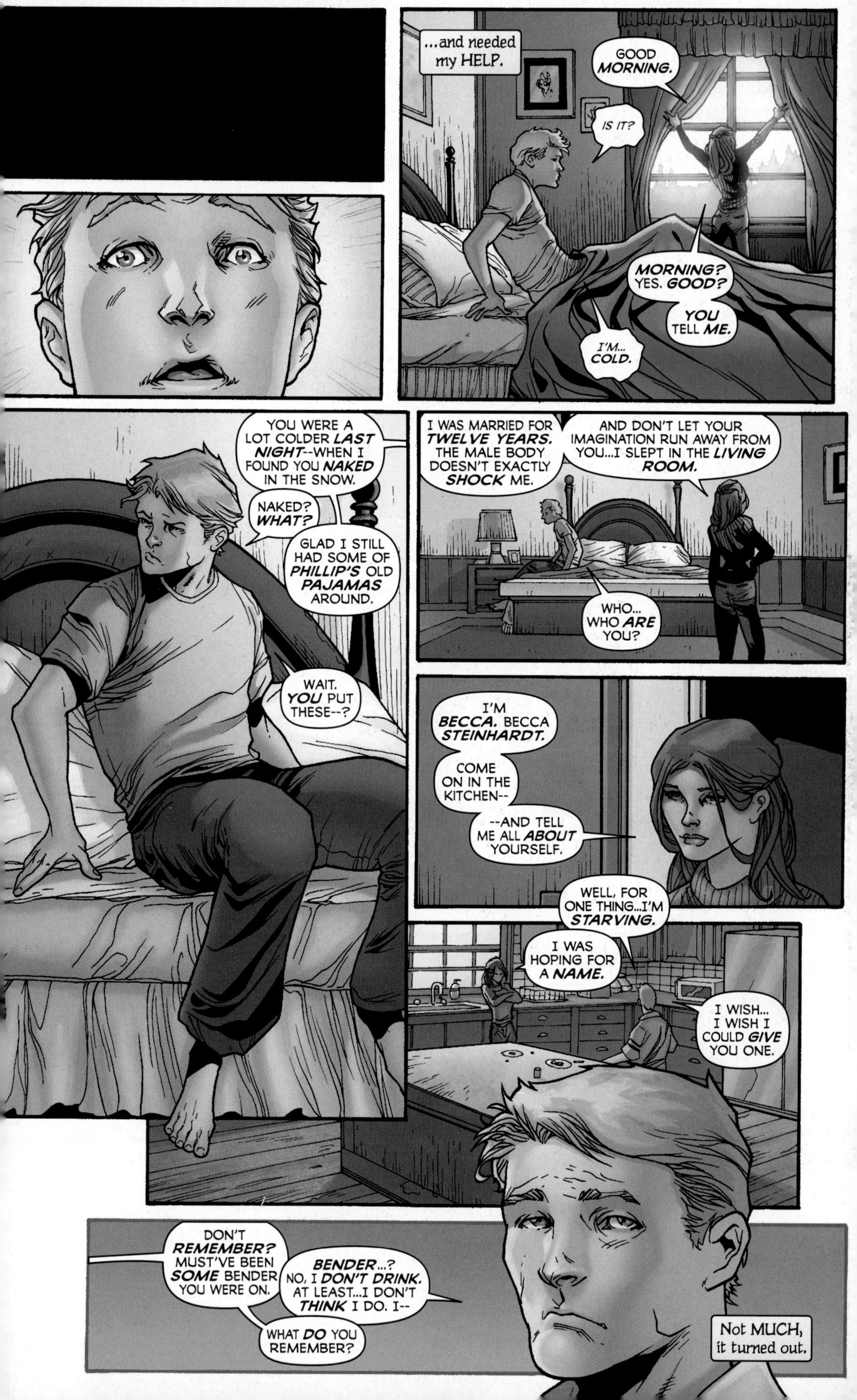

...and needed my HELP.
GOOD MORNING.
IS IT?
MORNING? YES. GOOD?
YOU TELL ME.
I'M... COLD.
YOU WERE A LOT COLDER LAST NIGHT--WHEN I FOUND YOU NAKED IN THE SNOW.
NAKED? WHAT?
GLAD I STILL HAD SOME OF PHILLIP'S OLD PAJAMAS AROUND.
WAIT. YOU PUT THESE--?
I WAS MARRIED FOR TWELVE YEARS. THE MALE BODY DOESN'T EXACTLY SHOCK ME.
AND DON'T LET YOUR IMAGINATION RUN AWAY FROM YOU...I SLEPT IN THE LIVING ROOM.
WHO... WHO ARE YOU?
I'M BECCA. BECCA STEINHARDT.
COME ON IN THE KITCHEN--
--AND TELL ME ALL ABOUT YOURSELF.
WELL, FOR ONE THING...I'M STARVING.
I WAS HOPING FOR A NAME.
I WISH... I WISH I COULD GIVE YOU ONE.
DON'T REMEMBER? MUST'VE BEEN SOME BENDER YOU WERE ON.
BENDER...? NO, I DON'T DRINK. AT LEAST...I DON'T THINK I DO. I--
WHAT DO YOU REMEMBER?
Not MUCH, it turned out.

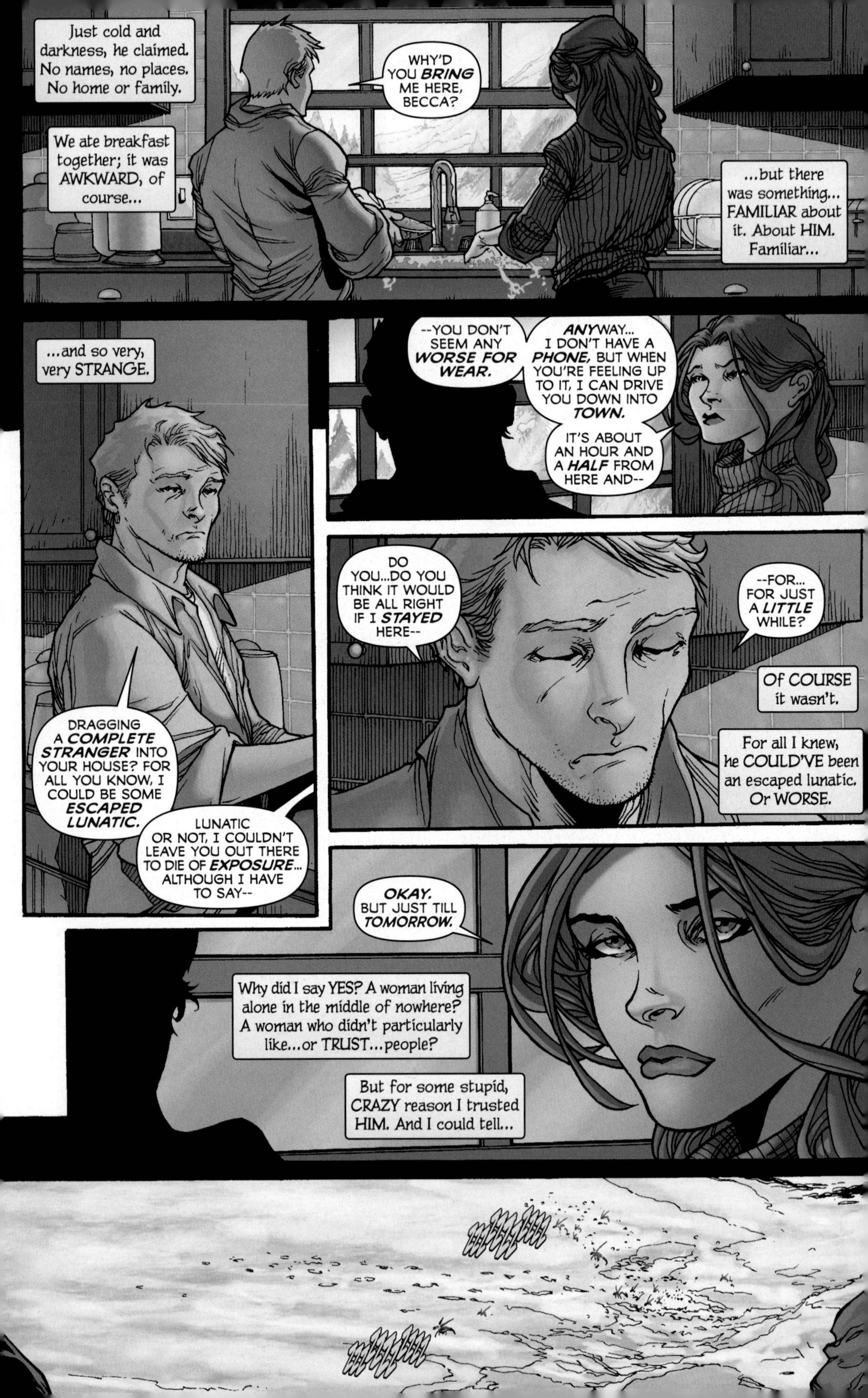
Just cold and darkness, he claimed. No names, no places. No home or family.
WHY'D YOU BRING ME HERE, BECCA?
We ate breakfast together; it was AWKWARD, of course...
...but there was something... FAMILIAR about it. About HIM. Familiar...
...and so very, very STRANGE.
DRAGGING A COMPLETE STRANGER INTO YOUR HOUSE? FOR ALL YOU KNOW, I COULD BE SOME ESCAPED LUNATIC.
LUNATIC OR NOT, I COULDN'T LEAVE YOU OUT THERE TO DIE OF EXPOSURE... ALTHOUGH I HAVE TO SAY--
--YOU DON'T SEEM ANY WORSE FOR WEAR.
ANYWAY... I DON'T HAVE A PHONE, BUT WHEN YOU'RE FEELING UP TO IT, I CAN DRIVE YOU DOWN INTO TOWN.
IT'S ABOUT AN HOUR AND A HALF FROM HERE AND--
DO YOU...DO YOU THINK IT WOULD BE ALL RIGHT IF I STAYED HERE--
--FOR... FOR JUST A LITTLE WHILE?
Of COURSE it wasn't.
For all I knew, he COULD'VE been an escaped lunatic. Or WORSE.
OKAY. BUT JUST TILL TOMORROW.
Why did I say YES? A woman living alone in the middle of nowhere? A woman who didn't particularly like...or TRUST...people?
But for some stupid, CRAZY reason I trusted HIM. And I could tell...

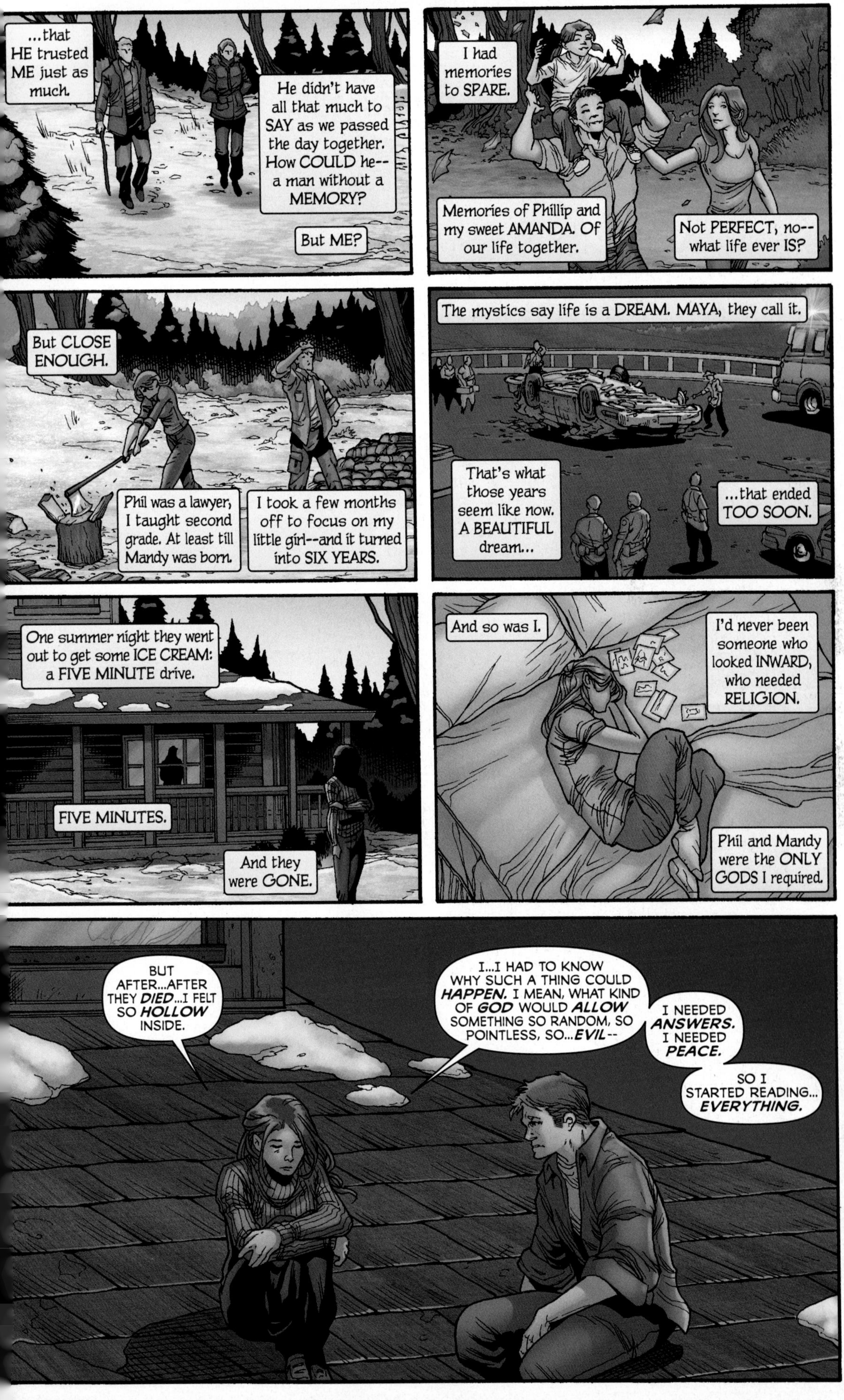

...that HE trusted ME just as much.
He didn't have all that much to SAY as we passed the day together. How COULD he--a man without a MEMORY?
But ME?
I had memories to SPARE.
Memories of Phillip and my sweet AMANDA. Of our life together.
Not PERFECT, no--what life ever IS?
But CLOSE ENOUGH.
Phil was a lawyer, I taught second grade. At least till Mandy was born.
I took a few months off to focus on my little girl--and it turned into SIX YEARS.
The mystics say life is a DREAM. MAYA, they call it.
That's what those years seem like now. A BEAUTIFUL dream...
...that ended TOO SOON.
One summer night they went out to get some ICE CREAM: a FIVE MINUTE drive.
FIVE MINUTES.
And they were GONE.
And so was I.
I'd never been someone who looked INWARD, who needed RELIGION.
Phil and Mandy were the ONLY GODS I required.
BUT AFTER...AFTER THEY DIED...I FELT SO HOLLOW INSIDE.
I...I HAD TO KNOW WHY SUCH A THING COULD HAPPEN. I MEAN, WHAT KIND OF GOD WOULD ALLOW SOMETHING SO RANDOM, SO POINTLESS, SO...EVIL--
I NEEDED ANSWERS. I NEEDED PEACE.
SO I STARTED READING... EVERYTHING.

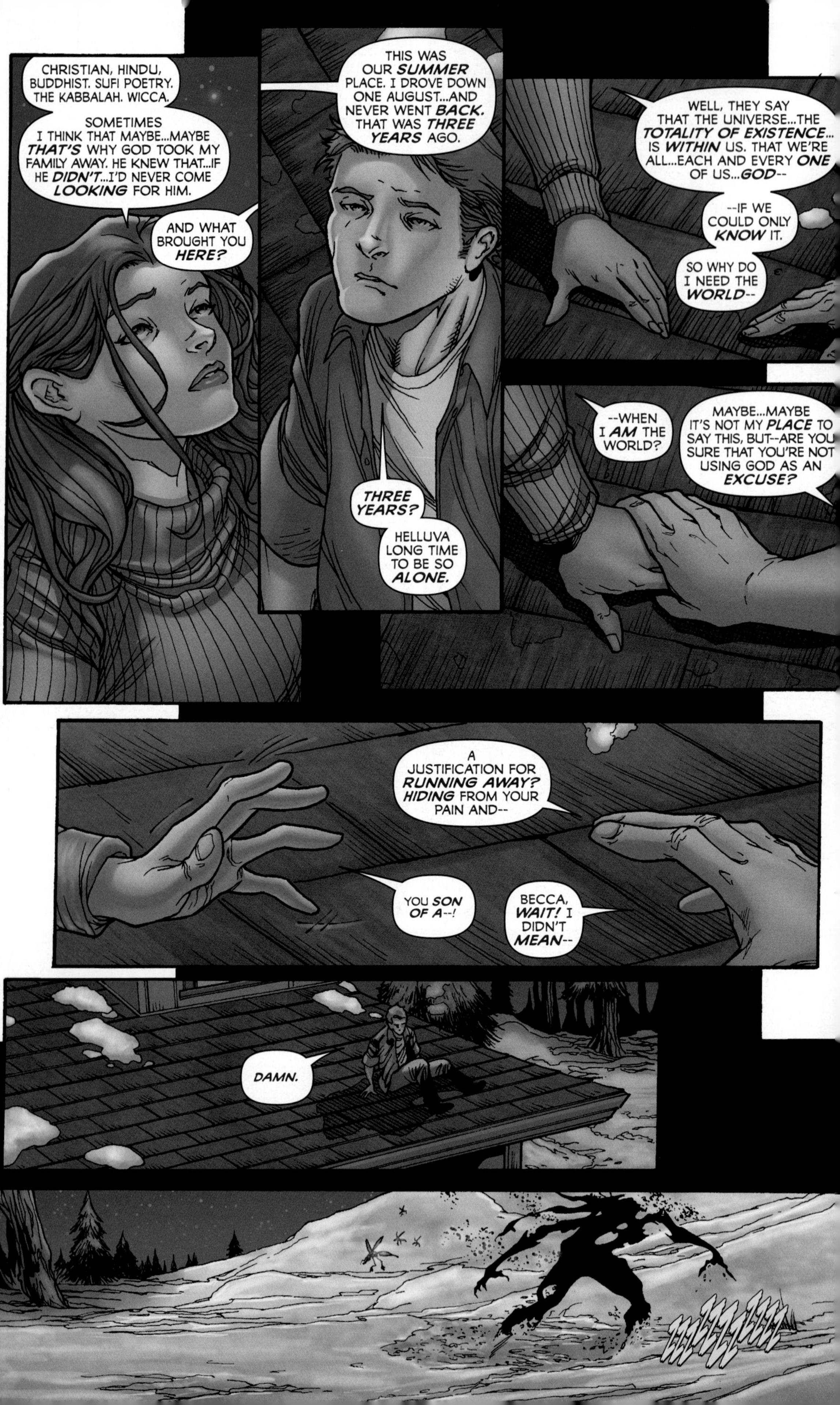
CHRISTIAN, HINDU, BUDDHIST. SUFI POETRY. THE KABBALAH. WICCA.
SOMETIMES I THINK THAT MAYBE...MAYBE THAT'S WHY GOD TOOK MY FAMILY AWAY. HE KNEW THAT...IF HE DIDN'T...I'D NEVER COME LOOKING FOR HIM.
AND WHAT BROUGHT YOU HERE?
THIS WAS OUR SUMMER PLACE. I DROVE DOWN ONE AUGUST...AND NEVER WENT BACK. THAT WAS THREE YEARS AGO.
THREE YEARS?
HELLUVA LONG TIME TO BE SO ALONE.
WELL, THEY SAY THAT THE UNIVERSE...THE TOTALITY OF EXISTENCE... IS WITHIN US. THAT WE'RE ALL...EACH AND EVERY ONE OF US...GOD--
--IF WE COULD ONLY KNOW IT.
SO WHY DO I NEED THE WORLD--
--WHEN I AM THE WORLD?
MAYBE...MAYBE IT'S NOT MY PLACE TO SAY THIS, BUT--ARE YOU SURE THAT YOU'RE NOT USING GOD AS AN EXCUSE?
A JUSTIFICATION FOR RUNNING AWAY? HIDING FROM YOUR PAIN AND--
YOU SON OF A--!
BECCA, WAIT! I DIDN'T MEAN--
DAMN.

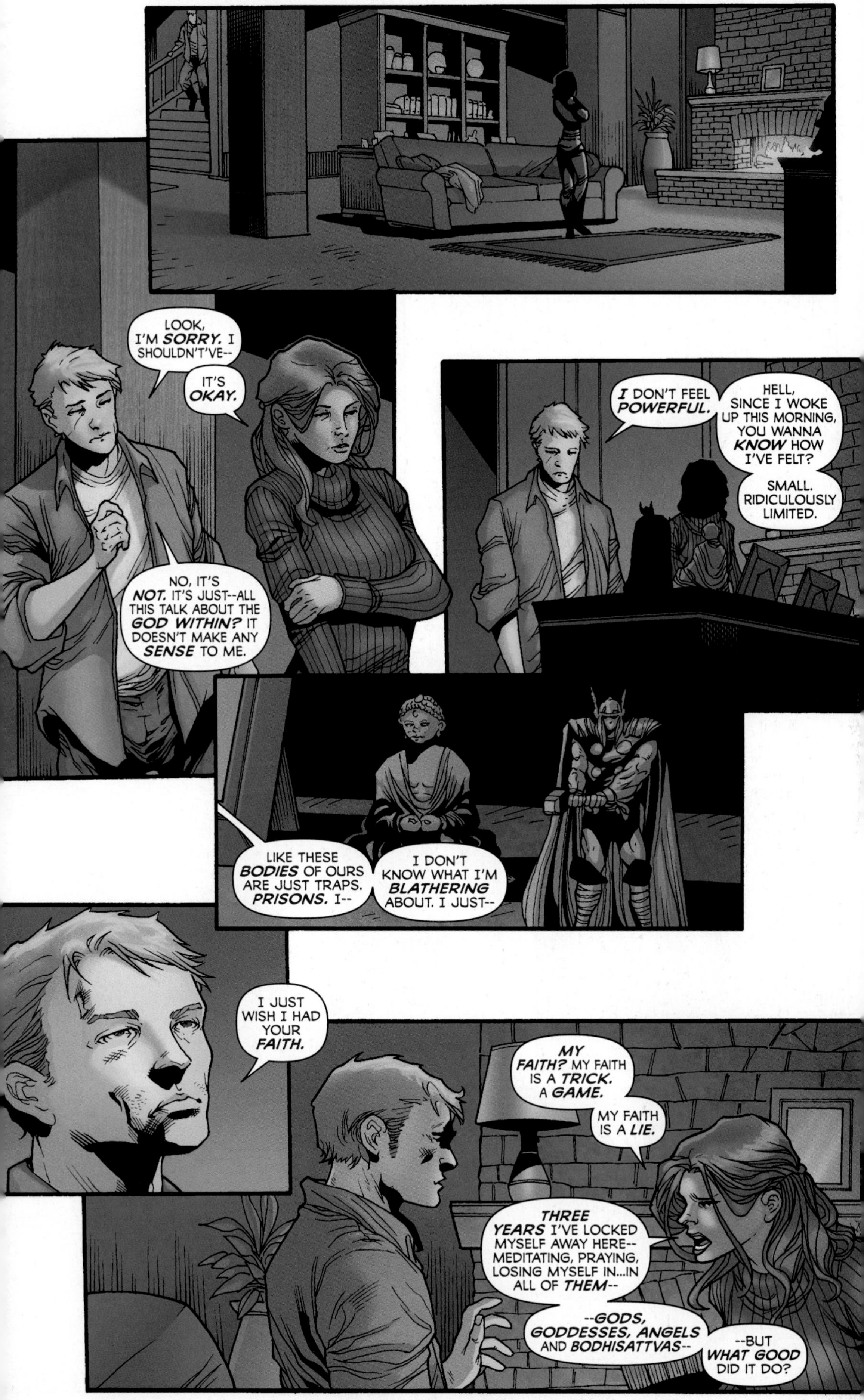
LOOK, I'M SORRY. I SHOULDN'T'VE--
IT'S OKAY.
NO, IT'S NOT. IT'S JUST--ALL THIS TALK ABOUT THE GOD WITHIN? IT DOESN'T MAKE ANY SENSE TO ME.
I DON'T FEEL POWERFUL.
HELL, SINCE I WOKE UP THIS MORNING, YOU WANNA KNOW HOW I'VE FELT?
SMALL. RIDICULOUSLY LIMITED.
LIKE THESE BODIES OF OURS ARE JUST TRAPS. PRISONS. I--
I DON'T KNOW WHAT I'M BLATHERING ABOUT. I JUST--
I JUST WISH I HAD YOUR FAITH.
MY FAITH? MY FAITH IS A TRICK. A GAME.
MY FAITH IS A LIE.
THREE YEARS I'VE LOCKED MYSELF AWAY HERE--MEDITATING, PRAYING, LOSING MYSELF IN...IN ALL OF THEM--
--GODS, GODDESSES, ANGELS AND BODHISATTVAS--
--BUT WHAT GOOD DID IT DO?

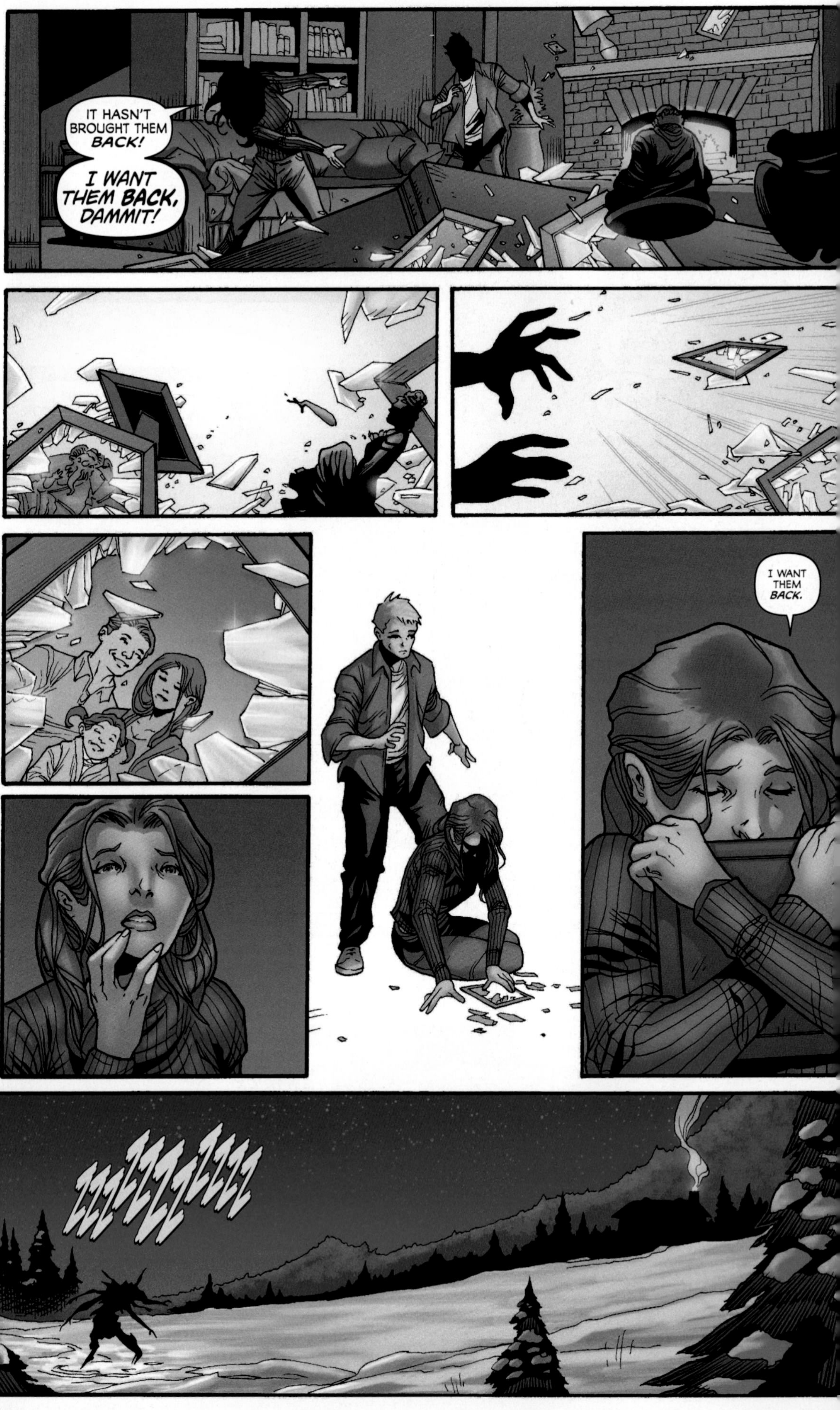
IT HASN'T BROUGHT THEM BACK!
I WANT THEM BACK, DAMMIT!
I WANT THEM BACK.
ZZZZZZZZZZZZZZ

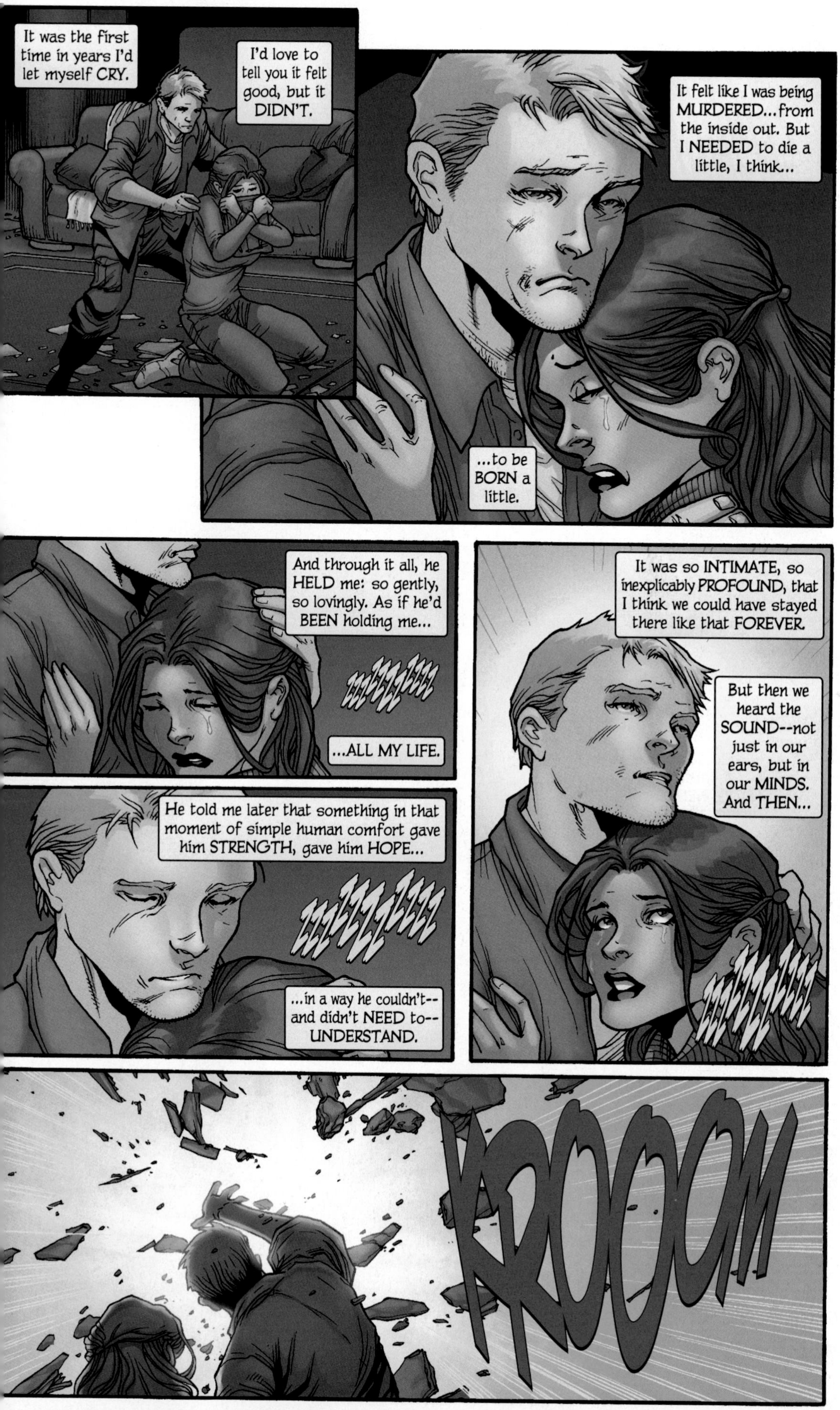
It was the first time in years I'd let myself CRY.
I'd love to tell you it felt good, but it DIDN'T.
It felt like I was being MURDERED...from the inside out. But I NEEDED to die a little, I think...
...to be BORN a little.
And through it all, he HELD me: so gently, so lovingly. As if he'd BEEN holding me...
zzzZZZzZZZZ
...ALL MY LIFE.
It was so INTIMATE, so inexplicably PROFOUND, that I think we could have stayed there like that FOREVER.
But then we heard the SOUND--not just in our ears, but in our MINDS. And THEN...
He told me later that something in that moment of simple human comfort gave him STRENGTH, gave him HOPE...
zzzZZZzZZZZ
...in a way he couldn't--and didn't NEED to--UNDERSTAND.
zzzZZZzZZZZ
KROOOOM

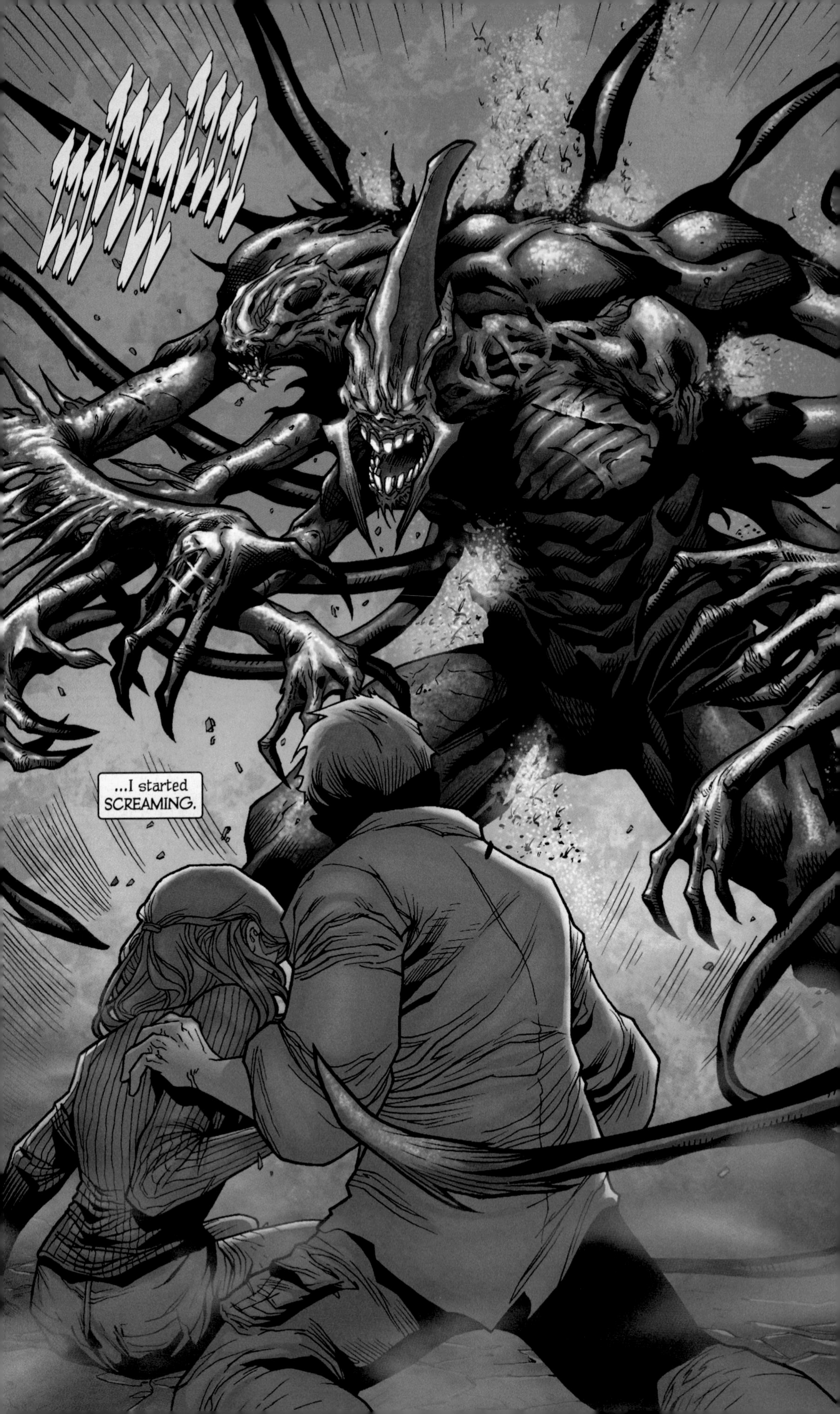
ZZZZZZZZZZZZ
...I started SCREAMING.

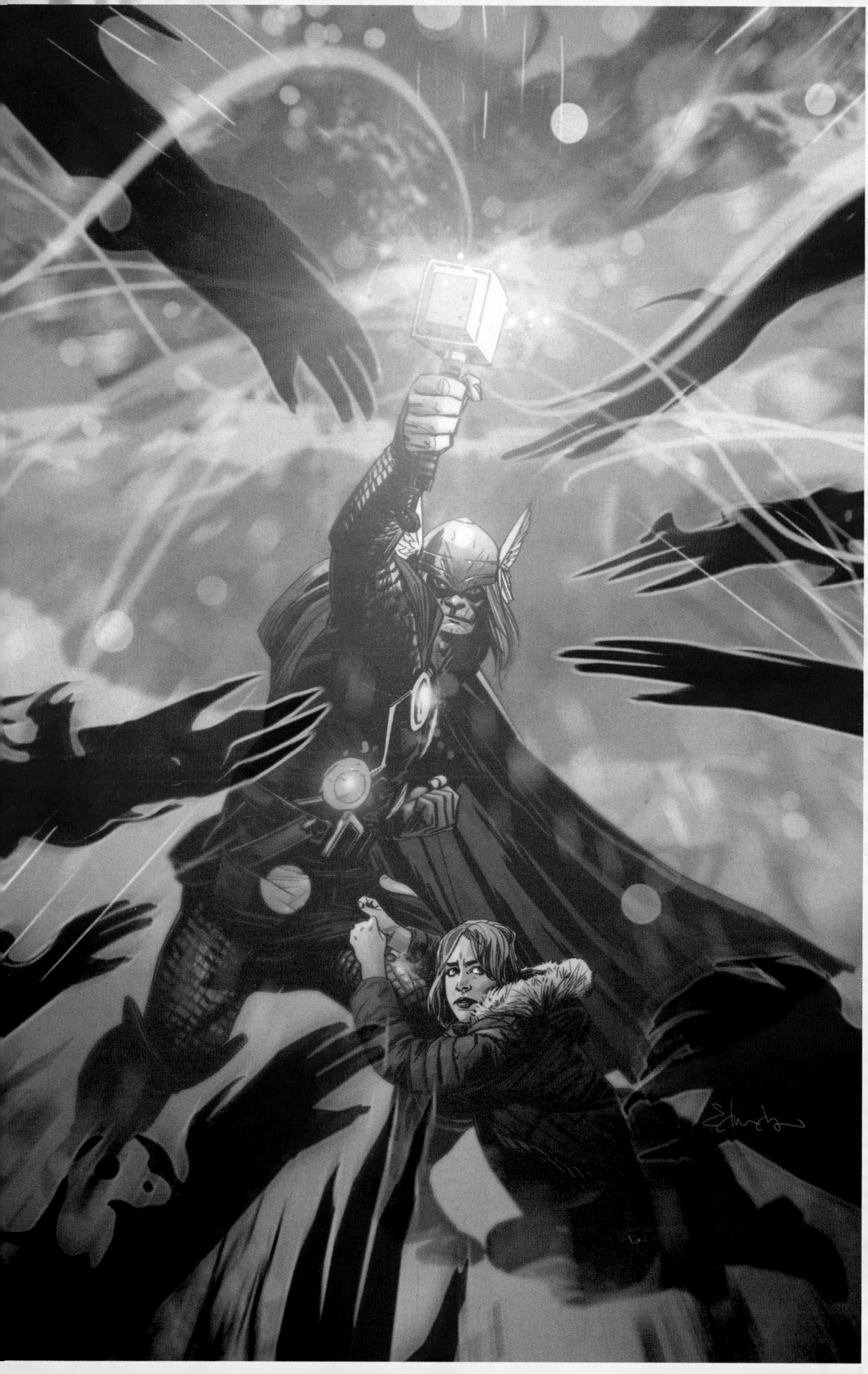

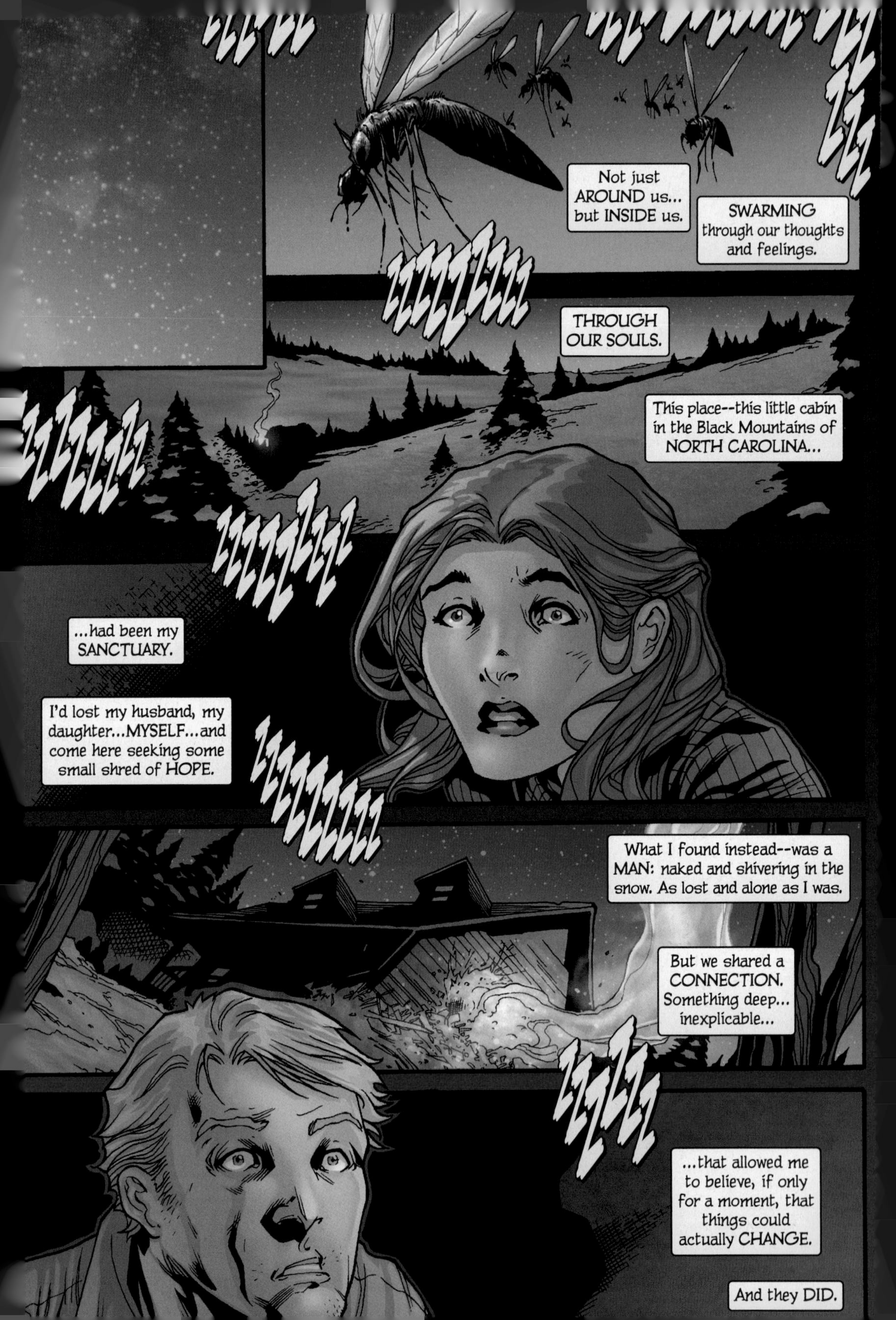
Not just AROUND us... but INSIDE us.
SWARMING through our thoughts and feelings.
THROUGH OUR SOULS.
This place--this little cabin in the Black Mountains of NORTH CAROLINA...
...had been my SANCTUARY.
I'd lost my husband, my daughter...MYSELF...and come here seeking some small shred of HOPE.
What I found instead--was a MAN: naked and shivering in the snow. As lost and alone as I was.
But we shared a CONNECTION. Something deep... inexplicable...
...that allowed me to believe, if only for a moment, that things could actually CHANGE.
And they DID.

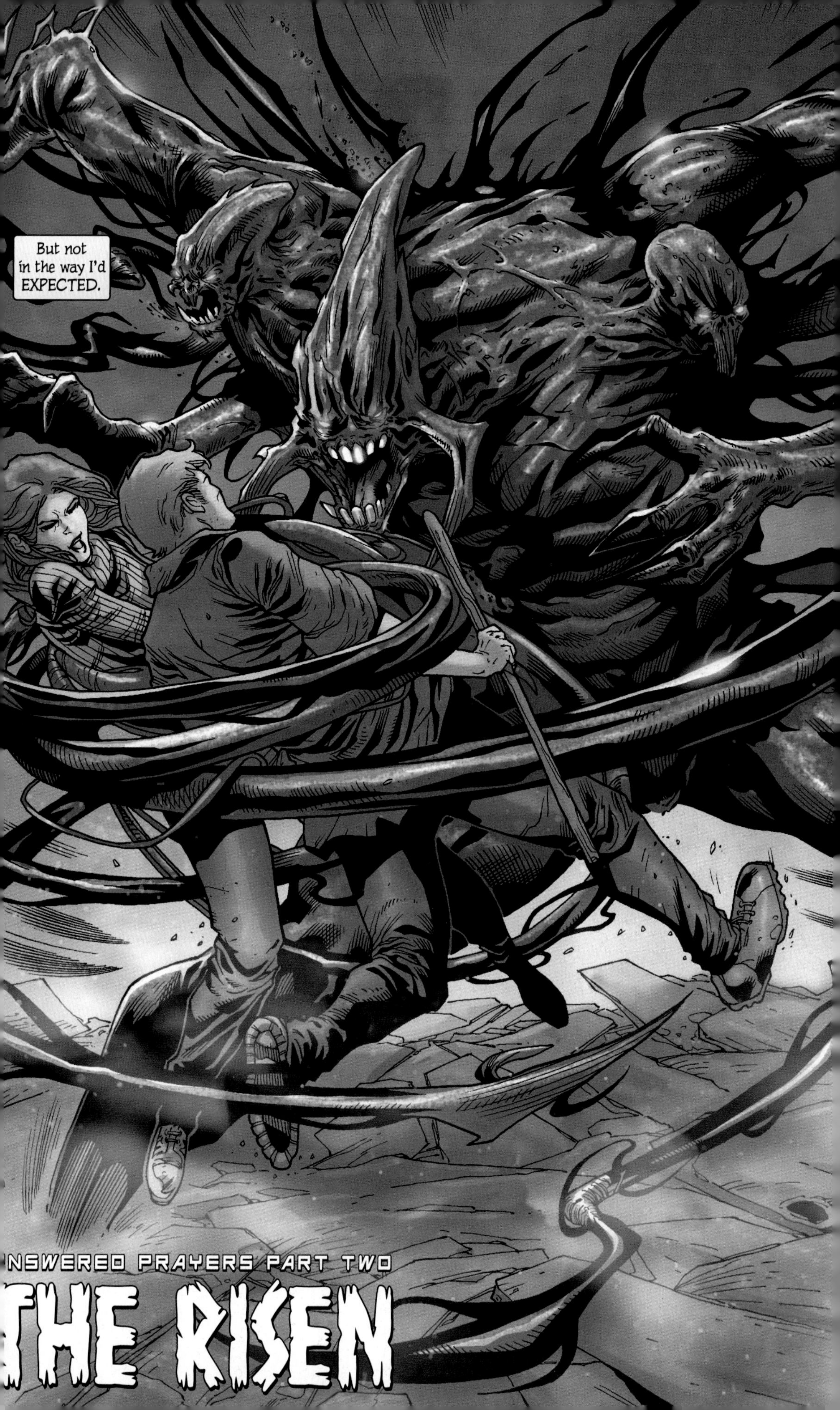
But not in the way I'd EXPECTED.
NSWERED PRAYERS PART TWO
THE RISEN

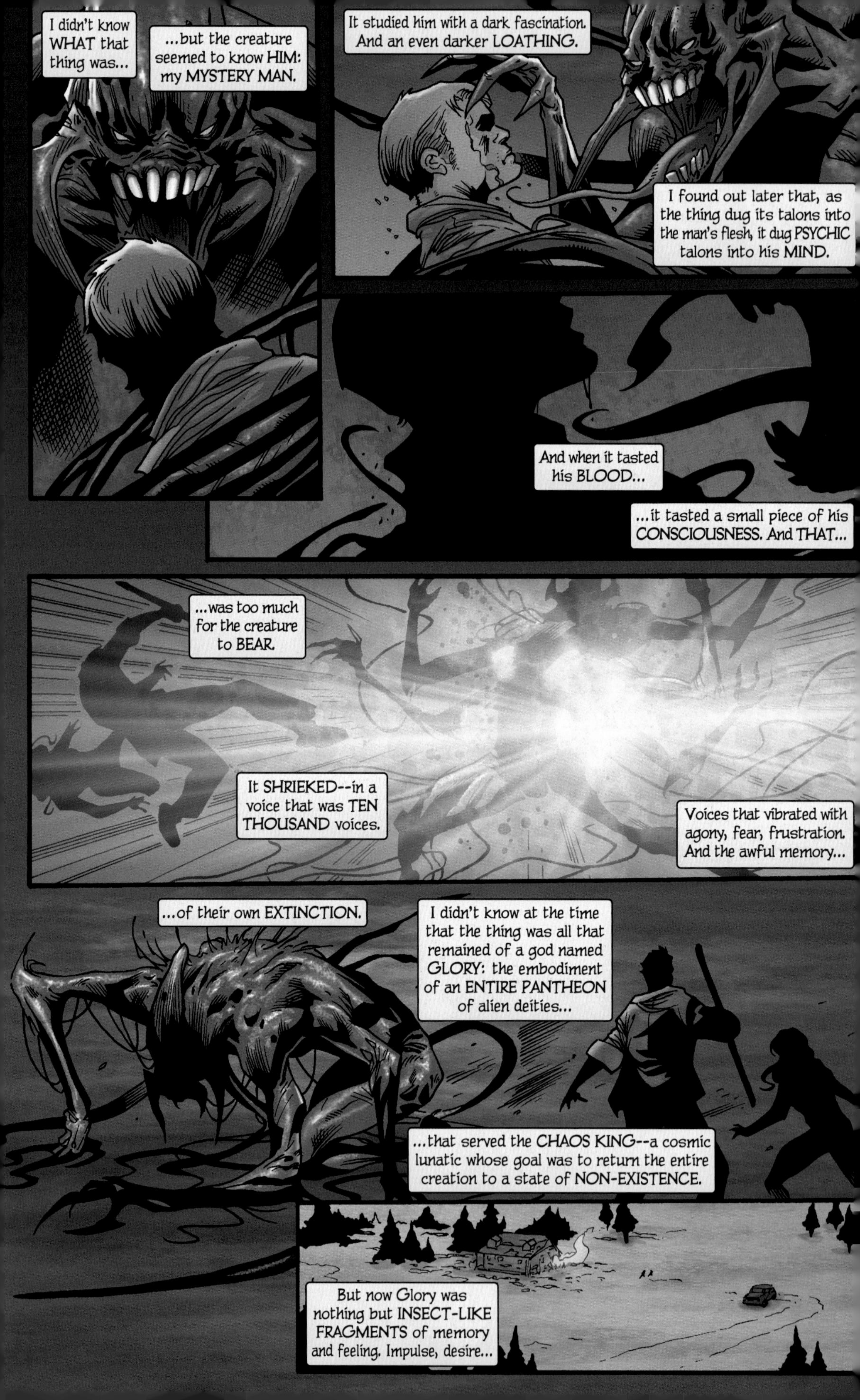
I didn't know WHAT that thing was...
...but the creature seemed to know HIM: my MYSTERY MAN.
It studied him with a dark fascination. And an even darker LOATHING.
I found out later that, as the thing dug its talons into the man's flesh, it dug PSYCHIC talons into his MIND.
And when it tasted his BLOOD...
...it tasted a small piece of his CONSCIOUSNESS. And THAT...
...was too much for the creature to BEAR.
It SHRIEKED--in a voice that was TEN THOUSAND voices.
Voices that vibrated with agony, fear, frustration. And the awful memory...
...of their own EXTINCTION.
I didn't know at the time that the thing was all that remained of a god named GLORY: the embodiment of an ENTIRE PANTHEON of alien deities...
...that served the CHAOS KING--a cosmic lunatic whose goal was to return the entire creation to a state of NON-EXISTENCE.
But now Glory was nothing but INSECT-LIKE FRAGMENTS of memory and feeling. Impulse, desire...

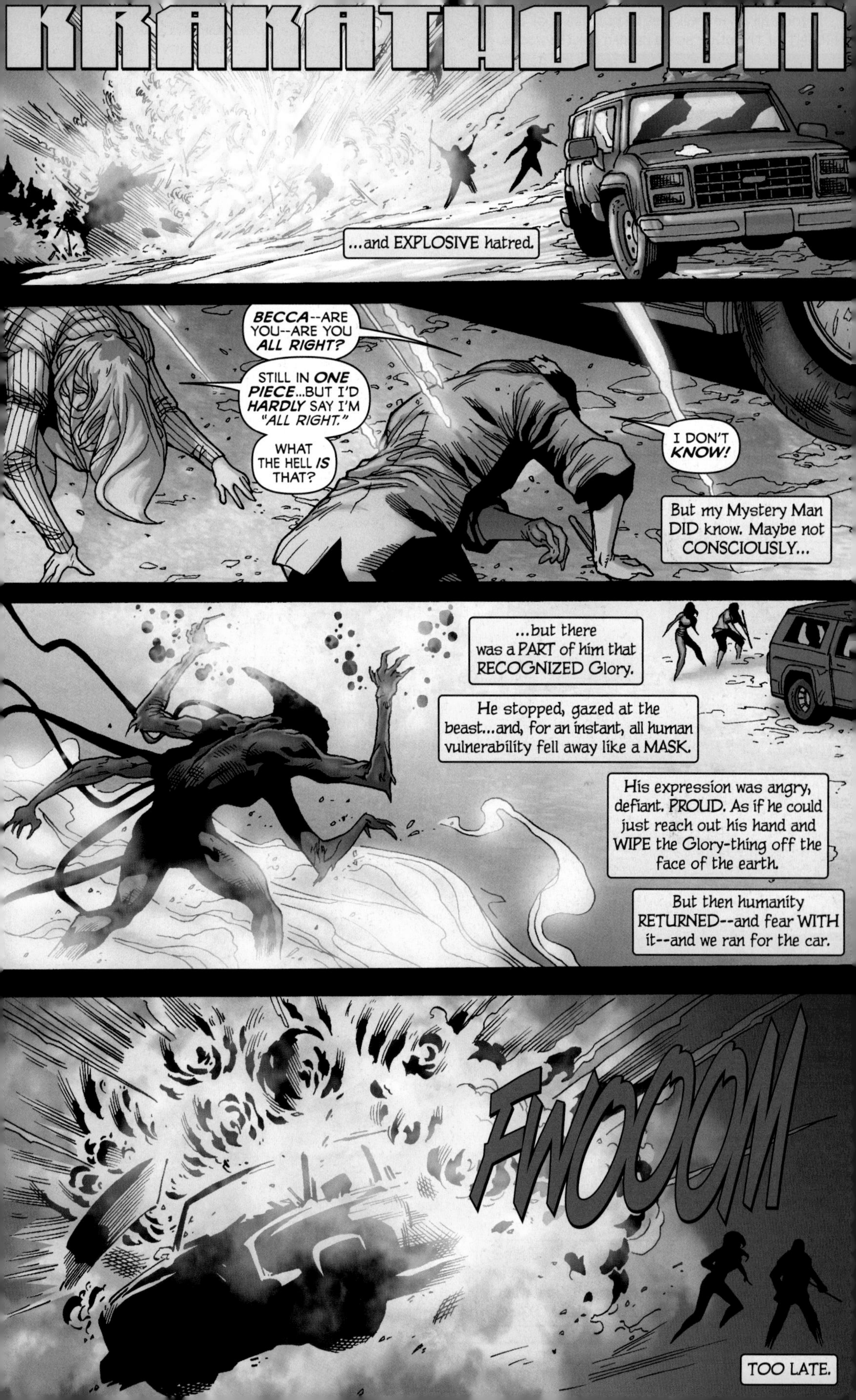

KRAKATHOOOM
...and EXPLOSIVE hatred.
BECCA--ARE YOU--ARE YOU ALL RIGHT?
STILL IN ONE PIECE...BUT I'D HARDLY SAY I'M "ALL RIGHT."
WHAT THE HELL IS THAT?
I DON'T KNOW!
But my Mystery Man DID know. Maybe not CONSCIOUSLY...
...but there was a PART of him that RECOGNIZED Glory.
He stopped, gazed at the beast...and, for an instant, all human vulnerability fell away like a MASK.
His expression was angry, defiant. PROUD. As if he could just reach out his hand and WIPE the Glory-thing off the face of the earth.
But then humanity RETURNED--and fear WITH it--and we ran for the car.
FWOOOM
TOO LATE.

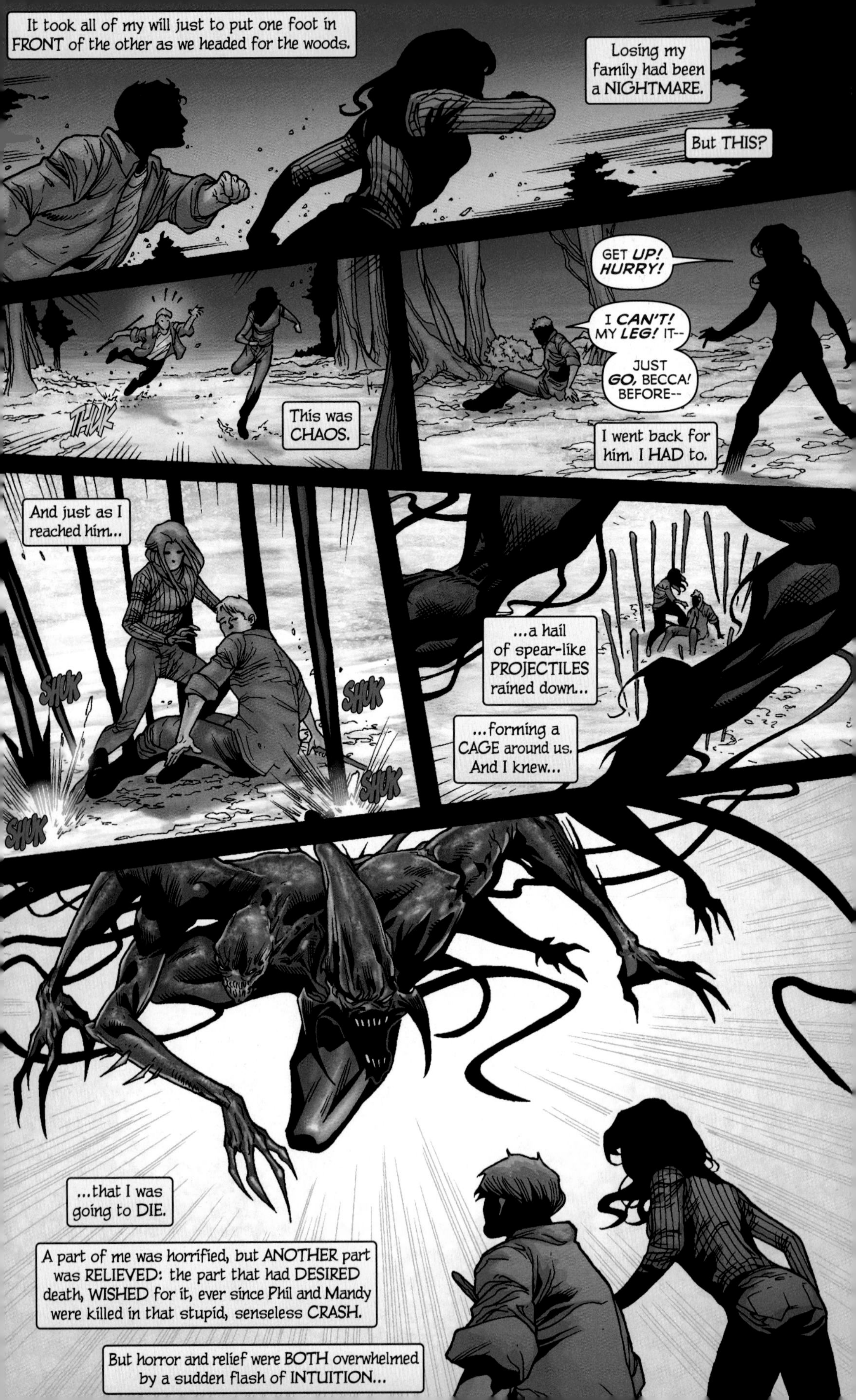
It took all of my will just to put one foot in FRONT of the other as we headed for the woods.
Losing my family had been a NIGHTMARE.
But THIS?
THUK
This was CHAOS.
GET UP! HURRY!
I CAN'T! MY LEG! IT--
JUST GO, BECCA! BEFORE--
I went back for him. I HAD to.
And just as I reached him...
SHUK
SHUK
SHUK
SHUK
...a hail of spear-like PROJECTILES rained down...
...forming a CAGE around us. And I knew...
...that I was going to DIE.
A part of me was horrified, but ANOTHER part was RELIEVED: the part that had DESIRED death, WISHED for it, ever since Phil and Mandy were killed in that stupid, senseless CRASH.
But horror and relief were BOTH overwhelmed by a sudden flash of INTUITION...

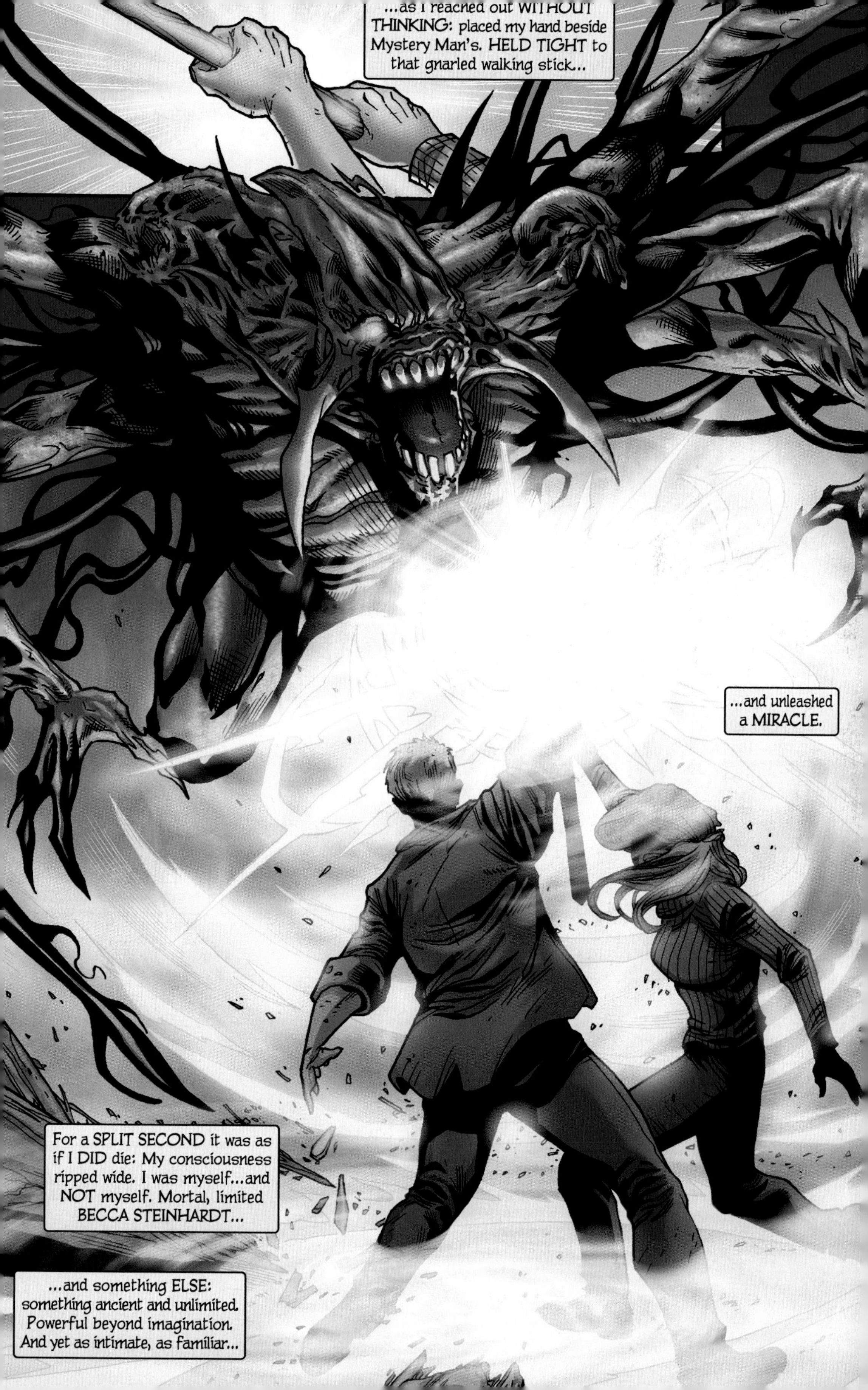
...as I reached out WITHOUT THINKING: placed my hand beside Mystery Man's. HELD TIGHT to that gnarled walking stick...
...and unleashed a MIRACLE.
For a SPLIT SECOND it was as if I DID die: My consciousness ripped wide. I was myself...and NOT myself. Mortal, limited BECCA STEINHARDT...
...and something ELSE: something ancient and unlimited. Powerful beyond imagination. And yet as intimate, as familiar...

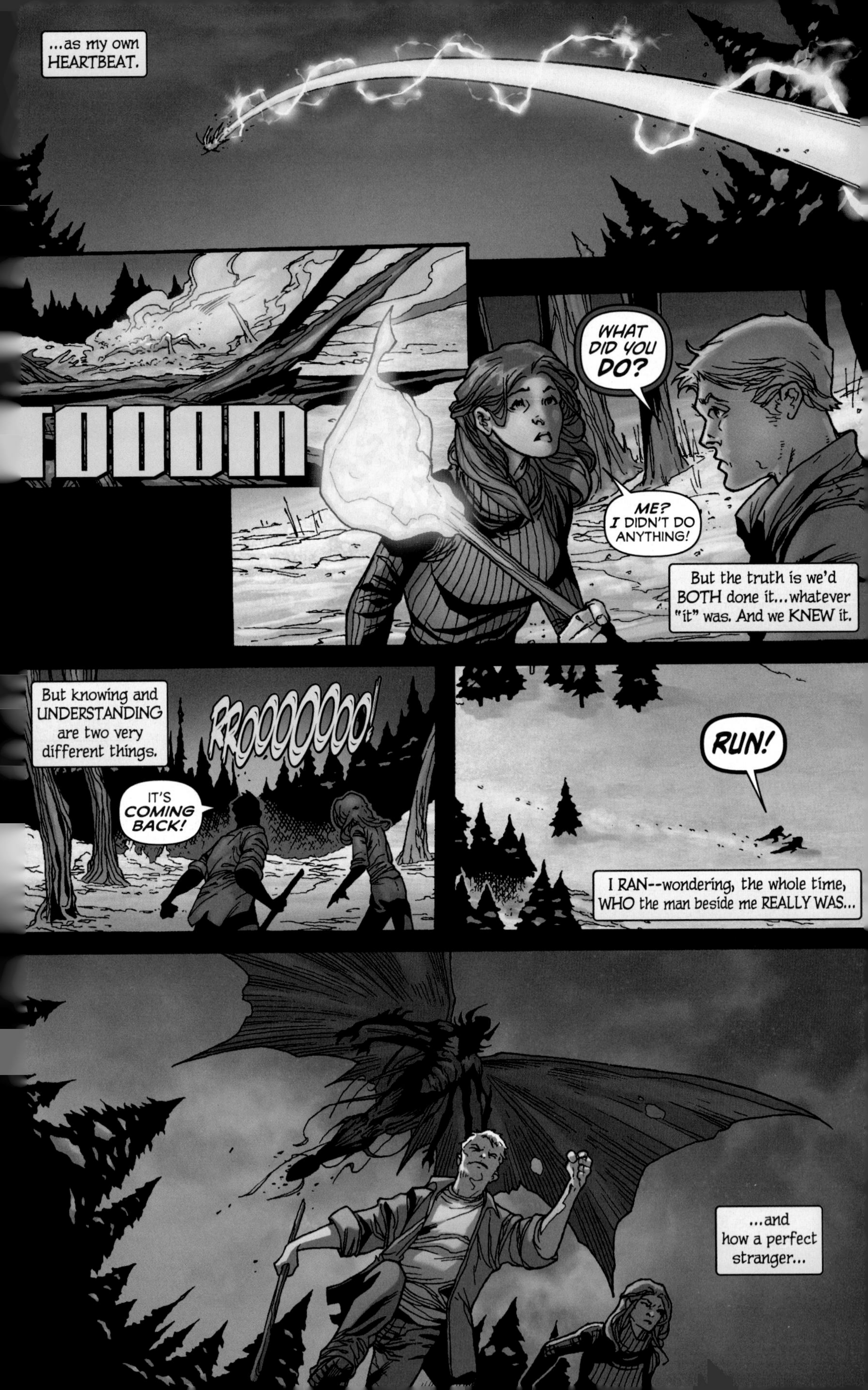

...as my own HEARTBEAT.
TOOOM
WHAT DID YOU DO?
ME? I DIDN'T DO ANYTHING!
But the truth is we'd BOTH done it...whatever "it" was. And we KNEW it.
But knowing and UNDERSTANDING are two very different things.
RROOOOOOO!
IT'S COMING BACK!
RUN!
I RAN--wondering, the whole time, WHO the man beside me REALLY WAS...
...and how a perfect stranger...

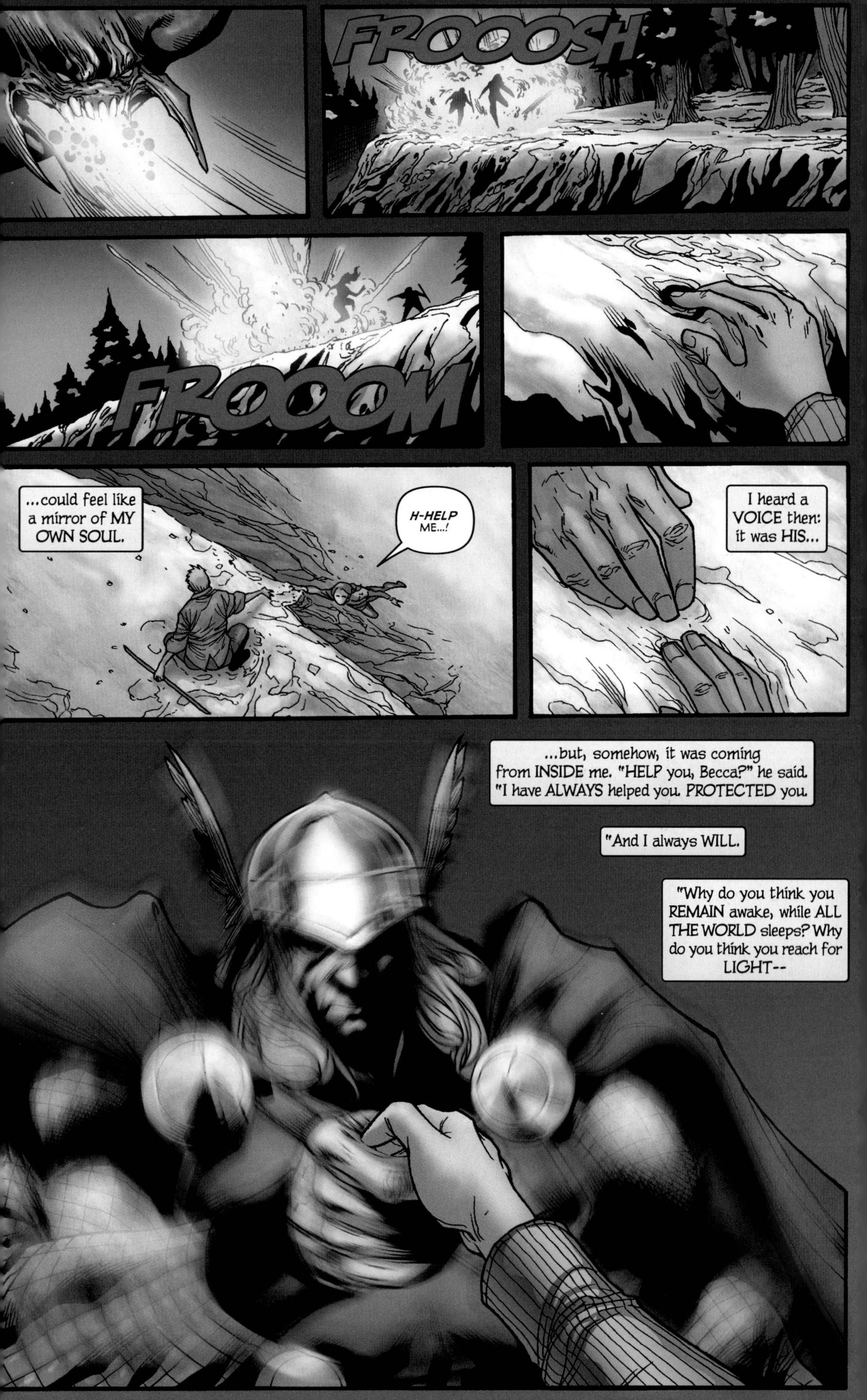
FROOOSH
FROOOM
...could feel like a mirror of MY OWN SOUL.
H-HELP ME...!
I heard a VOICE then: it was HIS...
...but, somehow, it was coming from INSIDE me. "HELP you, Becca?" he said. "I have ALWAYS helped you. PROTECTED you.
"And I always WILL.
"Why do you think you REMAIN awake, while ALL THE WORLD sleeps? Why do you think you reach for LIGHT--

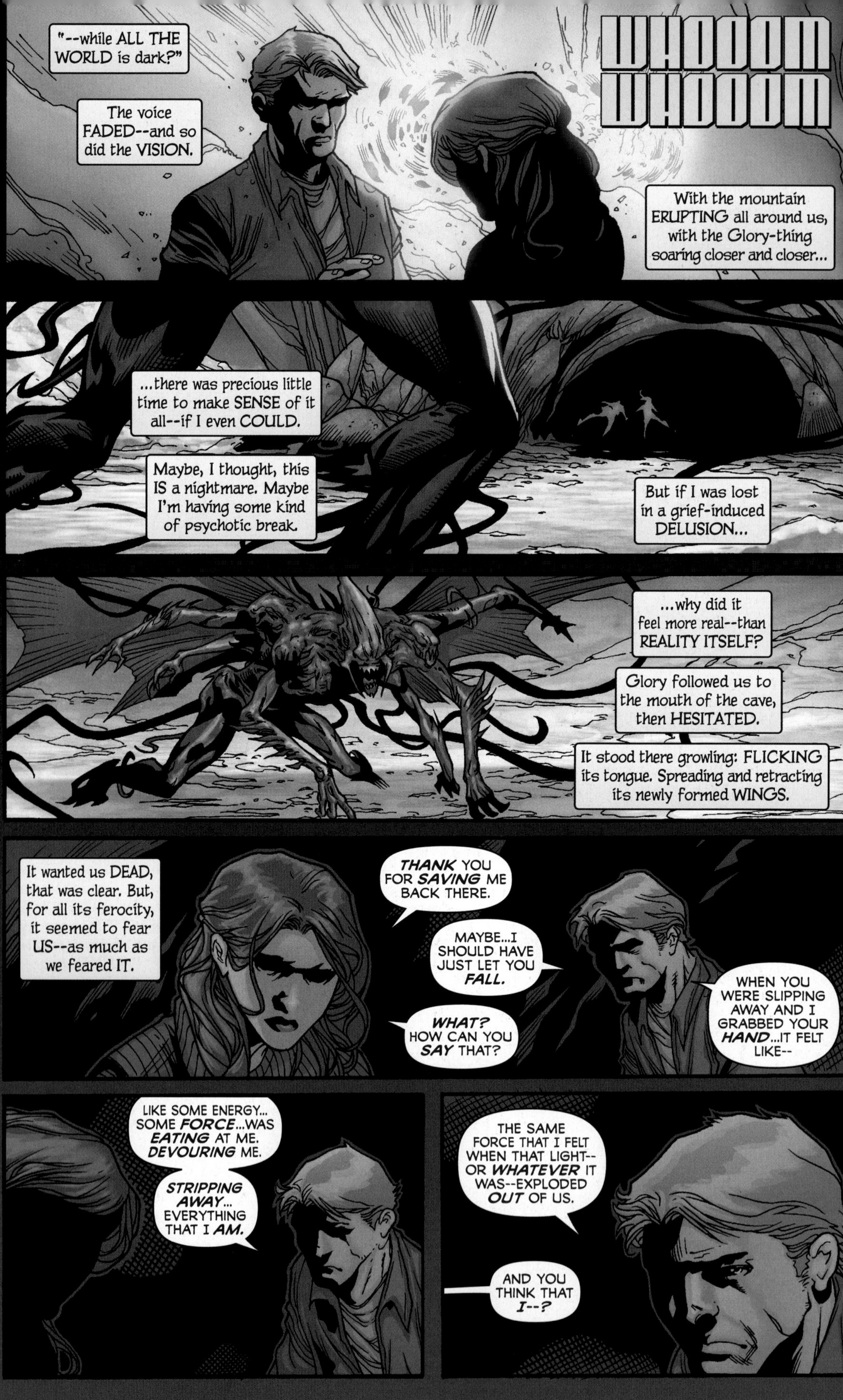
"--while ALL THE WORLD is dark?"
The voice FADED--and so did the VISION.
WHOOOM WHOOOM
With the mountain ERUPTING all around us, with the Glory-thing soaring closer and closer...
...there was precious little time to make SENSE of it all--if I even COULD.
Maybe, I thought, this IS a nightmare. Maybe I'm having some kind of psychotic break.
But if I was lost in a grief-induced DELUSION...
...why did it feel more real--than REALITY ITSELF?
Glory followed us to the mouth of the cave, then HESITATED.
It stood there growling: FLICKING its tongue. Spreading and retracting its newly formed WINGS.
It wanted us DEAD, that was clear. But, for all its ferocity, it seemed to fear US--as much as we feared IT.
THANK YOU FOR SAVING ME BACK THERE.
MAYBE...I SHOULD HAVE JUST LET YOU FALL.
WHAT? HOW CAN YOU SAY THAT?
WHEN YOU WERE SLIPPING AWAY AND I GRABBED YOUR HAND...IT FELT LIKE--
LIKE SOME ENERGY... SOME FORCE...WAS EATING AT ME. DEVOURING ME.
STRIPPING AWAY... EVERYTHING THAT I AM.
THE SAME FORCE THAT I FELT WHEN THAT LIGHT-- OR WHATEVER IT WAS--EXPLODED OUT OF US.
AND YOU THINK THAT I--?

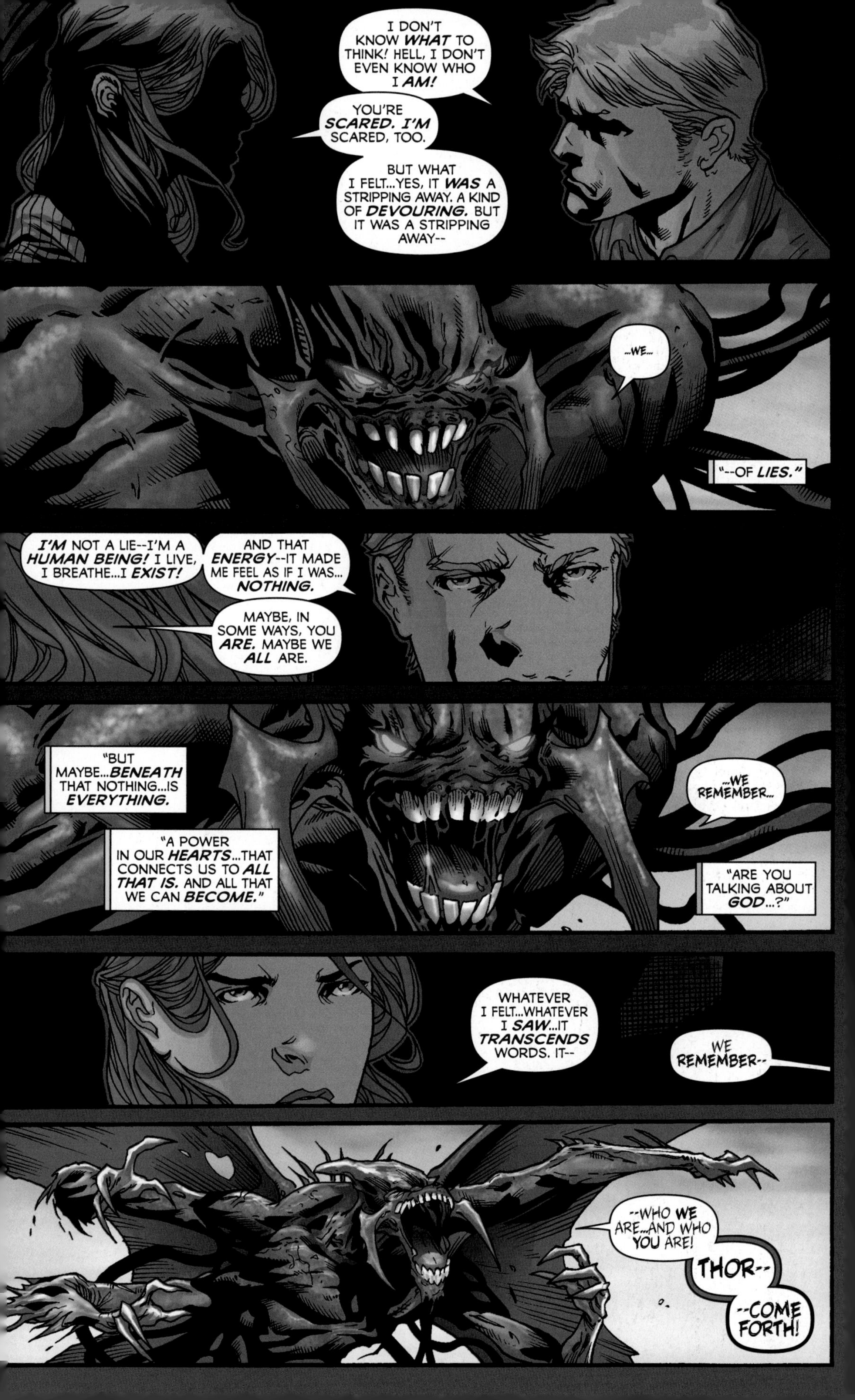
I DON'T KNOW WHAT TO THINK! HELL, I DON'T EVEN KNOW WHO I AM!
YOU'RE SCARED. I'M SCARED, TOO.
BUT WHAT I FELT...YES, IT WAS A STRIPPING AWAY. A KIND OF DEVOURING. BUT IT WAS A STRIPPING AWAY--
...WE...
"--OF LIES."
I'M NOT A LIE--I'M A HUMAN BEING! I LIVE, I BREATHE...I EXIST!
AND THAT ENERGY--IT MADE ME FEEL AS IF I WAS... NOTHING.
MAYBE, IN SOME WAYS, YOU ARE. MAYBE WE ALL ARE.
"BUT MAYBE...BENEATH THAT NOTHING...IS EVERYTHING.
"A POWER IN OUR HEARTS...THAT CONNECTS US TO ALL THAT IS. AND ALL THAT WE CAN BECOME."
...WE REMEMBER...
"ARE YOU TALKING ABOUT GOD...?"
WHATEVER I FELT...WHATEVER I SAW...IT TRANSCENDS WORDS. IT--
WE REMEMBER--
--WHO WE ARE...AND WHO YOU ARE!
THOR--
--COME FORTH!

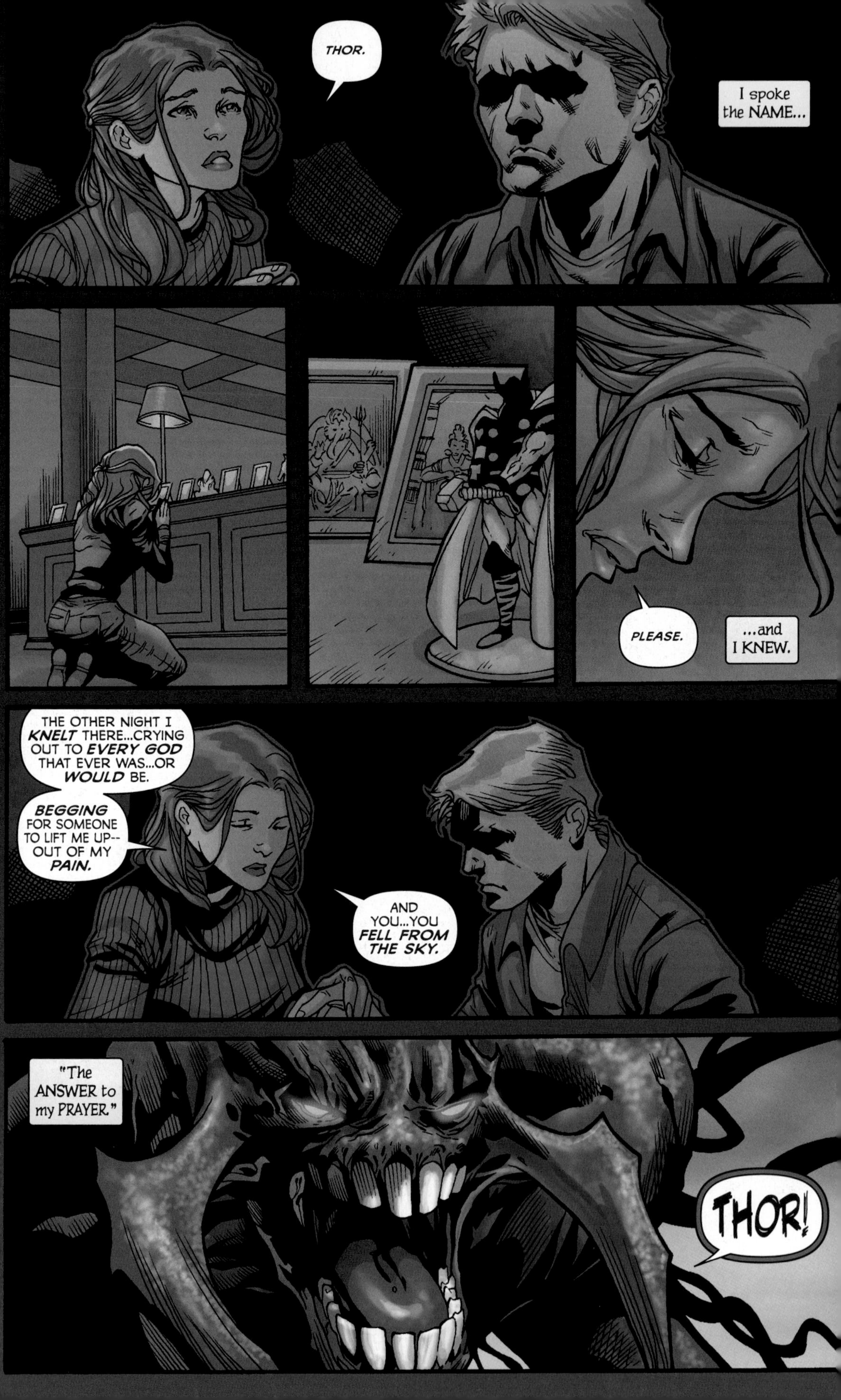
THOR.
I spoke the NAME...
PLEASE.
...and I KNEW.
THE OTHER NIGHT I KNELT THERE...CRYING OUT TO EVERY GOD THAT EVER WAS...OR WOULD BE.
BEGGING FOR SOMEONE TO LIFT ME UP-- OUT OF MY PAIN.
AND YOU...YOU FELL FROM THE SKY.
"The ANSWER to my PRAYER."
THOR!

IS IT...IS IT POSSIBLE?

NO. IT'S IMPOSSIBLE.

BUT IT'S TRUE.

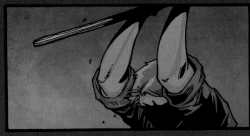

TOGETHER...?

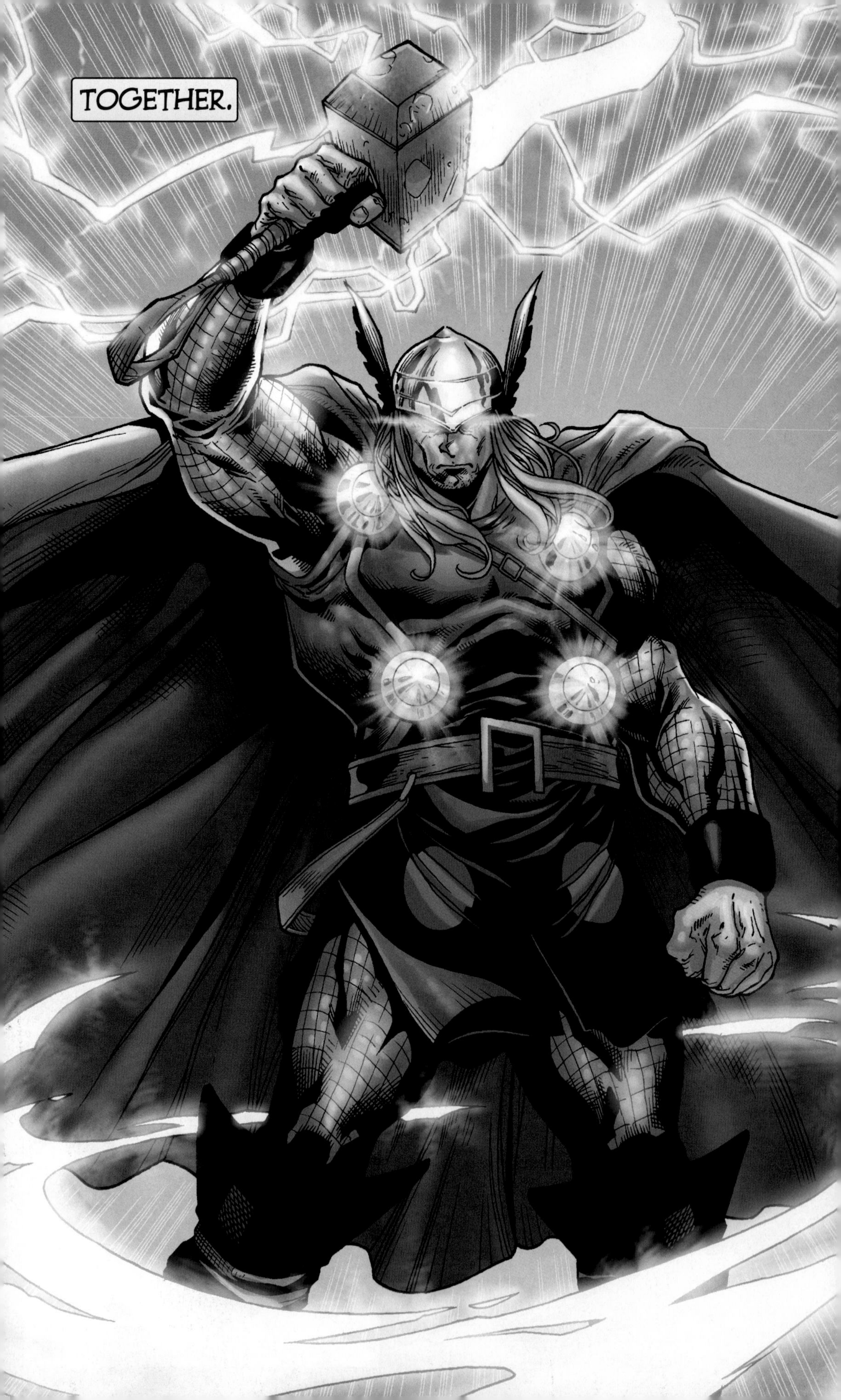
TOGETHER.

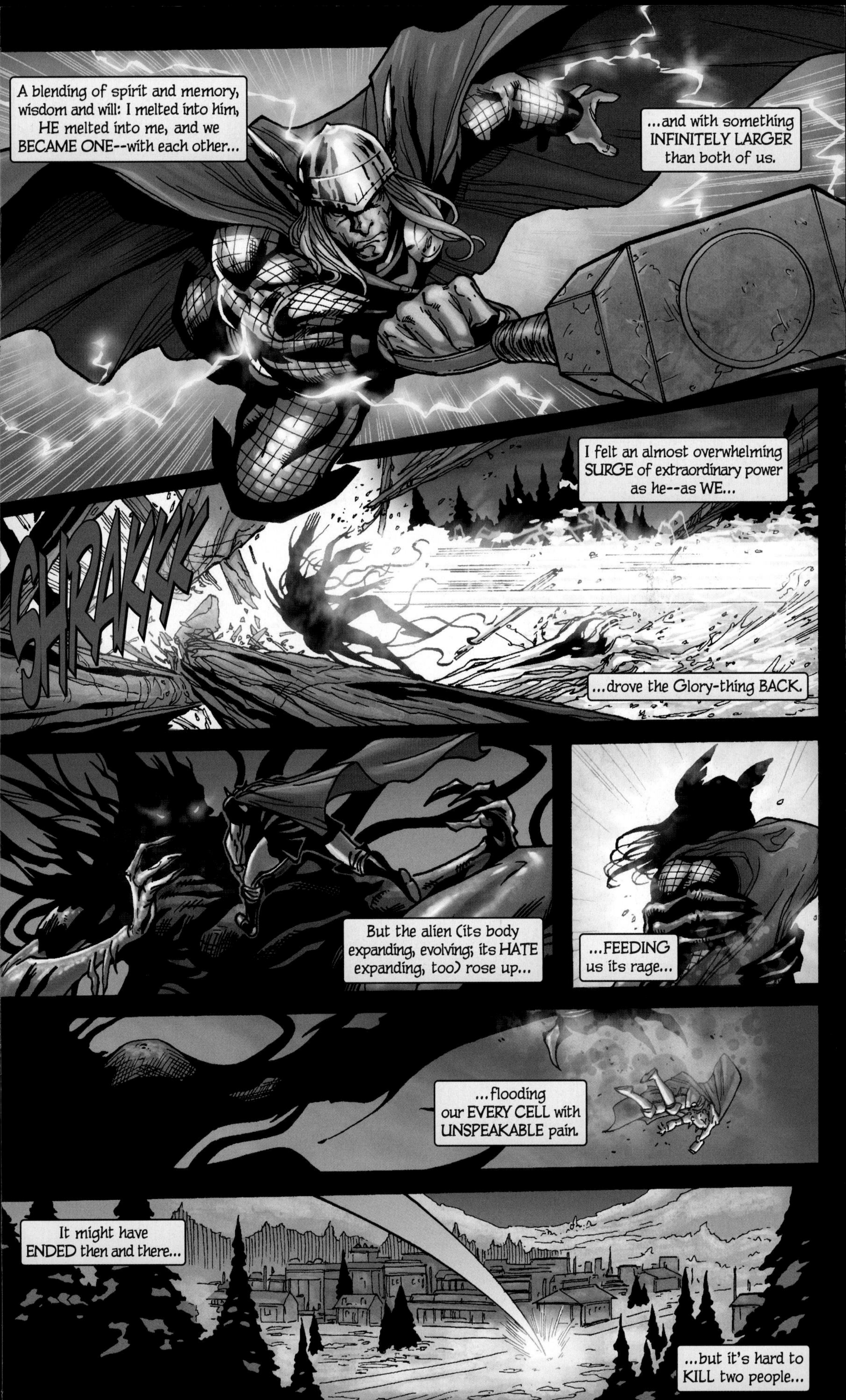
A blending of spirit and memory, wisdom and will: I melted into him, HE melted into me, and we BECAME ONE--with each other...
...and with something INFINITELY LARGER than both of us.
I felt an almost overwhelming SURGE of extraordinary power as he--as WE...
SHRAKK
...drove the Glory-thing BACK.
But the alien (its body expanding, evolving; its HATE expanding, too) rose up...
...FEEDING us its rage...
...flooding our EVERY CELL with UNSPEAKABLE pain.
It might have ENDED then and there...
...but it's hard to KILL two people...

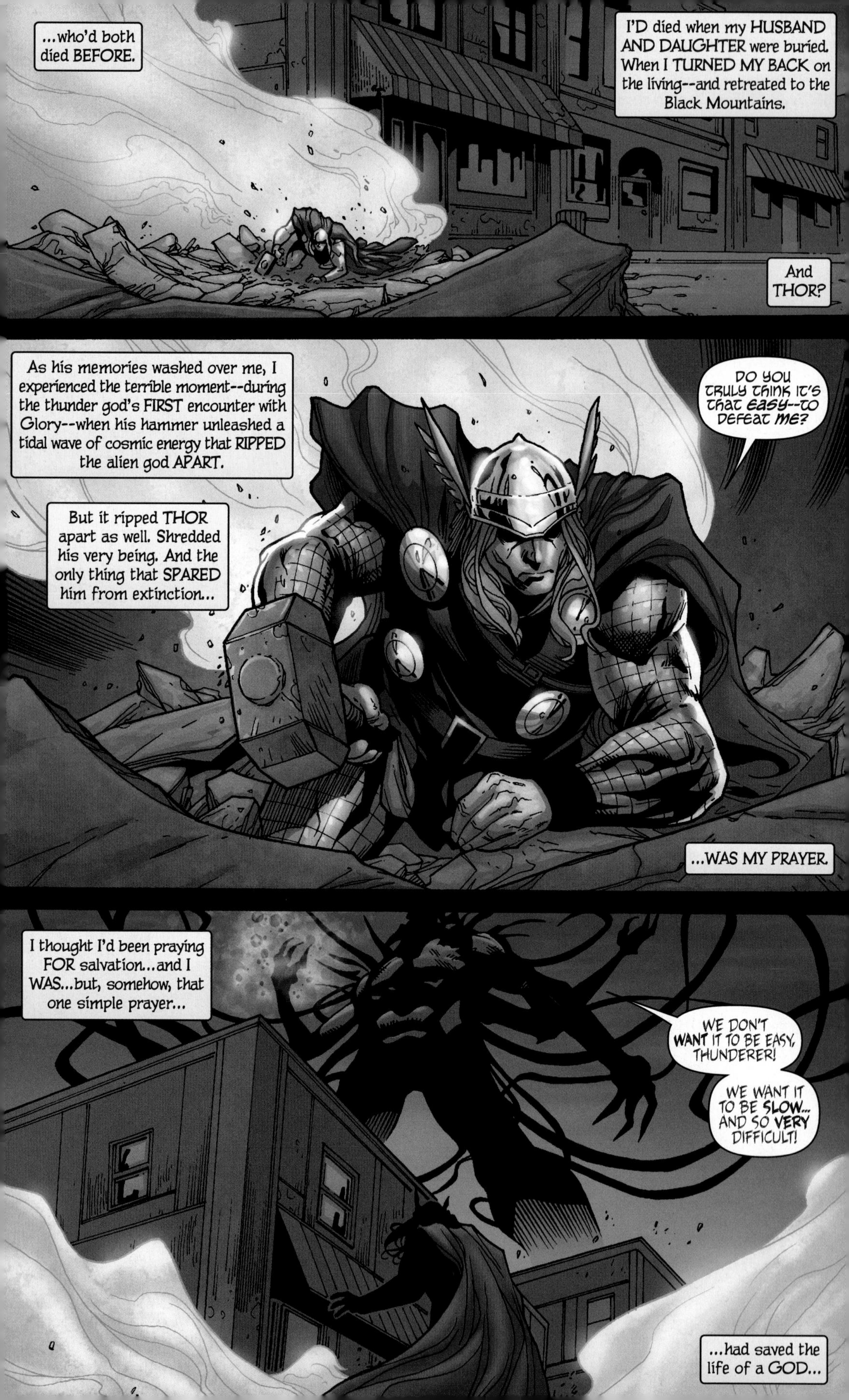

...who'd both died BEFORE.
I'D died when my HUSBAND AND DAUGHTER were buried. When I TURNED MY BACK on the living--and retreated to the Black Mountains.
And THOR?
As his memories washed over me, I experienced the terrible moment--during the thunder god's FIRST encounter with Glory--when his hammer unleashed a tidal wave of cosmic energy that RIPPED the alien god APART.
DO YOU TRULY THINK IT'S THAT EASY--TO DEFEAT ME?
But it ripped THOR apart as well. Shredded his very being. And the only thing that SPARED him from extinction...
...WAS MY PRAYER.
I thought I'd been praying FOR salvation...and I WAS...but, somehow, that one simple prayer...
WE DON'T WANT IT TO BE EASY, THUNDERER!
WE WANT IT TO BE SLOW... AND SO VERY DIFFICULT!
...had saved the life of a GOD...

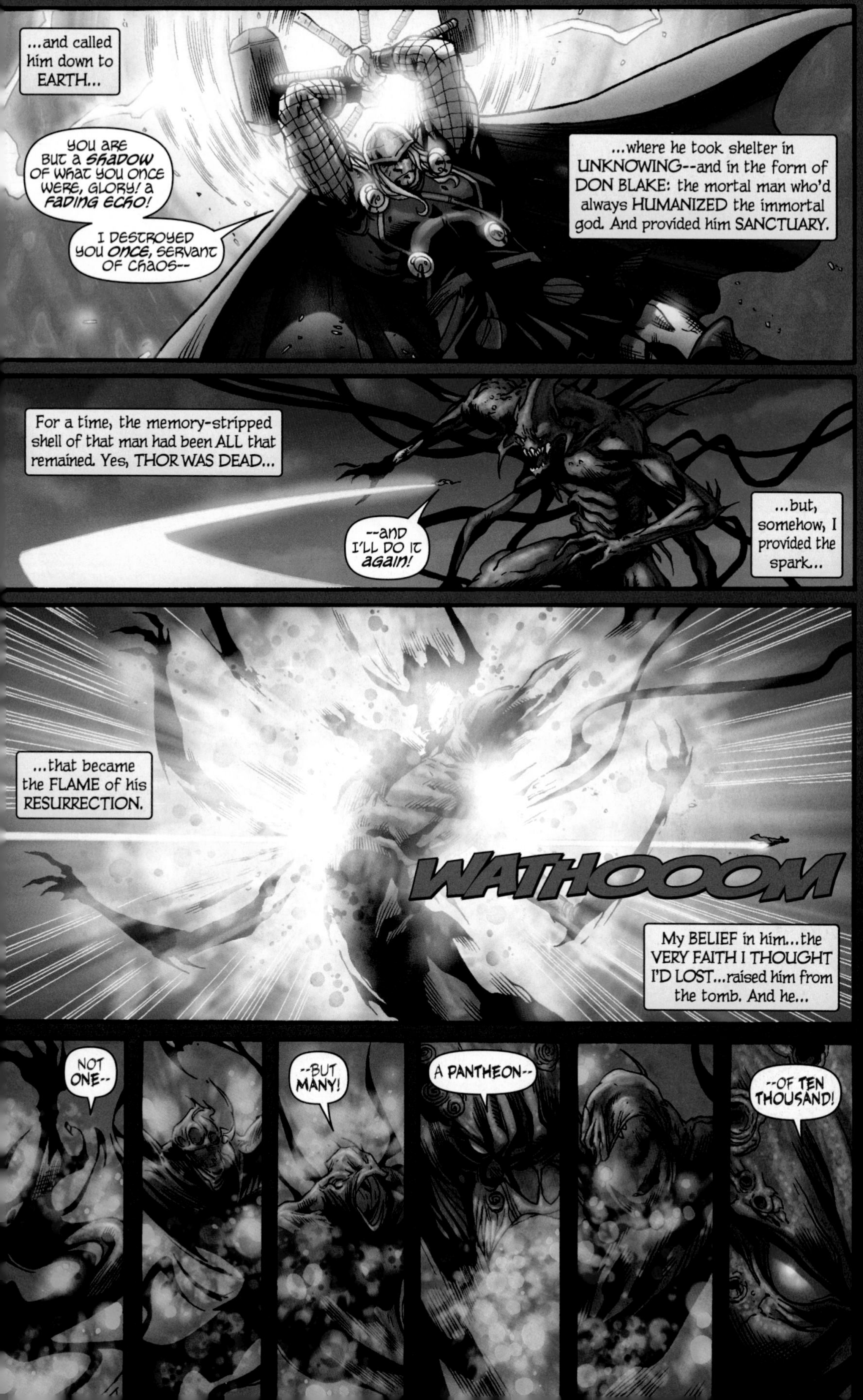
...and called him down to EARTH...
YOU ARE BUT A SHADOW OF WHAT YOU ONCE WERE, GLORY! A FADING ECHO!
I DESTROYED YOU ONCE, SERVANT OF CHAOS--
...where he took shelter in UNKNOWING--and in the form of DON BLAKE: the mortal man who'd always HUMANIZED the immortal god. And provided him SANCTUARY.
For a time, the memory-stripped shell of that man had been ALL that remained. Yes, THOR WAS DEAD...
--AND I'LL DO IT AGAIN!
...but, somehow, I provided the spark...
...that became the FLAME of his RESURRECTION.
WATHOOOOM
My BELIEF in him...the VERY FAITH I THOUGHT I'D LOST...raised him from the tomb. And he...
NOT ONE--
--BUT MANY!
A PANTHEON--
--OF TEN THOUSAND!

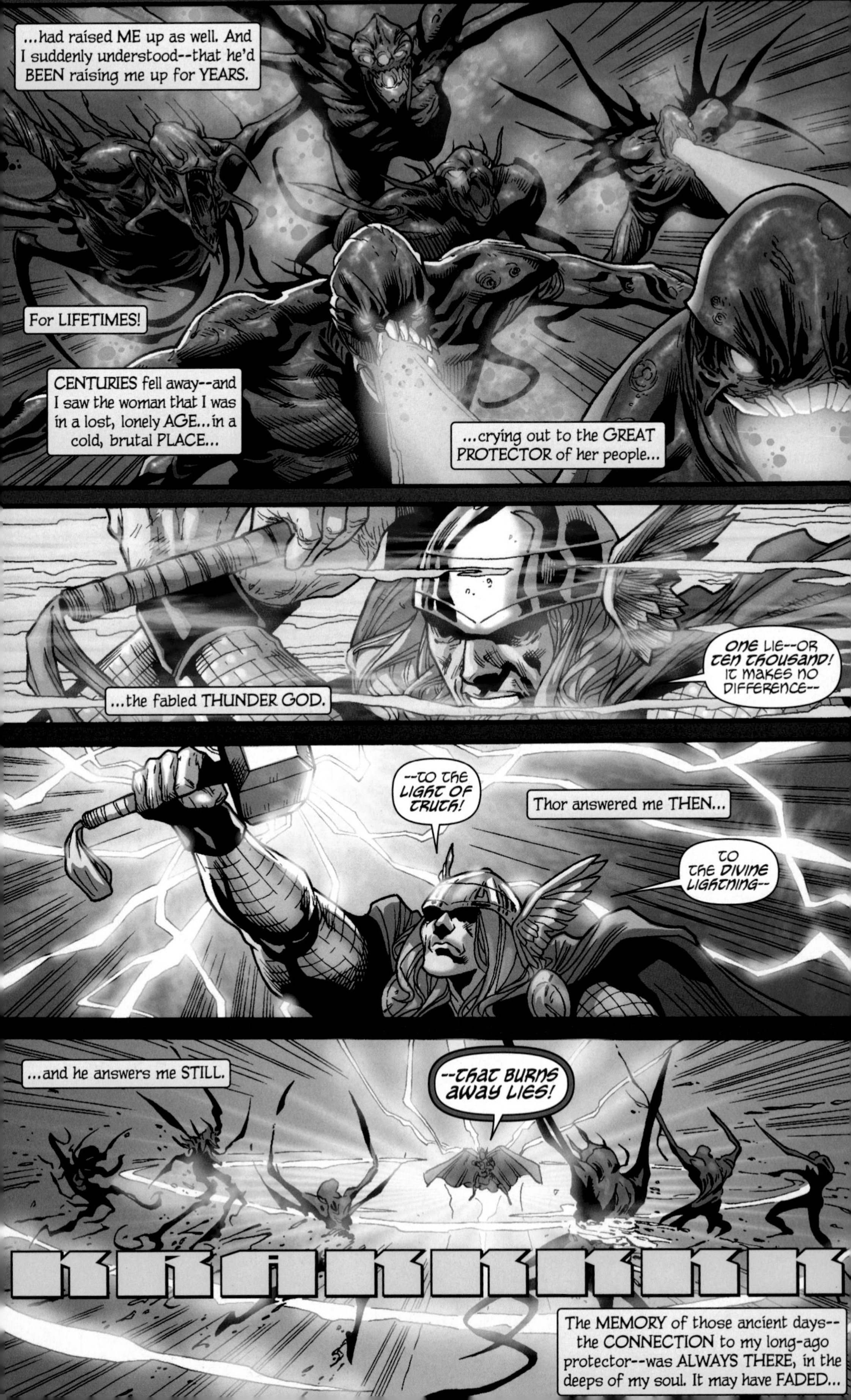
...had raised ME up as well. And I suddenly understood--that he'd BEEN raising me up for YEARS.
For LIFETIMES!
CENTURIES fell away--and I saw the woman that I was in a lost, lonely AGE...in a cold, brutal PLACE...
...crying out to the GREAT PROTECTOR of her people...
...the fabled THUNDER GOD.
ONE LIE--OR TEN THOUSAND! IT MAKES NO DIFFERENCE--
--TO THE LIGHT OF TRUTH!
Thor answered me THEN...
TO THE DIVINE LIGHTNING--
...and he answers me STILL.
--THAT BURNS AWAY LIES!
KRAKKKKKKK
The MEMORY of those ancient days--the CONNECTION to my long-ago protector--was ALWAYS THERE, in the deeps of my soul. It may have FADED...

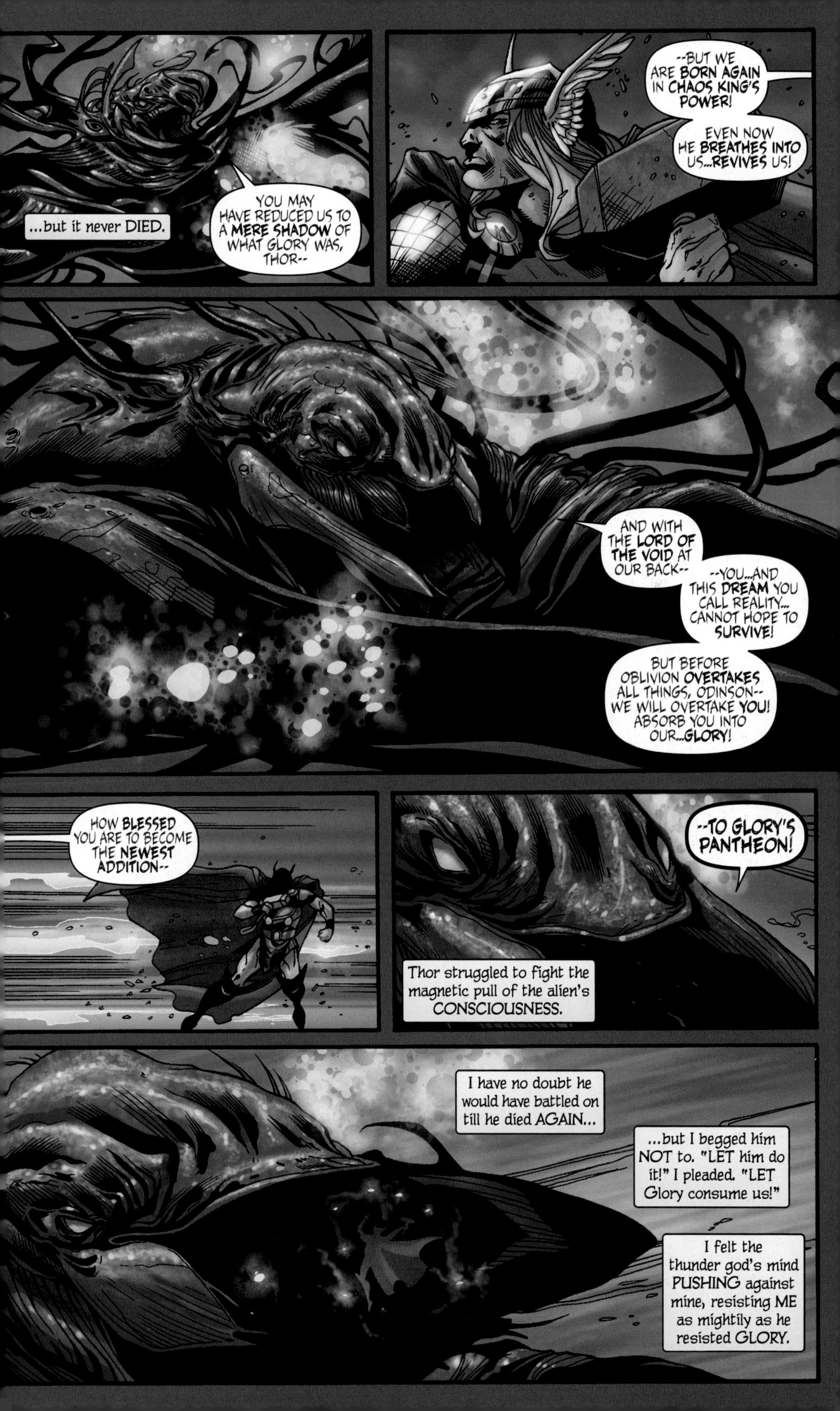

...but it never DIED.
YOU MAY HAVE REDUCED US TO A MERE SHADOW OF WHAT GLORY WAS, THOR--
--BUT WE ARE BORN AGAIN IN CHAOS KING'S POWER!
EVEN NOW HE BREATHES INTO US...REVIVES US!
AND WITH THE LORD OF THE VOID AT OUR BACK--
--YOU...AND THIS DREAM YOU CALL REALITY... CANNOT HOPE TO SURVIVE!
BUT BEFORE OBLIVION OVERTAKES ALL THINGS, ODINSON-- WE WILL OVERTAKE YOU! ABSORB YOU INTO OUR...GLORY!
HOW BLESSED YOU ARE TO BECOME THE NEWEST ADDITION--
--TO GLORY'S PANTHEON!
Thor struggled to fight the magnetic pull of the alien's CONSCIOUSNESS.
I have no doubt he would have battled on till he died AGAIN...
...but I begged him NOT to. "LET him do it!" I pleaded. "LET Glory consume us!"
I felt the thunder god's mind PUSHING against mine, resisting ME as mightily as he resisted GLORY.

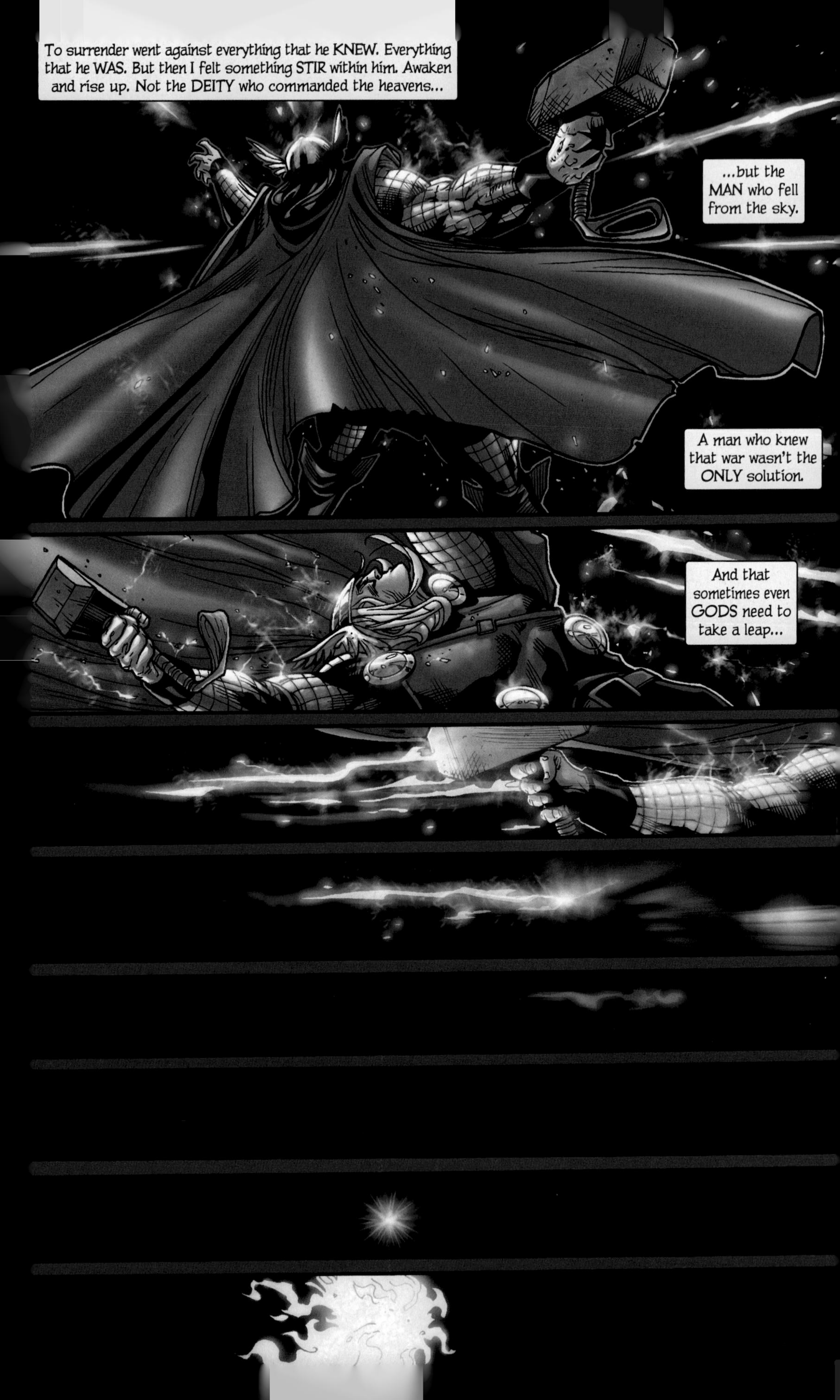
To surrender went against everything that he KNEW. Everything that he WAS. But then I felt something STIR within him. Awaken and rise up. Not the DEITY who commanded the heavens...
...but the MAN who fell from the sky.
A man who knew that war wasn't the ONLY solution.
And that sometimes even GODS need to take a leap...

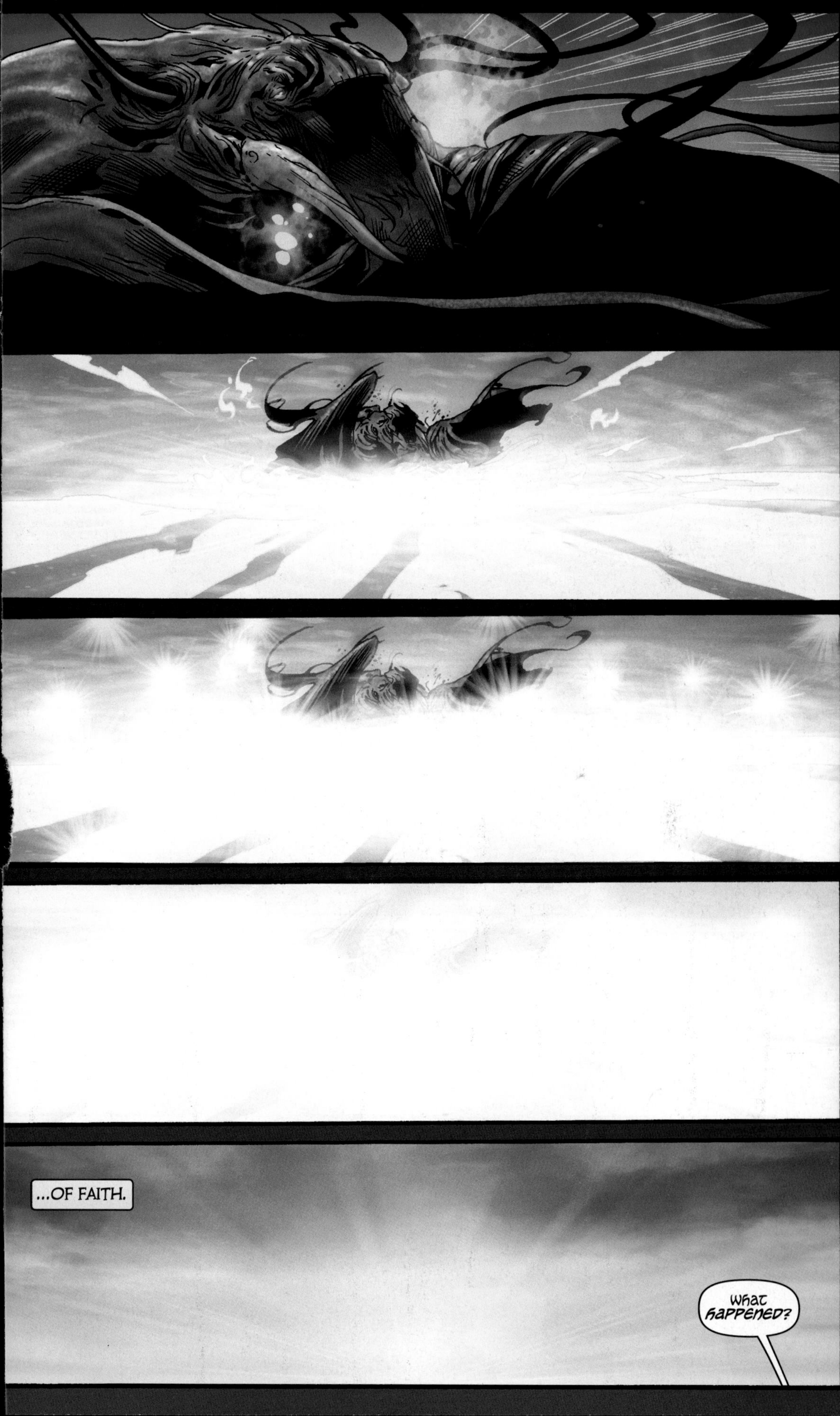
...OF FAITH.
WHAT HAPPENED?

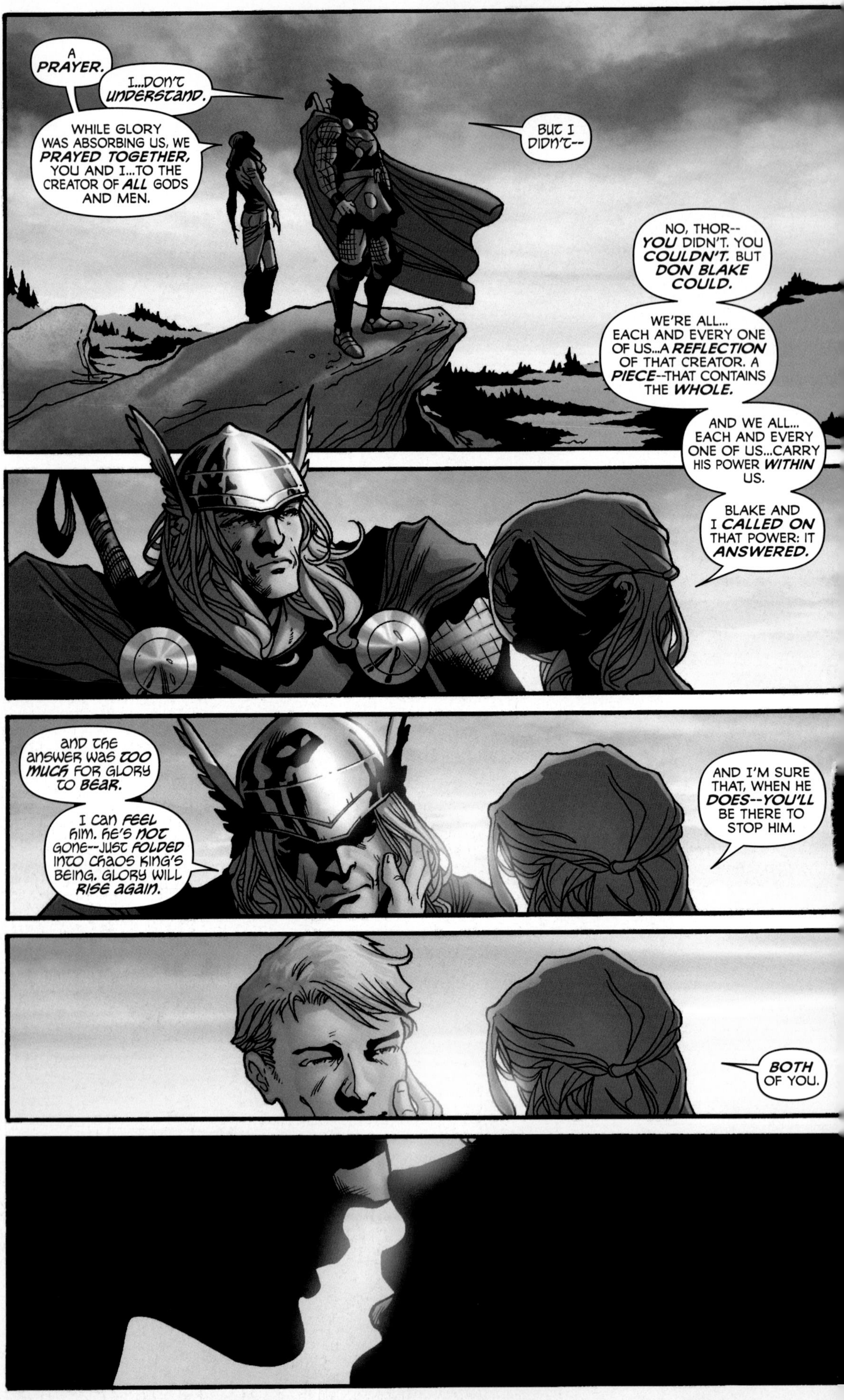
A PRAYER.
I...DON'T UNDERSTAND.
WHILE GLORY WAS ABSORBING US, WE PRAYED TOGETHER, YOU AND I...TO THE CREATOR OF ALL GODS AND MEN.
BUT I DIDN'T--
NO, THOR--YOU DIDN'T. YOU COULDN'T. BUT DON BLAKE COULD.
WE'RE ALL... EACH AND EVERY ONE OF US...A REFLECTION OF THAT CREATOR. A PIECE--THAT CONTAINS THE WHOLE.
AND WE ALL... EACH AND EVERY ONE OF US...CARRY HIS POWER WITHIN US.
BLAKE AND I CALLED ON THAT POWER: IT ANSWERED.
AND THE ANSWER WAS TOO MUCH FOR GLORY TO BEAR.
I CAN FEEL HIM. HE'S NOT GONE--JUST FOLDED INTO CHAOS KING'S BEING. GLORY WILL RISE AGAIN.
AND I'M SURE THAT, WHEN HE DOES--YOU'LL BE THERE TO STOP HIM.
BOTH OF YOU.

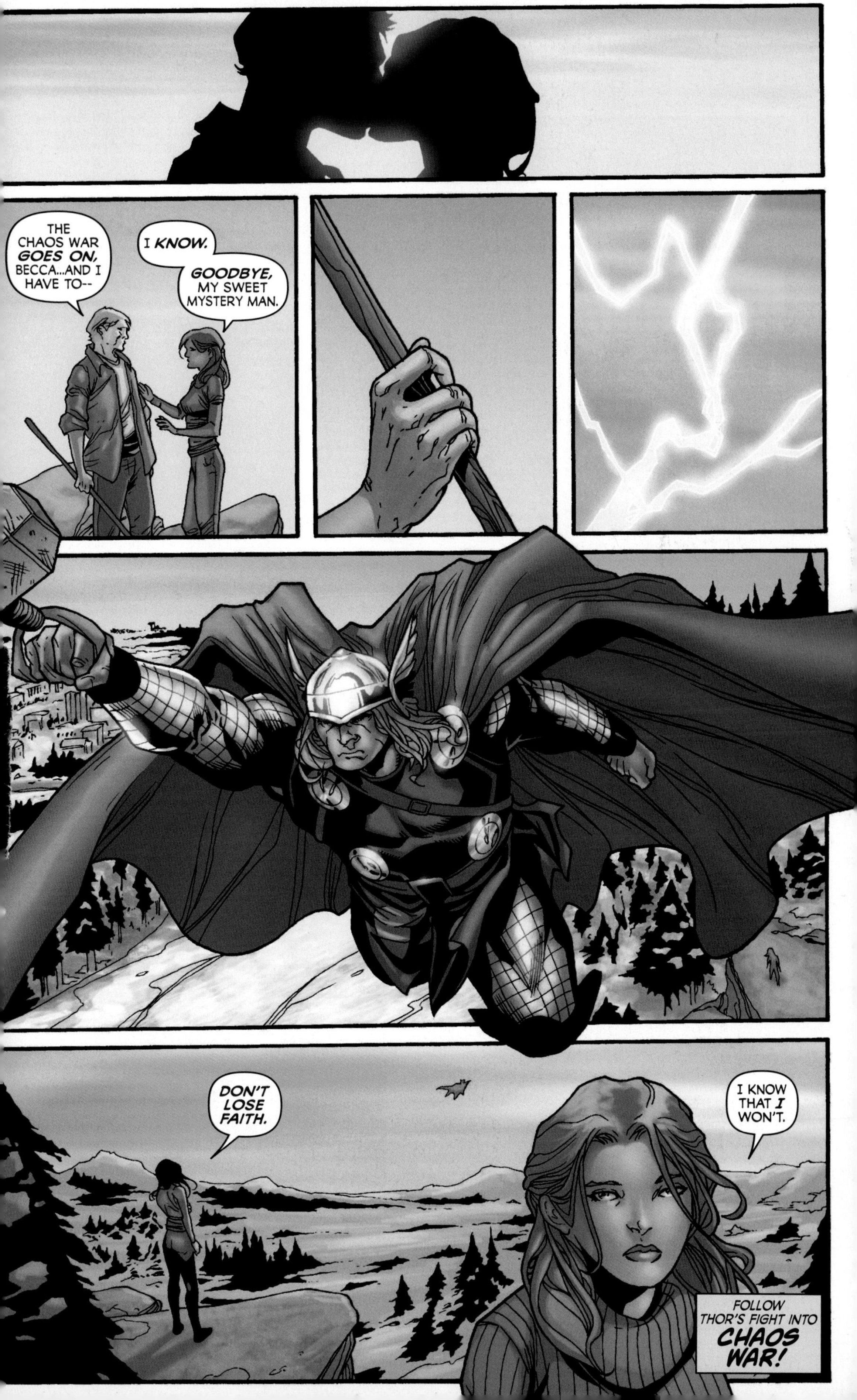
THE CHAOS WAR GOES ON, BECCA...AND I HAVE TO--
I KNOW.
GOODBYE, MY SWEET MYSTERY MAN.
DON'T LOSE FAITH.
I KNOW THAT I WON'T.
FOLLOW THOR'S FIGHT INTO CHAOS WAR!

CHAOS WAR: DEAD AVENGERS

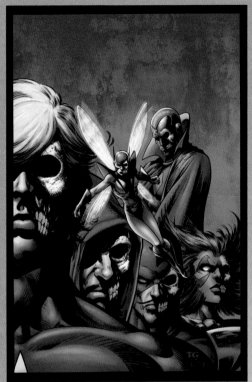

Cover to *Chaos War: Dead Avengers #3* by Tom Grummett.

Greg Pak isn't the only *Chaos War* architect playing double duty. Fred Van Lente is writing what is sure to be a hotly anticipated tie-in limited series, *Chaos War: Dead Avengers*. The three-issue series, with art by Tom Grummett, features some familiar deceased members of Earth's Mightiest Heroes as they make a stand against Chaos King ally — and classic Avengers foe — the Grim Reaper and his minions. We asked Fred to tell us a little about his team and what we can expect in the sure-to-be-cool *Chaos War: Dead Avengers*.

SPOTLIGHT: Dead Avengers, dead X-Men, Ares. There's a bunch of *Chaos War* tie-ins featuring dead characters. How was it decided to incorporate the deceased into *Chaos War*?

FRED: The Chaos King is destroying all of reality, piece by piece. As in *all* of reality. The dream realm of Nightmare. The pantheons where gods dwell. And the afterlife, too. When the realms of the dead are wiped out, the deceased don't have anywhere to go but the mortal realm.

SPOTLIGHT: Half the fun in hearing about Avengers teams is finding out the roster. Is it equally fun to pick a team? How did you decide who to use?

FRED: It is fun. I am an Avenger fan from way back, so I wanted to use folks from different eras. Swordsman from the Lee/Heck run, Vision is classic Thomas/Buscema, Roger Stern introduced Yellowjacket and Dr. Druid, Mar-Vell is a '70s mainstay, and Deathcry with her cleavage and bad attitude might as be well called the '90s. It's a great mix of high and low power, noble and rogue, mysticism and technology, the alien and the very human.

SPOTLIGHT: The Vision? So the synthezoid made it into the afterlife. Is this explained or is it just a matter of "a lot stranger things than this has happened in comics, just go with it"?

FRED: The former. It's quite a big deal to the story, actually. It's something Dr. Druid, say, who has a worldview based firmly in the natural world, has a very hard time accepting. Vision doesn't even entirely understand it himself.

SPOTLIGHT: Is everyone more or less his or her familiar personality? Are you writing them pretty much as though they were alive?

FRED: Yes. They're not zombies. That's another Marvel property I'm associated with.

SPOTLIGHT: It looks like you're using the Grim Reaper! Excellent choice — he hasn't been in the spotlight much lately and makes perfect sense. How does he hook up with the Chaos King?

FRED: Grim Reaper was dead himself for a while until he was resurrected by his psycho girlfriend Nekra, who's also along for this ride. And like many of the other monstrous entities in the Marvel U., they have sided with the Chaos King in his mad quest to destroy all existence. Grim Reaper is so consumed by his hatred for the Avengers, all he can see is the opportunity to destroy them once and for all.

SPOTLIGHT: Will any "Alive Avengers" be a part of the miniseries?

FRED: All of them. And the only ones standing between them and the Grim Reaper's limitless rampaging hordes of alien slaves are the Dead Avengers. This very much is *300* with super heroes. The Dead Avengers may be dead, but they can be wiped out of existence. And not all of them, and maybe none of them, will make it out of this last stand.

SPOTLIGHT: Any hints as to whether or not every member remains a "Dead" Avenger at the end of the story?

FRED: Keep reading.

CHAOS WAR: DEAD AVENGERS
is on stands now!

GRIM REAPER: Cover to *Chaos War: Dead Avengers #2* by Tom Grummett.

t from *Chaos War #2* by Khoi Pham.

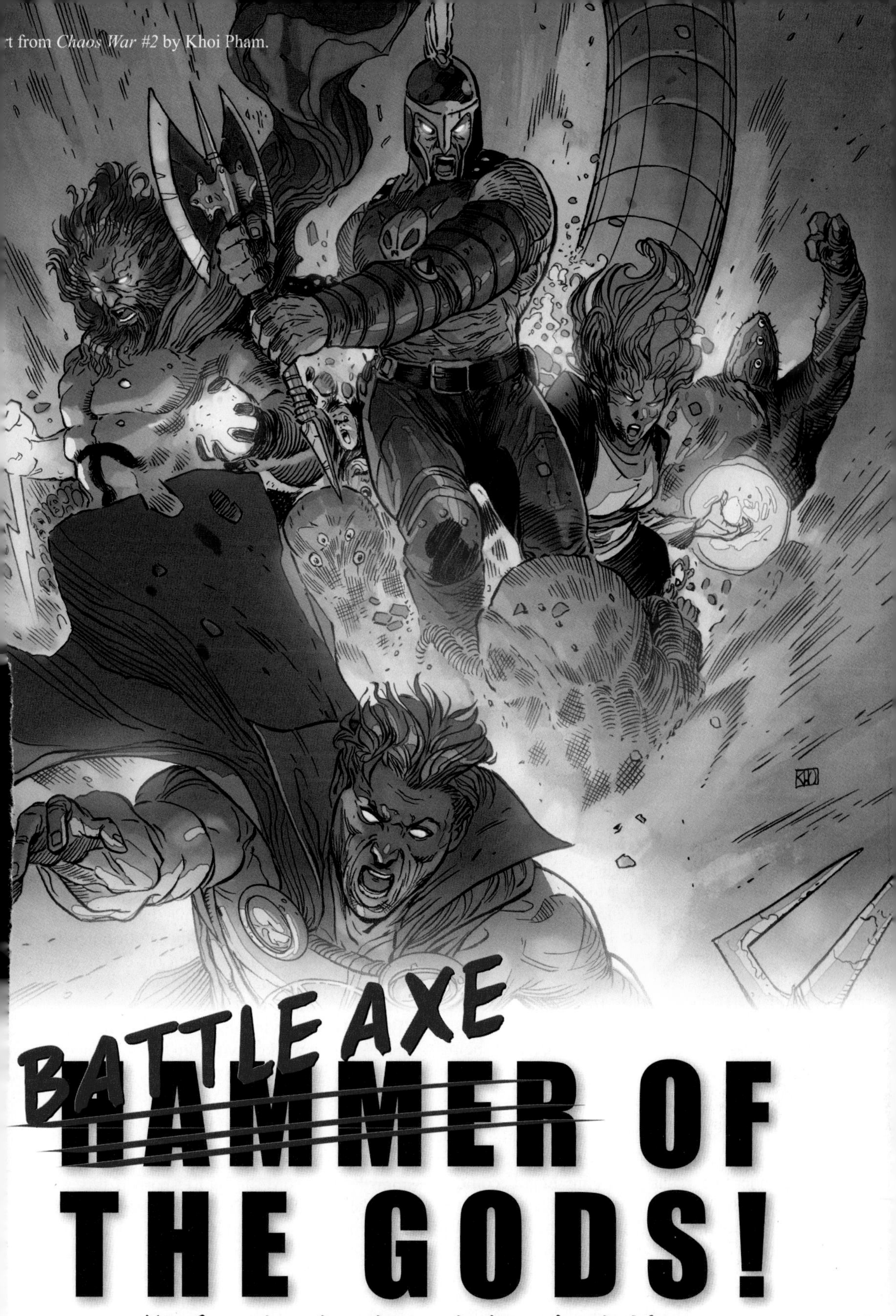

BATTLE AXE ~~HAMMER~~ OF THE GODS!

He Carries An Axe, A Sword, A Mace, A Machine Gun Into Battle — Whatever It Takes To Win!

Writer Michael Oeming Helps Us Understand Ares

HAVE GUN, WILL TRAVEL:
Michael Oeming updated Ares into an Earth-bound,
shotgun-wielding warrior in his 2006 miniseries, *Ares*.
(Art from *Ares* #1 by Travel Foreman.)

Michael Avon Oeming didn't know it at the time, but his 2006 *Ares: God of War* limited series put several important chess pieces in place. Not only did it position Ares as a character to be reckoned with, bring his son Alexander/Phobos to the Marvel Universe and destroy Olympus — but after introducing Amatsu-Mikaboshi in 2005's *Thor: Blood Oath* series, he established that character's prominence by making him the one who did the destroying. Ares went on to become a key figure in the Avengers books, both *Mighty* and *Dark*, before being killed by the Sentry during *Siege*; Alexander continues to be a member of Nick Fury's Secret Warriors. As for the destruction of Olympus and the presence of Mikaboshi — well, they've been important factors in *Incredible Hercules*. It's therefore only appropriate that Mike gets to be involved with *Chaos War*, and he does it by returning to the God of War in the *Chaos War: Ares* one-shot.

You'll notice a theme of many *Chaos War* tie-in books is that they star the deceased. That's because Mikaboshi has destroyed the realm of the dead itself in his quest to annihilate everything. That gives Mike a chance to again sink his teeth into his greatest Marvel legacy, Ares, this time joined by artist Stephen Segovia. Just check out our interview to see how excited Mike is.

> *"...it was not a death anyone will ever forget. I'm sure even Ares would approve of going out that way."*
> — Oeming on Ares' death in Siege

SPOTLIGHT: Your 2006 *Ares* miniseries really brought the God of War to a stature in the Marvel Universe he never had before despite being around for decades. Was it rewarding to see him become a fan favorite?

MIKE: Very much so! The reaction to the series was one thing, but it felt great to take a character from under the radar to seeing him become a player. It felt a little bit like giving back to Marvel for all the amazing stuff they've done in comics. It's a great honor to be part of it in some small way.

SPOTLIGHT: What do you find appealing about Ares and what do you think has caused him to strike a chord with readers?

MIKE: For me, it's the contrast between Warrior and Father. But besides that, I really thought about him being the *god of war*. And I looked at how the character was handled before and it became clear what to do with him. A god of war has to be *smart*. He has to plan; he knows you cannot win battles through pure muscle and rage. Look at the Spartans and the battle at the Hot Gates. That was strategy, intelligence and cunning that won that impossible battle. Honor is a part of that too. None of those attributes were written into Ares before — but once they are, he becomes infinitely fascinating.

SPOTLIGHT: What do you think of his journey since you last worked with him? Other than being, um, dead, how would you say the character has developed in the time between writing him?

MIKE: Brian (Bendis) did a great job with him in *Siege*. I thought his death was pretty sweet. He stood by his word; he told Osborn if this was a trick, he would kill him for it. It was a matter of honor, rules of war. And it was not a death anyone will ever forget. I'm sure even Ares would approve of going out that way.

SPOTLIGHT: There are several dead characters showing up throughout the *Chaos War*. How does Ares fit in? Is he on a particular side of the conflict?

MIKE: Without giving too much away, let me

MIGHTIEST AVENGER: Ares was Iron Man's "war machine" in his Mighty Avengers squad! (Art by Frank Cho from *Mighty Avengers #1*.)

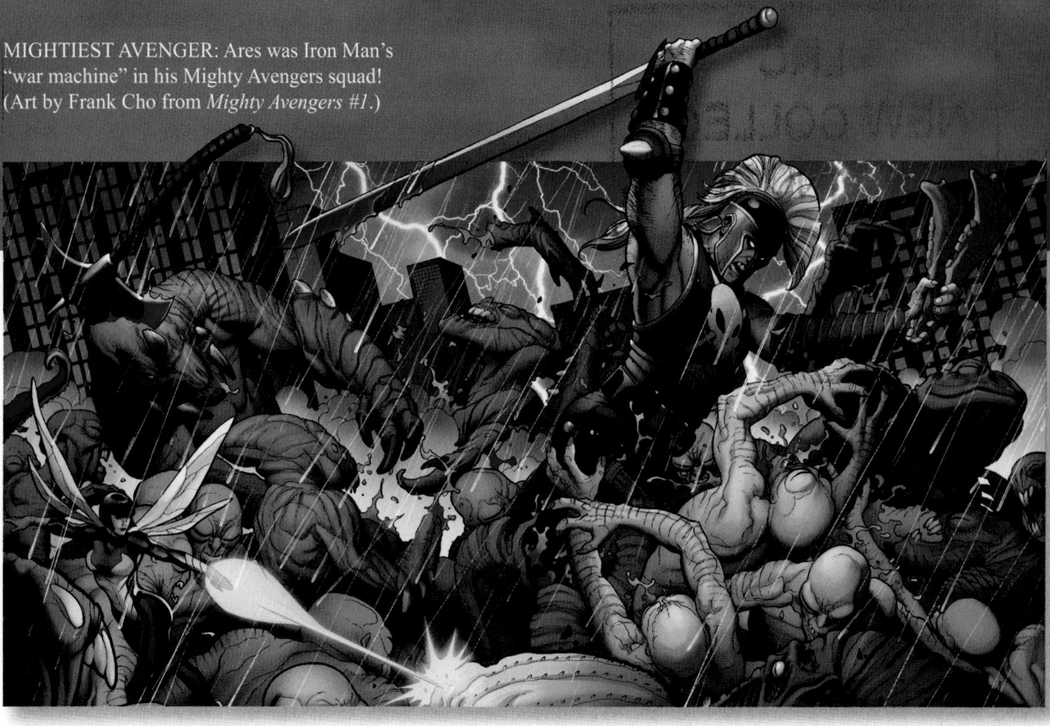

say that once a Greek is dead and is under the sway of Pluto, he's totally under his rule. Pluto has absolute godlike power in his realm of the dead, unless something goes horribly wrong…

SPOTLIGHT: Is there a specific adversary for Ares in this book?

MIKE: It's very nice that *Chaos War* goes back to the first *Ares* miniseries. It all ties together, both his companions and adversaries.

SPOTLIGHT: This is an odd question — but it is after all, about a comic whose star is deceased. How does Ares feel about being dead? It seems like part of life when you're a god to sometimes be "dead."

MIKE: I think he's pretty angry, but it can't be that bad. After all, several other mortals in Greek mythology have either escaped Hades or even went down into Hell, visited and came back. Where there is a will, there is a way.

SPOTLIGHT: In addition to reviving Ares, you brought Mikaboshi, the Chaos King, into the Marvel Universe in *Thor: Blood Oath* and established his prominence in the original *Ares* series. Now he's the central villain in a crossover event. Were you hoping he would be a character who would be followed up on after *Ares*?

MIKE: I had no idea! I honestly didn't. Again, I'm very honored. I was blown away when Stardust was used a few times after the *Beta Ray Bill* mini [see *Stormbreaker: The Saga of Beta Ray Bill TPB*], but this far surpasses that. I love creating new characters or reinventing forgotten ones. There's so much room and freedom for stories there.

SPOTLIGHT: How would you describe Mikaboshi and what does he represent as a god?

MIKE: Ego-driven evil. There's not enough room in this universe for him and anyone else.

SPOTLIGHT: Yet another character from your *Ares* series — his son, Alexander — has become a Marvel fixture as Phobos in *Secret Warriors*. Does he play a role in *Chaos War: Ares*?

MIKE: He's definitely on Ares' mind. Every father thinks about their children every day, so does Ares. He's a big motivation for him getting out of "dead."

SPOTLIGHT: You don't shy away from mythically large characters and stories. What do you enjoy about them, and what is the key to making them work?

MIKE: I've always been drawn toward fantasy for pretty classic reasons: to escape reality. You can trade bad feelings for feelings of wonder and mystery in fantasy. If you can take that feeling and combine it with human insights, you have something that works, and it can be pretty powerful.

SPOTLIGHT: You're a known Led Zeppelin junkie. What Zeppelin song would play over the title credits to your *Chaos War: Ares* one-shot if it were a movie?

MIKE: "Achilles Last Stand," of course! Speaking of which, when does *he* get a miniseries?

Just write one, Mike; we'll read it for sure! In the meantime, folks, look for CHAOS WAR: ARES *in December.*•

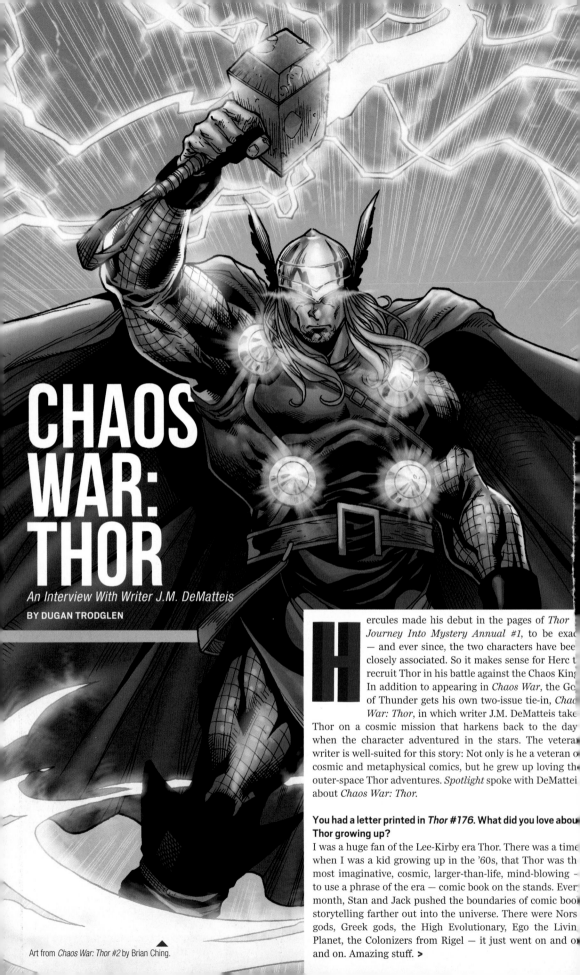

CHAOS WAR: THOR

An Interview With Writer J.M. DeMatteis

BY DUGAN TRODGLEN

Hercules made his debut in the pages of *Thor Journey Into Mystery Annual #1*, to be exact — and ever since, the two characters have bee closely associated. So it makes sense for Herc t recruit Thor in his battle against the Chaos King In addition to appearing in *Chaos War*, the Go of Thunder gets his own two-issue tie-in, *Chao War: Thor*, in which writer J.M. DeMatteis take Thor on a cosmic mission that harkens back to the day when the character adventured in the stars. The vetera writer is well-suited for this story: Not only is he a veteran o cosmic and metaphysical comics, but he grew up loving th outer-space Thor adventures. *Spotlight* spoke with DeMattei about *Chaos War: Thor*.

You had a letter printed in *Thor #176*. What did you love abou Thor growing up?

I was a huge fan of the Lee-Kirby era Thor. There was a time when I was a kid growing up in the '60s, that Thor was th most imaginative, cosmic, larger-than-life, mind-blowing – to use a phrase of the era — comic book on the stands. Ever month, Stan and Jack pushed the boundaries of comic boo storytelling farther out into the universe. There were Nors gods, Greek gods, the High Evolutionary, Ego the Livin Planet, the Colonizers from Rigel — it just went on and o and on. Amazing stuff. **>**

Art from *Chaos War: Thor #2* by Brian Ching.

In addition to things like Spider-Man and Daredevil, you've had a lot of success writing cosmic/metaphysical characters and stories in *Silver Surfer*, *Defenders* and others. Now, you have a full-on war of pantheons. What does it take to make these kinds of books work in a relatable way?

What it takes more than anything is to ground these stories in very relatable human characters and very relatable human issues. If you go so far out into the metaphysical landscape that your story loses its humanity, if it's all head and no heart, you're sunk.

▲ Writer J.M. DeMatteis.

While this story breaks off from the main *Chaos War* action, do we get any sense from your book how Thor feels about Hercules' new power and the fact that Herc, who has always seemed a clear notch below Thor in reputation, is clearly in charge of this conflict?

No. *Chaos War: Thor* is a very tightly focused tale, with the emphasis on Thor/Blake and his relationship with a woman named Becca — and the villain of the piece, an alien deity named Glory.

Thor's adventures lately have been very Asgard-centric. What does taking him away from that and into another milieu bring out in him?

In the case of this story, I think we get to strip Thor — and Blake — down to bare essentials and boil the story down to the elements that make the character really work. For me, it all comes down to the wonderful Thor/Blake metaphor: the idea that Blake seems like a normal guy — in fact, a guy with a handicap — and yet he's more powerful than he could have ever imagined. He's a god. I believe that's true for all of us: Every one of us, no matter our apparent weaknesses and limitations, contains the Divine — and like a hologram, each (seemingly) small piece of God contains the whole. We are the totality of the universe, and the totality of the universe is us.

The villain in *Chaos War: Thor* is a character named Glory. Who is Glory, and what is he up to that pits him against Thor?

Glory is one of the gods who's signed up for the Chaos King's battle to drag the entire Creation back to a state of Cosmic Nothing. Many of these alien gods have been coerced into the job — but Glory is such a raging, spiteful, black-hearted maniac that he's signed on voluntarily.

The thing that makes him such a formidable opponent is that fact that Glory isn't just "a god." He's the embodiment of an *entire pantheon* — hundreds, perhaps thousands, of mad alien deities in one body. Not an opponent that can be easily dispatched!

How is it working in the middle of a crossover event? Has it affected your approach?

Coming on board for one of these huge crossover events is — well, it's always intimidating. I've said many times over the years that I've never enjoyed participating in these things — not the least because, when you're working on a monthly book, these big events usually just intrude on your own carefully planned story. I may enjoy reading these big events, but writing them is something I've never been very enthused about. I can think of, perhaps, one or two over the years that have been fun. And I may be exaggerating by one.

That said, this one *is* fun. The story that Greg Pak and Fred Van Lente cooked up is terrific — it's Kosmic with a capital K — and they're playing with themes that I love. And that's what's important: that it's a good story, beyond the whole "event" aspect. As for my participation, what they've given me to play with — and these guys have been extremely generous collaborators — is just perfect. *Chaos War: Thor* ties in, very directly, to the main *Chaos War* story, but also stands outside of it, allowing me to tell a fairly self-contained story that is unique to the Thunder God. You can read this story on its own and be satisfied. But I suspect that, once *Chaos War* hits, people are going to be devouring the whole thing. And enjoying it immensely. ∎

"(WITH THOR) IF YOU GO SO FAR OUT INTO THE METAPHYSICAL LANDSCAPE THAT YOUR STORY LOSES ITS HUMANITY... YOU'RE SUNK."

– Writer J.M. DeMatteis

BATTLE IN THE COSMOS: Thor fights the Chaos King's eager footsoldier, Glory, in *Chaos War: Thor #1*. ▶

And lo, there came a day...

Avengers back from the grave! See where their stories began—and some of them ended—with these might collections!

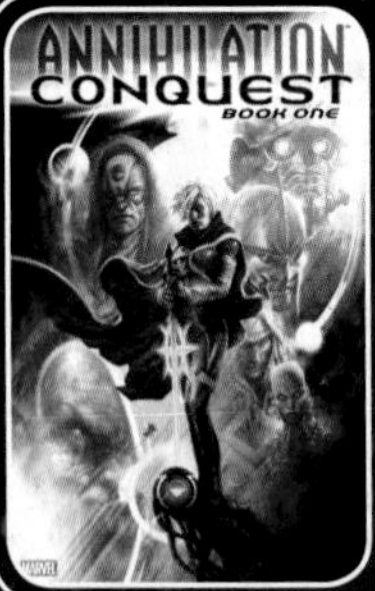
ANNIHILATION
CONQUEST
BOOK ONE

Annihilation: Conquest Volume One

In the grim aftermath of the Annihilation War, the galaxy struggles to rebuild. Gripped by fear and paranoia, civilizations have collapsed and entire worlds are now smoking ruins. Deathcry joins Starlord's band of outsiders to fight an invasion of the techno-organic Phalanx that could push an already devastated universe over the edge!

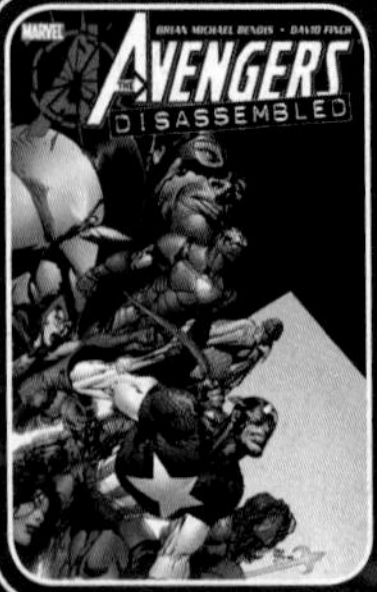
AVENGERS
DISASSEMBLED

Avengers Disassembled

It begins with the return of a team member thought dead - and by the time it's over, everything you know about the Avengers will have changed! The event that rocked the entirety of the Marvel Universe and set the stage for New Avengers begins here!

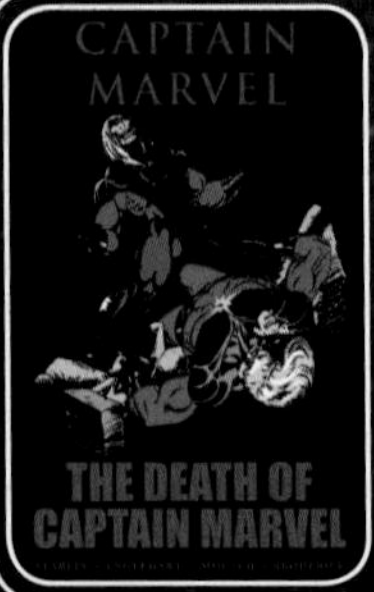
CAPTAIN
MARVEL
THE DEATH OF
CAPTAIN MARVEL

The Death of Captain Marvel

Witness the classic and tragic end of one of the greatest Avengers of all time, Mar-Vell of the Kree, who became the Earth hero Captain Marvel! After dozens of battles on our world and across space, Captain Marvel finally meets his fate in this deluxe hardcover.

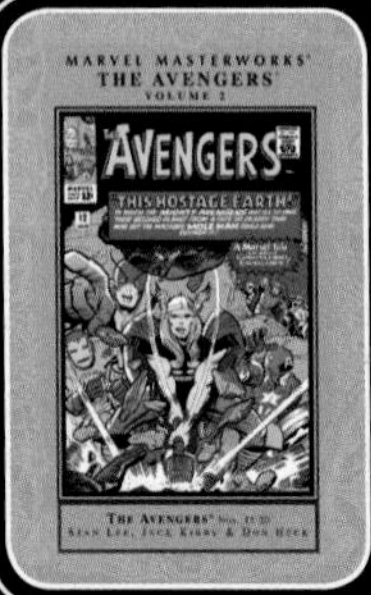
MARVEL MASTERWORKS
THE AVENGERS
AVENGERS
THIS HOSTAGE EARTH!

Marvel Masterworks: Avengers Volume Two

Comicdom's greatest assemblage of super heroes burst onto the scene in 1963 as Marvel Comics revolutionized the comic-adventure art form. Now, the epic story continues in Volume 2 with appearances by Quicksilver, Scarlet Witch, Spider-Man, and the first appearance of The Swordsman!

Echoes of Thunder!

The Chaos King has proven to be quite the foe for the Mighty Avenger.
But Thor's strength of
will have been measured before...

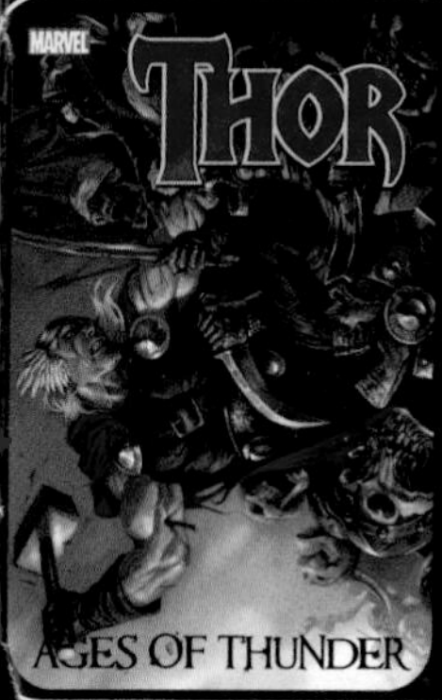
MARVEL
THOR
AGES OF THUNDER

Thor: Ages of Thunder. Matt Fraction. Patrick Zircher

In order to teach his fellow Asgardians a lesson, Thor must do something he has never done before: Stand down. Written by superstar Matt Fraction, Ages of Thunder is an epic story of one god's ultimate destiny toward humility through Humanity.

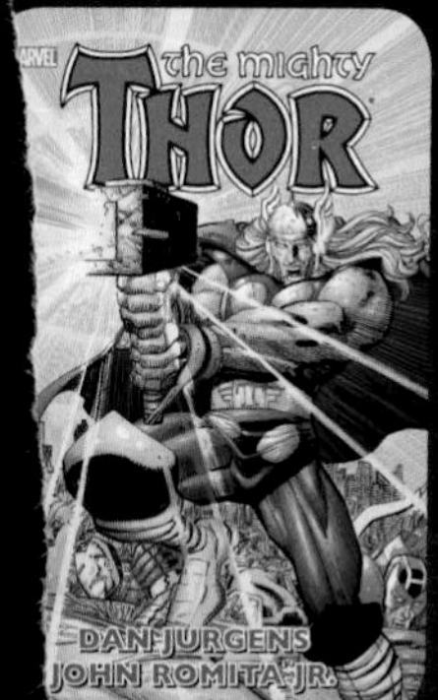
the mighty
THOR
DAN JURGENS
JOHN ROMITA JR.

The Mighty Thor. Dan Jurgens. John Romita Jr

Looking for a great place to start reading Thor? You've found it! Collecting the monumental run on Thor by Dan Jurgens and John Romita Jr, this first volume is all you'll need to get caught up on the Odinson himself. 'Nuff Said!

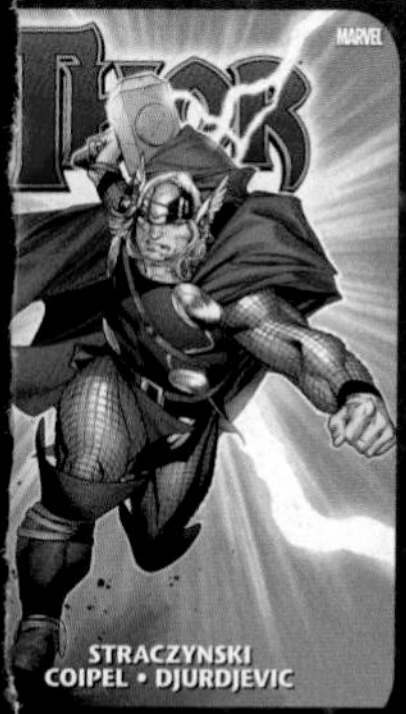
MARVEL
STRACZYNSKI
COIPEL • DJURDJEVIC

Thor Volume I. Straczynski. Copiel

Thor is back! Returned from the void and joined again to his human host, Donald Blake, Thor must find his Asgardian brethren and bring them into a world that may not want them there at all!

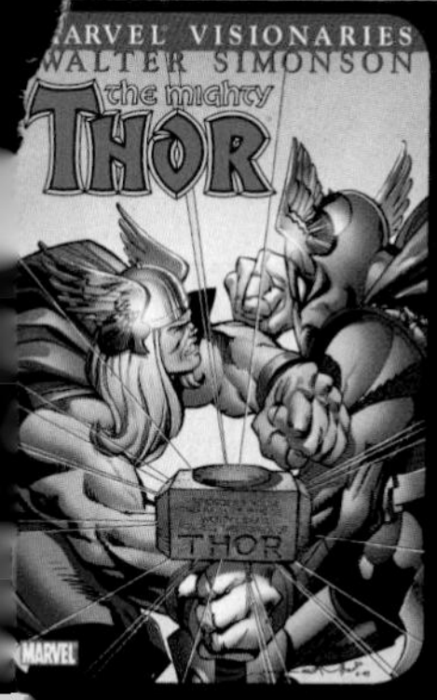
VISIONARIES
SIMONSON
the mighty
THOR
MARVEL

Thor Visionaries. Walter Simonson

Few creators left their mark on a single character quite the way Walter Simonson did with his run on Thor. From the majesty and mystery of fabled Asgard to the gritty streets of New York City, Thor was never the same. This collection is a must-read for Thor fans new and old alike.

Journey into History

As one of the premier heroes of the Marvel Universe, there is almost no end to the thrilling tales the thunder god has had! Here's another four history-spanning tales of the hammer-wielding wonder!

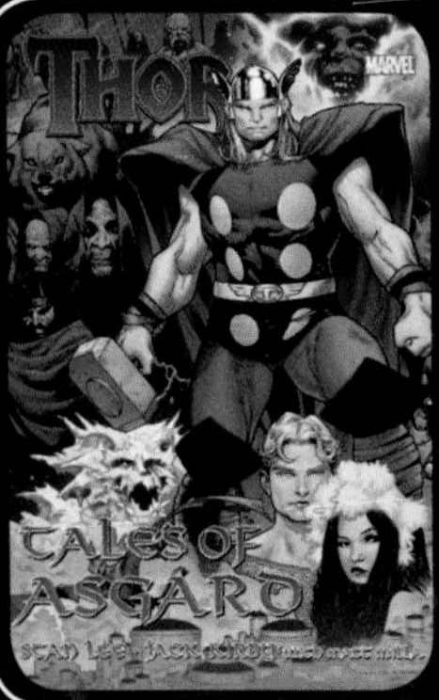
THOR
MARVEL
TALES OF ASGARD

Thor: Tales of Asgard

Never has Thor been more sensational than during these early tales crafted by Marvel's greatest, Stan Lee and Jack Kirby. Re-live Stan and Jack's stories of the Norse Gods and Thor before he came to Earth as Don Blake. Read these stories as never before with all-new, modern coloring and six interlocking covers by Olivier Coipel!

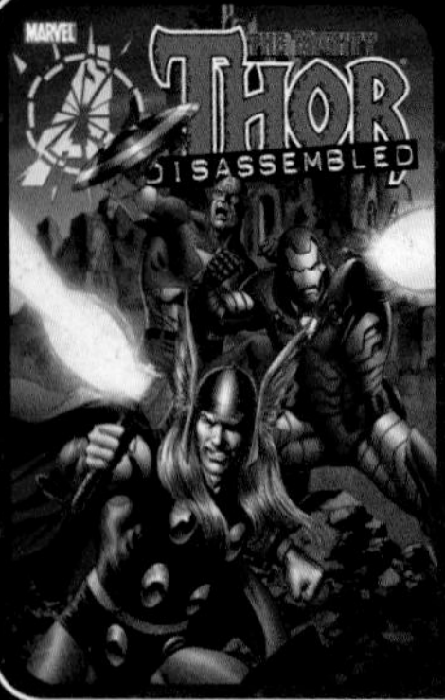
MARVEL
THE MIGHTY
THOR
DISASSEMBLED

Thor: Disassembled

Ragnarok appears to have come for the gods of Asgard, and only Thor and his Avengers allies are able to stave off that fate - but will the Thunder God be Asgard savior, or the architect of its downfall? Beset on all sides by treacherous foes from his past, the God of Thunder leads the tattered remnants of the forces of Asgard o a desperate quest, as the Realm Eternal burns.

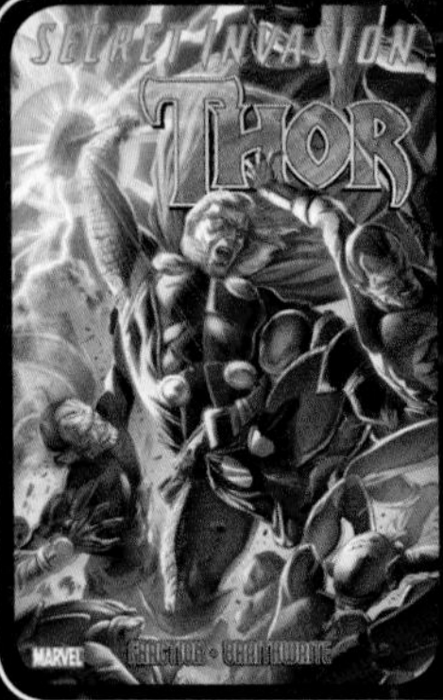
SECRET INVASION
THOR
MARVEL

Secret Invasion: Thor

The Skrulls are coming for Asgard!! But it's not just the pantheon who stand suffer the repercussions of the aliens' secret invasion - the citizens of small-tov Broxton, Oklahoma are about to become collateral damage in the attack, and the Gc of Thunder must defend two cites at once! For a job this big, Thor will have to tu to one of his oldest and closest allies - Beta Ray Bill!

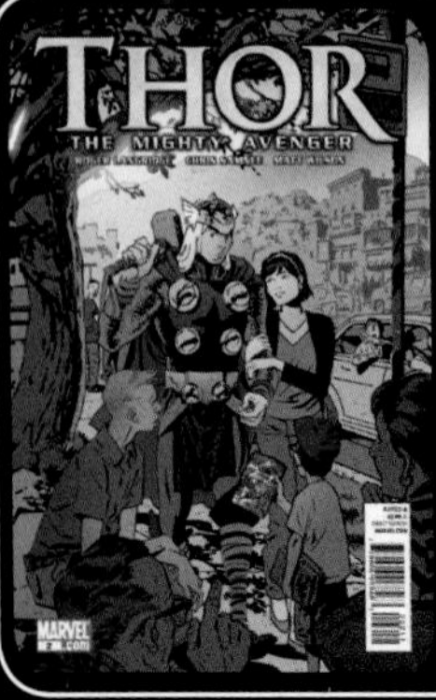
THOR
THE MIGHTY AVENGER
MARVEL

Thor: The Mighty Avenger

Thor's banished, he's mad, and he wants to **fight**. **Thrill** as he battles robots the size of cities! **Gasp** as he tames the mightiest sea creatures! **Swoon** as he rescues damsels from the vilest villains! It's Thor as you've **never** seen him before. If you're new to the mighty world of Thor, this collection of issues 1-4 is the **perfect** place to begin!